Knowles on

Local Authority Meetings

Knowles on
Local Authority Meetings

A Manual of Law and Practice

Eighth Edition

Philip J. F. McCourt
F.C.I.S., Solicitor

Chartered
Governance
Institute
UK & Ireland

This eighth edition published by

CGI Publishing Limited
Saffron House, 6–10 Kirby Street
London EC1N 8TS

First published as *The Law and Practice of Local Authority Meetings* 1978
First (revised) edition 1987
Second edition 1993
Third edition 1999
Fourth edition 2005
Fifth edition 2008
Sixth edition 2012
Seventh edition 2014
Eighth edition 2016

Typeset by Hands Fotoset, Bexhill, East Sussex

British Library Cataloguing in Publication Data
A catalogue record for this book is available from the British Library

ISBN: 978 186072 679 8

Contents

Preface

In the early editions of this book, Raymond Knowles expressed his gratitude towards the discussions and contribution provided by the residential committee administration course run by the National and Local Government Officers' Association (NALGO), at which both he and Charles Cross were tutors for many years and which provided the foundation for this book.

I must add my own such comments to his, for it was in attending that course that I first properly began to appreciate not just the continuing breadth of what local government does and seeks to achieve but the sheer complexities of fitting together the long list of requirements that go to achieve that: sound and lawful decision-making, good administration, development and delivery of functions and ambitions, public access, transparency and accountability, and the small and large 'p' in politics. In other words: governance.

Some 25 years later I remain perpetually amazed – not to say sometimes delighted and occasionally bemused and confused – by the plethora of rules, the continuing issue of new legislation, and the intricacies of law and practice that govern decision-making across the various forms of local government within the UK and elsewhere, all in an attempt to achieve that same end.

This publication is therefore as relevant now as when it was first published. For those approaching this subject anew, I would give the following four pieces of advice.

1. Use this book, of course.
2. Make the most out of the education, training and support provided by our professional associations, the Association of Democratic Services Officers (ADSO) and Lawyers in Local Government (LLG). This is essential for the continual learning and development we share via these associations. It is also for the access they provide to those programmes of training and qualifications now available, both as the successor to that old committee administration course and to the formal education leading to the Certificate, Diploma and to an MPA, MBA and/or ICSA. If you are reading this as a democratic services officer or clerk to a local authority and are not a member of ADSO (or SLCC if in a parish or town council), I recommend joining.
3. Make best use of those senior colleagues or managers who avail themselves as advisors or mentors. In my case, I was lucky enough to have as my ICSA training sponsor Jeffrey Greenwell, ICSA's former president and the then chief executive of Northamptonshire County Council, and in addition I had Roger Heath, the then chief executive of East Northamptonshire Council, as manager, co-sponsor and Law Society training principal. If you wish to make judicious use of the

knowledge and experience of others, you will find a number of such people in your career who will advise willingly and your knowledge bank and judgement will be well rewarded.

4. Discuss these topics not just with colleagues at your workplace, but with those at other authorities too. I cannot say this strongly enough. Local government is a small grouping in reality and we have a particular strength in being able to share the best of what we know and support each other. Beyond the training, this is where associations like ADSO and LLG really come into their own, not only through their formal structures but also through their informal local groupings. Access through the associations has enabled me to work on key projects with some key individuals, but more important by far has been being part of a group of colleagues who sat in the same place as myself in an opposite authority. Having the same problems and issues and being part of such a group of colleagues means that we can (so far as any of us are reasonably able to) be generous to each other in reassurance, support and guidance.

As ever, legislative changes, new case law and new (or even revived) practices continue unabated, and we have tried to keep up and incorporate the most useful of them here. This edition updates the previous text and attempts to answer some of the questions raised by previous editions. In doing so, I must acknowledge a debt of gratitude owed to Kim Sawyer, Gemma George and their teams at Peterborough City Council and to Kirsty Cole at Newark and Sherwood DC for their ideas, discussion and prompts in producing this edition.

The thanks of the publishers and myself go, as always, to Raymond Knowles and Tim Harrison, whose work has been updated in recent editions by Stephen Taylor and Deborah Upton.

Philip McCourt
April 2016

Table of Cases

References are to paragraph numbers and not to pages.

Table of Statutes

References are to paragraph numbers and not to pages.

Table of Statutory Instruments

References are to paragraph numbers and not to pages.

Table of Statutory Instruments

Table of Abbreviations

ACSeS	Association of Council Secretaries and Solicitors (now LLG)
ADSO	Association of Democratic Services Officers
AR	appellant's representative
CCG	clinical commissioning group
CfPS	Centre for Public Scrutiny
CR	council's representative
DCLG	Department for Communities and Local Government
DIP	Designated Independent Person
DLO	direct labour organisations
FOIA	Freedom of Information Act
FPTP	First Past the Post
H&SB	Health and Safety Board
H&SCA	Health and Social Care Act
H&SWA 1974	Health and Safety at Work, etc. Act 1974
H&WB	Health and Well-being Board
IP	Independent Person
JHWS	Joint Health and Well-being Strategy
JSNA	Joint Strategic Needs Assessment
LA(APM)A 1908	Local Authorities (Admission of the Press to Meetings) Act 1908
LACoRS	Local Authority Co-ordinators of Regulatory Services (a former body of the LGA)
LG&HA 1989	Local Government and Housing Act 1989
LG(AI)A 1985	Local Government (Access to Information) Act 1985
LG(MP)A 1976	Local Government (Miscellaneous Provisions) Act 1976
LGA	Local Government Association
LGA 1972	Local Government Act 1972
LGA 2000	Local Government Act 2000
LGFA 1988	Local Government Finance Act 1988
LGPIHA 2007	Local Government and Public Involvement in Health Act 2007
LLG	Lawyers in Local Government
LoGA 1939	London Government Act 1939
NALC	National Association of Local Councils
NDPB	Non-Departmental Public Body
O&S	overview and scrutiny
PA 1996	Police Act 1996
PB(AM)A 1960	Public Bodies (Admission to Meetings) Act 1960
PCCs	Police and Crime Commissioners
PCP	Police and Crime Panel
PGR	parent governor representative

Table of Abbreviations

PMCA 1994	Police and Magistrates' Courts Act 1994
RISE	Research and Information on State Education
RPA	Representation of the People Act
SLCC	Society of Local Council Clerks

Part 1
General Principles

Chapter 1
Current framework

Local government structure

1.1 This work is concerned with the law and practice relating to meetings of local authorities and associated bodies in England and of their committees and sub-committees. Though the local government system is broadly similar in Wales as to the principles which apply, there is increasing divergence in the detail from that of England as a result of the changes introduced by the Local Government (Wales) Act 1994 and the devolution of powers to the National Assembly for Wales by the Government of Wales Act 1998. The situation is somewhat different in Northern Ireland and different again in Scotland, although the meetings procedures of all the local authorities across the United Kingdom have much in common with the practice of the principal local authorities in England. For example, the Local Government Act (Northern Ireland) 2014 still contains many provisions that are identical or similar to those in the Local Government Act 1972 (LGA 1972), which – supplemented by Part I of the Local Government and Housing Act 1989 (LG&HA 1989) – remains the principal Act prescribing the relevant statutory provisions governing the conduct of local authority business in England. Readers in the UK outside England should, therefore, have little difficulty in applying what is said in these pages to their own perception of local differences of statutory and common law.

Administrative areas

1.2 In England – exclusive of Greater London (see 1.3) and the Isles of Scilly where there is a special council constituted by the Secretary of State[1] – the country is divided into counties and districts. The counties are either metropolitan or shire counties and within the former there are metropolitan districts and elsewhere non-metropolitan districts. Some districts are known as boroughs or cities, mostly for historical reasons.

Within the shire counties particularly there are rural parishes. Wales was previously divided into counties and districts, again under the LGA 1972, but local government in the principality was completely restructured by the Local Government (Wales) Act 1994, which created 11 new counties, and 11 county boroughs, each of which comprises one or more communities.

1.3 Greater London comprises the areas of the London boroughs, the City of London, and (of no real significance for local government purposes) the Inner and Middle Temples. The 12 London boroughs whose areas, together with the City, formed the former administrative county of London, are known as inner London boroughs; the remaining area of Greater London comprises outer London boroughs. A strategic Greater London Authority, comprising a directly elected executive mayor and members of the London Assembly, was created by the Greater London Authority Act 1999, resulting in a two-tier structure for the capital.

1.4 The structure of local government is often said to be predominantly two-tier because, in the greater part of the country, county and district councils operate over the same area. In many of the shire counties, however, it is really three-tier because of the existence of parishes. In parts of England, the structure is unitary or single tier, as in Wales, i.e. one local authority alone is responsible for all local government within its area apart from parished areas. In England these are the metropolitan authorities (constituted by the LGA 1972) and the unitary authorities (constituted under the LGA 1992 or the Local Government and Public Involvement in Health Act (LGPIHA) 2007). The number of unitary authorities has greatly increased over recent years both in terms of 'unitary counties' and in terms of 'unitary districts'. Where the new unitary authority is a former county area (e.g. Wiltshire), then the mechanism that is applied under the relevant Structural Changes Order is that existing districts within the county are abolished and their councils wound up and dissolved. A new district is then created, with its boundaries co-terminous with the county area, and the county continues to be administered by the county council. Where the new unitary authority is an existing district (e.g. Swindon), then the county functions for that area are transferred to the district, and a new county is constituted with its boundaries co-terminous with the district's boundaries, but without a separate county council having been created. Where a county area is to be split and two or more new unitary authorities are to be created (e.g. Cheshire), the existing county and districts are abolished as local government areas and the county council and existing district councils dissolved. The required number of new districts and district councils are then constituted, together with counties with co-terminous boundaries but with no county council. In this way the legal fiction is maintained that every district is within a county area, and that, although district councils, they are for some purposes classified as counties.

Local authorities

1.5 Local government legislation (in the LGA 1972 particularly) uses the term 'principal council' for the local authorities in Greater London, the metropolitan areas, and the counties and boroughs and districts. Where, throughout this work, the term 'local authority' is used, it means, as in legislation, a principal council or a local council. It is also used in respect of national park authorities and combined authorities, which may now be of a general kind established under the Local Democracy, Economic Development and Construction Act 2009 (as amended by the Cities and Local Government Devolution Act 2016) or more function-specific, as in the case of combined fire authorities, integrated transport authorities or combined waste authorities.

1.6 The term 'local government', however, will also refer to associated bodies that rely on the same or similar body of law, such as the Police and Crime Commissioners and associated scrutiny panels. All of these cross-authorities will comply with the same general principles and legislative compliance concerning their meetings as their principal councils (required of combined authorities under s. 99 of the LGA 1972) or will have regard to or cross reference the same provisions.

The Committee System

1.7 The above mentioned Localism Act 2011 amendments to the Local Government Act 2000 allow local authorities to 'return to' the committee system form of governance. That is, to operate under the form of governance arrangements permitted according to the Local Government Act 1972, which also remains applicable to ordinary committees of authorities operating executive forms of governance. If a local authority operates a committee system form of governance, the Secretary of State may now also specify functions and actions of the local authority which cannot be delegated (Local Authorities (Committee System) Regulations 2012 (SI 1020/2012)).

1.8 The term 'relevant authority', introduced in the LG&HA 1989 and used in this work to identify authorities referred to in that Act, includes principal councils and some others, e.g. waste disposal authorities and a joint or special planning board constituted for a National Park.[3]

1.9 Local authorities are creatures of statute, i.e. statutory corporations (though many municipal boroughs were originally incorporated by Royal Charter), whose constitution, obligatory duties and discretionary powers are derived directly from Parliament. They are the only democratically elected bodies outside the House of Commons and exist in their own right, not as agents of central government, although, increasingly over recent years, the government has initiated and obtained statutory powers restricting the freedom of action that the authorities previously enjoyed. Local authorities are, therefore, subject to the doctrine of *ultra vires* (see 1.49): they can only do those things that they are compelled or permitted to do by law.[4] Most of the services that local government provides are prescribed by particular Acts of Parliament. For example, county councils and metropolitan district councils and the London boroughs have responsibilities for major functions such as education, the personal social services and for regulatory tasks in, for example, planning and consumer protection, while the district councils discharge the major services of housing, environmental health and refuse collection, among a variety of others, and make bylaws for good rule and government. The new unitary authorities, as already indicated, have sole or joint responsibility for all functions within their area. Shire county councils and the unitaries have close links with or remain the relevant authority for fire services. They also have responsibilities for passenger transport and waste regulation and disposal; in metropolitan areas these services are, in general, provided by joint authorities. Parish and community councils have responsibility for a wide range of minor but important local services. In Wales, the distribution of services is somewhat similar. The services provided by local government change from time to time. There is, as it were, no prescribed constitutional dividing line between the functions of central government and those of local authorities: for example, responsibility for further and higher education has been transferred to independent corporations and much of that for housing is being transferred to housing associations. All local authorities act as a focus for local community action and aspirations:

in other words they have a leadership and coordination role that goes way beyond service delivery.

Local authority meetings

Definition of 'meeting'

1.10 The definition of a meeting as 'a gathering or assembly of two or more persons for a lawful common purpose' (see *Sharp v Dawes* (1876)) holds true in local government, for one person cannot in any sense constitute a meeting.[5] A meeting implies literally the coming together of two or more people; in the context of local government this is because there are certain legal formalities to be observed that require more than one person to be present in order for there to be a valid and lawful decision. These legal formalities include the need for a meeting to be properly convened.

1.11 Not only must there be at least two people present to constitute a meeting, but there ought also to be someone presiding to regulate deliberations. These requirements (that there must be at least two persons and ordinarily someone in control) have been said to be 'axiomatic and universal'.[6] In *R v Swansea City Council ex parte Elitestone Ltd* (1993) it was confirmed that for a local authority meeting, two members are enough. If a meeting of two is to proceed without a chairman (see 11.14) then the decision of the meeting to continue in this way should be clearly recorded – as, of course, with a larger number of members also (see 11.14). However, difficulties could arise where two members alone constitute a meeting and neither is appointed or specifically acts as the chair, because a decision could never be reached on an issue where there was an irreconcilable difference of view. In reality, therefore, normal practice dictates, for local government purposes, that no meeting should consist of fewer than three persons: because if there are two only, the one who is in the chair – and there will ordinarily be a chair – could decide every issue as they wished by exercise of their statutory power to give a casting vote in the event of an equality of votes.

1.12 The person entrusted with authority to regulate the conduct of a meeting is usually styled the chairman or chair, and in the case of council meetings the chair is the chair of the council. The ancient title of mayor for the chair of the council, enjoyed by the chairmen of borough councils, was preserved along with some other 'offices of dignity' by the LGA 1972, ss. 245, 246.

This includes the distinctive title of Lord Mayor conferred on holders of the mayoralty in certain boroughs. The 1972 Act has been amended to provide that in those local authorities where there is an elected mayor, the titles of Mayor and Deputy Mayor can only be used by the elected mayor and their chosen deputy mayor. The statutory Guidance issued following the 2000 Act makes clear, however, that in a very few cases such as where the title of Mayor derives from a Royal Charter, this title would continue whichever form of executive were chosen. In those instances, it is for the local authority to ensure that the two mayoral titles are distinguished from each other in some way. The chair of the council in a borough where there is an elected mayor is styled according to local preference: usually sometimes simply called the Chair of Council (London Boroughs of Lewisham and Newham) or Civic Mayor (Doncaster), or, where permitted, retaining Lord Mayor (Bristol), or, less obviously, called the Speaker (Bedford and the London Borough of Hackney).

Local authority meetings are private meetings

1.13 Generally, meetings may be either public or private. A public meeting has been defined[7] as 'Any meeting bona fide and lawfully held for a lawful purpose and for the furtherance or discussion of any matter of public concern, whether admission thereto be general or restricted.'

This is a wide definition. It includes any meeting in a public place[8] and any meeting on private premises[9] that the public or a section of the public are permitted to attend, whether on payment or otherwise. It might seem that local authority meetings could therefore be held to be public meetings but they are not; the public's right of admission is conferred by statute:[10] it is not a common law right. The fact that local authorities permitted the public to attend council and sometimes committee meetings before the law conferred upon the public a right of access did not affect the position: *Tenby Corporation v Mason* (1908), where the House of Lords held that the public had no right by common law to attend a council meeting: see 3.1.

Purpose of meeting

1.14 It is always important that the purposes of a meeting should be defined at the time it is convened. In the case of all formal meetings there will be an agenda or at least a clear understanding of the terms of reference of the committee or sub-committee, working party, panel or whatever it may be.

1.15 There are other meetings, less formally structured, where the objective may be less well defined, e.g. where local authority representatives receive a presentation of a developer's ambitions for the area, or seek to negotiate with a trade union on some matter in dispute. In those cases the authority's representatives must understand precisely what is to be their role: they must know the parameters within which discussion is to range, and obviously the extent of their power, if any, to bind the council. Unless these things are understood beforehand (with perhaps also a plan of tactics to be adopted depending upon the trend in discussion), the meeting may well be regarded as unsatisfactory on one or other or both sides, or the local authority representatives may find they have unintentionally committed their council to an unwanted course of action.

1.16 Where one local authority joins with another or others and/or with other agencies for the discussion or coordination of some matter in which each is interested, the need for a clear definition of the purpose of the meeting (or, if of continuing concern, the joint committee or other body set up) is particularly important. Such a meeting or committee or body has invariably a diffuse set of objectives that are not necessarily related to one another and not immediately identifiable in terms of responsibility to one set of decision-makers.[11]

1.17 Although in most cases the objective of a meeting will be to reach decisions, this need not always be so. For example, a number of councils are experimenting with holding occasional meetings for discussion only to give members of the council the opportunity of debating, without the pressure of the need for decision-taking, issues such as crime and disorder.

Regulation by law

1.18 The summoning, constitution and conduct of meetings (whether related to local government or not) is governed partly by statute and partly by common law.

The principal statute as regards local authority meetings is the LGA 1972, complemented now by the LG&HA 1989, Part I, and by the Local Government Act 2000 (as amended) and its various statutory instruments in respect of executive functions, but there are other enactments that regulate the constitution of particular committees of local authorities. In total, however, the statutory provisions (although extremely detailed in certain respects) affect a comparatively small part of the relevant law. The standing orders (see Chapter 2), that local authorities are required or empowered to make, seek to regulate matters that would otherwise have to be dealt with in accordance with the practices and conventions recognised at law.

Types of meeting

1.19 There are two broad categories of meetings within the sphere of local government. These can most easily, but not altogether satisfactorily, be termed 'formal' and 'informal'. A formal meeting is one convened in the manner prescribed by law to enable members to transact local authority business with the object of reaching decisions – or formulating recommendations as a basis for decisions – that are intended to commit the authority as a whole. An informal meeting is any other meeting for the consideration or transaction of business, which may or may not comprise councillors or at least comprise them exclusively.

It may be a meeting convened solely for exploratory discussions between councillors and officers or between councillors and representatives of other bodies, it is not intended to be given legal formality and by its nature cannot bind the local authority.

1.20 The main general principles governing formal meetings (of the full council particularly) are outlined in the paragraphs immediately following. Formal meetings of committees, and of gatherings akin to committees, are dealt with in Chapter 9, where there is a discussion of informal meetings of the kind increasingly common in recent years.

Formal meetings

1.21 Formal meetings are those of:

(a) principal councils, i.e. the councils of counties and districts in England and Wales and the London boroughs;
(b) statutory joint committees the authorities and the residuary bodies created, for

example, under the LGA 1985 and the LGA 1992, i.e. the statutory joint authorities, and the residuary bodies;

(c) parish councils and parish meetings in England and community councils and community meetings in Wales; and

(d) their committees and sub-committees.

Each must be convened and constituted in the manner prescribed by statute and/or standing orders.[12] There are other meetings, not of local authorities as such, of what might be termed constituent or associated bodies, which are formal in the sense that they are required to be held by statute.

Special meetings

1.22 There are, in effect, three types of special council meeting: the annual meeting; an extraordinary meeting; and a meeting convened for a specific purpose. Each is regulated by statute in varying respects, particularly as regards the convening of meetings (see Chapter 6).

1.23 The obligation on local authorities to hold an annual meeting in every year is referred to below. The law also requires that certain business shall be transacted at an annual meeting, i.e. the election of a chairman or mayor.

1.24 An extraordinary meeting of the full council is one that is convened other than by direction of the council as a whole, i.e. either by the chairman on their own initiative or upon the requisition of a prescribed number of council members.[13] There is provision also for the calling of meetings of a parish or community council in similar circumstances but the term 'extraordinary meeting' is not used. Although there was earlier provision in the LGA 1933 for such meetings, the term 'extraordinary meeting' was used in the LGA 1972 for the first time to refer to meetings convened in these circumstances. An example of a council meeting convened for a specific purpose is one called to consider a proposal of a local authority to promote or oppose any local or personal Bill in Parliament.[14] Meetings of this character are dealt with in Chapter 7.

1.25 Principal and parish councils are required to hold in every year an annual meeting of the full council;[15] and a parish meeting must assemble annually.[16] But a community meeting is under no such obligation.

The annual meeting of a principal and a parish council must be held within the period prescribed by statute, varying according to whether it is election year.

1.26 Except in the year of election of councillors or a mayor, a principal council may hold its annual meeting on such day in March, April or May as it thinks fit[17] and a parish council on such day in May as it may determine.[18] In the election year, the annual meeting of a principal council must be held 'on the eighth day after the retirement of councillors or such other day within 21 days immediately following the day of retirement as the council may fix': in the case of parish councils, on or within 14 days after the day on which the councillors elected at that election take office. The parish meeting must assemble 'on some day between March 1 and June 1 both inclusive'.

1.27 Each principal, parish and community council and parish meeting may hold in addition to the annual meeting (or any other meeting it is required to hold), such other, i.e. ordinary meetings of the full council, as it may determine.[19] It is difficult to understand why it was thought necessary to provide legislative power to do something that local authorities could surely do in any case. However, in the case of a parish council there is an obligation to hold not fewer than three meetings in addition to the annual meeting,[20] with discretion to determine the hour and days;[21] in the case of a parish that does not have a separate parish council, the parish meeting must (subject to any provision made by a grouping order) assemble at least twice a year.[22]

Some authorities fix the dates by standing orders; others determine them each year at the annual meeting.

Time of meeting

1.28 The time of meeting is not specifically prescribed by statute. In the case of principal councils the 'annual meeting . . . shall be held at such hour as the council may fix, or if no hour is so fixed at 12 noon',[23] which presumably means that, in the unlikely event of a principal council convening an annual meeting without specifying the time of the meeting, it would necessarily be at 12 noon, but the notice might surely still be held to be void for uncertainty. A parish and a community council's annual meeting may, somewhat similarly, be held 'at such hour as the council may fix or, if no hour is so fixed, six o'clock in the evening'.[24] The proceedings at a parish or community meeting must not commence earlier than 6.00 pm.'[25]

Meetings on Sunday

1.29 There appears to be no reason in law why a local authority should not meet on a Sunday, although there may be practical and other reasons why the practice should be regarded as undesirable.[26]

Frequency of meeting

1.30 Provided a local authority holds its statutory annual meeting and observes the requirements about other meetings (see 1.25), it can decide as it wishes upon the frequency of meetings,[27] i.e. it does not necessarily need to space out equally the ordinary meetings – though it may wish to do so in order to arrange a convenient and regular committee cycle: see 10.1. The frequency of meetings will obviously be determined by the volume and incidence of business. There has been a reduction in the amount of meetings of the full council in local authorities since the cabinet system was introduced. Most councils have a meeting of the full council approximately five to seven times per annum, although some have more (East Riding, for example, has ten). Most authorities usually dispense with meetings of the full council for the holiday period in the summer when, the expression goes, the council is 'in recess'. It is common practice for the dates of ordinary meetings to be fixed in advance at the annual meeting of a council, and this will be an extensive task for democratic services staff to get the calendar drawn up and agreed in advance.

Place of meeting

1.31 Meetings of a principal council must be held 'at such place, either within or without their areas as they may direct';[28] so, too, may meetings of a parish council and a community council except that the meetings must 'not be held in premises licensed for the sale of intoxicating liquor unless no other suitable room is available either free of charge or at a reasonable cost'.[29] This discriminatory prohibition against the holding of a meeting on licensed premises applies also to parish meetings, although the statute is otherwise silent as to place.

1.32 Where a local authority decides to hold a meeting outside its administrative area, it must take account of the accessibility of the venue for those entitled to be present. One authority, keen to foster its ties with a twin city across the Channel by holding a meeting there, prudently arranged for the proceedings – which were mostly of a ceremonial nature anyhow – to be confirmed at the authority's next ordinary meeting within its area in the UK.

1.33 These statutory provisions relating to place of meeting apply also to committee meetings.[30] Any local authority committee meeting may be held anywhere, either within or outside its area, as the council or committee may decide, except in the case of committees of a parish council or parish meeting or of a community council, which must not be held on licensed premises unless no other accommodation is available free or at reasonable cost.

1.34 It follows from the previous paragraph that if a number of councillors choose to meet of their own accord – as a political group or otherwise – their informal gathering together does not constitute a meeting for the lawful transaction of business. Notwithstanding this duality, for the purposes of this work, we assume that local authority meetings will take place ordinarily at the authority's offices.

Sometimes, however, particularly in the case of committees or sub-committees, a meeting will be arranged at a defined location out of the office on the highway for various purposes. For instance, there may be an inspection of a site that is the subject of a planning application. The reasons for meetings of this character are numerous. In all such instances, care must be taken to avoid obstruction of the highway, because that would constitute an offence. Highways exist for 'purposes of passage' and anyone using a highway for some other purpose is in theory a trespasser; but so long as the meeting is not likely to interfere with the right of passage or lead to a breach of the peace, then there is no reason why a local authority should not hold such a meeting. It may be prudent, of course, depending on circumstances, to advise people living in the vicinity of the meeting, so as to avoid unnecessary concern or speculation when they see a gathering outside their property.

Requisites of a valid meeting

1.35 In order to constitute a valid meeting there must be three essentials:

- at least two persons present – but see the comment above as to why this must normally be three;
- someone in the chair or a decision taken to proceed without a chair; and
- a lawful common purpose.

In addition, in relation to local authority meetings, there must be compliance with statutory requirements and standing orders, as to the time or period within which a meeting must be held and, in certain cases, as to the place of meeting. Each meeting must also be:

- properly convened, i.e. there must be public notice of the meeting and a summons sent to every person entitled to attend, which may now be by electronic means if the member consents to this in advance,[31] and papers must be available five clear days in advance; and
- properly constituted, i.e. (i) the proper persons must be present with the appropriate person in the chair, and (ii) the requisite quorum of members must be present.

Any irregularity in the convening, constitution or conduct of a meeting may, according to its nature (i.e. whether a council, cabinet, committee or sub-committee meeting), invalidate all or part of the proceedings. But want of service of the summons will not ordinarily affect the meeting's validity and there is a presumption in law (i.e. until the contrary is proved) that, once the minutes have been drawn up and signed, the meeting was properly convened and held and the members present duly qualified; even if there was a vacancy among the members or a defect in the election or qualification of any member, the proceedings are not thereby invalidated. This appears to be the effect of s. 82 of the LGA 1972, which provides that 'the acts and proceedings of any person elected to an office under this Act and acting in that office shall, notwithstanding his disqualification or want of qualification, be as valid and effectual as if he had been qualified'.

1.36 It follows from the previous paragraph that if a number of councillors choose to meet of their own accord – as a political group or otherwise – their informal gathering together does not constitute a meeting for the lawful transaction of business. Most local authorities allow the use of council accommodation for such informal meetings, although some make a charge to cover set-up costs, cleaning and heating. It is undoubtedly a matter for the local authority's discretion whether and when to allow the use of council-owned premises; and as a single councillor has few rights as an individual member, it may seem to follow that a number of them can claim no right by mere multiplication (although there might be some kind of right, extra-legal perhaps, in a number of councillors who wanted to meet for the purpose of framing a requisition for the calling of an extraordinary meeting of the council. Most local authorities now have an agreed code of practice governing the use of the council's resources, including use of council accommodation for informal meeting purposes, for example, the use for party group meetings and by individual councillors who wish to meet their constituents.

Decision-making

Determination of questions

1.37 As already indicated, most local authority meetings are held to reach a decision on an item or items of business: to decide a question.[32] This work is primarily concerned with procedural and associated matters, but it may be relevant to indicate briefly three stages in the process of decision-making: firstly, the need for a decision; secondly, an examination of the various lawful options that would lead to a solution, as well as consideration and analysis of the costs, consequences and risks; and finally, the choice of the most appropriate solution. This can be facilitated by careful preparation of the agenda at officer level beforehand. A rational or systematic approach to decision-making cannot always be pursued. There may be insufficient time to assemble and consider all the options, even if there could be perfect knowledge of all possibilities and their consequences. There is also the influence of politics on the decision-making. Much has been done, organisationally and otherwise, to improve the accountability and quality of decision-making in local government.

In 1991, the then Department of the Environment issued a consultation paper on The Internal Management of Local Authorities in England to encourage debate on the issue. This debate culminated in the Local Government Act 2000 (LGA 2000), which required those local authorities with populations of 85,000 or over as at 30 June 1999 to adopt executive arrangements whereby the management of the authority would be based on a separation of the executive, regulatory, scrutiny and representative roles of councillors. This Act also allowed the delegation of powers to individual members for the first time and had a profound effect on the style and format of local authority meetings, and on their decision-making. This issue is dealt with in more detail below.

Elements of a lawful decision

1.38 To be lawful a decision of a local authority, if taken by the full council or by a committee, must:

- comply with the cardinal principle of being reached by the required majority of councillors present and voting at a properly constituted meeting:;
- be one that the council is empowered or obliged to take, otherwise it is *ultra vires*;
- not offend against Wednesbury reasonableness, which in itself has several facets to consider, including that of bias or predetermination, discussed further below; and,
- if taken under delegated power, it must furthermore come within the scope of that power.

There are practical considerations, too. A decision must:

- if it is meant to lead to action (as opposed, for example, to a resolution merely expressing the council's view on an issue), obviously be capable of being executed, otherwise it will be of no effect; and
- not purport to undo what has already been done irrevocably, although it can rescind an earlier decision where this is feasible, provided standing orders allow this; and
- comply with the council's own internal processes for decision-making, and be in accordance with the council's own principles of decision-making, which are set out in the constitution of those councils operating executive arrangements.

General principles

A decision cannot ordinarily be impugned because of the lack of qualification of a councillor.[33] Ordinarily, too, a decision cannot be challenged because of the motive of a councillor or councillors who voted in favour of the proposition[34] or just because a councillor has not directed their mind in the meeting itself to the arguments for and against or to other relevant considerations: see *R v Waltham Forest London Borough Council ex parte Waltham Forest Ratepayers Association Group* (1987) and *Bishop's Stortford Civic Federation v East Hertfordshire District Council* [2014] EWHC 348 (Admin). A decision may come within the ambit of maladministration.

Majority present and voting

1.39 There is a general principle governing the manner in which an authority shall reach a decision. This is that, save where other prescriptions apply[35] in particular circumstances:

> '... all questions coming or arising before a local authority shall be decided by a majority of the members of the authority present and voting thereon at a meeting of the authority.'[36]

1.40 This means that every decision that falls to be taken by a local authority (unless it is one that an officer or individual member, including an elected mayor, has been empowered to make) can lawfully be reached only by the full council at a properly constituted council meeting or by a committee or sub-committee acting under delegated powers, and then only upon the affirmative vote of a majority of the members present and actually voting. Therefore, an authority of 100 members may properly be committed to a course of action at a council meeting at which no more than the prescribed quorum is present (say 25 council members, which represents the quorum in the case of a principal council of that membership), of whom only three trouble to put up their hand in favour when a vote is taken and two vote against: or – a more extreme example – if one member votes in favour and everyone else abstains.

1.41 Important consequences flow from this principle. It means that even where there has been extensive consultation with the public, including a local poll under s. 116 of the Local Government Act 2003, or where a referendum has been held under the provisions of the LGA 2000 in relation to the operation of executive arrangements, the local authority in full council or by a committee or sub-committee (or through the agency of another local authority or a joint committee) alone can make a decision on a matter that falls to be discharged by the authority and that has not been delegated to an individual; and it must do it at a properly constituted meeting. It cannot make a decision by asking councillors by letter to agree or reject a projected course of action. Nor can it do so by any informal gathering of its members: in, for example, a meeting of the majority group members of the council. Nor may any individual council member vote by proxy:[37] they must be present at a meeting if they wish their vote to count.

There must be a properly convened assembly of council members (in council or committee or sub-committee) so that a decision can be made in circumstances where the cut and thrust of debate and argument and counterargument can take place if members are so minded: the fact that most members may take no part in the proceedings or abstain from voting does not affect the position.

1.42 The questions to be decided are questions of every kind (except, as indicated already, those for which some special procedure and/or majority vote is required): the same principles apply whether the decision is concerned with major policy or administrative detail. The law does not make such distinctions but, of course, the local authority can do so by delegating to committees, sub-committees or officers, as it thinks appropriate, power to make decisions on matters that are less important. Even before the law permitted such delegation, officers in practice operated either under extra-legal authority to act within certain defined administrative areas or by presumption in law as agents of their authority.

Voting

1.43 Voting at every local authority meeting is ordinarily by show of hands or as otherwise prescribed in standing orders. This is expressly required by law in the case of parish and community councils unless standing orders otherwise provide, but no method of voting is laid down by statute in the case of principal councils (where in some cases an electronic system is used) or in the case of parish and community meetings. Every person presiding at any local authority meeting, whether of the full council, committee or sub-committee, may exercise a second or casting vote. The whole matter of voting is considered in detail later.

1.44 Ordinarily, no account is taken by the law as to the motives of those who vote, but the courts will look at those motives where they have led to a member voting other than in accordance with the duties that that member holds in coming to their decision. This happens when: the member allows their private interest to override the public interest, they have fettered their discretion in some way, they have taken into account an irrelevant consideration or they have failed to take account of a relevant consideration in coming to their decision on how to vote. All of this is discussed below concerning the Wednesbury principle, predetermination (not to be confused with predisposition) and bias. For example, a decision might be set aside where it is proved that the councillors who voted in a majority for a resolution were motivated by a malicious desire to damage a third party and so committed the offence of misfeasance in public office: see the House of Lords case *Jones v Swansea County Council* (1990).

There is no strict obligation imposed by law to say that members can only vote if present throughout a meeting and therefore have considered the arguments for and against a proposal. A member can come into the council chamber or committee room just as the chairman is calling for a show of hands and so cast a vote with little or no idea at all of the issue before the meeting. This is not dissimilar, of course, from what happens in the Commons.[38] Standing orders, however, often lay down that only those members present in the meeting when the proposition is put from the chair may vote. This only means present in the room and not necessarily seated, but can sometimes lead to an undignified rush after a lengthy debate. Putting the proposition means the moment when the chair asks for those voting in favour of it. There is, however, an important exception considered later: when a meeting is exercising a judicial or quasi-judicial role it would be improper, and potentially leave the council open to challenge on Wednesbury grounds, for a member to cast a vote without having been present to hear the submissions beforehand.

The Wednesbury principle

1.45 There is another procedural principle that a local authority must take into account in the course of arriving at a decision. If a decision is not to be challenged and declared of no effect on grounds of unreasonableness or, rather, irrationality, it must comply with what is known as the Wednesbury principle. This principle was enunciated in *Associated Provincial Picture Houses Ltd v Wednesbury Corporation* (1948). Lord Greene summarised it:

> '... the court is entitled to investigate the action of the local authority with a view to seeing whether it has taken into account matters which it ought not to take into account or, conversely, has refused to take into account or neglected to take into account matters which it ought to take into account. Once that question is answered in favour of the local authority, it may still be possible to say that the local authority, nevertheless, has come to a conclusion so unreasonable that no reasonable authority could ever have come to it. In such a case . . . the court can interfere. The power of the court to interfere in each case is not that of an appellate authority to override a decision of the local authority but is that of a judicial authority which is concerned, and concerned only, to see whether the local authority has contravened the law by acting in excess of the powers which Parliament has confided in it.'

The local authority's advisers clearly have a responsibility to ensure that, in reaching a decision, the council or a committee addresses its mind only to matters that it ought to take into account or does not refuse or neglect to take account of such matters and is not influenced by matters that are irrelevant. The minutes of proceedings at a meeting might usefully recite the considerations taken into account by the council, committee or sub-committee in reaching its decision. The need to demonstrate that the right reasons have been taken into account in reaching decisions puts a premium on accurate and comprehensive report writing: see *R v Camden Borough Council ex parte Cran and Others* (1995) where McCullough J was critical of the way in which the comments of residents had been conveyed to members considering the designation of a controlled parking zone and the designation was quashed; and *Costas Georgiou v Enfield London Borough and Others* (2004), where Richards J considered that the members of the planning committee were not given sufficient information to ensure the proper discharge of their functions in relation to the planning application and that the committee's decision was consequently flawed. In *R (on the application of Ware) v Neath Port Talbot County Borough Council & National Grid* (2008), where erroneous advice was given by a monitoring officer to a councillor and that advice was acted upon so that the councillor did not participate in a planning decision of a local authority, the court held that following advice from the monitoring officer, any decision reached through the absence of that councillor was liable to be quashed on the grounds that it had been reached by having regard to an immaterial consideration if the advice was incorrect. In this particular instance the correct advice had been given, but the Court of Appeal appeared to leave it open for such decisions to be quashed if the advice had not been correct. The court confirmed the approach that it is a matter for each individual member as to whether or not to take part in the decision-making process.

1.46 In *R v Waltham Forest London Borough Council ex parte Waltham Forest Ratepayers Action Group* (1987), the court had to consider the extent to which party political considerations can lawfully be taken into account in decision-making.

Members of the majority group on the council had discussed at a party meeting what policy should be pursued as to the setting of the rate at the forthcoming council meeting. The group agreed to support a rate increase of 62% for the domestic rate and 56.6% for the non-domestic rate. The group's standing orders required members of the group to refrain from voting in opposition to group decisions under penalty of the withdrawal of the party whip. A number of members who voted against this level of rate increase at the group meeting voted in favour at the council meeting at which the previously agreed amounts were passed by 31 votes to 26. A number of ratepayers sought judicial review on a variety of grounds but the Divisional Court rejected arguments to the effect that:

1 the councillors had fettered their discretion by regarding themselves as bound by the terms of their election manifesto to undertake expenditure that rendered such a rate inevitable;
2 the resolution was 'irrational' or Wednesbury unreasonable;
3 there was no genuine or adequate consultation with representatives of commerce and industry; and
4 six or seven councillors had voted contrary to their personal views.

The Court of Appeal dismissed an appeal confined to issue (4). The court held that had the councillors in question voted for the resolution not because they were in favour of it but because their discretion had been fettered by the vote at the group meeting, then the councillors would have been in breach of their duty to make up their own minds as to what rate was appropriate. That, however, was not established on the facts. The court noted that the sanction was only withdrawal of the party whip: there was nothing to prevent a councillor who voted against the party line continuing as an independent member. The court found that the councillors were entitled to take account of party loyalty and party policy as relevant considerations, provided they did not dominate so as to exclude other considerations. This is an example of a predisposition, rather than a predetermination, which is discussed below.

It is also a useful note, perhaps, on the role of the member: the member must take into account all relevant considerations, and it is arguable that it is the role of officers to place these before the members and also advise on the facts as to what is not a relevant consideration, but what comparative weight to place on those considerations is a matter for the members.

Bias and predetermination

1.47 In making decisions, councillors must observe the distinction between having a closed mind to arguments that may be contrary to the rules of natural justice and therefore unlawful, and simply having a predisposition to taking a certain view. The test was set out in *Porter v Magill* (2001) by Lord Hope who said that 'the question is whether the fair-minded and informed observer, having considered the facts, would conclude that there was a real possibility that the tribunal was biased'.

There have been a number of cases on apparent bias and closed minds. In *Mohammed Reza Ghadami v Harlow District Council and Sapphire Retail Fund Ltd* (2004), a chairman of a district council planning committee had been close to developers and had conveyed to an objector the threat of compulsory purchase of his land. The court held that a fair-minded and informed observer would be led to conclude that there was a real possibility that the councillor had made up his mind in favour of the development and that he would approach the decision on the planning application with a closed mind and without impartial consideration of all the planning issues. Such apparent bias or predetermination vitiated the grant of planning permission. Also, in *Bovis Homes Ltd v New Forest DC* (2002), the chairman's membership of a particular interest group would have caused a fair-minded observer to conclude that there was a real danger of bias on her part and that her presence at and participation in the relevant meeting vitiated the decision. In addition, committee members had attended the meeting with a draft resolution already prepared, which they adopted without amendment or qualification, thereby giving the impression that they had attended the meeting with closed minds. The committee's decision was quashed.

These cases highlight the importance of ensuring that the minutes of a meeting are clear as to the actual decision being made and record any other matters of importance. The cases also highlight the importance of members being clear as to the capacity in which they are taking part in any discussion. This is particularly crucial in 'dual-hatted' cases where they take part in various stages of the decision-making process as a member of more than one of the bodies involved. If this does occur, members must ensure that there is no conflict of interest or apparent bias.

This approach can be contrasted to that in *R v Hereford and Worcester County Council ex parte Wellington Parish Council* (1996) where members of the county council's gypsy liaison group who had put forward a particular location for a gypsy site voted for it in the planning committee when their application came up for consideration. Mr Justice Harrison had no doubts that such an action was proper and lawful provided that opportunity was given to all arguments to be put forward.

Members should be careful as to throwaway remarks that may be interpreted as bias or predetermination. *National Assembly for Wales v Condron* (2006) concerned a planning committee's decision to allow a planning application, following a public inquiry and an inspector's report recommending granting permission. It was contended that the decision was vitiated by the appearance of bias arising out of a remark made by the chairman of the committee in a casual meeting with an objector the day before the committee meeting to the effect that he was 'going to go with the report of the inspector'. It was argued that this indicated that he had already made up his mind to accept the inspector's recommendation. The court held that those words went no further than indicating a predisposition to follow the inspector's report and not a closed mind. It did not matter how the person to whom those words were addressed had interpreted them. The question was whether the fears expressed by the complainant were objectively justified. There was a clear distinction between a legitimate predisposition towards a particular outcome and an illegitimate predetermination of the outcome. The wider context of a chance meeting and a casual remark was also important in assessing the significance of the words used. Having regard to the terms of the inspector's report, the fact that the members of the committee had relevant training and were subject to a code of conduct, and the nature of the committee discussions, which were unusually prolonged, the court decided that a fair-minded and informed observer would not conclude that there was a real possibility that the chairman was biased.

In the case of *R (on the application of Island Farm Development Ltd) v Bridgend County Borough Council* (2006), Collins J follows a similar non-interventionist line, and confessed to some doubt as to the approach in the Georgiou case, when he decided that there was no apparent bias or predetermination by the cabinet of a newly elected local authority in reaching a decision to discontinue negotiations for the sale of land, as there was no positive evidence to show that the local authority had approached the decision with a closed mind. Mr Justice Collins considered that local authority councillors were entitled to have regard to and apply policies that they believed in, particularly if those policies formed part of an election manifesto. In considering bias and predetermination, it is apparent that the courts are generally reluctant to interfere in what they consider the political process – *R v Waltham Forest LBC ex parte Baxter* (1988) and *R v Amber Valley DC ex parte Jackson* (1985) – instances where members have decided issues based on a political predisposition. A Court of Appeal decision *R (Lewis) v Persimmon Homes Teesside Ltd* (2008) pointed out that 'clear pointers' will be required if a councillor's '. . . state of mind is to be held to have become a closed, or apparently closed, mind at the time of decision'.

The *Island Farm* decision can be said to have ended a period where over several years the judicial view moved from the prescriptive to the permissive. During this period, the government determined that it would end the pendulum swing and set the matter out in legislation. This resulted in section 25 of the Localism Act 2011, which contains provisions for dealing with allegations of predetermination or matters which otherwise raise an issue about the validity of a decision, where the decision-maker(s) had or appeared to have a closed mind when making the decision. The reality is a set of words which says much the same thing as the judgement in *Island Farm* did – only in many people's view, not as clear or as understandable. The legislation sets out that the decision-maker(s) is not to be taken to have had a closed mind 'just because' the decision-maker/s had previously done anything relevant to the decision, that directly or indirectly, indicated what view the decision-maker took, or would or might take, in relation to a matter. However, if there is a presumption of 'no closed mind', then it is arguable that this must be rebuttable. It may therefore be appropriate for Monitoring Officers to warn members against making extreme comments which could indicate a closed mind, and to provide them with guidance in respect of the new provisions.

The courts have already recognised to some extent the presumption against bias in relation to elected members, as was demonstrated in a number of cases including *R (Lewis) v Persimmon Homes Teesside Ltd* (2008) above. Key to the statutory provision appears to be the 'just because' provision. If a member is, for example, very clear about their position with strong language in support of their view, then the legal position that if a member approached a decision with a closed mind, it could affect the validity of the decision, must still prevail. Equally, if a member could show that when taking the decision they had approached it with an open mind despite making other views known, and taken account of all relevant information, they could reasonably participate in a valid decision. The more extreme and firm the views expressed by members, then the more difficult it is to show that they still have an open mind.

Decision must not be ultra vires

1.48 Although a decision may have been made in a procedurally correct manner, it will be *ultra vires* if it is one that the local authority has no power to make. A detailed discussion of the doctrine of *ultra vires* would be beyond the scope of this work, but briefly it means that a local authority can lawfully do only those things that it is obliged to do by law or that it is permitted or assumed to be permitted to do by law. In the course of years, the courts have adopted a more liberal attitude to the assumed powers of a local authority – in tune, it might be said, with present-day recognition that local government is concerned with more than the mere carrying out of specific powers and duties.[39] In s. 111 of LGA 1972, authorities have power to do anything (whether or not involving expenditure, borrowing or lending money or the acquisition or disposal of any property or rights) calculated to facilitate or be conducive or incidental to the discharge of any of their functions. Local authorities and the Audit Commission did not always agree over the extent of powers conferred by s. 111; and the dangers of relying on the section as a basis for exercising powers has been shown in cases involving the giving of guarantees to banks: see *Credit Suisse v Allerdale Borough Council* (1994) and *Credit Suisse v Waltham Forest London Borough Council* (1996). Furthermore, there is power in s. 137 enabling any local authority, subject to certain restrictions (particularly the exclusion of expenditure that the authority is otherwise permitted or obliged to make), to incur expenditure not otherwise authorised.

In order to ensure that local government is able to act in the widest possible way, the Localism Act 2011 introduced a general power of competence. Section 1 introduced a general power of competence, subject to certain restrictions, under which local authorities can do anything that an individual with full capacity (a 'natural person') could do. The power is very wide and may be exercised 'in any way whatever' and anywhere – i.e. it is not tied to the benefit of the inhabitants of an authority's own area or its residents. The concept of *ultra vires* also used to apply to all companies, until a similar provision enabled the need for a 'memorandum of association', specifically setting out what a company existed to achieve (its objects), to be done away with. Anyone who thought that the Localism Act general power of competence was an equivalent provision and a panacea for all thoughts of legal restraints that existed on local authority activities should think again. The exercise of the power is obviously subject to express statutory restraints, for example, s. 149 of the Equality Act 2010, where the power is one of the 'functions' to the exercise of which the s. 149 duty applies. Any existing prohibition on local authority powers will continue to apply. Where the exercise of the general power is 'overlapped' by an existing power, any restrictions imposed on the latter will apply to the general power. Arrangements for the discharge of the authority's functions, governance and contracting out of functions are expressly excluded from the general power. Use of the power for doing things for a commercial purpose are limited in that they must be carried out through a separate company (currently under Part V of the LG&HA 1989). Restrictions on local authority powers in future legislation will only apply to the general power where expressed to do so. However, there are still 140 reserve powers ('Henry VIII clauses'), where the government gives itself the power to repeal or amend a bill once it becomes an act.

Before the coming into force of the general power of competence, a job of the governance lawyer and democratic services officers in support was to search through all of local government law to see if there are legal powers that allow the local authority to carry out a desired action. However, that role has now been changed, to search through all of local government law to see if there are legal powers that do not allow the local authority to carry out a desired action. This may seem slightly tongue-in-cheek, but this is not the case. Without denigrating what a huge step forward the general power of competence is, and how tremendously useful it has been in allowing us to help achieve the aims of our authorities, the express and inherent restrictions are many. For example, having the power to do all of the things that a natural person can leaves out many functions that are part and parcel of being a local authority: a natural person cannot raise taxes, cannot force entry onto someone else's land, cannot do works in default, cannot issue licences to operate taxis, gamble or serve alcohol, cannot take children or adults into care without their consent, cannot operate blue-light services and so on (and quite rightly so). For these functions, we must fall back on s. 111 referred to above. The power also does not do away with the common-law duties associated with local authority decision-making, such as fiduciary interest and natural justice.

It also remains a general principle of administrative law that a public body must exercise a statutory power for the purpose for which the power was conferred by Parliament, and not for any unauthorised purpose. An unauthorised purpose may be laudable in its own right, yet it is still unlawful. The issue is not whether or not the public body has acted in the public interest, but whether it has acted in accordance with the purpose for which the statutory power was conferred. Where a statutory power is exercised both for the purpose for which it was conferred and for some other purpose, the public body will have acted unlawfully unless the authorised purpose was its dominant purpose.[39]

In *Porter v Magill* [2002] 2 AC 357, Lord Bingham set out the general principle at [19]:

'(1) Powers conferred on a local authority may be exercised for the public purpose for which the powers were conferred and not otherwise. A very clear statement of this principle is to be found in Wade & Forsyth, Administrative Law, 8th ed. (2000), pp 356–357. The corresponding passage in an earlier edition of that work was expressly approved by Lord Bridge of Harwich in *R v Tower Hamlets London Borough Council, Ex p. Chetnik Developments Ltd* [1988] AC 858, 872:

> "Statutory power conferred for public purposes is conferred as it were upon trust, not absolutely – that is to say, it can validly be used only in the right and proper way which Parliament when conferring it is presumed to have intended."

The principle is routinely applied, as by Neill LJ in *Credit Suisse v Allerdale Borough Council* [1997] QB 306, 333 who described it as "a general principle of public law".

To underline this point, the ruling in *Attfield, R (on the application of) v London Borough of Barnet* [2013], where the council had increased "the charges for resident parking permits and visitor vouchers . . . to generate additional income to meet projected expenditure for road maintenance and improvement, concessionary fares and other road transport costs" was challenged by a local resident. This led to the court finding that the relevant legislation was "not a fiscal measure and does not authorise the authority to use its powers to charge local residents for parking in order to raise surplus revenue for other transport purposes funded by the General Fund".'[40]

'Blanket' resolutions on policy

1.49 One other matter relating to the effectiveness of a decision needs to be touched upon here. It is in order – indeed, there is much to commend the practice – for a local authority to pass a resolution setting out its general policy on any issue in order to ensure consistency in decision-making. But whatever rules or guidelines on policy the authority may establish in this way, the general principle (though there is an exception: see 1.47) is that a local authority must not apply them so rigidly that it precludes proper consideration of the merits or otherwise of individual questions that arise for decision within the general policy or guidelines. See, for example, among cases on fettering discretion in self-created rules of policy: *R v Port of London Authority ex parte Kynoch* (1919); and *R v Bexley London Borough Council ex parte Jones* (1994) compared with *R v Southwark London Borough Council ex parte Udu* (1995).

1.50 There is, however, at least one instance where the law permits the passing of a rigid blanket resolution. The Lotteries and Amusement Act 1976, sch. 3, para. 2, and the Gaming Act 1968, sch. 9, para. 3, concerned with the licensing of permits for commercial provision of amusements with prizes and permits for gaming machines, expressly allow policy resolutions by the local authority declaring, for example, that it will not issue or renew any permits in respect of premises of a specified class. It is evident, however, that the court will interpret the statutory rules strictly: see *R v Herrod ex parte Leeds City District Council* (1976) and *Walker v Leeds City Council* (1976).

Maladministration

1.51 A further factor to be mentioned in relation to decision-making is the possibility of a local authority being found guilty of maladministration by a local government ombudsman. The term 'ombudsman', not used in the statute, comes from the Swedish and means 'people's defender'. Under the LGA 1974, Part III as amended,[41] it is open to an aggrieved individual to take a complaint of maladministration, direct or through a councillor, against a local authority (but not a parish or community council or a parish or community meeting), a police authority, or one of the authority's committees, to a local commissioner of either the Commission for Local Administration in England or the Commission for Local Administration in Wales, as the case may be. The Act does not define maladministration (it is for the ombudsman to decide whether maladministration has occurred) but it refers, for example, to the way in which an authority's decision has been made.[42] It covers administrative action or inaction based on or influenced by improper considerations or conduct (e.g. arbitrariness, malice or bias, including unfair discrimination), neglect, unjustified delay, incompetence, failure to observe relevant rules or procedures, failure to take relevant considerations into account, failure to establish or review procedures when there is a duty or obligation to do so, and the use of faulty systems. There are certain matters expressly excluded from the ombudsman's jurisdiction and they have no power to compel a local authority to redress or compensate anyone whose interests have been prejudiced through maladministration; but clearly most local authorities do act on what the Ombudsman says.

Variation of decisions

1.52 Decisions once made may, so far as practicable and lawful, be subsequently varied or rescinded although standing orders ordinarily seek to limit the frequency of change in this respect. Clearly it would be impracticable for an authority to purport to rescind a resolution upon which action has been taken that could not be undone; and unlawful to purport to rescind a resolution so as to disadvantage a third party who has properly relied on the decision unless, of course, the law permits the revocation or amendment of the decision when compensation may be payable. As to the position regarding committee and sub-committee decisions.

When does a resolution become effective?

1.53 In most instances the decision of a local authority takes effect immediately the resolution is properly passed, unless there is provision in the council's constitution that a certain number of days must elapse before a decision can be acted upon to allow it to be 'called in' or referred back to the decision-maker either by a specified number of members, or by an overview and scrutiny committee or council, depending upon the precise arrangements adopted by the particular local authority concerned. In certain circumstances, however, a decision cannot be acted upon until specific formalities have been observed; a compulsory purchase order made by an authority is not valid until confirmed by the confirming body;[43] a decision to sell land is ineffective until the formal deed has been executed; and in some cases a decision does not take effect until formal notification has been served upon those affected by it, e.g. a decision to dismiss an employee, or a decision granting planning permission.

1.54 There have been several cases on whether resolution or notification amounts to a grant of planning permission: see *Slough Estates v Slough Borough Council* (1969). In *R v West Oxfordshire District Council ex parte C. H. Pearce Homes Ltd* (1986), however, the issue was clearly decided. Woolf J said:

> 'Suffice it to say that even in the absence of authority I would, from my examination of the [planning] code, find a clear indication that it is the notification which amounts to the grant, and that where the notification is proceeded by a resolution of the authority that resolution should be regarded as a resolution that planning permission should be granted and that the resolution is intended to be implemented by the notification which amounts to the grant. Accordingly, until there has been notification, an applicant for planning permission has not received permission.'

This distinction between the resolution and the administrative act that gives the resolution full effect is important for several reasons. The local authority can change its mind after the resolution and before formal notification to revoke its decision. In *R v Yeovil Borough Council ex parte Trustees of Elim Pentecostal Church* (1972), there was a change of heart by the planning authority, which had previously resolved to grant planning permission, and the applicant's application for an order of mandamus requiring the council to issue planning permission was refused. Thus, of course, compensation for any revocation of planning permission cannot arise until after formal notification of the decision.

1.55 While it is important that, as a general rule, where a decision is to take effect on a certain future date, the resolution should specifically include that date, the resolution may not necessarily be defective if it does not, provided that the local authority's intention is clear, e.g. in the minutes as distinct from the resolution itself. In *Sheffield City Council v Graingers Wines Ltd* (1977), it was held that there had been sufficient compliance with statute even though a resolution under s. 17 of the General Rate Act 1967 (relating to the rating of unoccupied property) did not in its terms state when the resolution was to take effect and despite provision in s. 17(2), as amended by the LGA 1972, s. 15(1), that:

> '. . . the day to be specified in a resolution under subs. (1) of this section shall be . . . the first day of a rate period for that area beginning after the date on which the resolution is passed.'

The Court of Appeal considered this was a serious omission but, while the trial judge held that it was fatal, the Court of Appeal took the view that, in the circumstances of the case, it was not: neither justice nor common sense required the court to isolate the resolution from its context to 'make that violent extraction of the kernel from the nut in which it shelters'.

Continuing validity of resolution

1.56 As a general rule there is no need for a local authority to pass a new resolution to replace one passed under legislation that, though repealed, is re-enacted to similar effect. For example, a resolution to apply the provisions of s. 19 of the Local Government (Miscellaneous Provisions) Act 1982 (which concerned the registration of food hawkers and premises) is of continuing effect by virtue of the Interpretation Act 1978, ss. 16 and 17, despite the repeal of s. 19 of the 1982 Act and its re-enactment in Pt IV of the Food Act 1984.

1.57 The IA 1978 provides in s. 16 that where an Act repeals an enactment the repeal does not, unless the contrary intention appears, affect the previous operation of the enactment repealed or anything done thereunder; and s. 17 provides that where an Act is repealed, with or without modification, then unless the contrary intention appears, any reference in any other enactment to the Act repealed is to be constructed as a reference to the re-enacted provisions.

Inaccurate notification of a decision

1.58 What if an officer of the local authority misinterprets the terms of a decision to a third party or provides an inaccurate notification of the decision? Is the authority bound by its decision as minuted or by the officer's notification of its terms? A discussion of the concept of estoppel is outside the scope of this book but, so far as planning is concerned, this view of Michael Albery QC[44] is of interest:

> 'It is submitted . . . that where planning permission is granted or refused by a corporate body, the grant or refusal is constituted by the appropriate resolution of that body or of its delegated committee. On the other hand, the applicant is entitled to assume that notice of such decision received from the officer of such body entrusted with the conduct of such matters correctly represents the decision. He is not bound to call for a minute of the resolution in order to check such accuracy. If the applicant acts, as will usually happen, to his detriment on the faith of such notice, and perhaps even if he does not, the planning authority

> will be estopped from denying the accuracy of such notice. This estoppel will ensure for the benefit of the applicant's successors in title, in that for conveyancing purposes the notice can be treated as conveying the terms of the permission. But an applicant who has reason to suspect that the notice is less favourable to him than the resolution of which it purports to give notice is entitled to obtain copies of and to rely on the resolution itself, but not of course the application or surrounding correspondence unless these are incorporated into the resolution by reference.'

Conduct of local authority business

Official reports

1.59 The ways in which local authorities conduct their business, i.e. through the traditional processes of democratic machinery, have been the subject of several important inquiries over the past half-century or so. The 1960s saw the publication of the twin reports of *Maud on The Management of Local Government* and *Mallaby on Staffing of Local Government*. Later, prior to the reorganisation of local government outside Greater London in the 1970s, there was the Bains report on *The New Local Authorities: Management and Structure* and the complementary Patterson report *The New Scottish Local Authorities: Organisation and Management Structures* and the Layfield Report in 1976 into Local Government Finance. Then came the Widdicombe Report: *The Conduct of Local Authority Business* in 1986. These reports were concerned with wider issues than those that relate to local authority meetings, but many of their observations, conclusions and recommendations impinge on the decision-making process. Finally Nolan, in its Third Report of the Committee on Standards in Public Life (July 1997, Cm.3 702), looked at a number of issues relating to the subject matter of this work.

Party organisation

1.60 The political organisation and greater political intensity of local government has been an aspect that came late to many parts of local authority working and has had a profound effect on the conduct of local authority business, seen particularly in the LG&HA 1989, which made provision for political balance in the membership of a local authority to be translated into committees and sub-committees, but not the cabinet. There have been other changes: councillors have a greater control now than formerly, and policy issues arise for consideration more often nowadays from the initiative of councillors through the majority party group than from officers. After a local election, members of the political party that has secured the largest number of seats will 'form an administration' to run the authority politically, decide whom to appoint as committee chairs, and significantly discuss and often virtually make the more important decisions in group meetings. It is for the senior executive member (elected mayor or leader) to decide who will be members of their cabinet, but this is invariably also agreed to some extent by members themselves. Control of the authority means that the group decisions can be carried through the formal meetings procedure and translated lawfully into effective action. Members of minority parties will also hold group meetings and, either in concert or separately, will provide a focus of 'opposition' in the council chamber if not in committees. Where an election has resulted in a no overall control – or balanced – council, then the parties may seek to arrive at some accommodation between themselves. One party group will form an administration with the support, tacit or otherwise, of another; committee chairs may in these circumstances preside over committee meetings but with greater influence on the business of the meetings coming from political group spokespersons who receive, with the chair, the pre-committee briefing that in other circumstances might be provided by officers to committee chairs only. There is no one pattern of political organisation common to all hung councils. Sometimes the committee chairs rotate on a meeting-by-meeting basis between the groups. In other authorities, a chair is appointed each time the committee meets. Effective member control is sometimes operated through a representative panel of group representatives who meet informally before meetings for a pre-committee briefing. Devices such as these prove helpful to officers in seeking inter-party views and act as a sounding board for the chief executive's management team.

Governance models

Traditional dispatch of council business

1.61 For many years, the traditional way in which local authorities conducted their business was through 'the appropriate channels', which meant that:

> 'Each matter – often irrespective of character or importance – that arises for consideration from an external source (a complaint from an individual if it cannot be dealt with at officer level or a petition from a group of aggrieved electors, representations from a local pressure group, the circulars and directions and guidance that issue forth from government departments) is ordinarily routed by way of a departmental head to the appropriate committee for consideration and subsequent report to the council sitting in full assembly and then back to the departmental head for any necessary executive action. So, too, projects which originate internally (proposals, for example, formulated by departmental heads of their own initiative or, increasingly, projects formulated by the political group which controls the local authority): these follow through the same channels.'[45]

This basic procedure, still discernible in almost every authority, has become modified over the years, particularly as a result of the 'cabinet system'. There has been less propensity to 'put things to committee [cabinet]', individual officers and members have been given more delegated powers, procedures have been streamlined and, more recently because of the impact of party politics, members have concentrated their attention on policy issues. These are described in more detail later on in this book.

For obvious reasons, the full council could not possibly deal with the totality of business that falls to be discharged by a local authority. Hence, because the law compelled authorities to appoint certain committees, and the volume and pressure of business in any event made it unavoidable, authorities conducted their business through committees. The committee system has immense advantages and served local government well; but not inconsiderable disadvantages also, and the expansion of local authority business and the demands for more effective and efficient administration highlighted the weaknesses of the committee system, particularly its fragmentation of an authority's organisation.

Executive arrangements under the Local Government Act 2000

1.62 This all changed following the introduction of Part II of the 2000 Act, which introduced a complete new system of executive arrangements for all but the smaller shire districts. Since its introduction, these governance models have had their own weaknesses highlighted.

The 2000 Act as originally enacted contained the option of three principal executive forms:

- directly elected mayor and executive (cabinet)
- leader and executive (cabinet)
- directly elected mayor and council manager.

Only one authority (Stoke-on-Trent) adopted the elected mayor and council manager form of executive, in which the executive consists of the elected mayor and the council manager only. The LGPIHA 2007 prescribed that all local authorities were to review their executive arrangements, and that the mayor and council manager model was no longer an option.

The 2000 Act also gave some freedom over the form of leader model that was adopted, which allowed for a 'weak leader' model, as was preferred by many councils operating non-mayoral executive arrangements because it retained several controls over the leader and executive by full council, along a spectrum to a 'strong leader' model. Under the provisions of the LGPIHA 2007, most local authorities had to review their executive arrangements and adopt only one of two executive arrangements: either a mayor and cabinet executive or the new-style leader. The latter was a prescribed 'strong leader' model, whereby the leader is appointed for a four-year term (or until his/her term of office expires, if the council elects by halves or thirds) and is defined in the legislation as 'the senior executive member', a shared terminology with the directly elected mayor.

The Localism Act 2011 has since reintroduced the option to return to the committee system and also allows for the possibility of a hybrid system, in which an authority can put to the Secretary of State an alternative for adoption in relation to itself. In the following sections, the role of full council and the different models are outlined.

1. Current framework

Under Part II of the 2000 Act, a local authority with a population of at least 85,000 as at 30 June 1999 was required to operate one of three models of executive arrangements. These were: an elected mayor and cabinet; a leader and cabinet; or an elected mayor and council manager. The intention behind the models was to separate clearly the executive from the other functions of the council in order to increase the efficiency and accountability of local authorities. In addition, local councils could delegate decision-making to individual councillors for the first time. In this way, decisions might be taken more quickly and efficiently, the individuals who make decisions should be more easily identifiable, those individuals will be publicly accountable and their actions subject to regular scrutiny, and councillors would have more time to represent their communities because they will not be spending as much time in committee meetings.

Those authorities that did not have a population of at least 85,000 as at 30 June 1999 had to make alternative arrangements (sometimes called the fourth option), which need not involve a separate executive but should nevertheless have provided for review and scrutiny of the discharge of the executive function.

Also, for the first time, every local authority had to prepare, publicise and keep up to date a written constitution that sets out its governance arrangements. These arrangements go far beyond what is covered by its standing orders and include setting out the roles of councillors and officers; the function and terms of reference of full council, the cabinet and various other council bodies; the principles of decision-making; and also incorporate various codes and protocols in the constitution. The Secretary of State issued a model modular constitution and statutory Guidance to which local authorities had to have regard when implementing Part II of the 2000 Act.

The role of the council in executive arrangements

1.63 Under the Local Authorities (Functions and Responsibilities) (England) Regulations 2012 (SI 2012/2853), the full council must set the budgetary and policy framework of the authority within which the executive will operate. These Regulations, which were made under ss. 9EA, 9EB and 105 of the Local Government Act 2000 (in England), make provision for local authorities to discharge of executive functions by another local authority or the executive of another local authority. Specifically, the Regulations require the full council to:

- adopt or approve specified plans and strategies of the local authority;
- adopt or approve the budget and any plan or strategy for the control of the authority's borrowing or capital expenditure; and
- determine the scheme of members' allowances.

Examples of plans or strategies to be approved or adopted by the full council are the crime and disorder reduction strategy; development plan documents; licensing authority policy statement; local transport plan; plans and alterations that comprise the development plan; the sustainable community strategy; and the youth justice plan.

Elected mayor and cabinet

1.64 Under the LGA 2000 as enacted, this model could only be adopted following a referendum. Given the political commitment to elected mayors by central government, however, the Localism Act 2011 enables the Secretary of State, by order, to require a specified local authority in England to hold a referendum on whether it should operate a mayor and cabinet executive (s. 9N). This provision was to be applied to the 12 largest cities (outside London). As Liverpool and Leicester had already agreed to have elected mayors, and the referendums in the ten remaining cities took place on 3 May 2012. Voters in nine cities (Birmingham, Bradford, Coventry, Leeds, Manchester, Newcastle-upon-Tyne, Nottingham, Sheffield and Wakefield) rejected a mayoral system of governance. Bristol alone voted in favour.

It is also possible to hold a referendum to abolish an elected mayor. There have been three such referendums so far. Two (Stoke-on-Trent in 2008, and Hartlepool in 2011) have resulted in the elected mayor being abolished. Electors in Doncaster voted to retain the mayoral system in a referendum on 3 May 2012.

Where a mayor has been created by resolution of the council, five years must elapse before the council may resolve to abolish the mayor. However, where a referendum (whether initiated by the council or by a petition) is held to reverse the decision of the resolution, there is no time limit.

1.65 Under this model, an elected mayor must appoint between two and nine members of the authority to be members of the executive (i.e. a cabinet). The elected mayor: provides the political leadership; proposes the policy framework and budget to the full council; and takes executive decisions within the policy framework. The cabinet implements the policy framework under the political guidance of the elected mayor and takes such decisions as a group or as individuals as may be delegated to them by the elected mayor. The council approves the constitution, agrees the policy framework and the budget, and makes certain appointments. Amendment or rejection of the budget and of a policy or strategy forming the policy framework requires a two-thirds majority, which is set out in the Local Authorities (Standing Orders) (England) Regulations 2001, whereas only a simple majority is required to amend a leader's proposals. The other such provision specific to a mayor is where the council resolves to vary executive arrangements so that they differ from the existing arrangements but still provide for the same form of executive (i.e., short of changing from mayor and cabinet but, for example, altering the executive procedure rules). Under section 9NB(2) inserted by the Localism Act 2011, this requires the mayor's written consent before the full council's changes can come into force.

Whilst many of the other differences between an elected mayor and a leader were removed by the introduction of the 'strong leader model', so that the 2000 Act refers to them both simply as the 'senior executive member', the principal difference remains. The mayor, unlike the leader, is not a councillor and does not have an electoral ward to represent, but works full time as the mayor. Indeed, s.9H(3) of the LGA 2000 (as inserted by the Localism Act 2011) expressly states that a 'reference in any enactment (whenever passed or made) to a member of a local authority or a councillor of a local authority does not include a reference to an elected mayor of the authority'. This is subject under s.9H(4), however, to regulations, of which there are none yet, or 'any other contrary intention that appears in any enactment (whenever passed or made)'. Such a contrary intention is provided for the purpose of voting under the Local Government Act 1972, whereby s.2B provides that the mayor is to be treated as a member of the council. Since the mayor is not appointed by the council, it is possible that they may not be a member of the majority or any political party.

A directly elected mayor may not be removed from office by a vote of no confidence, and there is no mechanism to force them to resign, and they can only be removed at an election.

As referred to earlier, where councils already have a chair of council that is styled as mayor, there needs to be a change in the latter's title to reflect the difference, be that 'civic mayor', 'chair of council' or even 'speaker'.

Under the changes through the Localism Act, if a local authority has a mayor and cabinet executive, it may not resolve to vary its governance arrangements in a way that changes the arrangements but still provides for the same form of executive, unless the elected mayor has given written consent to the proposed change.

Leader and cabinet

1.66 This is by far the most common form of executive arrangement under the 2000 Act, and it has been adopted by most authorities. Under this model, the executive leader is elected (or removed) by the full council. In the 2000 Act, it was for each local authority to set out in its executive arrangements how the appointment of the cabinet should work. Broadly, this was either where the cabinet is appointed by the executive leader who also determines the scheme of delegations (strong leader model), or where the cabinet is appointed by the full council, which also determines the delegations. In both cases, the cabinet must consist of between three and ten councillors (including the leader). The division of responsibilities between the leader, the council and the cabinet is much the same as for the elected mayor and cabinet model above with the leader exercising similar powers to the elected mayor in the strong leader model.

Under the Local Government and Public Involvement in Health Act 2007, the basis on which the executive is appointed was changed for authorities in England. A 'new style' leader and cabinet executive was prescribed, and this means that the election of the leader by the council now runs for a term of four years, as opposed to being renewed annually. The leader may, however, be removed by a vote at a full council meeting or may choose to resign, and indeed the council itself may prescribe the circumstances in which the leader is to be removed from office in mid-term.

It is now for the leader to decide their own cabinet rather than it being agreed by the full council, and similarly the leader must appoint a deputy leader who will act in their absence. Their term of appointment also lasts for four years but they can be removed from office by the leader in mid-term.

Role of councillors not on the executive

1.67 In all of the models set out above, the role of the councillors who are not on the executive is to assist the executive in policy development, propose new policy to the executive or the council, represent their electorate, and review and scrutinise policy and executive decisions.

Overview and scrutiny arrangements

1.68 Executive arrangements must also provide for the appointment for one or more overview and scrutiny committees. Sometimes these are called panels or commissions, to distinguish them from the regulatory committees, but they remain an ordinary committee of council under s. 102 of the LGA 1972, albeit with amending regulations and powers. In the statutory Guidance, the Secretary of State advised that these overview and scrutiny committees should meet frequently and be 'cross-cutting' rather than service based. The committees must have the power to review or scrutinise decisions taken by the executive or any other part of the council, and make reports to the council or to the executive. They can also report on any matters that affect the authority's area or its inhabitants. Their role includes both developing and reviewing policy and holding the executive to account.

1.69 These committees are politically balanced, which ensures that a political party with an overall majority on the council and hence forming the administration of the council also has control of the overview and scrutiny committees. Where there is a majority administration, there is a logical inconsistency between providing that these committees should hold the executive to account and ensuring that they are controlled by members of the same party as the executive. Accordingly, while acknowledging that this is a matter for local political groups, the statutory guidance recommends that whipping is incompatible with overview and scrutiny, and should therefore not take place.

Regulatory and other committees

1.70 A local authority must also maintain a number of regulatory and other committees to deal with functions such as the determination of applications for planning permission that cannot be dealt with by the executive. These are committees carrying out functions delegated from full council in the sense of ordinary committees established under s. 102, with functions delegated under s. 101. As such, there is no bar on members of the cabinet being members of such a committee, although it is recommended that they are not a member of the audit committee. Indeed, it is a recommendation that the cabinet executive member with the portfolio for development of planning policy should also be a member of the development control (or planning) committee to gain that cross-over insight. Further, there are also committees that must be set up under powers other than in the 1972 Act, often referred to as statutory committees, an example of which is the committee that a local authority is required to establish under the Licensing Act 2003.

Changes under the Localism Act 2011

1.71 The Local Government Act 2000, as amended by the Localism Act 2011, allows local authorities to operate the following forms of governance:

(a) executive arrangements (as above);
(b) a committee system; and
(c) arrangements prescribed by the Secretary of State.

The Secretary of State has the power under these changes to prescribe governance arrangements that local authorities in England may operate. A local authority may propose to the Secretary of State that they should exercise this power if the local authority considers that the operation of the proposed arrangements would be an improvement on its current governance arrangements and that they would be likely to ensure that the decisions of the authority are taken in an efficient, transparent and accountable way, and would be appropriate for all local authorities or any particular description of local authority to consider.

The Act provides that a local authority must pass a resolution if it wishes to change governance arrangements. If a local authority passes a resolution to change from one form of governance to another or from one form of executive to another, it may not pass another resolution to make such a change for another five years, unless the later resolution is approved in a referendum. Once such a resolution has been passed, the local authority must make copies of a document setting out details of the arrangements available for inspection by the public at its principal office. It must also publish in a local newspaper a notice giving details of the change in governance arrangements.

A change in governance arrangements proposed by a local authority is subject to approval in a referendum if the local authority's existing arrangements were approved in a referendum, or if the local authority resolves that a proposed change in governance arrangements should be subject to approval in a referendum.

The committee system

1.72 These amendments to the Local Government Act 2000 allow local authorities to vernance arrangements, rate the following forms of e which local authorities operated before the Local Government Act 2000, governed according to the Local Government Act 1972, which also remains applicable to ordinary committees of authorities operating executive forms of governance. If a local authority operates a committee system form of governance, the Secretary of State may specify functions and actions of the local authority which cannot be delegated (Local Authorities (Committee System) Regulations 2012 (SI 1020/2012)).
1.73 While a local authority operates executive arrangements, it must appoint one or more overview and scrutiny committees and provide for members to be able to refer matters of relevance to an overview and scrutiny committee, a local authority that operates the committee system form of governance does not; the position is only that they may appoint overview and scrutiny committees, under s. 9JA.
1.74 Those councils that have moved back to the committee model of governance since the reintroduction through the Localism Act 2011 amendments have reported that the advantages for them, in adopting a 'modern committee system', have been:

- enhanced backbench member engagement;
- improved transparency and accountability of decision-making;

- scrutiny at the point of decision-making;
- enhanced opportunities for public in engagement;
- more consensual approaches to decision-making and the opportunity to bring the opposition into the decision-making process, demonstrating whole-council commitment to issues where there is cross party support; and
- ability to disengage from structures that are extensive but unproductive in terms of scrutiny.

The councils go on to report that the following points remain to be addressed:

- The absence of individual member decision and lesser frequency of meetings of the relevant committee, as opposed to an executive/cabinet decision-making, could potentially lead to the need for decisions to be delayed or taken by urgency procedures which are less open to public or opposition scrutiny. In practice, however, urgency powers have been reported as very seldom needing to be used.
- There remains some confusion among the public and local authority colleagues when governance arrangements do not fit their understanding and assumptions around the more common executive leader and cabinet or directly elected mayoral model.
- Work remains to be done on reducing the number of reports duplicated across committees and referrals between committees.
- There still remains an appetite among many members for more involvement in decision-making.

Retention of lead members retains a single-member focus for policy making and clear point of referral for offices.

The hybrid system (prescribed arrangements)

1.75 An authority may make use of the third permitted form of governance for local authorities in England set out at s. 9B(1) of the Local Government Act 2000 as inserted by the Localism Act 2011. That is the option of 'prescribed arrangements', better known as 'hybrid arrangements'. This provides that the Secretary of State may, by regulations made under s. 9BA, prescribe the governance arrangements that local authorities may operate, which must include provision about how, and by whom, the functions of a local authority are to be discharged; may include provision enabling functions to be delegated; and, in so doing, may include provisions which apply or reproduce (with or without modifications) any of the other provisions of that part of the LGA 2000 – thus the reference to a hybrid. Such regulations would be made as a result of a proposal being put to the Secretary of State that describes the provisions that the authority considers should be made and explains why the operation by the authority of the proposed arrangements would be an improvement on the arrangements which the authority has in place currently for the discharge of its functions and why the proposed arrangements would be likely to ensure that the decisions of the authority are taken in an efficient, transparent and accountable way.
1.76 At present, no such regulations have been made. That small fact has nonetheless not stopped a number of authorities from organising their governance

arrangements under one of the other two options in such a way that they resemble a hybrid system of governance and that they also refer to themselves in that way. The difference, however, is that their hybrid relies on the acquiescence of the leader (if an executive version) and the members to allow it to continue rather than it being fixed under a set of regulations. These include examples, which look remarkably alike, whereby there is:

- a leader (or mayor) and cabinet system, but where there are no decisions made by individual executive members and that the cabinet meetings resemble something of a committee, to the point where opposition members are invited to attend and debate or may even be members on a proportional basis, and all key decisions are subject to a function-related O&S committee; and
- a committee system, but where there is an executive or P&R (policy and resources) committee that resembles a cabinet (but opposition members attend and vote), there remain lead members who hold portfolio for officers to contact and brief in relation to that P&R executive committee and there are advisory functional or cross-cutting committees that consider 'key' decisions before they are submitted to the executive committee.

The ethical framework

1.77 The law relating to the conduct of members was completely changed by the 2000 Act and a new ethical framework introduced based on the General Principles set out in the Relevant Authorities (General Principles) Order 2001. These were categorised in the Order as selflessness, honesty and integrity, objectivity, accountability, openness, personal judgement, respect for others, duty to uphold the law, stewardship and leadership. In order to give the General Principles some teeth, and to ensure that members would be subject to sanction should they not observe them, each authority was obliged to adopt a local code of conduct for members based on a model code of conduct issued by the Secretary of State. These principles applied to the conduct of members and co-opted members when they were acting as members of the authority, including in meetings of the authority, except that honesty and integrity and duty to uphold the law applied on all occasions.

1.78 The part of the mandatory code of conduct concerning interests was largely designed as a reflection of that law on bias, except that it allowed the law to deal with the individual councillor concerned and not just the decision in which he or she was wrongfully a participant. This meant that the authority could be subject to a challenge where a member allowed personal interests to conflict with his or her duty to act in the public interest under the law on bias (see above), which remains the case and is the principal means of advice to a committee or meeting, and to its chair in controlling the meeting, rather than to the individual. The problem was that some members and officers felt that this overly complicated matters and made it difficult to explain matters and separate in members' minds the two tests, being only very slightly different from each other.

1.79 In England, the mandatory code and sanctions provisions of the 2000 Act, the 'standards regime', was repealed by the Localism Act 2011. Local authorities are now required by s. 28 of the Act to adopt a code whose contents must be consistent with the seven 'Nolan' principles of standards in public life, and must set out the rules that the authority wants to put in place with regard to requiring members to register and disclose pecuniary and non-pecuniary interests.

1.80 Prior to the 2000 Act and the standards regime, there was a statutory national code of conduct, the breach of which would amount to maladministration if a complaint were made to the Ombudsman. Acting when prevented from doing so when a member had a direct or indirect pecuniary interest was also a criminal offence under s. 94 of the LGA 1972 (something that remains for officers under s. 117) and where a member wilfully wasted the resources of the authority, it could be claimed back by the Audit Commission (district auditor) under their powers of surcharge, first introduced in legislation in 1844. All of these provisions were repealed when the mandatory code and sanctions provisions were introduced. This is worth noting, particularly the latter point, for while the Localism Act 2011 did introduce the sanction of a new criminal offence on interests, it is not as wide as was previously the case, and offers no sanction concerning public resources other than that which the authority might bring itself for breach of trust or under the continuing common law offences and action for malfeasance in public office. It is this, together with the abolition of the Audit Commission and the district auditor, which has led critics to say that the conduct of members in local authorities is now subject to the least amount of control or redress by the public since the imposition of surcharge was applied fully to local government in 1925 (which is also a good example of the fiduciary duty in action).

Duty to promote and maintain high standards and the code of conduct

1.81 Section 27 of the Act requires relevant authorities to promote and maintain high standards of conduct by members and co-opted members of the authority. There is considerable local power to determine how do to do this, but it must be done within the context of a duty to establish and maintain a code of conduct, also to be determined locally. The Code must, however, be based on the Committee on Standards in Public Life's seven principles of public life, which were revised as an outcome of their report of January 2013 as follows.

Principle	**Revised description**
Preamble	The principles of public life apply to anyone who works as a public office-holder. This includes all those who are elected or appointed to public office, nationally and locally, and all people appointed to work in the civil service, local government, the police, courts and probation services, NDPBs (Non-Departmental Public Bodies), and in the health, education, social and care services. All public office-holders are both servants of the public and stewards of public resources. The principles also have application to all those in other sectors delivering public services.

Selflessness	Holders of public office should act solely in terms of the public interest.
Integrity	Holders of public office must avoid placing themselves under any obligation to people or organisations that might try inappropriately to influence them in their work. They should not act or take decisions in order to gain financial or other material benefits for themselves, their family or their friends. They must declare and resolve any interests and relationships.
Objectivity	Holders of public office must act and take decisions impartially, fairly and on merit, using the best evidence and without discrimination or bias.
Accountability	Holders of public office are accountable to the public for their decisions and actions, and must submit themselves to the scrutiny necessary to ensure this.
Openness	Holders of public office should act and take decisions in an open and transparent manner. Information should not be withheld from the public unless there are clear and lawful reasons for so doing.
Honesty	Holders of public office should be truthful.
Leadership	Holders of public office should exhibit these principles in their own behaviour. They should actively promote and robustly support the principles and be willing to challenge poor behaviour wherever it occurs.

In accordance with the legislation, there is no longer an 'official' model code. Instead, each local authority must determine their own local code of conduct; and how they fulfil the duty in the Act of promoting and maintaining high standards of conduct. The code applies to members and co-opted members of the authority when acting in that capacity, and the definition of 'co-opted member' does not include non-voting members.

Authorities are free to determine what they put in or leave out of a Code, though s. 28(2) does require the inclusion of the provisions the authority considers appropriate in respect of the registration (in its register) and disclosure of interests. Any decision to adopt a local Code must be taken at full council, and all standards matters are to be non-executive functions.

The abolition of the Model Code means that different authorities may have different Codes. A councillor who is a member of more than one authority is likely to be subject to different Codes, according to which authority they are currently acting on. Different members of the same joint committee will be subject to the varied Codes of their different parent authorities.

The requirement for members to give an undertaking to comply with the code of conduct is removed, although it might be considered reasonable to expect compliance from responsible members of a public body! The previous consequence of not being able to act as a member where the undertaking was not provided has gone.

General principles

Drafting the Code

1.82 The councils in Wales remain subject to a mandatory code and have the advantage, or disadvantage, of complaints going to the Ombudsman in Wales rather than the authority. In England there exists a model code for parishes developed by NALC (National Association of Local Councils) and three alternative templates for principal authorities. These are the existing old code, a model developed by the Local Government Association and a templates produced by DCLG (Department for Communities and Local Government). These are reproduced in Appendix 2.

The Code of Conduct provisions seek to do two separate things. The first is to set out rules of good conduct for Members of the Council and its committees in carrying out their functions. This is to protect the good order and administration of the Authority and the reputation of the Members. This is sometimes easier said than done and, while the rules are all to be consistent with the Nolan principles, when viewed as a whole there are currently four models in circulation on which councils have based their own code.

The second objective is to deal with transparency and member interests. The transparency element is dealt with through a requirement to establish a register of interests for public inspection. This openness allows the public to see where a member 'is coming from', to make clear where a conflict of between the public interest and a private interest might occur, and as a safeguard against abuse of one's position for personal benefit. The Act provides (see below) that the Register:

- must deal with a mandatory set of personal interests, Disclosable Pecuniary Interests (DPI) backed by potential criminal offences; and
- can deal with any other interests that the authority feels should be disclosed through the register, backed by the potential for a finding of breach of the Code under local arrangements, referred to as 'Other Interests'.

In seeking to tackle conflicts of interest, the Act and the resulting Code seek to enshrine the principle of integrity in decision-making as a personal responsibility of the member. It also establishes the means by which integrity is maintained and how potential conflicts of interest are to be handled by the member and by the authority.

From the member's point of view, not resolving a conflict between their personal interest and the public interest may result in public censure at the least and a criminal conviction at the worst. The Code therefore deals with how the member should behave when faced with such a conflict of interest. As noted above, the Act requires, in effect, that the Code contains a mandatory element to deal with potential conflicts of interest caused by a member's most direct personal interests, 'Disclosable Pecuniary Interests' (DPI), backed by potential criminal offences for failing to follow the required steps.

The Act also provides, if the council so chooses, for the Code to deal with potential conflicts of interest caused by a member's less-direct personal interests, referred to in the Act as 'Other Interests'. These would be backed by the potential for a finding of breach of the Code under local arrangements, referred to as 'Other Interests'. The Act also gives the Council discretion over some of the actions a member should take when faced with such conflicts of interest through the express power to adopt standing orders.

For the council, this part of the Code seeks to place a personal responsibility upon members for their actions in relation to public law matters. For the council, if a decision is made in the face of a conflict between the council's obligation to act in the public interest and the individual decision-maker's personal interest, then the resulting decision is at risk of challenge. That duty is set out under the heading of bias and a separate heading of predetermination. Both are grounds for challenging a council decision.

- The test for bias is: would a fair-minded and informed observer (i.e. the court), having considered the facts, conclude that there was a real possibility that the decision-making would be biased?
- The test for a 'prejudicial interest' under the old mandatory code tried to reflect this test in terms of the individual member duty.

Predetermination is normally a matter associated more specifically with Development Control, and referred to directly in planning guidance/codes, but it is a legal concept related to all areas of local government decision-making. (See above.)

Many authorities have simply kept the previous Code, coming to the conclusion that it met these objectives, but have amended it to incorporate the DPI rules. Some have adopted the LGA template, preferring its purposive style over the 'dos and don'ts' style of the old code that some felt verged on the patronising. Others still opted for the bare adoption of the Nolan principles.

In the latter case, more pertinently, both of these replacement codes tend to be used by authorities that felt that the old code confused the interest provisions of the code and the common law on bias to an extent that was not helpful. These authorities have therefore decided not to adopt any set rules concerning members and where they hold other interests. Rather, they have sought to deal with these issues as an explanation of a common law duty on the council. This does not mean, however, that the principle could not be applied to a member who actively ignores the duty on the council in terms of common law and bias, given that the principle of integrity places on the member a duty to 'declare and resolve any interests and relationships'.

Dealing with member interests

1.83 The government produced a guidance document for councillors on personal interests in August 2012, which was updated and reissued in March 2013. This is intended to give basic practical information about how to be open and transparent about one's personal interests. This sets out also the choices open to councils when adopting a local Code. This contained the following advice:

– 'The national rules require your council's code of conduct to comply with the Seven Principles of Public Life, and to set out how, in conformity with the rules, you will have to disclose and register your pecuniary and your other interests. Within these rules it is for your council to decide what its code of conduct says.'

- 'Within the requirements of the national rules it is for your council or authority to determine what is to be entered in its register of members' interests . . . Disclosable pecuniary interests, and any other of your personal interests which your council or authority, in particular through its code of conduct, has determined should be registered.'
- 'Where your council's or authority's standing orders require this, you must leave the room.'

A problem most councils have had to wrestle with is that this guidance is a little at odds with itself in respect of those places where the legislation and stated policy do not necessarily stand up to close scrutiny. In this regard, the guidance refers to two major issues and two minor irritants, as follows.

The DCLG indicative code and the guidance text provides guidance for Disclosable Pecuniary Interests only, but does note that that does not account for any interest beyond the immediate interests of the member and their spouse/civil partner. The guidance also advises:

> 'They [Members] should not act or take decisions in order to gain financial or other material benefits for themselves, their family, or their friends. They must declare and resolve any interests and relationships.'

There is a similar approach in terms of remaining or not in the chamber where there is an interest:

> 'Even where there are no such standing orders [requiring that you leave the room], you must leave the room if you consider your continued presence is incompatible with your council's code of conduct or the Seven Principles of Public Life.'

The law is quite clear that a DPI is only required to be registered, unless it is a matter before the Council, in the period after a Member is elected. The hiatus caused by this oversight is handled by the statement that:

> 'All sitting councillors need to register their declarable interests. Any suggestion that you should tell the monitoring officer about your pecuniary interests only in the immediate aftermath of your being elected is wholly incompatible with this duty, with which you must comply.'

The DPI provisions contain no general exemptions in the way there used to be in respect of budget setting, school transport, etc. It was presumed by many that it was left to a local regime to deal with this. When legal advice was circulated that these generic exemptions should be put in place locally, and some members quite rightly complained, the response was that it is gold plating and that 'council tax liability applies to the generality of the population; councillors have no unique position in that regard'. The letter and guidance, in repeating this in a clarified form in the guidance below, in effect replaces general exemptions with the concept of *de minimis* (the principle that trivial matters may be disregarded). While this is a view with which many of us would agree, it is missing as an expression of the Act, causing some to feel vulnerable, and is therefore another factor to bear in mind.

Appendix 3 may assist when advising members in taking them through a flow-chart of considerations, depending on whether they rely on the old code style of both DPI and other interest provisions or the alternative separation of DPI and common law considerations.

Registration of interests

1.84 Localism Act 2011 s. 29 requires monitoring officers of relevant authorities to establish and maintain a register of members' and co-opted members' interests, to make the register available for inspection and to publish it on their authority's website. The content of any such register must be approved by the full council. It also requires the monitoring officer of a principal council to make the register of members' interests for parish councils in its area available for inspection and publish it on the website of the principal council. In addition, parish councils are required to publish the register on their own website, if they have one. The absence of standard definitions of such interests, and the degree of local discretion, creates scope for considerable local variation, so that a councillor may be subject to very different requirements in different capacities.

Section 30 requires members of relevant authorities to notify the monitoring officer of any disclosable pecuniary interests of them or a spouse or civil partner they live with, within 28 days of taking up office. The section allows the Secretary of State to make regulations defining a 'disclosable pecuniary interest', and requires the monitoring officer to enter any notified disclosable pecuniary interest in the authority's register, as well as any other interest notified to them, whether or not it is pecuniary.

A member of a relevant authority is required (s. 30) to disclose a disclosable pecuniary interest that they are aware of (apart from a sensitive interest – see s. 32), at a meeting or if acting alone, where any matter to be considered relates to their interest. If the interest is not already registered, members are required to register it within 28 days. The monitoring officer must then enter the interest in the authority's register. It prohibits a member from participating in discussion or voting on any matter relating to their interest or, if acting alone, from taking any steps in relation to the matter (subject to any dispensations – see s. 33). Local authorities may also, should they so wish, amend their standing orders to require a member to leave the room when a matter in which they have a disclosable pecuniary interest is debated or voted on. Once a member has made the initial registration, there is no requirement to update such registrations for changes of circumstances, such as the acquisition of development land, unless and until a relevant item of business arises at a meeting which the member attends (unlike the pre-2000 Act regime in s. 19 Local Government and Housing Act 1989 and the regulations under that Act).

The requirement for disclosure of interests at meetings applies to the same range of 'disclosable pecuniary interests' as the initial registration requirement, plus any non-disclosable pecuniary interests and non-pecuniary interests which the authority's Code requires to be disclosed. The duty to disclose only arises if the member is aware of the interest. However, where the interest is already on the authority's register of interests, or is in the process of entry onto the register having been notified to the Monitoring Officer, the member is under no obligation to disclose the interest at the meeting, so members of the public attending meetings might well not be aware of a member's interests in a matter under debate unless they had also previously inspected the authority's register. Where it is an unregistered interest, the member is required both to disclose it at the meeting and to register it within 28 days of the meeting at which relevant business is considered.

The duty to disclose arises if the member attends the meeting, as opposed to the present Code requirement to disclose 'at the commencement of' consideration of the matter in which the member has an interest. In future, the member cannot avoid the need to disclose merely by withdrawing during that part of the meeting when the particular item of business is considered. Failure to disclose a disclosable pecuniary interest is a criminal offence. There is no such sanction for failing to disclose non-disclosable pecuniary interests or non-pecuniary interests, even where disclosure is required by the authority's code of conduct.

Disclosure and withdrawal are required to cover a member's disclosable pecuniary interest in any item of business at a meeting, or in any matter which they would deal with as a single executive member or ward councillor. If they have a disclosable pecuniary interest in such a matter, they are simply barred from participating in discussion or voting on the matter at the meeting, or (as a single member) taking any steps in respect of the matter, other than referring it to someone else for determination. Participation in the discussion of the matter, or taking steps in respect of the matter, in the face of these prohibitions is made a criminal offence. The equivalent of merely personal interests, requiring disclosure but not withdrawal, will be covered by the requirement for the authority's Code to make some provision for disclosure of non-disclosable pecuniary interests and of non-pecuniary interests.

The requirement for the member to withdraw from the meeting room may be dealt with in the authority's standing orders. Indeed, it is left open to authorities to make no provision for such members to withdraw, leaving them present and liable to influence other members during the discussion. This means that a member who fails to withdraw as required in standing orders does not commit any criminal offence and the sanction, if the member became disruptive, would be the standard provision enabling a meeting to vote to exclude such a member.

Section 34 of the Localism Act makes it a criminal offence if a member or co-opted member fails, without reasonable excuse, to comply with requirements under ss. 30 or 31 to register or declare disclosable pecuniary interests. It is also a criminal offence to take part in council business at meetings, or act alone on behalf of the council, when prevented from doing so by a conflict caused by disclosable pecuniary interests. The magistrates' court, upon conviction, can impose a fine of up to level 5 (currently £5,000), and an order disqualifying the person from being a member of a relevant authority for up to five years. A prosecution must be brought within three years of the offence, but it cannot be prosecuted by the local authority itself, only by the Crown Prosecution Service.

There are no requirements in relation to private life, though disqualification as a result of a sentence of imprisonment for three months or more (whether suspended or not) in s. 80 of the Local Government Act 1972 remains.

Committees and sub-committees dealing with standards

1.85 Local authorities no longer need to have standards committees, although they must put in place arrangements to deal with complaints of breach of its code of conduct, including arrangements for investigation of complaints and arrangements 'under which decisions on allegations can be made'. In the case of district and unitary authorities, this also applies to allegations in respect of parish councillors in their areas. Most authorities have retained a standards committee of some nature to undertake these functions at member level, even if some sanctions, such as removal from committees, will have to be applied by full council. Others have added the functions to an existing committee such as a governance or, more commonly, the audit committee.

District and unitary authorities are responsible for having arrangements in place to investigate and determine allegations against parish councillors, but the Act does not provide how this might be done (other than requiring the views of an Independent Person). Specifically, parish councils are under no obligation to have regard to any findings of the district or unitary authority or its standards committee.

Authorities have discretion to set their own processes and to delegate more of the process. There is no requirement for a review stage. The statutory requirement for a hearing has gone and the authority can find that a member has broken the Code without even having conducted an investigation (although it would be usual to expect local authorities to ensure that the principles of natural justice are observed).

There is greater scope now for the Monitoring Officer to seek local resolution of a complaint before a decision is taken as to whether the complaint merits investigation. This will hopefully enable the more minor or tit-for-tat complaints to be taken out of the system without the full process previously required.

The Act gives no explicit powers to undertake investigations or to conduct hearings (any such action required would be implied as appropriate). So there is no power to require access to documents or to require members or officers to attend interviews, and no power to require the member to attend a hearing.

The Act gives authorities no explicit powers to take any action in respect of a breach of the local Code. Authorities have been given no powers to impose alternative sanctions, such as requiring an apology or training. Accordingly, other than naming and shaming the individual member, it is unclear whether the authority can take any action beyond administrative actions to secure that it can continue to discharge its functions effectively. This takes us back to reliance on *R v Broadland DC ex parte Lashley* (2001) All ER (D) 71, where the principle of local action through a common-law standards committee and council, to ensure no disruption to the proper administration of the council's affairs, was upheld.

The Independent Person

1.86 Every principal authority must appoint one or more Independent Persons.

Independent Persons are appointed by advertisement and application, and there are very strict rules preventing a person from being appointed if they are a friend or relative of any member or officer of the authority or of any parish council within the authority's area. They can they be paid a fee and/or expenses and the Act provides that a person does not cease to be independent merely because such payments are made.

A person cannot be appointed as an Independent Person if they have within the past five years been a co-opted voting member of a Committee of the authority. The functions of the Independent Person (IP) are as follows.

- The IP must be consulted and their views taken into account before the authority takes a decision on any allegation it has decided to investigate.
- The IP may be consulted by the principal authority in circumstances where the authority is not taking a decision whether to investigate the allegation.
- The IP may be consulted by a member of the authority against whom an allegation has been made.
- The IP may be consulted by a parish councillor against whom an allegation has been made.

It is important to ensure that the impartiality of the Independent Person is not compromised by undertaking more than one of these roles where it would be inappropriate to do so. Hence the appointment of more than one is sensible, and most local authorities have recruited two.

The appointment of independent members must be agreed by a majority of the whole number of Councillors (s. 28(8)(c)(iii)).

Sanctions

1.87 Local authorities no longer have any sanctions available beyond 'naming and shaming', which may be taken to the point of the standards hearing purchasing an advert in a local paper to set out their findings in full. The potential of this modern form of pillorying forms a largely effective deterrent for poor behaviour short of the criminal in members but, for a well-documented few it has been most ineffective or indeed a perverse badge of honour.

There does remain, however, the position established in common law for local authorities to regulate themselves in the manner described in the case of *R v Broadland ex parte Lashley 200 EWCA Civ 179* (2001). This expressly may not be any action taken to punish a member but is, rather, actions undertaken to ensure the good administration of the authority. The actions of the council, after due process and to counter a particular mischief, might include:

- naming and shaming – by reporting the committee's findings to council for information;
- recommending to the member's group leader (or, in the case of un-grouped members, recommending to council or to committees) that he/she be removed from any or all committees or sub-committees of the council;
- recommending to the leader of the council that the member be removed from the cabinet, or removed from particular portfolio responsibilities;

- instructing the monitoring officer to arrange training for the member;
- removing from all outside appointments to which he/she has been appointed or nominated by the authority;
- withdrawing facilities provided to the member by the council, such as a computer, website and/or email and internet access; or
- excluding the member from the council's offices or other premises, with the exception of meeting rooms as necessary for attending council, committee and sub-committee meetings.

Notes

1 LGA 1972, s. 265.
2 See 9.39.
3 LG&HA 1989, s. 21.
4 For a comprehensive list of local authority functions see *Cross on Local Government Law*, 8th edn.
5 The few exceptional cases where one person can constitute a meeting (e.g. as under the Companies Act, which provides that 'one member of the company present in person or by proxy shall be deemed to constitute a meeting') have no application to local government.
6 Sebag Shaw and Dennis Smith, *The Law of Meetings* (1947).
7 Law of Libel Amendment Act 1888, s. 4.
8 A 'public place' is any highway, public park or garden, any sea beach and any public bridge, road, lane, footway, square, court, alley or passage, whether a thoroughfare or not, and includes any open space to which, for the time being, the public have or are permitted to have access, whether on payment or otherwise: Public Order Act 1936, s. 9(1).
9 'Private premises' are defined as 'premises to which the public have access (whether on payment or otherwise)' only by permission of the owner, occupier or lessee of the premises': ibid.
10 LGA 1972, ss. 100A, 100E, added by LG(AI)A 1985, as regards principal councils: see generally Chapter 3.
11 For a discussion of the problems inherent in multi-organisations (outside the scope of this work), see: R. J. P. Harris and D. J. Scott, 'Perspectives on Multi-Organizational Design', *Local Government Studies*, 8, p.31.
12 See generally LGA 1972, s. 99, and sch. 12.
13 LGA 1972, sch. 12, paras. 3, 9, 25.
14 Ibid., s. 239.
15 Ibid., sch. 12, paras. 1, 7, 23.
16 Ibid., para. 14.
17 Ibid., sch. 12, para. l(2)(b).
18 Ibid., sch. 12, para. 7(2).
19 Ibid., paras. 2, 8 and 24.
20 Ibid., para. 8.
21 Ibid., para. 8(2).
22 Ibid., para. 14(3).
23 Ibid., para. 1(4).
24 Ibid., paras. 7(3), 23(3).
25 Ibid., paras. 14(4), 32(1).
26 An opinion to the contrary appeared in the *Justice of the Peace and Local Government Review* of 21 September 1963, but no grounds for the opinion were advanced.
27 LGA 1972, sch. 12, paras. 2(1), 8(1), 24(1).
28 Ibid., paras. 10(1), 26(1).
29 Ibid., paras. 10(1), 26(1).
30 Ibid., s. 99 applies the provisions of sch. 12 to committees and sub-committees.

31 LGA 1972, sch.12, para 1B(b)(iii) [inserted by SI 2015/5].
32 Ibid., sch. 12, Pt VI, para. 39(1).
33 Ibid., s. 82, but the position may be different where the council is acting in a quasi-judicial capacity.
34 A decision could be set aside if the council were guilty of the rarely invoked offence of misfeasance in public office because councillors voted with the object of maliciously damaging a third party: see 1.44.
35 For example, a majority of the whole number of council members is required for a resolution to promote or oppose a Bill: LGA 1972, s. 239, and see 7.144.
36 LGA 1972, sch. 12, para. 39.
37 A proxy is a person appointed by someone to act and vote for them at a meeting. The term is also applied to the instrument by which such person is appointed. There is no common law right to vote by proxy (*Harben v Phillips* (1883) and no statutory right conferred in respect of local authority meetings.
38 House of Commons standing order No.37 provides that an MP can vote in a division without having heard the question put, i.e. there is no need even to know what is being voted on!
39 'Local government is more than the sum of the particular services provided. It is an essential part of English democratic government.' Report of the Royal Commission on Local Government in England (1969), Cmnd 4040, p. 146 – a sentiment endorsed by the Widdicombe Committee in its interim report (see 1.60).
40 LGA 2000, s. 2.
41 LGA 1988, s. 29 and sch. 3, and LG&HA 1989, ss. 22–28.
42 'If circumstances are not properly reported or if facts are omitted from a report to a committee the authority itself might be found guilty of maladministration in its decision-making. The ombudsman may find maladministration if serious complaints are not reported to the appropriate committee. Promises made by the authority and not fulfilled may result in a finding of maladministration. Procrastination and even, perhaps, undue haste may also produce an adverse finding by the ombudsman. These issues have now to be kept very much in the forefront of the mind of those who write reports and draft minutes.' R. G. Brooke, 'Modern Approach to Committee Practice' (1979), 143 *Local Government Review* 3.
43 Bylaws for good rule and government are made by simple resolution of the local authority, but the bylaws must be 'made under the common seal of the authority' and do not have effect until confirmed by the appropriate confirming authority: LGA 1972, s. 236(3).
44 (1974) 90 Law Quarterly Review 351, 360; and see 'The Legal Effects of Statements by Planning Officers', ibid. in which it is quoted. See also *Southend-on-Sea Corporation v Hodgson (Wickford) Ltd* (1961); and *Lever Finance Ltd v Westminster (City) London Borough Council* (1971).
45 *Roberts Appellant; And Hopwood and Others Respondents. 3 April 1925* [House of Lords].

Chapter 2
Standing orders

Statutory provisions

Discretion and obligation

2.1 All local authorities have statutory power to make discretionary standing orders if they choose, under the LGA 1972:

- for the regulation of council proceedings and business; and
- regarding the quorum, proceedings and place of meeting of their committees and sub-committees.

But 'relevant authorities' must incorporate certain mandatory standing orders into their constitution with respect to staff and regulating certain aspects of their proceedings and business, and for contracting purposes: see 2.4–2.5.

Standing Orders must be contained in the Constitution of a Local Authority (LGA 2000, s. 37), as well as the Code of Conduct and such other information as the Secretary of State may direct or the council might require.

Model standing orders

2.2 A model set of standing orders for the guidance of local authorities in regulating their proceedings and business was issued by the former Ministry of Housing and Local Government in 1963 and reprinted in 1973. These were then updated in the Modular Constitution in 1999. The National Association of Local Councils (NALC) revised its model standing orders for parish and town councils in 2011, but there has been no revision of those set out in the Modular Constitution for local authorities. As to standing orders that the law compels local authorities to adopt and observe (mandatory standing orders), see 2.4.

2.3 In 1995, the Association of District Secretaries (which then became the Association of Council Secretaries and Solicitors (ACSeS) and is now Lawyers in Local Government (LLG)) published a set of draft Standing Orders, ostensibly written in plain English, for the guidance of local authorities in devising their own standing orders to meet local circumstances and local methods of working.

2.4 The standing orders in the modular constitution were then updated by a working group from ACSeS and a law firm from 2011. The intention was to keep a bank of sample and preferred best practice standing orders, but the scale of the task proved too expensive. What resulted is a revised set of standing orders, designed around a county council structure, which, it has to be said, does contain some flaws. It is nonetheless very useful and is available to LLG members through their website.

Mandatory standing orders

General principles

2.5 The Widdicombe Committee had recommended that local authorities should be statutorily required to include in their standing orders a number of matters of a procedural character. It favoured also the codification of conventions and established practices: see 2.24. Following the coming into force of the LG&HA 1989, which gave effect to several of Widdicombe's proposals, the DoE set up a working party of local government officers and civil servants, to prepare a new model set of standing orders and to distinguish between those that were core and mandatory, i.e. not revocable, alterable or suspendable by authorities other than in prescribed circumstances, and those that were non-mandatory, free to be adopted, revoked, amended or suspended or not as an authority wished – as, indeed, was and is currently still the position of discretionary standing orders made under the 1972 Act: see 2.2.

The working party dutifully produced a set of draft standing orders that, for some four years, were the subject of consultation and inconclusive discussion. What emerged – apart from mandatory standing orders as to staff – were no more than two procedural core standing orders of comparative triviality. However, several of the standing orders drafted by the working party are reproduced in this book and are referred to in each case as 'one of the draft core standing orders' to distinguish it from an 'old model standing order'.

2.6 Various statutory instruments have, since the LG&HA 1989, required local authorities to make or modify standing orders so that they include the provisions set out in the regulations or provisions.

The Local Authorities (Standing Orders) Regulations 1993 accordingly came into force on 1 April 1993. The appointment of chief officers and meetings has now largely been repealed with the exception of national park authorities.

2.7 Following the LGA 2000, the Local Authorities (Standing Orders) (England) Regulations 2001 came into force on 7 November 2001. These replace or amend the 1993 Regulations that provide that an authority must make standing orders in relation to staff, regulation of its proceedings and disciplinary action against the three statutory chief officers with responsibility for governance, being the Head of Paid Service, Chief Finance Officer and Monitoring Officer. The 2001 Regulations have themselves been amended in 2014 and 2015 to account for those authorities now running committee systems and changes.

A feature of these mandatory standing orders is that the regulations require that an authority 'incorporate in standing orders relating to x the provisions set out in Part n of Schedule n or provisions to the like effect'. This last part has had the impact that a number of authorities took a little poetic licence with the phrase 'to like effect' and produced something slightly different and which, in some authorities, was then subject later to tidying up. This resulted some years later in a standing order to a potentially quite a different effect from that required by law. An example is of voting annually on budgets where, with the mayoral model in particular, the mandatory standing order is counter-intuitive to the traditional standing order and operation of voting; it is therefore worth going back and checking current wording against the regulations from time to time.

That provision can also be useful, however, as in the example of the recent changes to disciplinary matters and the statutory governance chief officers. The changed procedures have been seen by many as difficult to operate and counter-productive to the mischief they were intended to address. They are also, perhaps more importantly, more expensive in the long run. The provision 'to like effect' has therefore been achieved by melding the previous standing orders to the new to give a satisfactory outcome (see Newark and Sherwood DC for a good example).

2.8 In the absence of standing orders, either discretionary or mandatory, governing a local authority's procedures then, except so far as statutory provisions may apply, common law rules must be followed. In other words, common law applies wherever standing orders are silent on a particular point.

If an authority does not make standing orders affecting its proceedings (or if two or more authorities appointing a joint committee do not make standing orders governing the joint committee), or if the standing orders made in either case do not cover such matters, then the executive, committees (or joint committee) or sub-committee of either may themselves determine the quorum, proceedings and place of meeting.

In determining its own quorum, proceedings and place of meeting, however, the committee, joint committee or sub-committee should – on the analogy of *Picea Holdings v London Rent Assessment Board* (1971) – follow the practice of the parent local authority or authorities. By common law if no quorum is fixed, all acts of a committee must be done in the presence of all members of the committee (*Re The Liverpool Household Stores Association Ltd* (1890)), but in local government this is clearly overridden by the statutory provision that all questions coming before the local authority must be decided by a majority of those present and voting at a properly constituted meeting (LGA 1972, sch. 12, para. 39, as applied to committees by s. 99).

Variation and revocation

2.9 A local authority may vary or revoke or, within certain restraints, suspend its discretionary standing orders, i.e. those made under the general enabling power of the 1972 Act. A relevant authority cannot, however, vary or revoke or suspend mandatory standing orders. As standing orders, whether discretionary or mandatory, are made by simple resolution of the authority (subject to requisite notice of intention: see 2.18), so, too, may the variation or revocation of discretionary standing orders. Where a discretionary standing order has been revoked the resolution effecting the revocation may itself be rescinded, in which case the original standing order becomes again operative: *Weir v Fermanagh County Council* (1913).

2.10 Some authorities stipulate that standing orders shall be altered or rescinded only upon the recommendation of the standards or other committee with responsibility for making recommendations for the review of standing orders, while others require that a certain period of prior notice shall be given before formal amendment. In *R v Flintshire County Council, ex parte Armstrong-Braun* (2001), the council made a standing order preventing any one councillor from putting a matter on the agenda for discussion at a council meeting without being seconded by another council member.

One of the arguments for judicial review was that a councillor who was not a member of a party or group would be excluded if they could not get the support of other councillors. As part of his judgement, Schieman LJ found that the council had not fully considered the democratic implications of their alterations to standing orders.

Suspension

2.11 Although there is no specific power enabling an authority to suspend its discretionary standing orders, i.e. to decide, by resolution that for a special purpose or for a period of time one or other of its standing orders shall be of no effect, there is general acknowledgement that this can properly be done, and there was a provision to this effect in Article 16 of the Modular Constitution (DETR Modular Constitution for English Local Authorities).

The suspension must be by resolution: it cannot be implied (*R v Hereford Corporation ex parte Harrower and Others* (1970); and see 2.13). Widdicombe expressed this view:

> 'We think it undesirable that procedural rules should be capable of change in mid-meeting by suspension of standing orders. Some safeguards are required.
>
> We are not convinced that . . . the model standing orders . . . are of themselves sufficient, and propose that standing orders should not be capable of suspension or amendment without advance notice of motion except on the vote of two-thirds of the membership of the council. All standing orders should be statutorily required to include such a limitation.'

A two-thirds majority would need a change in the law because a local authority needs only a majority of those present and voting at a meeting to reach a decision. In *R v Teddington UDC* (1928) a standing order requiring a two-thirds majority to rescind a resolution was held *ultra vires*.

Validity

2.12 Local authorities could quite properly make standing orders without express statutory power or obligation to do so: every constituted body has an inherent right to regulate its own proceedings, though necessarily within the law. The fact that standing orders are made under statutory power and authority does not give them the force of law, they are not bylaws, nor can they impose penalties; and if they purport to override or are in conflict with the law they are ultra vires: see *R v Teddington UDC*, above. Even a standing order that goes beyond what the law strictly requires may be *ultra vires*, e.g. a standing order that requires a councillor to refrain from speaking rather than simply declaring and not voting when in arrears with council tax payments. In other words, where a statute deals specifically with a subject matter, standing orders cannot lawfully go further; but where this is not so the local authority is free to apply a standing order to the subject matter (see *R v Newham London Borough Council ex parte Haggerty* (1986), in which it was held that as there is no statutory framework for the eligibility of councillors for committee membership, it is open to an authority by standing orders to establish its own criteria for membership provided they are not irrational).

The question of validity was considered at length in *R v Flintshire County Council, ex parte Armstrong-Braun* (2001) and it was held that, in principle, a standing order could be quashed as falling outside the policy of the LGA 1972.

Compliance and enforceability

2.13 There is authority for the view that a local authority is bound to observe its discretionary standing orders (see *R v Woolwich Borough Council* (1922)). In *R v Hereford Corporation ex parte Harrower & Others* (1970) at p. 1427, Lord Parker CJ said:

> 'It is quite clear that there is a statutory duty on the local authority to comply with standing orders as they exist at the time and if those standing orders have not been suspended then there is a duty to comply with them.'

This case was concerned with standing orders in respect of contracts and not in regard to the regulation of internal domestic business.

However, in *R v Rushmoor Borough Council ex parte Crawford* (1981) the court made an order of *certiorari* to quash a decision of the majority Conservative group on the council suspending all Labour opposition councillors from committee membership because the decision to do so contravened the council's standing orders. In *R v Educational Services Committee of Bradford City Metropolitan Council ex parte Professional Association of Teachers* (1986), the court held that a resolution passed by the committee to rescind a previous decision of the council to afford recognition to the applicant trade union was *ultra vires* for lack of compliance with standing orders.

2.14 In *Hereford*, above, the local authority had suspended its standing orders by implication. The council had decided, quite openly, to invite tenders for the installation of central heating in certain flats from only the local electricity and gas boards and the National Coal Board, but omitted to suspend its standing orders that provided for open competitive and not select tendering. The court held that although the council could properly suspend its standing orders it could do this only by formal resolution of the council and not by implication. It also emerged from this case that if an authority acts contrary to its standing orders, the ratepayers have sufficient legal right to enable them to seek an order of mandamus against the authority.

2.15 The effective power of a local authority to enforce compliance with standing orders upon its individual council members is limited. It would therefore be unwise for an authority to make a standing order that could be flouted with impunity. As an example, banning members from leaving their seats at meetings might well be held to be unreasonable and it would therefore be unlawful for the council to order a member out of a council meeting who persisted in walking around the chamber in defiance of a standing order prohibiting it, because he has a lawful right to be present subject to temporary exclusion for disorderly conduct. It is at least open to doubt whether walking around the chamber in contravention of a standing order could be classed as disorderly conduct.

The position as regards officers is quite different: compliance with standing orders can be an express or implied part of their employment contract, and a breach of standing orders could be dealt with as a disciplinary matter.

2.16 Where a local authority is in breach of a mandatory standing order, if the breach is so fundamental that the substance of a statutory requirement has not been complied with, any decision affected by the breach may be void and, in principle, susceptible to judicial review. Breach of standing orders is likely to be significant in the context of maladministration and unquestionably breach by an authority of its own internal procedures and of mandatory standing orders, will be regarded as failing in an administrative as well as a legal context. Haggerty, above, shows that the courts will use compliance with standing orders as a measure of the validity of a council's action.

2.17 Most political groups recognise that the discipline of internal procedural rules is necessary, and are therefore disposed towards persuading their members to keep in line. However, in the event of difficulties with members who continually disregard standing orders, discussing the issues with the political group leaders or party whips may be a good starting point.

Procedural considerations

Formal making of standing orders

2.18 Standing orders are made by simple resolution, by the full council as regards standing orders that apply to the authority's proceedings and business generally; or by the executive or a committee or sub-committee where the council itself has not made standing orders relating to its committees and the committee or sub-committee wishes formally to regulate its proceedings. Standing orders made by a committee or sub-committee cannot override the standing orders of the local authority. The form that standing orders take is dealt with below: see below.

2.19 Although there are no special formalities for making standing orders (there is no approval of a confirmatory body to be sought), the democratic implications of the standing orders should be explained. The general law affecting the convening of a council meeting requires notice to be given of the intention to make standing orders in the summons to the council meeting at which the motion is to be put. An authority can decide that, before any amendment of a standing order comes into force, it is confirmed by a subsequent meeting and this provision was included in the Modular Constitution. A simple majority is necessary: *R v Teddington UDC*, above.

2.20 In practice, the standing orders will be drafted by officers to meet the wishes and needs of the local authority, and may first need to be approved by the constitutional or governance committee or other committee set up for this purpose (or often combined with or a sub-committee or even working group of standards or audit committee), and submitted by recommendation to the full council for approval. Mandatory standing orders do not necessarily need to follow the precise wording of the requisite regulations: they can be 'of like effect' (see above).

Amendment of standing orders

2.21 Where the standing orders themselves prescribe the procedure for amendment, the procedure should be followed, provided it does not purport to override the law. Mandatory standing orders can be amended, to such limited extent as may be necessary to correct any ambiguity or other misstatement, provided they remain 'of like effect'.

Periodical review

2.22 Each local authority should undertake a regular review of its discretionary standing orders, annually or at some other predetermined interval of time, as part of the Monitoring Officer's review of the Constitution. It is unlikely that major changes will be needed in those that deal with the rules of debate, but it may be necessary to take account of changes in the law and organisational structure during the past year, and any practical procedural difficulties that have arisen that could be helped by amending or modifying standing orders.

Supply to members

2.23 Councillors (and co-opted, i.e. non-voting, members, too) must be provided with an up-to-date copy of standing orders.

Members should be provided with a copy of the Constitution, as should any member of the public on request (LGA 2000, s. 37). In practice, most if not all authorities make their Constitution available on their website.

Content

What should be included

2.24 What is included in discretionary standing orders is entirely a matter for determination by each local authority, although enforcement is a necessary consideration. The main purpose is to provide for the better regulation of proceedings but most authorities now incorporate staffing and financial regulations and a variety of standing order provisions relating to the corporate structure and organisation of the authority into their Constitution. However, there are often well-established practices or conventions governing the conduct of local authority business that are not incorporated in formal standing orders.

General principles

Conventions

2.25 Widdicombe said, '. . . it saw an important role for local conventions in dealing with those matters where the need is for clear rules but which are not sufficiently susceptible to legal definition to lend themselves to standing orders and on which there is too great a variety of local circumstances for national codes of conduct to be appropriate.' It recommended that each local authority should draw up and make publicly available a list of the conventions it observes in relation, for example, to:

- the basis on which committee places are apportioned among councillors (now governed by LG&HA 1989, s. 15);
- channels for councillors' contact with officers;
- the relationship between committee chairmen and chief officers;
- responsibility for the agenda;
- the rights of councillors to obtain information and advice from officers;
- any arrangements for informal working groups or regular briefing meetings with officers that are not formally constituted as committees of the council;
- attendance of officers at party groups;
- the allocation of support services to councillors; and
- the status of any staff attached to the political groups or individual councillors.

Widdicombe did not believe that conventions should necessarily be given the force of law. The danger of giving them a statutory status would be that the conventions would be over cautious and avoid some of the more problematic relationships. Even without statutory status, the local government ombudsman would generally take such conventions into account in deciding whether maladministration had occurred.
2.26 There are advantages in having conventions in a single document, and some or all of the above are often incorporated into the Constitution of a council. There will also be the Code of Conduct and so forth, usually including the code of practice on planning.
2.27 It has also become customary for hung, or balanced, councils to produce conventions to govern the handling of business where there is no overall political control or even any council leader. Among items commonly covered are: dealing with business between meetings; procedure on equality of votes and use of the casting vote; briefing meetings; and the use of delegated powers of officers. These questions will vary from council to council depending on the approach adopted.

Form

2.28 Standing orders should be easy to understand, though often they are not for a variety of reasons. Sometimes, because they are couched in the words of a statute or, in a misguided attempt to be precise, the wording is so difficult that an authority has to produce an explanatory note for the convenience of council members to show the intention. A useful tool for the convenience of members is a summary of the standing orders or the use of a flowchart.
2.29 The date when the standing orders were made or last reviewed should be shown in the Constitution, together with the date when they became effective. Most

authorities use a loose-leaf system where printed copies are offered (which makes for easier updating) and there should always be an indication of the date when each standing order was approved. The orders should be grouped in a logical sequence, and – a recommendation made in the model standing orders – it is a convenient practice for appropriate extracts from statutes to be printed in a distinctive typeface, such as italics, at the head of each standing order. Mandatory standing orders might be treated similarly.

Chapter 3
Admission of press and public

Introduction

Origin of right of admission

3.1 The right of members of the public to attend local authority meetings has been acquired gradually over the years. At the beginning of the twentieth century, council meetings were regarded by common law as private meetings, even though the local authority in full assembly was transacting public business. The local authority's entitlement to exclude the public, and press representatives, from their meetings was affirmed in *Tenby Corporation v Mason* (1908), which arose out of the Tenby authority's refusal to allow a local newspaper reporter to attend council meetings after, it was alleged by the council, the reporter had produced seriously inaccurate reports of the proceedings. As a result of the court judgement, Parliament passed the Local Authorities (Admission of the Press to Meetings) Act 1908 (LA(APM)A 1908), which gave a right to 'duly accredited representatives of the press' to be admitted to council meetings, but in s. 5 provided that 'nothing in this Act shall be construed so as to prohibit a local authority from admitting the public to its meetings'. Even earlier it had been held in *Purcell v Sowler* (1877) that by common law an authority might expressly or impliedly consent to the attendance of non-members at its meetings, so council meetings were open meetings only so far as the local authority thought fit to allow the public to attend.

3.2 It was nearly 50 years later, in the Public Bodies (Admission to Meetings) Act 1960 (PB(AM)A 1960),[1] that the public was accorded a specific right to be admitted to the meetings of local authorities and certain other bodies to which it applied. This remains the legislation that is applicable only to parish and community councils, parish meetings and certain other bodies set out in a schedule to the Act.

3.3 Then, in the reorganisation of local government in the 1970s, the LGA 1972 extended that right to permit the public to attend meetings of principal local authority committees. A major development occurred when the Local Government (Access to Information) Act 1985 (LG(AI)A 1985), extended this right of admission to sub-committees from 1 April 1986 by additions to LGA 1972, and made detailed provisions obliging those authorities to supply the public with agenda and reports in advance of all meetings, again by adding new provisions to the LGA 1972. As to what constitutes a committee or sub-committee. The Act also applies to meetings of joint boards or joint committees, combined authorities and other local government bodies as specified.

Admission of the public and press

General principle

3.4 Every principal council and its committee and sub-committee meetings must be open to the public, except when the public is excluded – as it must be – because confidential information might otherwise be disclosed during an item of business or – as it may be – if information within one of the statutorily specified categories of exempt information might be disclosed. The general principle underlying the 1985 Act is that meetings should in general be open to the public, including the press. Widdicombe, however, suggested some restriction according with its view that purely deliberative committees (including, significantly, the policy and resources committee) that do not make decisions could comprise councillors of one party only. It said:

> 'What concerns us about the 1985 Act is that it applies equally to committees that have no decision-taking powers but are purely deliberative. We think that this is misconceived, and that the same distinction between decision-taking and deliberative committees should be made with regard to access to information as with regard to committee membership. It is a simple reality, which no legislation can alter, that politicians will develop policy options in confidence before presenting the final choice for public decision. We do not think this unreasonable. If the law prevents them from conducting such discussions in private in formal committees, then they will conduct them less formally elsewhere. We have heard that some local authorities have been creating new informal mechanisms expressly to avoid the effects of the 1985 Act. It is unsatisfactory to force policy deliberation out of the formal committee system into groupings of indeterminate status. It is also unnecessary. No decision can be taken by a local authority without it eventually being referred to a decision taking committee or the council, where there will be full public access to the meeting and the documentation. Given this basic safeguard, we can see no benefit in applying the Act also to deliberative committees. We would not in any way wish to discourage individual local authorities from opening deliberative committees to the public and press if that is appropriate to their particular circumstances, but do not believe that they should be required by law to do so.'

In reality, those policy deliberations are now often made at briefing sessions or 'informal meetings' for cabinet/executive members and relevant committees or scrutiny bodies, which are informal in nature and have no legal status.

Application

3.5 The transaction of business likely to involve disclosure of confidential information that requires principal councils to exclude the public means:

- information furnished to the council by a government department upon terms, however expressed, which forbid the disclosure of the information to the public; and
- information the disclosure of which to the public is prohibited by or under any enactment or by the order of a court.

In either case, the reference to the obligation of confidentiality is to be construed accordingly. Because there is a statutory requirement upon the local authority or a committee or sub-committee to exclude the public in these circumstances, the generally accepted view is that there may be no need for a resolution to that effect to be passed beforehand: it is sufficient for the chair to ask the public to withdraw so that confidential information can be dealt with.

3.6 The question of who makes the decision on exempt information can get a little confusing and sometimes a little frustrating for some members and officers alike. This is because the exclusion of the public and press on the grounds that it may reveal exempt information is, in reality, a two-stage process. The first concerns the publication of the report, which is a decision made by the officers (or, rather, the proper officer), and the second the actual exclusion of the press and public, which is a decision made by the council or committee, but working backwards.

3.7 The decision on whether or not information is exempt is one for the council or committee deliberating on that item of business, not officers.

3.8 The duty to allow members of the public and press access to a meeting, and also the papers provided to that meeting, are contained in the Local Government Act 1972 as amended by the LG(AI)A 1985 (as described above). The power to decide that an item of business on an agenda is 'exempt' from this duty resides with the committee deliberating on that item. These provisions are now set out at s. 100A (Admission to meetings of principal councils), which states that:

> (1) A meeting of a principal council shall be open to the public except to the extent that they are excluded, whether during the whole or part of the proceedings, under subsection (2) below or by resolution under subsection (4) below.
>
> ...
>
> (4) A principal council may by resolution exclude the public from a meeting during an item of business whenever it is likely, in view of the nature of the business to be transacted or the nature of the proceedings, that if members of the public were present during that item there would be disclosure to them of exempt information, as defined in section 100I below.

3.9 It is for this reason that each meeting that takes this action must make a positive decision in the form of a resolution, set out as an item on the agenda, and that this is the case whether or not a member of the press or public is actually present. Such a resolution must (a) identify the proceedings, or the part of the proceedings, to which it applies, and (b) state the description, in terms of Schedule 12A to the Act, of the exempt information giving rise to the exclusion of the public, and where such a resolution is passed this section does not require the meeting to be open to the public during proceedings to which the resolution applies.

3.10 It should be noted that the list in Sched. 12A has since been amended, so that after some delay it now accords with the exemptions permitted under the Freedom of Information Act 2000, including the important element of the application of the public interest test to which members must apply their minds, under which information can be considered exempt if and so long as, in all the circumstances of the case, the public interest in maintaining the exemption outweighs the public interest in disclosing the information. There is no statutory definition of what constitutes the 'public interest' but in May 2013, the Information Commissioner issued updated guidance on public interest entitled 'Public Interest Test: Freedom of Information Act' (Version 2), which sets out relevant factors to be considered.

3.11 This decision is one for that meeting alone. The process for officers in preparing the agenda and publishing the reports is, in effect therefore, to work backwards from that prospective decision. The officers are in the position that they must consider whether or not a meeting is likely, or even that they may resolve to go into private session and, therefore, not publish the papers in advance as they would normally do. The process before a meeting thus reflects the possible decision to be made by the meeting and, all importantly, the legal tests associated with that.

In this instance, the law places that responsibility upon the 'proper officer' who, in constitutional terms, is usually the monitoring officer. These provisions are set out at s. 100B (Access to agenda and connected reports). While what is likely or not likely to be determined as being exempt information at the meeting will be discussed in the chair's pre-meeting, it is normally the monitoring officer, who is the final arbiter as proper officer, who must take the decision over what is or is not likely to result in a resolution to exclude the public and press. That translates in practical and real terms to a professional determination over what will or will not meet the (now fairly clear) legal tests in terms of what is exempt from public access in a report before a meeting takes place.

3.12 The key word in the above, however, is 'before'. That role then changes from one of arbiter to one of advisor at the committee meeting itself. The proper officer will duly advise on the matter, but the law is quite clear that the decision on the application of the legal test set out above is one for the committee or cabinet to make in voting on whether or not to exclude the public.

3.13 If a meeting makes a decision to remain in public session, the reports and papers previously marked 'not for publication' in the likelihood of them being exempt, would be duly made available to the public with immediate effect, and then published in the normal way.

3.14 If a member is unhappy with that decision of the committee or cabinet, there are two potential courses of action. The first is judicial review of the committee or cabinet's decision, dependent on the nature of the decision. The second is a request for the information under FOI. As the access to information regime is aligned with the provisions of the Freedom of Information Act 2000, the response should be the same. That process has the advantage of complaint and recourse to the Information Commissioner's Office, which may ultimately lead to the Information Tribunal(s).

3.15 Once made, the effect of passing of such a resolution is it removes the provision that the meeting is open to anyone but the membership of that committee and those persons expressly invited to attend. This decision includes Members of the Council who are not members of that committee. Each council will have its own protocol on how other members may or may not then be a party to that exempt discussion, but the law is clear that is does exclude any other member not part of that committee.

3.16 There are separate rights for overview and scrutiny committees to demand information about executive meetings. There are also rights for individual Members, which are discussed elsewhere.

Meetings of the executive and other decision-making bodies

3.17 So far as those councils with executive arrangements are concerned, the LGA 2000, as amended by the Localism Act 2011, provides that, subject to regulations made by the Secretary of State, it is for a local authority executive to decide which of its meetings, and which of the meetings of any committee of an executive, are to be open to the public and which of those meetings are to be held in private. The Local Authorities (Meetings and Executive Arrangements) (Access to Information) (England) Regulations 2012, which came into force on 10 September 2012, provide that a meeting of a 'decision-making body' (which includes the executive, a committee of the executive and a joint committee all of whose members are executive members) must, subject to exceptions, be held in public. Regulation 4 of the 2012 Regulations set out the circumstances in which a meeting of a decision-making body must or may exclude the public. The 2012 Regulations provide that the public must be excluded from a meeting during an item of business whenever it is likely that confidential information would be disclosed in breach of the obligation of confidence if members of the public were present during that item. The decision-making body may, by resolution, exclude members of the public from a meeting during an item of business if it is likely that exempt information would be disclosed if members of the public were present during that item. In addition, the decision-making body may exercise a lawful power to exclude a member or members of the public in order to maintain orderly conduct or prevent misbehaviour.

3.18 A decision-making body must provide at least 28 clear days' notice of a meeting to be held in private. The notice must include a statement of the reasons for the meeting to be held in private. It must be made available at the local authority's offices and published on its website (if it has one). During the notice period, members of the public may make representations about why the meeting should be held in public. Then, at least five clear days before the private meeting, the decision-making body must make another notice available at the local authority's offices and on its website (if it has one). The further notice must include a statement of the reasons for the meeting to be held in private, details of representations received about why the meeting should be held in public, and the response of the decision-making body to those representations. If the date by which the meeting must be held makes the publication of the notices impracticable, a meeting may be held in private only if the decision-making body has obtained the agreement of the chair of the relevant overview and scrutiny committee – or, if there is no such person or the chair is unable to act, the chair of the local authority or, if there is again no such person, the vice-chair of the local authority – that the meeting is urgent and cannot be deferred. Where this occurs, the decision-making body must, as soon as is reasonably practicable after obtaining the required agreement, make available at the local authority's offices and on its website (if it has one) a notice explaining why the meeting is urgent and cannot reasonably be deferred.

Notice of meetings of decision-making bodies

3.19 Decision-making bodies must give at least five clear days' notice of the time and place of a public meeting, unless the meeting is convened at shorter notice. If a meeting is convened at shorter notice, the notice of the time and place must be given at the time that the meeting is convened. The notice must be displayed at the local authority's offices and published on its website (if it has one). The agendas and reports for such meetings must also be made available to the public, except where they relate only to matters during which, in the proper officer's opinion, the meeting is likely to be a private meeting. A reasonable number of copies must also be available for the use of members of the public at the meeting. Following a request made by a member of the public or on behalf of a newspaper and on payment of postage, copying or other necessary charges for transmission, a copy of the agenda and reports must be supplied.

Notice of key decisions

3.20 The 2012 Regulations set out additional requirements with regard to notice of key decisions. A decision-maker who intends to make a key decision on behalf of a local authority must publish a document publicising this. The document must include the following details:

- that a key decision is to be made;
- the matter in respect of which the decision is to be made;
- where the decision-maker is an individual, their name and title;
- where the decision-maker is a body, its name and members;
- the date on or period within which the decision will be made;
- the documents to be considered before the decision is made;
- the address from which those documents are available;
- confirmation that other documents may be submitted to the decision-maker; and
- the procedure for requesting details of such documents as they become available.

Where the matter is such that exclusion of the public from meetings at which the matter is to be discussed or exemption from the disclosure of documents relating to the decision is permitted, the document publicising the intended key decision must contain particulars of the matter, but may not contain confidential or exempt information or details of the advice of a political adviser or assistant.

3.21 The document publicising an intended key decision must be made available for public inspection at the local authority's offices and on its website (if it has one) at least 28 days before a key decision is made. If it is impracticable to comply with the publication requirements before a key decision is made, the decision may be made if:

(i) the proper officer has informed the chair of the relevant overview and scrutiny committee, or, if there is no such person, to each member of the of the relevant overview and scrutiny committee by written notice of the decision to be made, and
(ii) the proper officer has made that notice available for public inspection at the local authority's offices and published it on its website (if it has one), and
(iii) five clear days have elapsed following the day on which the proper officer made the notice available.

As soon as reasonably practicable after complying with those requirements, the proper officer must make available at the local authority's offices and on its website (if it has one) a notice explaining why compliance with the publication requirements before making a key decision is impracticable. In cases of special urgency, where compliance with the prior publication set out above is impracticable, a key decision may still be made if the decision-maker has the agreement of the chair of the relevant overview and scrutiny committee – or, if there is no such person or the chair is unable to act, the chair of the local authority or, if there is again no such person, the vice-chair of the local authority – that the making of the decision is urgent and cannot reasonably be deferred. As soon as is reasonably practicable after obtaining such agreement, the decision-maker must make available at the local authority's offices and on its website (if it has one) a notice setting out the reasons why the decision is urgent and cannot reasonably be deferred.

Meetings that are convened for the sole purpose of an officer briefing members, such as cabinet briefing meetings, need not be open to the public.

Other meetings open to the public

3.22 With the exception of meetings of a local authority decision-making body as referred to in paras. 3.4 and 3.5, the meetings required to be open to the public and press are those of principal councils as defined in the LGA 1972, of the authorities established by the LGA 1985, and of certain other authorities[2] and of the committees and sub-committees of all such authorities. Parish and community councils remain subject, as regards the admission of the public to meetings, to the provisions of the PB(AM)A 1960 as extended by the LGA 1972, s. 100.[3] This means that parish and community councils and their committee meetings must be open to the public unless by resolution excluded from the whole or part of any meeting whenever publicity would be prejudicial to the public interest by reason of the confidential nature of the business to be transacted or for other special reasons stated in the resolution and arising from the nature of the business or of the proceedings. The National Association of Local Councils (NALC) has recommended that the spirit and letter of the 1972 legislation should be accepted at parish and community council meetings.

3.23 Some councils have developed ideas to increase public participation and to increase the entitlement of the public to attend committee meetings. Some local authorities now have a public question time at cabinet or committee meetings and, for example, applicants or objectors to planning applications are increasingly permitted to attend and address planning committee meetings.[4] Some councils limit such participation to residents of that local authority's area. Commonly, where members of the public are allowed to speak, there is a time limit for public participation in a general question time of around 15 minutes. Also, how long an individual is allowed to speak is usually limited to, say, five minutes. Wherever possible, groups or individuals are encouraged to nominate one representative, who can be a councillor, to speak on behalf of all. Advance notice of appearance is usually requested to be given to the council so that officers can brief members on the facts and, in the case of a planning matter, on the relevant planning issues, and provide proper advice on how to respond. Once the committee begins its decision-making discussion on a particular application the public are not permitted to speak again. The advantages to such participation are that it does enable the public to make direct representations to the decision-making body and ensures that all members are aware of the issues involved.

There are recognised disadvantages, however, in that the process can be time consuming in relation to contentious matters; objectors can be inarticulate or verbose, even unreasonable and unpleasant particularly if, having taken the time and trouble to attend, the decision is not one that they are seeking. Inevitably, this does make meetings longer, but is a price worth paying for public engagement and evidence gathering. It is good practice for the chair to ask any subsequent objectors if they have anything new to add, to ensure that the committee do not have to sit through a number of objectors all making the same point.

3.24 It is also common for local authorities to allow local electors or other members of the public, under procedures set out in standing orders, to ask questions at council meetings. As to the submission of petitions or the hearing of deputations at council meetings.

3.25 In order to increase access to those members of the public who are not able to attend the meeting, there are also a number of councils who now broadcast their own meetings via the internet.

Notice of other meetings

3.26 Public notice must be given of meetings of a principal council and its committees and sub-committees,[5] and copies of the agenda and accompanying reports must be made available to the public: otherwise the transaction of business is prohibited (see more particularly Chapter 6). These requirements, arising out of the LG(AI)A 1985,[6] are of particular significance in the case of committee and sub-committee meetings because there is elsewhere already an obligation upon local authorities to give public notice of council meetings. Separate arrangements relate to meetings of an authority's cabinet if operating executive governance arrangements.

Closed meetings

3.27 A procedural difficulty can arise where a committee is conducting quasi-judicial business that is not concerned with an item of exempt information and, having heard the representations, wishes to consider its decision in private. The committee may find it difficult to find a reason for excluding the public. Some argue that it would seem reasonable – although in the final resort only the courts can decide – for all the proceedings to be conducted in public session until the parties have concluded their statements when the chairman should say, or words to like effect: 'We will now retire to consider the representations that have been made and will reassemble shortly to announce our decision.' In other words, there would be no resolution to exclude the press and public. This is an uncomfortable place to be in and very likely to be unsustainable. It is better to have reasons to go into exempt session that cover the whole meeting and pass a resolution in respect of deliberation on those exempt matters, if this is what is wished, which may also be affected by the committee withdrawing rather than the press and public. Given that any such meeting is likely to be only relevant to regulatory or employment (i.e. appointment by interview or disciplinary matters), and will therefore involve information concerning a person's personal or business, or the need to obtain privileged advice, affairs this would not seem an unreasonable approach to take.

In the case of hearings under the Licensing Act 2003, this has been dealt with by expressly providing in the Licensing Act 2003 (Hearings) Regulations 2005 that the licensing authority may exclude the public from all or part of a hearing where it considers that the public interest in so doing outweighs the public interest in the hearing, or that part of the hearing, taking place in public. Parties and their representatives may be treated as members of the public. This follows on from the case of *R v London Borough of Wandsworth, ex parte Darker Enterprises Limited* (1999) EWHC Admin 34, where the court held that 'it is hard to see how sub-committees could effectively conduct their discussions, in relation to decisions whether to grant or renew licences, if they were required to do so in public'.

It is important, therefore, that the statutory authority under which the committee is acting is checked to see if there is any specific power applicable to exclude the public, if it is likely that a committee will be seeking to exclude the public from all or part of its proceedings.

Exclusion must be reasonable

3.28 Local authorities may well regard it as important that the spirit of the law should be observed and that their proceedings should be as open as practicable. In any case, an authority must act reasonably when exercising its discretion to exclude the public from a meeting and must justify its action by reference to the statutory list of items of exempt information or other statutory authority. An authority clearly cannot by subterfuge exclude the public in circumstances where it is required to admit it, e.g. by failure to give requisite notice of the meeting or by deciding to meet in a place that is manifestly inadequate to accommodate members of the public. In *R v Kensington and Chelsea London Borough Council and another, ex parte Stoop* [1992]

1 PLR 58, in an application for judicial review of a decision of the council, it was held that where a local authority committee votes to refuse planning permission and then adjourns into private session to receive advice from its solicitor about the chances of successfully resisting an appeal and the likelihood of an award of costs against the authority in the event of the appeal being successful: (a) the solicitor's advice is exempt information within the meaning of the 1972 Act, Sch. 12A, and therefore the committee is entitled to receive it in private; and (b) the requirement of fairness in decision-making does not require that an objector to the grant of planning permission should be given an opportunity to make further representations between the committee's receipt of that advice and its decision to change its mind and grant planning permission. Moreover, the applicant himself did not have a right to remain in the meeting when the public was excluded.

Who are the public?

3.29 The right of admission to local authority meetings applies to the public generally,[7] i.e. it is not restricted to council tax payers or electors or local residents alone, except in the case of a parish meeting or a community meeting.[8]

Adequacy of accommodation

3.30 There are obviously practical limits to the right of the public to be admitted. How much space is set aside is a matter for the local authority's discretion. During the passage of what was to become the PB(AM)A 1960, it was said that:[9]

> '. . . the duty imposed on a local authority... will be to choose a room big enough to take some members of the public and some reporters. It will not have to provide accommodation for an unlimited number of each . . . The usual way in which anybody whose deliberations are open to the public complies with its obligations is by providing reasonable but limited accommodation for members of the public and then allocating it on the basis of first come, first served.'

3.31 If a local authority or committee or sub-committee decides to meet in a very small room and then says in effect 'We cannot have the public in because there is no room', it would be acting in bad faith; and in such an event, the Lord Chief Justice said in *R v Liverpool City Council ex parte Liverpool Taxi Fleet Operators' Association* (1975), the authority would not be beyond the long arm of their Lordships' court. It would seem, therefore, that where a council or committee or sub-committee is to discuss a matter in which it knows there is considerable public interest, it must either provide more accommodation for the public than is ordinarily available or at least ensure that the accommodation is no less than that ordinarily available.

3.32 On occasions, some local authorities change the normal venue for a meeting if it is known that a particular matter is likely to generate a large public attendance. For example, one council moved its planning committee meeting to a local theatre when considering a major planning application affecting a significant part of the borough.

Admission of press representatives

Substantially same rights as public

3.33 Representatives of the press enjoy no rights of admission to local authority meetings greater than those conferred upon the public[10] except that an authority is required, as far as practicable, to provide 'duly accredited representatives of newspapers' with reasonable facilities. The term 'duly accredited representatives of newspapers' is not defined in the LGA 1972 (nor in the LG(AI)A 1985 which amended it), but 'newspaper' includes: (a) a news agency that systematically carries on the business of selling and supplying reports of information to newspapers; and (b) any organisation that is systematically engaged in collecting news (i) for sound or television broadcasts; or (ii) for programmes to be included in a cable programme service that is or does not require to be licensed.

Facilities for the press

3.34 While a meeting of a principal council is required to be open to the public, duly accredited representatives of newspapers attending the meeting for the purpose of reporting the proceedings for those newspapers must, as far as practicable, be afforded reasonable facilities for taking their report and, unless the meeting is held in premises not belonging to the council or not on the telephone, for telephoning the report at their own expense.[11] Similar provisions apply to meetings of decision-making bodies (see 3.4): if a meeting of a decision-making body is open to the public, any person attending the meeting for the purpose of reporting proceedings should be afforded reasonable facilities for taking their report.[12]

Principal authorities and decision-making bodies must, on request and on payment of postage or other necessary charges for transmission, supply for the benefit of any newspaper:

- a copy of the agenda for a meeting and accompanying reports;
- such further statements or particulars, if any, as are necessary to indicate the nature of the items included in the agenda; and
- if the proper officer thinks fit in the case of any item, copies of any other documents supplied to members of the council in connection with the item.[13]

In relation to the meetings of principal councils, the LGA 1972 permits a charge to be made for postage and transmission of the above documents, not a charge for the documents themselves. In relation to the meetings of decision-making bodies, however, the charge can also include a copying charge.

Photography, live broadcasts and tape recordings

3.35 It is expressly provided that: nothing in this section shall require a principal council to permit the taking of photographs of any proceedings, or the use of any means to enable persons not present to see or hear any proceedings (whether at the time or later), or the making of any oral report on any proceedings as they take place.[14] This is now subject, however, to the provision inserted by the Openness of Local Government Bodies Regulations 2014 (SI 2014/2095) reg. 4, that:

> (7A) While a meeting of a principal council in England is open to the public, any person attending is to be permitted to report on the meeting.
> (7B) Subsection (7A) does not require a principal council in England to permit oral reporting or oral commentary on a meeting as it takes place if the person reporting or providing the commentary is present at the meeting.
> (7C) A person attending a meeting of a principal council in England for the purpose of reporting on the meeting must, so far as practicable, be afforded reasonable facilities for doing so.
> (7D) Subsection (7C) applies in place of subsection (6)(c) in the case of a principal council in England.
> (7E) Any person who attends a meeting of a principal council in England for the purpose of reporting on the meeting may use any communication method, including the internet, to publish, post or otherwise share the results of the person's reporting activities.
> (7F) Publication and dissemination may take place at the time of the meeting or occur after the meeting.

3.36 'Reporting' is widely defined. There is an express provision, however, that this is to be without prejudice to any power of exclusion to suppress or prevent disorderly conduct or other misbehaviour at a meeting.[15]

Other considerations

Qualified privilege of documents provided

3.37 Where any accessible document (defined by LGA 172 s. 100H(6)) of a meeting of a principal council or a committee or sub-committee of principal council:

- is supplied to, or open to inspection by, a member of the public; or
- is supplied for the benefit of any newspaper,

the publication thereby of any defamatory matter contained in the document is privileged unless the publication is proved to be made with malice. Care should always be taken with items such as motions set down for debate in council particularly when sensitive subjects that may refer to the actions of individual members are being dealt with.

Exclusion of public and press in event of disorder

3.38 The statutory obligation upon principal councils to admit the public and the press to their meetings is 'without prejudice to any power of exclusion to suppress or prevent disorderly conduct or other misbehaviour at a meeting' (and see chapter 7, where the whole question of disorderly conduct at meetings is considered).

3.39 If the chair of a meeting thinks it desirable or necessary to adjourn the meeting because of disorder among the public present, the council, committee or sub-committee cannot afterwards resume proceedings with the public still debarred from admission on the assumption that readmission would again lead to disorder, because this would be a contravention of the public's right of admission. But those persons, whether individuals or a group, can properly be excluded if persisting in disorder when business proceeds.

3.40 There appears to be no right for the press or public upon readmission, or at the end of the meeting, to be told what business was transacted in their absence,[17] although the chair might think it appropriate to outline what has been decided.

Standing orders

3.41 There is no provision in the existing model standing orders or mandatory standing orders in respect of the admission or exclusion of the public from local authority meetings,[18] but there is no reason why standing orders could not be made regulating, within the law, local arrangements.

3.42 It is not uncommon for local authorities to include in standing orders pro forma motions that may be moved without notice, e.g. motions to exclude the public and the press. Thus in the case of a principal council when exempt information is to be considered:

> 'That under s. 100A(4) of the Local Government Act 1972, the public be excluded from the meeting for the following item(s) of business on the grounds that it (they) involve(s) the likely disclosure of exempt information as defined in paragraph(s)... (respectively) of Part 1 of schedule 12A of the Act.'

Or, in the case of, say, a parish or community council:

> 'That the public be excluded from this meeting during consideration of... as publicity would be prejudicial to the public interest because of the confidential nature of the business to be transacted.'

Access to information

Extended access to documents

3.43 The LGA 1972, as amended by the LG(AI)A 1985, provides the right of the public (and the press) to inspect the documents of principal local authorities and of their committees and sub-committees,[19] and conferred on councillors, as members of those authorities, a statutory right of access to council papers.[20] The rights of the public in this respect are mentioned briefly here because in many ways the rights are closely identified with the right of access to local authority meetings: indeed, in *R v Hackney London Borough Council ex parte Gamper* (1985), it was said that for councillors with a 'need to know' there is no logical distinction between access to documents and attendance at meetings. Public access to documents (agenda and reports) prior to a meeting is dealt with later in this book, as is the statutory right of councillors in this connection. The introduction of the Freedom of Information Act 2000, and its full implementation on 1 January 2005 in relation to access to information held by local authorities, further extended the range of information and documentation able to be accessed by the press and the public, considered further below.

Duty to publish other information

3.44 Each principal council is also required to publish the following information and to keep it available for public inspection:[21]

- a register giving the name and address of every councillor and the ward or division represented, and the name and address of every member of each committee and sub-committee; a list specifying the powers exercisable by officers under delegated authority, and the title of the officer where the power is exercisable for a period of more than six months;
- a document summarising the rights that the law confers[22] upon members of the public to attend local authority meetings and council, committee and sub-committee meetings, and to inspect and copy and be furnished with documents; and
- a register of interests of members and co-opted members.[23]

Review of past practice

3.45 The Policy Studies Institute carried out a research project during 1995 to evaluate the first ten years of the operation of the LG(AI)A 1985. The result, published in its report Public Access to Information, in general complimented local government on the manner in which authorities had applied the legislation and had in many cases gone beyond it. The report contained recommendations and a list of suggested 'best practices' as follows:

- publicity: more active steps to publicise rights including special leaflets;
- awareness: use of targeted publicity for the press and training for members;
- background papers: listing on committee papers with contact numbers;

- committee papers: seven days' advance notice wherever possible and available at local centres;
- documents: official jargon should be avoided and use of plain English encouraged;
- exempt information: minimal use encouraged to enable policy matters to be discussed in public;
- agenda: public items should be taken first;
- venues: larger accommodation should be used when necessary; and
- charging: charges should be kept as low as possible.

Good practice

3.46 Also in 1995, the then local authority associations circulated a 'good practice note', *Open Government*. It recommended that each local authority should draw up a policy on access to information by the public, assisted by the advice contained in the note, which also set out an updated, but not comprehensive, list of statutory provisions providing access rights for the public. In 2000, the modular constitution issued by the Secretary of State included a section on access to information and this has been adapted by each council to provide a summary of how information can be accessed in terms of its own decision-making structure.

Freedom of Information Act 2000

3.47 The Freedom of Information Act 2000 provides a general right of access to recorded information held by public authorities. It is intended to promote a culture of openness and accountability within the public sector by providing a right of access to information held by it. These rights are also to help promote public involvement in the decision-making process by allowing the public access to relevant information, and facilitate better understanding of how public authorities carry out their duties, make their decisions and spend public money.

3.48 The general right of access to information, however, is subject to exemptions. There are 23 categories of exemptions, some of which are absolute and others that are not (qualified exemptions). If an absolute exemption applies, then the local authority need not disclose the information. Although some absolute exemptions relate to obvious matters of secrecy, such as the intelligence services or information whose disclosure is positively prohibited by law, most of the absolute exemptions are designed to carve out from disclosure under the Act information whose availability is governed by some more specialised set of rules, and that may be accessible to the applicant by other means. For example, personal data of which the applicant is the data subject will be dealt with under the Data Protection Act 1998, disclosure of information that is subject to a duty of confidence by common law will be governed by common law principles, and disclosure of information in court documents is a matter for the rules of the court concerned. In these cases, the exemption is made absolute not to place it beyond the public gaze, but to prevent a potentially uncomfortable interaction between two specialised and potentially incompatible regimes for its disclosure.

3.49 If a qualified exemption applies, then information is only exempt from disclosure if in all the circumstances of the case, the public interest in maintaining the exemption outweighs the public interest in disclosing the information. Examples of such exemptions are law enforcement, audit functions or where it is argued by the local authority that disclosure would prejudice the effective conduct of public affairs. In the latter case, such an exemption would only apply if this were the reasonable opinion of a qualified person who, so far as local authorities are concerned, must be the monitoring officer or, in their absence, the chief executive.

3.50 The Information Commissioner is the enforcing authority for the FOI Act 2000 and various guidance has been issued to assist local authorities in implementation. It is clear that since the FOI Act 2000 the public have become far more aware of their right to access information, and in a recent study by the Information Commissioner, 84% of people were aware of their right to access information held by public authorities, compared to only 73% in 2005.

With regard to councillors, the Information Commissioner decided that a local authority had to release details of those telephone calls a councillor had claimed for in his expenses, although the phone numbers could be redacted (case ref: FS50074146).

The Information Commissioner has decided a case in respect of the quorum needed for a licensing sub-committee, when the council sat with a quorum of two but refused to provide a copy of its legal advice (case ref: FS50098767). The local authority relied on the s. 41 exemption as they claimed the information was provided in confidence, as it was part of legal advice obtained by another public authority and shared 'in confidence'. As the s. 41 exemption is an absolute one, there was no need for the Information Commissioner to consider whether the public interest test applied, and a different decision may well have been reached if he had had to decide whether the public interest test had been correctly applied.

Notes

1 Under the PB(AM)A 1960, s. 1(2), which previously applied to all local authorities but no longer to principal councils, the power to exclude the press and public was very widely drawn in general terms (see 3.5). When the Bill was before the Commons on 5 February 1960, Margaret Thatcher, one of the sponsors of the Bill, said it had been found impossible to draft a clause that would cover all individual cases where the public should be excluded.

The 1985 Act sought to overcome that 'impossibility' but it is interesting now to see how closely the terms of the exempt information follow what Mrs Thatcher, now Baroness Thatcher, said in the Commons in 1960:

> 'There are two prongs to this clause. Publicity would be prejudicial for two main groups of reasons. The first group is where the matters under discussion are of a confidential nature. They may relate to personal circumstances of individual electors. They may relate to a confidential communication from a government department asking local authorities for their opinion on a subject which the minister would not like to be discussed in open session until he is a good deal further on and has received the views of local authorities. There is another group of subjects which perhaps could not be strictly termed confidential but where it would be clearly

prejudicial to the public interest to discuss them in open session. They may relate to staff matters, to legal proceedings, to contracts, the discussion of which tender to accept and other such matters. On this prong the press has to be excluded for a special reason which would need to be stated in the resolution for exclusion. Where the matter is confidential it would not need to be specified further in the resolution for exclusion. Where it was for a special reason that reason would need to be specified in broad general terms in the resolution for exclusion.'

2 This means, in addition to the principal councils listed at 1.5: a joint authority, a joint board or joint committee if a body corporate discharging the functions of two or more principal councils, a police authority which is a body corporate, and a combined fire authority (LGA 1972, s. 100J, added by LG(AI)A 1985), and joint consultative committees with health authorities: LG(AI)A (Extension) Act 1986.

3 So, too, do the council of the Isles of Scilly and joint boards or joint committees that discharge functions of any of these bodies (or of any of these bodies and of a principal council or a new authority established under the LGA 1985): LG(AI)A 1985, s. 4 and sch. 2, para. 4(2).

4 See 'Permitting the public to speak at planning committees' by Alec Samuels: an experiment by Southampton City Council: (1993) 162 *Local Government Review* 161.

5 LGA 1972, s. 100A(6), added by LG(AI)A 1985.

6 LGA 1972, s. 100A(5), added by LG(AI)A 1985.

7 The point was made by Sir Jocelyn Simon, Solicitor-General, during the passage of the Bill through Parliament: House of Commons Official Report, col. 162: 30 March 1960.

8 LGA 1972, ss. 13(1), 32(1).

9 By the Solicitor-General: House of Commons Official Report, cols. 119–20; 30 March 1960. Note, too, the words 'so far as practicable' in LGA 1972, s. 100(1).

10 During the passage of the Public Bodies (Admission to Meetings) Bill through Parliament, the Solicitor-General made it clear in the Commons on 30 March 1960 that the press should not be admitted at the expense of the public, nor vice versa. At an earlier occasion, Henry Brooke, the then Minister of Housing and Local Government, said: 'If the public gallery is full, that does not entitle members of the public to occupy the seats set aside for the press, nor would it be proper if members of the press attended . . . in enormous numbers, to say that only reporters could come in and that provision could not be made for the public.'

11 LGA 1972, s. 100A(6)(c), added by LG(AI)A 1985.

12 Local Authorities (Executive Arrangements) (Meetings and Access to Information) (England) Regulations 2012, reg. 4(6).

13 LGA 1972, s. 100B(7), added by LG(AI)A 1985 and Local Authorities (Executive Arrangements) (Meetings and Access to Information) (England) Regulations 2012, Reg. 7(7).

14 Ibid. s. 100A(7).

15 Ibid. s. 100A(8),(9).

16 Department of Communities and Local Government *Your council's cabinet – going to its meetings, seeing how it works: a guide for local people* (June 2013).

17 A view expressed at 137 JPN 153 but, of course, the public can always inspect the minutes of the meeting.

18 But the old model standing order no. 11 was to this effect: 'If any question arises at a meeting of the council (or of a committee thereof to which the Public Bodies (Admission to Meetings) Act 1960 applies by virtue of section 2(1)) as to the appointment, promotion, dismissal, salary, superannuation or conditions of service, or as to the conduct of any person employed by the council, such question shall not be the subject of discussion until the council or committee, as the case may be, has decided whether or not the power of exclusion of the public under section 1(2) of the Public Bodies (Admission to Meetings) Act 1960 shall be exercised.'

3. Admission of press and public

19 Access to documents of a limited range of other local authorities, i.e. parish and community councils, the council of the Isles of Scilly and joint boards or joint committees which discharge functions of any of these bodies (or of any of these bodies and a principal council) is still governed by the LGA 1972, s. 228 as amended, and is thus exercisable by electors and not members of the public generally.

20 LGA 1972, s. 100F, added by LG(AI)A 1985. The rights are in addition to any common law or other rights. Widdicombe suggested that these rights should all be contained in statute with no reliance on common law: Widdicombe Report. para. 5.71. A council constitution will include a section on rights of access to information.

21 LGA 1972, s. 100G, added by the LG(AI)A 1985, and amended by the LG&HA 1989, s. 194 and sch. l.

22 This means not only the rights conferred by Pt VA and Pt XI of the LGA 1972 but under 'such other enactments as the Secretary of State by order specifies': and the Local Government (Inspection of Documents) (Summary of Rights) Order 1986 specifies for this purpose the several enactments listed in the schedule to the Order. See also: Appendix 1 of a good practice note, *Open Government* (1995), published by the then local authority associations.

23 The Localism Act 2011, s. 29 (in England) and the LGA 2000, s. 81 (in Wales) requires the monitoring officer to establish and maintain such a register. The register must be available for inspection by the public at an office of the authority at all reasonable hours. In England, the register must be made available on the authority's website. In Wales, once the register is established, the council should publish in one or more local newspapers a notice stating the availability of copies of the register and where it may be inspected. This requirement applies to all relevant authorities, including parish councils.

Chapter 4
Local authority membership

Election of councillors

General considerations

4.1 Members of a local authority are those persons who have been elected in accordance with the statutory rules relating to local elections[1] to serve for the requisite term of office in a representative capacity on one of the authorities referred to earlier, sometimes on more than one, as a person may be a member of the county council, district council and parish council within the administrative county. When submitting themselves for nomination for election and, if elected, then throughout their membership, the person must be of full age and a British (or Irish) citizen and possess certain qualifications linking them with the area of the authority.[2] In addition, they must be free from a number of disqualifications.[3] So long as a councillor remains qualified they cannot be removed from office, though they may resign voluntarily at any time. The whole process of election and the detailed rules relating to qualification and disqualification are for the most part matters outside the scope of this work.

4.2 Some reference needs to be made in general terms, however, to the position of persons who may act as councillors though strictly disqualified from office and of the consequences of their attendance at meetings of the council and committees and sub-committees. In this respect, s. 82 of the LGA 1972 is important; it provides that:

> 'The acts and proceedings of any person elected to an office under this Act and acting in that office shall, notwithstanding his disqualification, be as valid and effective as if he had been qualified.'

'Office' means the office of councillor or chairman or vice-chairman of the council or elected mayor or executive leader, but not membership or the chairmanship or vice-chairmanship of a committee or sub-committee, none of which is of itself an office within the Act. Nevertheless, there is a presumption elsewhere in the Act, in sch. 12, para. 41(3), applied to committees and sub-committees by s. 99, that a local authority meeting has been properly constituted.

Until the contrary is proved, a meeting of a local authority a minute of whose proceedings have been made and signed in accordance with this paragraph shall be deemed to have been duly convened and held, and all the members present at the meeting shall be deemed to have been qualified.

4.3 The vacation of office by councillors who do not secure re-election and the coming into office of new councillors can pose administrative and procedural difficulties for local authorities. Standing orders as a rule provide for the transitional period between the day of election and the annual meeting and the appointment of newly constituted committees. Most authorities avoid holding meetings during this period but sometimes, of course, urgent business demands that decisions must be made by councillors. The normal practice that appointments to committees are made for the council year, i.e. until the start of the next annual meeting, is necessarily conditioned by the rule that persons not re-elected at the end of their term of office cease to be councillors 'on the fourth day after the ordinary day of election' and that newly elected councillors 'shall come into office on the day on which their predecessors retire'.[4] The exception is the chairman of the council, who may continue until a successor is elected at the annual meeting (but who may not vote unless using his or her casting vote). His means that councillors not re-elected may lawfully attend meetings of committees and sub-committees and meetings of outside bodies on which they represent the council on the second and third day after the date of election.[5] A councillor not re-elected may, as chair of a committee, for example, properly act as such during this period. But a newly elected councillor cannot in practice attend to any council business until the annual meeting following their election, when committee membership is decided, and in any case cannot act as a councillor until they have made a declaration of acceptance of office.

Under the Local Government Act 2000, s. 52(2), the form of declaration of acceptance of office under this section may include an undertaking by the declarant that in performing their functions they will observe the authority's Code of Conduct for the time being under s. 51 of the 2000 Act. The Local Elections (Declaration of Acceptance of Office) Order 2012 (SI 2012/1465) sets out the form of declaration, and it no longer requires councillors to agree to be bound by their authority's code of conduct.

Rights, duties and obligations

Introduction

4.4 It is appropriate to consider briefly the rights, duties and obligations assumed by councillors following election, because these are significant in relation to local authority meetings. If, for example, councillors en bloc ceased to attend meetings then the business of the local authority could not continue for very long: how long would depend upon a number of factors. Supposing the members failed to attend the first meeting of the council after their election so that the council's annual meeting could not take place: the council would not be properly constituted because it would not have a chairman.[6] On the other hand, if the members met at the annual meeting, elected a chairman, conducted such other business as the law required and passed resolutions delegating considerable executive power to officers,[7] it is conceivable that the authority could function effectively and legally for some time: until no doubt some specific act required the council's formal resolution. In the absolute extremity, i.e. if through the failure of members to attend meetings it became impossible for local government to be carried on, the government would invoke the default powers available.[8]

4.5 It is also worth noting the title of this chapter and why a councillor (or elected mayor or co-opted member) is referred to internally as a 'member'. The reason is that he or she is a member of the corporation that is the local authority. It is by no accident that this is the same term used by companies to describe their shareholders, because in many ways the legal separation and situation between the member and the corporation is the same. Being referred to as a 'member' is a useful reminder for both the councillor and the authority's officers of the different roles that a councillor fulfils and helps explains when, how and why the relationships are different. In the literal and legal sense:

- any actual power a councillor has derives only from when they are making a decision as a member of the council, i.e. acting as a part of the whole in council or committee or by specific delegation under executive arrangements; but
- at all other times, from the corporation's point of view and the law, a councillor is simply a member of the public, albeit one with substantial and varying degrees of influence and who, for certain members under executive arrangements or in certain circumstances concerning their ward (under s. 236 of the LGPIHA 2007), may make individual decisions, but only within a set legal framework.

4.6 Widdicombe[9] had divided 'the various activities that councillors undertake' into four main areas:

1. activities directly related to council business, that is, attending meetings of the council and its committees and sub-committees; preparation for such meetings; meetings with council officials; travelling to and from council meetings; membership of committees;
2. meetings with organisations or bodies on which councillors represent the council;
3. attendance at party meetings in relation to council activities; and
4. meetings with the public, including dealing with electors' problems, surgeries and pressure groups; attending public consultation meetings.

The National Census of Local Authority Councillors carried out by the LGA in 2010 found that councillors spent an average of 23 hours per week on council business, and that, in general, ten hours per week were spent at meetings. These figures have been broadly consistent and are in line with the 2006 and 2008 census information.

Rights and duties generally

4.7 A councillor when elected to office possesses certain rights conferred by law, e.g. is entitled to attend council meetings without hindrance; and if they can show a 'need to know' in relation to a particular item of business, can claim a common law right to attend the meeting of the committee or sub-committee concerned. They have otherwise only a limited right as an individual councillor.

A councillor also assumes certain other obligations on gaining office, e.g. they undertake in their declaration on acceptance of office to fulfil the duties as councillor to the best of their judgement and ability and may conceivably have some personal responsibility for maladministration; but does not incur any general legal duty to attend to their voluntarily imposed tasks, e.g. they are not bound to attend meetings, although it could be argued in making the declaration of acceptance of office a councillor undertakes to discharge their duties, and there are instances where liability may be incurred if they fail to attend a meeting that they ought to attend. However, if a councillor neglects to attend meetings over a prescribed period, they forfeit the office of councillor. A councillor's common law right to information – which has statutory backing – is discussed below.

Right to attend meetings

4.8 A councillor has an absolute right throughout his term of office to attend every full council meeting of the local authority to which he has been elected. Nowhere is this right expressly so stated but an authority would be acting unlawfully if it sought to exclude a member from a meeting of the full council, e.g. either by failing to summon them to the meeting or by denying them admission; even the exclusion of a councillor for disorderly conduct or other misbehaviour can only be for a strictly limited period. But a parish or community councillor, if not on the electoral roll for the parish or community concerned, has no right to attend and take part in the proceedings of a parish or community meeting. This arises because a person, though not on the electoral register, is qualified to be a parish or community councillor if, for example, they live 'outside the parish or community but within three miles of it'. The National Association of Local Councils regards this as an absurdity because it means, for example, that a councillor who may have taken a leading part in a parish or community council's decision has no right to explain or defend it at an electors' meeting (although they may be invited to attend and address the electors present), nor may they vote. The law does, however, permit a parish or community council chairman to take part in the proceedings and they must preside if present; and although they cannot vote with the body of electors, they have a casting vote.

4.9 However, where a member:

- ceases to be qualified for membership of the authority; or
- becomes disqualified for membership of the authority; or
- ceases to be a member of the authority by reason of failure to attend the meetings, and the authority has, where necessary, declared the member's office to be vacant, the authority could properly deny them admission as a member – though the member could, of course, attend as a member of the public.

4.10 The right of a councillor to attend committee meetings is, however, a qualified one. In the first place a councillor need not serve on any committee at all: they cannot be appointed to a committee if unwilling to serve (see *R v Sunderland Corporation* (1911), where it was held that a person who is appointed to serve on a committee may lawfully resign against the will of the council); nor can they dispute the council's decision if it does not appoint them to any committee or, having appointed them, deprives them of committee membership (*Manton v Brighton Corporation* (1951), although the council must be scrupulous in observing its standing orders in this respect: *R v Rushmoor Borough Council ex parte Crawford* (1981). Nevertheless, so long as they remain a member of a committee, they are entitled to attend all the committee's meetings for the duration of their local authority membership.

4.11 A councillor who has not been appointed to a particular committee can claim a right to attend a meeting of the committee, but not to vote, if able to show a 'need to know'. This appears to be a result of *R v Hackney London Borough Council ex parte Gamper* (1985),[10] where the court applied the principle set out in *R v Birmingham City District Council ex parte O* (1983), which related to a councillor's entitlement to information. It has always been open to a local authority (in circumstances usually prescribed by standing orders) to permit a councillor to attend meetings of committees of which they are not a member, but prior to the *Gamper* case it was thought that no councillor could claim a right to attend – except insofar as they could be present in the public gallery as a member of the public. In Hackney, however, the court took the view that there was really no logical distinction between access to documents and access to meetings, i.e. the common law was the same if access was necessary in order to enable the councillor to perform their duties as a councillor. The court also decided that members of parent committees had an automatic right to attend all of that committee's sub-committees. This was further developed in *R v Sheffield City Council ex parte Chadwick* 1985 [84 LGR 563], where the Council had refused to allow a member to attend meetings of a budget sub-committee or supply him with reports, on the grounds that attendance of opposition members would make it difficult for members to seek advice from officers. Woolf LJ held that it was unlawful to use a sub-committee for party political purposes in this way.

Right with others to call meetings

4.12 A councillor has no right, as an individual member, to demand a meeting of the full council. They can, however, join with others in requisitioning a council meeting. Any right they may possess of calling a meeting of a committee is dependent on standing orders.

Access to information

4.13 It has long been recognised that a councillor has a common law right to be provided with or to inspect council documents that it is reasonably necessary for them to see in order to carry out their duties as a councillor. That common law right has now been restated in important respects and in 1986, for the first time, the councillor if a member of a principal council was given a statutory right of access to prescribed categories of document. A councillor has always, of course, been able to exercise the same power of inspection of documents that members of the public or electors possess.

4.14 A councillor's statutory right of access to documents is provided by s. 100F of the LGA 1972, added by the LG(AI)A 1985, which came into effect on 1 April 1986. This provides that 'any document which is in the possession or under the control of a principal council and contains material relating to any business to be transacted at a meeting of the council or a committee or sub-committee' must be open to inspection by any member of the principal council. This means that a councillor's statutory right of access is limited to documents concerned with business about to be transacted at a meeting. A member cannot, for example, demand to see a document that relates to business not yet due to come before a meeting; and it is submitted that if they wish to delve into a matter that has been dealt with in the past they must resort to the right of access available to the public generally or to their common law entitlement, or through the Freedom of Information Act 2000. Indeed, it is expressly stated that the statutory rights are in addition to any other rights that a councillor might have.

In respect of executive functions where councils are operating an executive form of governance, the above is replicated, by virtue of the LGA 2000 s. 22 providing that the Secretary of State may make regulations in respect of access to information, in regulation 16 of the Local Authorities (Executive Arrangements) (Access to Information) (England) Regulations 2012 (SI 2012/2089).

4.15 A councillor's common law right of access to council documents is dependent (and always has been though not expressed in precisely the same terms) upon a 'need to know' in order to enable them properly to perform their duties as a councillor: *R v Barnes Borough Council ex parte Conlan* (1938). But it has never been an absolute right. Humphrey J said in Barnes it could not extend to all documents 'since in the case of a large local authority it would be an impossible burden to become acquainted with all the council's business'. And there is no right to 'a roving commission to go and examine the books or documents of a corporation'. Mere curiosity or desire to see and inspect documents is not sufficient: see *R v Southwold Corporation* (1907). Nor can a councillor properly exercise the right for some indirect motive, e.g. to assist someone in litigation with the council: see *R v Hampstead Borough Council* (1917).

4.16 In the case of *R v Hackney London Borough Council, ex parte Gamper* (1985) the applicant was a councillor on the respondent council, and was also a member of the council's public services and housing committees, and chairman of a housing services sub-committee. The council created three new sub-committees of the public services committee, two of which were responsible for looking after the direct labour organisations (DLO) employed by the council. The applicant, in his capacity as a member of the parent committee and of the housing services sub-committee, requested access to certain documents and meetings of the DLO sub-committees. The council refused him access to the documents and to the meetings. He applied for an order to quash the council's decision.

The court decided that the principle that a council member had a right of access to committee documents provided he could show that he had a 'need to know' and that where he was a member of the committee in question he would generally be assumed to have such a need to know, were equally applicable to sub-committee documents. The council should have considered whether the applicant had a need to know in respect of the confidential documents; and since the council had merely considered whether the documents were confidential, and not whether the councillor had a need to know, the council's decision was quashed. It was also held that, even if the council had considered the applicant's individual need to know, its decision to refuse the applicant access to the documents was a decision that no reasonable council could have reached if properly directed in law. Furthermore, there was no logical distinction between access to documents and attendance at meetings and therefore since, on the facts, the applicant needed to attend the meetings of the DLO sub-committees in order to perform his duties properly as a member of the council, the council's decision would be quashed.

4.17 This followed the decision taken by the House of Lords in *City of Birmingham District Council v O and another* (1983). In that case a member of the city council's housing committee had asked to see the papers of the social services committee concerning the adoption proceedings of a child in the council's care. The councillor, as a member of the housing committee, had become aware that the prospective adoptive parents had a bad record of rent arrears and that the husband had previously served a prison sentence. The councillor believed that to allow the adoption proceedings to continue could constitute a serious error of judgement by the social services committee. The councillor's request for access to the social services committee's papers was not opposed by the council but by the prospective adoptive parents, who sought judicial intervention through an order of prohibition to prevent disclosure. The House of Lords held that the general principle was that a councillor was entitled by virtue of his office to have access to all written material in the possession of the council provided he had good reason for such access, and that a councillor *ex hypothesi* normally had good reason for such access to all written material in the possession of a committee of which he was a member and, second, that a councillor had no automatic right of access to material in the possession of a committee of which he was not a member. In the case of information in the possession of a committee of which he was not a member, a councillor had to demonstrate a need to know such information in order to be able to carry out duties as a councillor properly. This decision was ultimately a decision for the council itself, although the council was entitled expressly or impliedly to delegate this function. Applying those principles, there were undoubtedly grounds for questioning the wisdom of the proposed adoption, and the council itself would ultimately be responsible if the adoption should prove unsuccessful. It was therefore not unreasonable for the council to permit the councillor to have access, in confidence, to the files of the council's social services department relating to the child and the applicants. The position was not altered by the fact that the council had delegated its functions in relation to adoption to the social services committee, because the council itself had a residual responsibility for the committee's actions and an obligation, in appropriate circumstances, to exercise some degree of control over the committee. (See 1.46 as to the Wednesbury principle.)

4.18 In *R v Clerk to Lancashire Police Committee ex parte Hook* (1980), the question arose as to whether a councillor elected after a highly confidential report had been considered and acted upon had a right to see the document to enable him to perform his duties as a councillor. The Court of Appeal (Lord Denning MR dissenting) upheld the decision of the divisional court refusing to grant an order directing the clerk of the police authority to provide an unabridged copy of the report to the new councillor. The report was the result of an inquiry conducted by the Chief Constable of Hampshire. It disclosed serious shortcomings in the Lancashire police force and leading counsel had advised the police authority that, as the report contained defamatory statements, publication might endanger the privilege that would otherwise attach to it and that the safest course would be to refuse new members access to it. The report was leaked, however, and a police officer was awarded substantial damages for libel. The new councillor in good faith sought through the courts to compel the clerk to supply him with an unabridged copy of the report. Waller LJ, citing *Stuart v Bell* and *Adam v Ward* (1917) held that the committee had not decided on improper advice and said the final decision must in the last resort be that of the committee, which could take into consideration possible adverse effects on innocent people of allowing the inspection of documents. It was not reasonably necessary for the new councillor to have access to matters not disclosed to enable him to carry out his duties: he was not concerned with the daily management of the police force. Lord Denning dissented. He said the new councillor simply wanted to be better informed at any subsequent consideration of the matter. A member has a right to see all a committee's documents and this included a new member.

4.19 This area can present difficulties when faced with requests by members to see file papers and confidential reports. However, the above cases make it clear that an officer faced with a request is required to satisfy themselves that the member is entitled to the information. The crucial questions are: is it necessary for the member to see that particular document or paper to get the information they are seeking; and are the duties they are seeking to carry out those which they have 'as a councillor'; are they, in other words, consistent with their responsibilities as an elected member of the council in question? These can be difficult questions to answer – and a difficult position for the member to understand. Because of this, it is good practice for there to be a written code and for any necessary appeals machinery to be set up in advance.

Obligations generally

4.20 The obligations of councillors at a meeting are the same whether the meeting is that of the full council, executive or a committee or sub-committee. They must avoid doing anything that might encourage a complaint of maladministration against the council and are expected to:

- comply with standing orders;
- behave in an orderly manner;
- declare a disclosable pecuniary interest they may have in a contract or other matter that is the subject of consideration (where not on the register of interests);
- refrain from taking part in the consideration or discussion and voting on matter in which they have a prejudicial interest or in respect of which they are otherwise prohibited from voting (e.g. being in excess of two months in arrears of council tax at budget setting), and
- observe the law.

Compliance with standing orders

4.21 If a councillor fails to comply with standing orders they should be:

- called to order by the person presiding at the meeting if the omission to comply is a breach of the order of debate at a meeting; and
- interviewed by the chairman of the council or the leader/mayor, and asked to comply if the offending member is in breach of some other standing order.

If a councillor behaves in a disorderly manner at a meeting, the chair can, with the consent of the meeting (*Armour v Macrea* (1886) 13 R (J) 41), order them to leave temporarily. In the case of *John v Rees* (1969) Ch 345 at 382, it was held that the chairman of a meeting had an inherent power to adjourn it in the event of disorder if they acted bona fide with the purpose of forwarding and facilitating the meeting, and if the adjournment were for no longer than necessary for the restoration of order. In an extreme case of persistent disregard, the council could show its displeasure by depriving the member of all committee membership (see below). However, it could not properly deny them a right to be present at any committee or sub-committee meeting if he can show a 'need to know' and it is probable that the council could not impose its will on a political group that insisted on appointing a particular member to a committee under the proportionality provisions.

Confidentiality of council papers

4.22 Councillors are expected to treat as confidential all papers that they receive in the course of council business unless made public by law or by the authority's express or implied consent. The now repealed model Code of Conduct provided that a member must not:

- disclose information given to them in confidence by anyone, or information acquired that they believe is of a confidential nature, without the consent of a person authorised to give it, or unless they are required by law to do so; or
- prevent another person from gaining access to information to which that person is entitled by law.

A sensible summary code or no code

4.23 All reports made or minutes kept by any committee or cabinet must, as soon as the committee has concluded action on the matter to which such reports or minutes relate, be open for the inspection of any member of the council.

Payment of allowances

4.24 An entirely different system of allowances for councillors was introduced under s. 18 of the LG&HA 1989 with these three purposes in mind:

- to give each council greater freedom, within an overall ceiling on remuneration, to adopt a system of allowances suited to its own circumstances;
- to end the apparent incentive to multiply the number of days on which councillors undertake approved duties; and
- to restrict the ability of councils to pay allowances in respect of party political activities.

Certain former allowances under the Local Government Act 1972 now apply only to community councils. The principal provisions have been disapplied and only relate in respect of expenses connected with receiving courtesy visits (England only).

The Local Government Act 2000 introduced new categories for members, and the current position, set out in the Local Authorities (Members' Allowances) Regulations 2003 (SI 1021/2003), which came into effect on 1 May 2003, briefly summarised, is:

- special responsibility allowance, for leader, deputy leader, cabinet members and chairmen of committees, and leaders of political groups;
- basic allowance;
- dependant carers allowance;
- co-optees allowance; and
- travelling and subsistence allowances.

The position for Wales is different and is set out in the Local Government (Wales) Measure 2011. Councillors were also given access to the Local Government pension scheme from 2003, where permitted to do so by their remuneration panel.

4.25 Entitlement to special responsibility, basic and travelling and subsistence allowances depends on a scheme made by each principal authority concerned. The Local Authorities (Members' Allowances) Regulations 2003 require councils to establish an independent remuneration panel to make recommendations on the levels and types of allowances to be paid. Councils are responsible for formulating a scheme of allowances taking into account those recommendations, although they may choose not to follow them. The Regulations require that a panel's recommendations must be published, as must a council's scheme of allowances. There should be an indication of any differences from the recommendations put forward by an independent remuneration panel.

4.26 Allowances payable under the LG&HA 1989[11] must be in accordance with a scheme made by the principal councils concerned. The scheme must provide for payment of a basic allowance of the same amount to each member and special responsibility allowances, which need not be the same, and fall into one or more categories specified, i.e. acting as leader or deputy leader of a political group; presiding at meetings; representing the authority at meetings of, or arranged by, any body; membership of a committee or sub-committee that meets with exceptional frequency or for exceptionally long periods; acting as spokesman for a political group on a committee or sub-committee; and other activities requiring at least the same time and effort as any of the foregoing.[12]

4.27 Principal councils are also responsible, under the Local Authorities (Members' Allowances) Regulations 2003, for establishing an independent parish remuneration panel (based on their own independent remuneration panels) to recommend the level of parish basic, chairman's, and travelling and subsistence allowances for parish and town councils within their area. It will be up to the individual parish or town council to determine whether it wishes to adopt the panel's recommendations. It is also required to publish details of any scheme of allowances adopted.

4.28 Councillors' allowances are now coming more increasingly under the spotlight as employees' salaries are being frozen. Grant Shapps, the then Minister for

Local Government, said in 2010, 'The new government will let the sunlight of openness into councillor allowances to allow the press and public to hold elected officials to account more.' This was followed, in December 2012, by Local Government Minister Brandon Lewis setting out proposals to limit access by councillors to the local government pension scheme from April 2014.

Duty to disclose interests

4.29 Probably the most important obligation imposed upon a councillor by law is that which requires them to act on any disclosable pecuniary interest in a matter that is before a meeting at which they are present and to refrain from participating in the discussion thereon and from voting.

Code of conduct – historical context

4.30 The provisions of s. 94 of the LGA 1972 provided that if a member of a local authority had any pecuniary interest, direct or indirect, in any contract, proposed contract or other matter, and is present at a meeting of the local authority at which the contract or other matter is the subject of consideration, they should at the meeting and as soon as practicable after its commencement disclose the fact and shall not take part in the consideration or discussion of the contract or other matter or vote on any question with respect to it.

4.31 The statutory regime governing declarations of interests was sharply criticised by the Nolan Committee. It recommended that all pecuniary and non-pecuniary interests should be treated together; that they should be registered and declared where members were 'likely to be influenced' in their consideration of the issue; and that members should withdraw where there was a real danger of bias: in other words where the member was affected more than the generality of people by the decision being taken. Nolan took the view that the existing statutory position was difficult to understand and even more difficult to comply with.

4.32 Following on from the Nolan recommendations, the LGA 2000 gave power to the Secretary of State to issue and revise a model code of conduct in respect of local authorities. The Local Authorities (Model Code of Conduct) (England) Order 2001 (SI 2001/35 75) came into force on 27 November 2001 and set out a model Code of Conduct both for those authorities operating executive arrangements and for those who operate alternative arrangements. This has subsequently been revoked by the Local Authorities (Model Code of Conduct) (England) Order 2007 (SI 2007/1159) and the Local Authorities (Model Code of Conduct) (Wales) Order 2008 (SI 2008/788). The provisions of the model code set out in the Schedules were mandatory, and every local authority had to adopt the Code of Conduct for members and co-opted members.

Code of conduct – content

4.33 This was discussed in more depth in Chapter 1, but under the Localism Act 2011, each local authority must adopt a code of conduct for their members and co-opted members; however, there is no longer a prescribed model code to which members must sign up. To varying degrees there are three model codes of conduct in place across principal authorities in England (plus one that has been drafted specifically for parish and community councils). These are:

(a) a variation of the preceding mandatory code, which is seemingly the most popular and remains a list of 'do and don't' actions;
(b) a model template produced by the Local Government Association (after protracted negotiation with ACSeS (Association of Council Secretaries and Solicitors, now LLG), SOLACE (Society of Local Authority Chief Executives) and other professional representative bodies), which is largely purposive in tone and content; and
(c) a template produced by the government (partly as a result of the delay in the LGA production above), which is a bare listing of the Nolan principles from which the authority's code can be hung.

4.34 Under the Localism Act 2011, 'personal and prejudicial interests' have been repealed and replaced from 1 July 2012 by a new test of a 'disclosable pecuniary interest' under s. 30. This is defined in the Relevant Authorities (Disclosable Pecuniary Interests) Regulations 2012 (SI 2012/1464). Disclosable pecuniary interests are not the same as personal and prejudicial interests, and some local authorities have chosen to include definitions similar to these in their codes, together with associated constraints.

Members with a disclosable pecuniary interest will not be able to speak or vote, but do not have to leave the room unless, as is indicated in the Act, the authority's standing orders provide that they should do so.

4.35 Dispensations are available under the Localism Act 2011 (s. 33) and the reasons for the grant of the dispensation are wider than the previous standards regime, and give greater flexibility and discretion to the Authority. A dispensation can be granted where the council considers that:

(a) without the dispensation, the number of persons who could not take part due to their disclosable pecuniary interest would be so great as to impede the transaction of the business. In practice, this means the decision-making body would be inquorate;
(b) without the dispensation, the representation of different political groups on the body transacting any particular business would be so upset as to alter the likely outcome of any vote relating to the business. In practice, this is assuming that members will vote along party lines, and in the case of overview and scrutiny committees, this is assumed not to be the case, as no whip can be applied;
(c) granting the dispensation is in the interests of persons living in the authority's area;
(d) without the dispensation, each executive member would be prohibited from participating in any particular business to be transacted by the authority's executive as they would have a disclosable pecuniary interest; or
(e) it is otherwise appropriate to grant a dispensation.

A dispensation under this section must specify the period for which it has effect, and the period specified may not exceed four years.

The effect of a dispensation is that it allows councillors to participate in any discussion and/or vote on any matter in which they have a disclosable pecuniary interest.

Personal liability

4.36 As referred to above, under the concept of being a 'member', responsibility for decisions made in council or committee meetings is, politically at least, a collective responsibility: the responsibility is that indivisibly of the members as a whole and the decision made is taken in the name of the local authority, granted under s. 265 of the Public Health Act 1875 and incorporated further under s. 39 of the Local Government (Miscellaneous Provisions) Act 1976: see 5.14 as to the immunity of both councillors and officers in this respect, including the scope of further protection that may be provided under s. 101 of the Local Government Act 2000 and the resulting Local Authorities (Indemnities for Members and Officers) Order 2004.
There are, however, circumstances in which a council member incurs personal and even criminal liability at law. There are specific local government provisions, e.g. for failure to register a disclosable pecuniary interest or for not acting as required in respect of declaring council tax arrears at the budget meeting. There are also applications of more generic law, including:

- offences under the Bribery Act 2010;
- misconduct in public office, a common law criminal offence (and, on the face of it, the most common criminal conviction for offending members);
- misfeasance in public, the civil common law equivalent;
- particular personalised orders, such as those made in employment tribunals; and
- breach of trust, most controversially, an outcome of *Westminster City Council v Porter* (2003).

4.37 It has always been the function of an authority's advisers to alert members to any possible illegality of a course that the council or committee wishes to pursue. Where an authority persists in pursuing what the officers believe may be an unlawful course of action, the officers should do what they properly can to protect the interests of the authority and its individual members. In *R v Browne* (1907) and *Davies v Cowperthwait* (1938), it was held that it was not necessarily misconduct for a councillor to ignore the advice of the town clerk if the councillor honestly believed the advice to be erroneous; but this view now needs to be related to the duties of the monitoring officer and the chief finance officer, and the action that the law requires to be taken by the local authority on their report. Because expenditure on items that are lawful in themselves can be so excessive and unreasonable in amount as to render the expenditure unlawful, the committee clerk should ensure that the grounds for the decision and the reasoning are fully recorded; and it may be useful to include a phrase to this effect:

> '... and the council/committee therefore considered it reasonable in all the circumstances [to take the action decided upon].'

Maladministration

4.38 The view has been expressed that 'the acts of individual members . . . may become the subject of maladministration'.

Statutory Chief Officers and governance

4.39 Relevant local authorities have a duty[13] to designate one of their officers, to be known as the monitoring officer, who cannot be the head of paid service nor the (s. 151) finance officer. The monitoring officer is responsible under s. 5A(2) LG&HA 1989 for preparing a report if they consider that any proposal, decision or omission, in the course of the discharge of functions of the relevant authority, by or on behalf of the relevant authority's executive, constitutes, has given rise to or is likely to or would give rise to any of:

- a contravention, by the relevant authority's executive or any person on behalf of the executive of any enactment or rule of law; or
- any such maladministration or injustice as is mentioned in the Local Government Act 1974 Part 3 (local government ombudsmen): no duty arises unless the local government ombudsman has conducted an investigation in relation to the proposal, decision or omission concerned.

4.40 The monitoring officer must consult so far as practicable with the head of paid service and the chief finance officer when preparing a report, and as soon as practicable after a report has been prepared they must arrange for a copy of it to be sent to each member of the authority and, where the authority has a mayor and council manager executive, the council manager: s. 5A(5).

4.41 The council's executive must consider any report by the monitoring officer (or deputy) at a meeting held not more than 21 days after copies of the report are first sent to members of the executive; and to ensure that no step is taken for giving effect to any proposal or decision to which such a report relates at any time while the implementation of the proposal or decision is suspended in consequence of the report: LG&HA 1989 s. 5A(6) (s. 5A, as added). In the absence of a successful application for judicial review, the findings of the Ombudsman are binding on the authority (*R v Local Commissioner for Administration ex parte Eastleigh Borough Council*). As soon as practicable after the executive has finished considering the monitoring officer's report, it must itself prepare a report that specifies: what action (if any) the executive has taken in response to that report; what action (if any) the executive proposes to take in response to it and when it proposes to take that action; and the reasons for taking the action specified in the executive's report or, as the case may be, for taking no action: s. 5A(8) (s. 5A as added). As soon as practicable after the executive has prepared that report, it must arrange for a copy of it to be sent to each member of the authority and the authority's monitoring officer.

The same powers exist for the chief finance (s. 151) officer in relation to expenditure (s. 114 and s. 114A of the Local Government Finance Act 1988). A similar process also exists in respect of the responsibilities of the head of paid service under s. 4 LG&HA 1989.

Co-option

General power of co-option

4.42 Local authorities have long been able to include within the membership of their committees persons who are not elected members of the appointing authority. The position now is that the general effect of the power to co-opt in the LGA 1972, s. 102(3), has been modified by the LG&HA 1989, s. 13, by defining, in somewhat complex terms, the two categories of voting and non-voting members of a committee, sub-committee or joint committee.

4.43 Local authorities have a general power[14] to co-opt persons from outside their membership to any committee, other than a committee for regulating or controlling finance, appointed under the enabling power of the 1972 Act to set up committees.[15] The provisions as to co-option do not apply to statutory committees where the constitution of the particular committee and the duty or power to co-opt are regulated by the enactment concerned. The power to co-opt rests with the full council and not with committees,[16] although the selection of persons to serve as co-opted members is usually left to the committees. There is no power to co-opt to the full council.[17]

4.44 Co-opted persons appointed under the general enabling power must not be disqualified from membership of the appointing authority[18] but do not need to be positively qualified to be a councillor of the authority. The law is silent as to the qualification of persons for co-option. In practice, local authorities that, for example, invite voluntary bodies to appoint a representative to serve on a committee as a co-opted member do not ask (although presumably they could do) whether the representative is of full age or a qualifying citizen or fulfils the requirements as to residential qualifications. The former restriction on the number of co-opted members to not more than one-third of the membership of a committee no longer applies.[19] Although persons holding politically restricted posts are prohibited from membership of a local authority, this prohibition does not appear to affect co-option on to committees.

Rights and obligations

4.45 A co-opted member of a committee has, in general, no voting rights (but see below); nor do they possess any rights or privileges in respect of any other committee of the council, nor may they attend council meetings (other than in their capacity as a member of the public, of course). A co-opted member is, however, under the same obligations as members of the council that appoints them: they must observe the council's standing orders and, most importantly, must comply with the rules relating to the Code of Conduct. Co-opted members sign the same acceptance of office as members of the council. Co-opted members are entitled to travelling and subsistence allowances on the same basis as councillors[20] but not to an attendance allowance, although a financial loss allowance is payable in lieu.

4.46 The general rule is that, with some exceptions, co-opted members have no voting rights.[21] Co-opted members of overview and scrutiny committees may vote provided the council has a voting rights scheme in place under the Local Government Act 2003 (s. 115) which amends the Local Government Act 2000 (Schedule 1, paragraphs 12–14). The purpose of the change was to meet a commitment given in the Local Government White Paper of December 2001 (*Strong Local Leadership – Quality Public Services*).

A scheme may include:

(a) provision for a maximum or minimum in relation to the number of co-opted members of an overview and scrutiny committee entitled to vote at meetings of the committee; and
(b) provision for giving effect to any maximum or minimum established under paragraph (a).

If a voting rights scheme is in place, then this must be publicly available and a public notice needs to be published in at least one local newspaper publishing the fact that there is a voting rights scheme. Similarly, if the scheme is varied, then the same process has to be followed. The Secretary of State may make regulations in respect of a voting rights scheme, but to date, none are in force.

In respect of overview and scrutiny committees which deal with education functions, then there are provisions under Schedule A1 Local Government Act 2000 (paragraph 7), which mean that the committee must include at least one person nominated by the Diocesan Board for Education, if the council area contains at least one Church of England-maintained school. The committee must similarly include at least one person nominated by the Bishop for the diocese if the area contains at least one Roman Catholic-maintained school.

Parent Governor Representatives were introduced under the School Standards and Framework Act 1998, and under the Parent Governor Representatives (England) Regulations 2001 an overview and scrutiny (O&S) committee exercising education functions must include between two and five parent governors, for a term of two to four years. Parent Governor Representatives may speak on any subject but can only vote on education matters. There is a good practice guide available for PGRs on the RISE (Research and Information on State Education) trust website (www.risetrust.org.uk). This suggests that PGRs are provided with the same support as elected members, but research carried out in 2004 suggests that this is far from the case in practice. It is likely that PGRs can continue in position in their position even if they belong to a school that takes 'Academy' status – i.e. is no longer a local authority-maintained school – as the legislation does not provide for disqualification in this event.

Co-opted member as committee chair

4.47 In the past it was acknowledged that a co-opted member of a committee could be elected as its chair, although it was recognised there were disadvantages. Even in the different circumstances of today a committee could, if so minded, elect a co-opted member as its chairman but, except when the business before the committee was business on which the co-opted member was entitled to vote, the member could not otherwise exercise the power of a person presiding to give a second or casting vote. A co-opted member cannot fulfil the full tasks of the chair in any case: they could not as such attend council meetings as a member, and get their committee's proposals through full council, nor answer questions put to them there, nor indeed represent the committee on other committees. A councillor vice-chair can conceivably deputise for a co-opted member chairman in such circumstances.

Removal of co-opted member

4.48 It would seem that a local authority can always remove from committee membership any person whom it has co-opted to a committee on the analogy of *Manton v Brighton Corporation*. As it has power to remove a council member from one of its own committees (or a joint committee to which it is a party), then it must be presumed to have similar power over a co-opted member, other than a Parent Governor Representative. This view is reinforced by the decision in *R v Peak Planning Board ex parte Jackson* (1976), in which a distinction is made between nomination and appointment. If the outside body upon whose nomination the person has been co-opted notifies the local authority that it wishes to replace its nominee, then, always assuming that the co-opted person has not become disqualified, the local authority alone can determine whether to accede to the nominating body's request.

Representation on other local authorities and public bodies

General considerations

4.49 Local authorities are often invited, and in some instances have a right, to be represented on other bodies, both statutory and voluntary, i.e. other than those to which the rules relating to political balance apply, although, of course, where the numbers of representatives allow, there is no reason why an authority should not appoint on the basis of political proportionality. The role to be exercised by the representatives on these other bodies depends upon the terms of their appointment. Any conflict of interest that might arise as between the aims and objectives of the council and those of the other body could have severe repercussions for members or, indeed, officers. In *Burgoine and Cooke v London Borough of Waltham Forest and McWhirr* (1996), the court held that officers representing the council on an outside body were unable to take advantage of an indemnity given by the council, thus rendering them personally vulnerable when the outside body went into liquidation. This position changed as a result of the Local Authorities (Indemnities for Members and Officers) Order 2004. In addition, members have to bear in mind whether they need to declare an interest when discussing matters that relate to outside bodies to which they are appointed, although only a requirement of some authorities' code of conduct, remains an issue in terms of the common law on bias.

4.50 It is good practice for the local authority to know the terms of reference of each body to which a member (or officer) is appointed, and whether that body carries indemnity insurance in respect of the member (or officer). Members need to know whether they are merely attending as an 'observer' and taking no part in the governance or management of the outside body, or whether they are appointed in a position of general control or management. Indeed, insurance companies may require the authority to show that they have managed the risk by vetting activities and maintaining accurate records, as only members with 'observer' status are able to be indemnified by the council.

4.51 The appointment or nomination of representatives on other bodies is ordinarily reserved to the full council, unless they are executive appointments, and dealt with at the annual meeting. Model standing order no. 17 (DETR Modular Constitution) suggests the voting on appointments in this manner:

> 'If there are more than two people nominated for any position to be filled and there is not a clear majority of votes in favour of one person, then the name of the person with the least number of votes will be taken off the list and a new vote taken. The process will continue until there is a majority of votes for one person.'

Nomination or appointment?

4.52 It is a matter dependent upon the circumstances of each particular case whether the representative is an appointee or a nominee. In all cases of co-option, as we have already seen, the submission of a person's name is mere nomination and it is the local authority on whose committee the person is to serve that makes the actual appointment. In such a case the nominating body cannot recall the nominee or revoke the appointment: the nominee's continuation in office is solely for the appointing local authority to decide. In other cases where the local authority or other body itself appoints its representatives on another local authority or other public body, the local authority can always revoke the appointment and substitute another representative at any time. However, in *Regina v Brent London Borough Council, ex parte Assegai* (1987), it was held that a local authority could not summarily dismiss a school governor before the end of their term without first informing them of the proposed dismissal and giving them the opportunity to reply in writing to the complaints made against them.

Defamatory statements in council and committee

General principle

4.53 Statements in council and committee meetings are subject to the general principles of law relating to defamation:[22] that is to say, a person who makes a defamatory statement (one exposing a person to hatred, ridicule or contempt, or which causes them to be shunned or avoided, or which has a tendency to injure them in his office, profession or trade) commits a tort and is liable for the consequences that flow from such an act.

Privilege

4.54 It is a general defence in an action for defamation for the defendant to show that the statement was made on a privileged occasion. There are two kinds of privileged occasion: absolute and qualified. Local authorities do not enjoy absolute privilege even when acting judicially: see *Royal Aquarium and Summer and Winter Gardens Society v Parkinson* (1892). Where the privilege is absolute, as in certain judicial and parliamentary proceedings, it is a complete defence to an action for defamation.

4.55 Qualified privilege attaches to: an occasion where the person who makes a communication has an interest or a duty – legal, social or moral – to make it to the person to whom it is made, and the person to whom it is so made has a corresponding interest or duty to receive it.

4.56 Qualified privilege will attach to statements made in council, cabinet and committee. Where pleaded in an action for defamation, the author of the defamatory statement must prove: (a) a duty to make the statement; and (b) an interest on the part of the recipient to receive it. The plaintiff may still succeed if able to prove malice on the defendant's part because an essential feature of qualified privilege is the absence of malice. Reckless disregard as to whether what is said is true or not will also destroy qualified privilege. It was held in *Horrocks v Lowe* (1972), affirmed by the House of Lords (1975), that where an alderman honestly believed in the truth of their assertions but had no reasonable grounds or was hasty in jumping to conclusions or was irrational or prejudiced, this did not destroy their privilege. Lord Denning said:

> 'It is of the first importance that the members of a local authority should be able to speak their minds freely on a matter of interest in the locality. So long as they honestly believe what they say to be true, they are not to be made liable for defamation. They may be prejudiced and unreasonable. They may not get their facts right. They may give much offence to others. But so long as they are honest, they go clear. No councillor should be hampered in his criticisms by fear of an action for slander. He is not to be forever looking over his shoulder to see if what he says is defamatory. He must be allowed to give his point of view, even if it is hotly disputed by others. This is essential to free discussion.'

4.57 In *Royal Aquarium and Summer and Winter Garden Society v Parkinson* (1892), above, Lord Esher MR described a statement made by a county councillor at a meeting to which privilege attached as made by one 'utterly regardless of the truth, or of any personal injury he might be inflicting, perfectly reckless whether what he was saying was true or false'.

4.58 It seems probable, though not free from doubt, that informal meetings on council business are not occasions to which qualified privilege attaches, such as, for example, a party group meeting, and meetings of officers. The position as regards working parties is also uncertain, but there would seem to be greater prospect of being able to show the identity of interest between the giver and receiver of information that is necessary to support a defence of qualified privilege. Working parties are now so much an accepted part of the machinery of local government that the principles set out by Lord Denning, in *Horrocks v Lowe*, above, are likely to apply. Whatever the status of the meeting, the defence of qualified privilege would not, of course, extend to remarks made once the chairman had closed proceedings.
4.59 The Local Authorities (Indemnities for Members and Officers) Order 2004 states that an indemnity cannot be provided to an officer or a member in respect of any claim to defamation that they may wish to make against another, but an indemnity may be given in respect of any claim brought against them.
4.60 The rise of Twitter and other online fora has seen an increase in the number of defamation/libel claims against councillors.

Other defences

4.61 There are certain other defences. Justification can be pleaded if the words are true and justification provides a complete answer. It is also a good defence to show that what was said was fair comment on a matter of public interest, honestly believed to be true, relevant and not inspired by malicious motive, and that the statements of fact on which the comment was based were materially true.[23] Fair and accurate reports of meetings of local authorities and their committees are privileged unless the publication is proved to be made with malice.

Chairing a committee

4.62 The most significant change in a councillor's role, from the viewpoint of the law and practice of local authority meetings, is upon becoming chair/mayor of the council, portfolio holder or a committee chairman, although politically they may regard leadership of the council as of paramount importance.[24] The duties and responsibilities of a portfolio holder, council chair/mayor are discussed later (see 7.30 et seq.). There are, of course, other political offices apart from that of leader: each party will ordinarily appoint a number of whips.

Differing conceptions

4.63 The role adopted by a committee chairman is influenced partly by their own conception of what it should be both in committee and outside the committee room, and by the degree of authority ordinarily bestowed upon the chairmanship by local custom. Nowhere today does a committee chairman restrict themselves solely to presiding at meetings of their committee and to acting as spokesperson at council meetings. Even within a narrow concept of their role, varying attitudes are adopted: some members see their task as chairman as a mere interpreter of the committee's collective will; but others think it proper that they should influence and guide the committee in the decisions it makes. Where it is the authority's practice to re-elect the same committee chairman year after year as long as they are willing to serve, there is greater likelihood of the chairman becoming the shaper rather than the interpreter of the committee's views.

4.64 The choice of committee chairmen lies in the gift of the majority party on the council, but in some authorities the parties arrive at an understanding to share the chairmanships in rough proportion to their strength on the council – although very often the minority party will not allow any of its members to accept a committee chairmanship so as not to jeopardise its opposition role and clear itself of any responsibility in the application of the policy of the dominant group. However, good practice sets out that at least some of the chairs of overview and scrutiny committees should be given to minority parties to give weight to the independence of the role.

4.65 The principle of rotating or shared chairmanship has gained much credence with the development of hung, or balanced, councils in recent years. Such authorities where no one party has overall control produces great problems for chairmen in committee and conventions often need to be formulated in order to allow business to proceed. There is nothing inherently unlawful in having chairmen change from meeting to meeting. In such cases the first item of each agenda will be 'Appointment of chairman for the meeting'. When operating a system of this kind, it is important to be clear as to the extent of the chairman's powers and the length of time they will hold office: is it purely for the duration of the meeting at which they are elected or do they hold office until the next such appointment is made – presumably at the next meeting? Either course of action can be taken, but it must be clear at the time of the appointment. When the chairman's authority ceases at the end of the meeting, it is usual to have a convention that the various group spokespersons for each committee will be given authority to be consulted on action required between meetings. However, this can cause difficulties in the case of overview and scrutiny committees because of the Local Authorities (Executive Arrangements) (Meetings and Access to Information) (England) Regulations 2012, which set out that the chairman of the relevant overview and scrutiny committee must be consulted on various matters. Therefore, for these meetings, if there is to be a chairman for each meeting, it must be clear that they retain the chairmanship until the next meeting.

4.66 Another difficult question is whether a meeting can proceed if no chairman has been appointed at all. There may be no nominations or an equality of votes for rival candidates. Legal opinion is divided on whether the meeting can properly proceed, but probably on balance it can do provided the meeting itself passes a resolution to that effect. By common law a committee meeting can control its own proceedings, subject to compliance with standing orders, so if it expresses a clear wish to proceed, then there seems no reason why it cannot do so. In such circumstances the clerk will simply call over the agenda items, ensuring that there is a resolution passed to decide any issues and proceed to the next item, while taking care not to play any part in the debate itself. A pragmatic solution such as this, to keep business flowing, is not to be recommended and every effort should be made to appoint a chairman for every meeting. Insofar as council meetings are concerned, there must be someone presiding.

Chairman's action

4.67 In practice, a committee chairman is invested with considerable power and influence. But the authority with which they are endowed and the power they exercise are based on convention: 'probably', it was once said, 'the only example in local government of a convention analogous to the constitutional convention.' The practice of chairman's action – now largely fallen into disuse since it was challenged in the courts (see below) – began as a convenient arrangement whereby officers in circumstances of urgency between meetings sought authority from the committee chairman before taking this, that or some other course of action. It avoided delay and was a convenient, workable arrangement that facilitated the despatch of business but rested solely on mutual trust and confidence and good faith. It was purportedly clothed with legality by ensuring that, at the next ensuing meeting of the committee, the chairman's action was confirmed. Strictly speaking, an individual council member cannot be empowered to make decisions because it was unlawful for an individual councillor to be given delegated authority, since in respect of committees this would be outside the powers conferred by statute. This position is different in respect of executive functions as a result of the LGA 2000, which allows delegation of decision-making to individual members of the executive, and the Local Government and Public Involvement in Health Act 2007 (s. 236), which allowed local authorities to give a delegation to all members in certain circumstances.

4.68 The practice of chairman's action was examined judicially in *R v Secretary of State for the Environment ex parte Hillingdon London Borough Council* (1986).[25] That case put one question beyond doubt (indeed there was probably little doubt anyhow) but left at least one other unsettled. The question settled is that there can be no valid delegation to an individual councillor because s. 101 of the LGA 1972, while it permits delegation to a committee, sub-committee, officer or another local authority, does not empower a committee chairman to act alone – even if purportedly comprising a committee of one.

4.69 *Hillingdon* was decided on circumstances that may not ordinarily arise. The local authority had sought judicial review of the Secretary of State's refusal to determine appeals against enforcement notices issued by the council on the authority alone of its planning committee chairman. The council had purportedly clothed the chairman with delegated powers to give 'instructions regarding the institution or defence of legal proceedings or the representation of the council in any matters referred to him by the director of law and administration, and expressly to make decisions on a number of matters including enforcement procedure under the Town and Country Planning Act'. In other words, the chairman was not merely as a matter of administrative practice required to be consulted in circumstances of urgency and to approve a course of action that an officer wished to take, but was purportedly empowered to make decisions on a continuing basis in a specific sphere of the local authority's functions. Furthermore, the council had sought to justify its standing orders provision on the argument that it had fixed at one the membership of a committee to which it had delegated decision-making powers. The standing orders did not provide for ratification of the committee chairman's action and in the particular circumstances that gave rise to the court proceedings, there had been no ratification.

4.70 What then, are the implications of *Hillingdon* on the practice of chairman's action? It could be argued that the judgement does not rule out chairman's action, provided its operation is well regulated and any decision made by a committee chairman is subsequently confirmed by resolution of the council or committee or sub-committee with delegated powers. Woolf J in *Hillingdon* said:

> 'There may be difficulties in overcoming the problem by a duly authorised committee . . . ratifying the *ultra vires* action of the chairman retrospectively. As to this, I need to express no conclusive view because there was no ratification in this case.'

4.71 That there was no ratification in *Hillingdon* is understandable. On the authority's contention that the delegation was lawful, it followed logically that there was no requirement for confirmation because any decision, properly made under valid delegated authority, becomes effective from the time it is made. That said, however, there is authority for the view that there can be no effective ratification of action that is in itself unlawful. As to that, in relation to chairman's action, the law remains unclear and, as Widdicombe has pointed out, 'unsatisfactory'.

4.72 It may be that, so long as a committee chairman is not asked to make a decision that affects or prejudices third-party interests, it is not unlawful for officers to continue to seek a committee chairman's concurrence with a projected course of action in circumstances of urgency, where it would be impracticable within the time available to call together the full committee or sub-committee. The court in *Hillingdon* appears to have recognised that this might be perfectly lawful within limits. Referring to *R v Brent Health Authority ex parte Francis* (1985) (in which the chairman of the health authority had made a decision about the exclusion of the public from its meetings), Woolf J said:

> 'In this case . . . urgent action was subsequently ratified by the authority when the meeting was held . . . However, this decision related to the internal procedures of the authority and I can see a very real distinction between a chairman acting alone in exercising this sort of function in relation to its own proceedings and a chairman purporting to take a decision which legislation such as the Town and Country Planning Act requires to be taken by the authority before enforcement proceedings are commenced.'

4.73 Difficulties of the kind discussed here can be overcome, as the judge in *Hillingdon* himself observed, by delegating the necessary authority to an officer:

> 'I . . . accept that it would be difficult to fault a procedure where the decisions are taken by a fully authorised officer pursuant to s. 101 in consultation with the

> elected chairman... this would be a simple way of dealing with these urgent matters which could not go before an elected committee or sub-committee but for which it is undesirable for a single officer to take sole responsibility . . .'

Hillingdon does not reflect the current position in respect of executive functions; the LGA 2000 s. 15(2) provides that decision-making may be delegated to an individual member of the cabinet, as well as to officers. However, where an individual member intends to make a key decision, the rules in respect of access to information apply (SI 2000/2372) and any report in respect of the decision to be taken must be made public for at least five clear days (subject to the usual rules as to exempt information). In addition, a copy of the report should be supplied to the relevant overview and scrutiny chairman, or where there is no chairman to every member of the committee. In addition, there are requirements for the recording of decisions taken by individual cabinet members (see 12.20).

4.74 As to delegation to an officer, a local authority can in certain circumstances be bound by the act of an officer within their ostensible authority but beyond the scope of their delegated authority. There could well be contentious matters or issues of political sensitivity where a local authority would be reluctant to allow an officer complete freedom to act, though willing to make the delegation conditional upon consultation with the appropriate councillor. It is important that consultation alone is envisaged and not prior approval, for that would be indistinguishable from purportedly conferring delegated authority upon an individual member.

4.75 The importance of getting right both the form and the procedure of delegation was shown in *Fraser v Secretary of State for the Environment and the Royal Borough of Kensington and Chelsea* (1987). This, again, was an enforcement notice case, but here the action had been taken by an officer acting under the council's standing orders, which required them to obtain 'the written approval of the mayor or the chairman of the appropriate committee or sub-committee with delegated powers'. The director of planning and transportation drafted a letter that was sent to the chairman of the planning committee for approval. A discussion then took place on the telephone after which the director signed the letter. Mr Justice Nolan, as he then was, considered this to be a valid exercise of the discretion vested in the officer concerned, who had clearly made up his mind before discussing the matter with the chairman: the action came within the phrase 'in consultation with' used by the judge in *Hillingdon* (see 4.72).

4.76 These circumstances can be contrasted with those in *R v Port Talbot Borough Council ex parte Jones* (1988). Here the action under review was the allocation of a council house and the housing officer, Mr Hale, made it clear in evidence that without pressure from the chairman of the housing committee, Mr Lewis, he would not have allocated it as he did. Mr Justice Nolan found this to be the wrong side of the line in terms of legality:

> 'The discretion to allocate the house . . . could only lawfully be delegated to Mr Hale. In the light of his affidavit, to describe the decision as made by him as the authorised delegate of the council would be a travesty of the facts.'

4.77 Given the fairly generous guidelines approved in *Kensington and Chelsea* (see 4.75), there is little need for a chairman to be asked to act alone. Legally there is no reason why an officer who has delegated powers which are exercisable 'in consultation' with one or more members cannot change their mind in the event of disagreement with the member or members concerned. The central fact must always be that the decision itself is made by the officer, and care must be taken to ensure that politically sensitive issues, such as in *Port Talbot* (see 4.76) are not left to be dealt with under delegated powers.

4.78 It is hardly surprising that Widdicombe took the view that the position as regards chairman's action is 'unsatisfactory'[26] and sought to devise a solution that 'is consistent with the corporate framework of local government and at the same time is consistent with sensible administrative practice'. It concluded:

> 'We believe . . . that the law should allow the possibility of delegation of decisions to chairmen themselves . . . Such delegation should not be at large: it should not become a device for avoiding decision-taking by committees, nor a means of chairmen adopting a ministerial style of administration. The legislation should set clear limits on the scope of delegation to chairmen. It should be permissible only where a decision is required because of urgency. In other circumstances the legislation should state that any decision of the chairman is unlawful, irrespective of whether the council or committee purport to ratify it retrospectively. This should remove the legal doubt about ratification . . . The chief executive either directly or by delegation to one of his chief officers, should be required to agree in each case that the matter is urgent before any decision can be taken . . . We propose furthermore that the decision taken under delegated powers should be reported to the next meeting of the committee or sub-committee in question, that the provisions introduced by the Local Government (Access to Information) Act 1985 should apply to the report and other documents on which the decision is based, and that the chairman should not be able to take a decision where he or she has a pecuniary interest in the matter.'

Widdicombe's proposals were only adopted in respect of executive functions (see 4.72).

Implied authority

4.79 It must be apparent from all that has been said in the foregoing paragraphs that a committee chairman must be careful not to overreach their implied authority. If the scope of that authority is set down in writing, there is less risk.

It is generally recognised, but again only as a convention, that a committee chairman may, by virtue of their office, make suggestions – even, perhaps, in exceptional circumstances, give directions – to an officer. It is also recognised that, by virtue of their chairmanship, the chairman may enjoy a certain limited freedom of access to property under the control of their committee on the assumption that they are doing what the committee would direct them to do. But legally a committee chairman, like any other individual council member, has no power or authority other than that expressly conferred upon them by resolution and thus can only properly give orders through a decision made at a properly constituted meeting.

Failure to attend meetings

Statutory provisions

4.80 Section 85 of the LGA 1972, carried over directly from s. 63 of the Local Government Act 1933, expressly provides that where a council member fails throughout a period of six consecutive months from the date of their last attendance to attend any meeting of the authority, then, subject to certain exceptions, they cease to be a member of the authority, at which point the authority is under a duty to declare the office vacant under s. 86, unless the failure was due to some reason approved before the expiry of that period. The authority's approval, it is submitted, if not limited in time (and most authorities in giving approval will specify both the reason to which the approval relates and the period for which it will run), lasts until it ceases to have effect because the councillor has resumed attendance, or the reason to which the approval relates no longer applies, or the councillor's term of office has ended.

4.81 Attendance as a member at a meeting of any committee or sub-committee, or at a meeting of any joint committee, joint board or other body by which for the time being any of the functions of the authority are being discharged, or that was appointed to advise the authority on any matter relating to the discharge of those functions, and attendance as representative of the authority at a meeting of any body of persons, is deemed to be attendance at a meeting of the authority. It does not matter how informal the meeting is, so long as an attendance is recorded.

4.82 Failure to attend a committee is extended to failure by a member of the executive to attend an executive (cabinet) meeting. Continuing the vein of generous application, for these purposes exercising delegated authority as an individual member is counted as attendance (ss. (2A),(2B)).

4.83 Equally, a councillor cannot fail to attend meetings if there were none, as in *Re Neeson's Application* (1986) 13 NIJB 24, where the Court of Appeal in Northern Ireland found that removing a councillor from all committees and then not holding a council meeting within the time period was not grounds to declare his office vacant.

4.84 A member of any branch of the naval, military or air forces when employed during war or any emergency on any naval, military or air force service, and a person whose employment in the service of the Queen in connection with war or any emergency is such as, in the opinion of the Secretary for the Environment, to entitle them to relief from disqualification on account of absence, does not cease to be a member of the authority by reason only of a failure to attend meetings of the authority if the failure is due to that employment.[27]

Practical considerations

4.85 There is some argument as to whether it is an officer's duty to alert a councillor to risk of forfeiture of office because of failure to attend meetings. Sooner or later the authority's attention will need to be directed to the position and it would be an act of courtesy on the officer's part to warn the member concerned of the near approach of the expiry of the six months' period. But ought an officer to assume that a member is going to default? It may be that a member, instead of being grateful for the kindly warning, would take exception to what they might regard as precipitate action on the officer's part. And just when should the matter be reported to the council? No later than the member is approached? That hardly seems appropriate, for no question can yet arise of disqualification. Does the authority need to be informed at all unless and until the member defaults and so disqualifies themselves? These questions suggest that there should be a locally acceptable code of practice that can be put into effect automatically.

4.86 An authority cannot retrospectively approve an excuse for failure to attend meetings after the six-month period has expired. This was thought permissible formerly because s. 63 of the Local Government Act 1933 did not contain the words 'before the expiry of that period' – provided the authority acted before declaring the office vacant. If a member once loses their office through failure to attend for the six-month period, the disqualification cannot be overcome by their subsequently resuming attendance: see *R v Hunton ex parte Hodgson* (1911). Nevertheless, the office becomes vacant only when the authority declares it to be vacant,[28] which the authority must do, and a casual vacancy arises.[29]

Political group meetings

4.87 There has been earlier reference to the significant politicisation of local authorities over the past several years and the consequent removal of effective decision-making to majority group councillors meeting away from public gaze in the party group. This means that many important decisions on policy are first made by the majority group of a local authority and afterwards translated into effective and lawful action through the formal cabinet system. It was said (prior to the LGA 2000):[30]

> 'The effect . . . has been most marked. With decisions settled by a political process beforehand, the purpose of the committee has changed from one of decision-making to a debating forum where the minority parties and the public can be informed of the decisions of the majority party. The opposition can use the meetings to challenge the policies of the majority party and to seek information from officers. The recommendations before committees will be defended politically by the chairmen and other members and not by officers, whose role will be confined to presentation and interpretation of the facts and the submission of professional judgements.'

However, this is still a common criticism in most instances, and there appears to be a perception that the cabinet system rubber-stamps decisions that are taken beforehand. Minority group councillors also hold group meetings to organise, if they can, a cohesive approach in opposition to the majority group policies.

4.88 Political group meetings are not local authority meetings and are outside the scope of this book for several reasons. The decisions taken in group meetings cannot bind the authority. Strictly speaking, no officer can be called upon to attend and/or advise such meetings; and in practice they are often wholly informal in character and the decisions, even when not disputed (as frequently they are), cannot bind any of the party members. However, in practice, officers are often asked to attend group meetings to provide advice or updates to members.

4.89 It is common practice for members of each political party on the local authority to hold a group meeting before each council meeting to discuss business on the council meeting agenda, decide upon the party line to be pursued on at least the more important items, and apportion out responsibility for speaking in support or opposition as the case may be. The efficiency and effectiveness with which party business is conducted 'behind the scenes' appears to depend, first, upon the strength of the particular party within the authority (a party with an overwhelming majority tends not to be over-meticulous in its organisation; but where the parties are narrowly balanced each plans its tactics with considerable care); and, second, upon the personal qualities of the party whips and other party officials.

4.90 The proprieties ought to be and generally are observed. The activities of the party groups are restricted to determining the course of action to be taken at formal meetings of the authority: no group, even when composed of all the council members of the majority party on the council, can by decision in the group meeting legally bind the local authority. However, where members of the majority party on a particular committee or sub-committee decide to defer action pending discussion 'in another place', there is always the possibility (inadvertently rather than by design) that officers may find themselves under pressure to take action following a political decision in a group meeting or, more rarely (but it can happen), for officers to be asked to take account of the views of the majority group rather than, say, the appropriate committee chairman in the event of the opposition parties holding chairs. Officers must, of course, act with tact and discretion in such circumstances: they must be realistic and recognise that the leader individually or the group collectively has or can secure the support of the majority of councillors, but at the same time the officers must require compliance with due formality and insist – in practice, invariably through the chief executive or the monitoring officer – that any political decision so made shall be properly reported to and confirmed by the appropriate committee/cabinet or the council, and therefore taken legally.

Regularisation of party control

4.91 Widdicombe addressed itself to political activity of this character. Its recommendation for pro rata representation on committees was substantially implemented by the LG&HA 1989, s. 15 and this, it believed, would 'help remove any sense that such groups are somehow improper or alien to local government' – a point made to it in written evidence:

> 'It has been said that the political parties should also do more themselves to remove any sense of mystery surrounding party groups, particularly where they are discussing issues which will come before the council or its committees for decision.'

4.92 Widdicombe expressed the view that:

- there needs to be greater openness about groups and their proceedings so that unnecessary suspicions are avoided: party groups should not meet in a hole-and-corner atmosphere;
- the formulation of decisions in party groups outside the formal local government system should not be allowed to undermine the statutory safeguards that apply within the system; and
- there should be adequate access to the advice of officers so that the policy of the majority group does not become predetermined without full knowledge of the facts and law.

On this last point, Widdicombe said that officers' terms and conditions of service should be amended so that no special inhibition is placed on the attendance of officers at party groups.

4.93 It is impossible here to recite in full all that Widdicombe had to say about the incursion and operation of party politics in local government. In summary, however, it proposed that the national political parties (and local parties and groups) should take steps to:

- ensure that party groups keep a publicly available list of those attending their meetings;
- ensure observance of their model standing orders insofar as they limit the number of non-councillors attending meetings of party groups, preclude non-councillors from voting at such meetings and prevent non-councillors from determining the policy to be followed by the party group on matters before the council for decision;
- debar from attendance at party group meetings persons disqualified from council membership following surcharge proceedings by the auditor; and
- ensure that the Code of Conduct is implemented in respect of conflicts of interests arising at meetings of party groups and to amend their model standing orders accordingly.

Group meetings, not 'committees'

4.94 The distinction between group meetings and formal meetings of the local authority and its committees and sub-committees is important. Usually this is clear, but not always. Thus in *R v Hyndburn Borough Council* (1985),[31] a decision of a group leaders' meeting (comprising the leader and deputy leader of the Conservative Group and the leader and deputy leader of the Labour Group on a local authority) not to allow SDP/Alliance Group councillors to attend was held to be lawful on the grounds that the meetings, designed for purposes of informal consultation between the political parties and chief officers, formed no part of the formal committee machinery of the council: 'Any decision which it was felt goes beyond this category, whether as a matter of political prudence or to avoid any doubts about legalities, is referred to committee for ratification,' acknowledged Woolf J.

4.95 Political group meetings of the kind discussed here, because they are not local authority meetings, are not obliged to be open to the public and nor are the contents subject to the provisions of the Freedom of Information Act 2000.

Notes

1 Widdicombe, paras. 7.15–7.30, recommended a simplification of the electoral system to provide for single-member wards or divisions and a uniform period of office of four years. This proposal was not pursued.

2 In *Parker v Yeo* (1992), it was held that the town or county hall could be a councillor's 'principal or only place of work' for the purposes of qualification for election. This decision has been criticised and Labour Party headquarters advise its candidates not to rely on it.

3 Disqualifications now include employment in a politically restricted post in any local authority in the country: LG&HA 1989, s. 1.

4 LGA 1972, ss. 26(1) and (7)(b).

5 Unless a contrary intention appears, a provision of an Act comes into force at the beginning of the day in question: see IA 1978, s. 4(a). Thus a person not re-elected at an election held on a Thursday goes out of office at the moment after midnight on the Monday following, i.e. at the start of the fourth day after the Thursday, and must cease to act as a councillor not later than during the Sunday.

6 LGA 1972, s. 2, provides that for every county and every district there shall be a council consisting of a chairman and councillors; s. 3 provides that the chairman of a principal council shall be elected annually; and s. 4 that the chairman's election shall be the first business transacted at the annual meeting of a principal council.

7 A local authority may properly arrange for the discharge of its functions by an officer: LGA 1972, s. 101 (see 5.9).

8 The power of the central government to act in default is related to particular statutory functions. There is no legislative power to replace the local authority in its entirety.

9 Widdicombe Research Volume II: The Local Government Councillor, p. 41.

10 See also *R v Sheffield City Council ex parte Chadwick* (1985) and *R v Hyndburn Borough Council ex parte Strak* (1985). All three cases had been brought by Alliance councillors who had been excluded from committees.

11 S. 18 and Local Authorities (Members' Allowances) Regulations 1991, 1993 and 1995.

12 1991 Regulations, reg. 9(1).

13 LG&HA 1989.

14 LGA 1972, s. 102(3).

15 Ibid., s. 102(1).

16 Committees cannot determine their own constitution but a committee can be empowered by the council to decide who to appoint to fill co-opted places.

17 The aldermanic system, abolished long ago, whereby persons could be brought in from outside the council's membership, was, in effect, a system of co-option.

18 LGA 1972, s. 104(1).

19 This restriction was removed by the LG&HA 1989, s. 13(8).
20 LGA 1972, ss. 173–178.
21 LG&HA 1989, s. 13, which prescribes the basic division into voting and non-voting co-opted persons.
22 See e.g. *Clark & Lindsell on Torts*.
23 Defamation Act 1952, s. 7.
24 See s. 19.
25 The practice was also examined – and the view was the same – in *R v Secretary of State for Education and Science ex parte Birmingham District Council and Another* (1984).
26 *Widdicombe Report*, para. 5.74.
27 LGA 1972, s. 85(3).
28 Ibid., s. 86.
29 Ibid., s. 87(1).
30 See R. G. Brooke, 'Modern Approach to Committee Practice', (1979) 143 *Local Government Review* 3.
31 Unreported, but see (1986), 150 *Local Government Review* 57.

Chapter 5
The role of officers

Introduction

The local government service

5.1 Each local authority separately and independently appoints and employs staff for the discharge of its functions:[1] on 'single-status' terms and conditions settled locally but incorporating common core conditions negotiated at national level through collective bargaining by local authority and trade union representatives. Local authority employees collectively comprise the local government service,[2] which is a concept rather than a clearly defined entity, i.e. it is unlike the civil service, which represents identifiable and integrated central government employment in the service of the Crown, but it ensures interchangeability of employees between local authorities and continuity of service for several purposes. This work refers to officers associated in one way or another with the local government decision-making process in meetings. This means the chief executive in particular in advising on and giving effect to policy; the monitoring officer who, has responsibility for the legality of the decision-making process (often this includes the democratic services function); and the chief officers who also have a role in policy advice and an operational role in service delivery (whether or not this is externalised) and in the public protection and regulatory services. As to the head of the paid service, the monitoring officer, proper officer and chief finance officer; and as to the role of officers in quasi-judicial proceedings.

Authorities, other than parish or community councils, have power to appoint assistants for political groups on the council provided they meet certain criteria, and subject to stringent conditions and safeguards.[3] These political assistants are the only local government officers who are able to be appointed having regard to their political activities or affiliations – all other members of staff must be non-political in their work. A political group cannot have more than one political assistant and the number of political assistants is limited to three in each council. There are strict rules set out in s. 9 of the LG&HA 1989 on how a political group qualifies for a political assistant. The pay and political activities of a political assistant, once appointed, are restricted by statutory regulation. The political assistant's purpose is to provide assistance, in the discharge of any of their functions as members of a relevant authority, to the members of any political group to which members of the authority belong. As the political assistants have much contact with the leadership and membership of their group, it can often be useful for democratic services staff to liaise with them on the various operational matters that need to be arranged, or matters of policy clarified with the political groups.

5.2 Beyond that exception, officers are appointed by the local authority as a corporate body; s. 112 of the LGA 1972, which provides the power that 'a local authority shall appoint such officers as they think necessary for the proper discharge by the authority of such of their or another authority's functions as fall to be discharged by them and the carrying out of any obligations incurred by them in connection with an agreement made by them [with another local authority]'. This is subject to a limitation concerning the pay policy statement under s. 41 of the Localism Act 2011 and, with greatest impact, the Local Authorities (Standing Orders) (England) Regulations 2001, which sets parameters around member involvement in the appointment and dismissal of staff of chief officers and those below deputy chief officer level as defined in the LG&HA 1989.

5.3 There are also certain posts that fulfil the requirement of 'proper officer' (discussed below). Other posts are named and carry set roles, responsibilities and liabilities, such as the returning officer and electoral administration officer. Other posts are also named, such as the scrutiny officer (discussed below). There is also a set of posts named in the LG&HA 1989 and LGA 2000 that must be appointed to and known as statutory chief officers. These posts currently include:

- Head of Paid Service (ref. LG&HA 1989, s. 4);
- Monitoring Officer (ref. LG&HA 1989, s. 5);
- Chief Finance Officer (ref. LGA 1972, s. 151/LG&HA 1989, s. 6);
- Director of Children's Services (ref. Children Act 2004, s. 18);
- Director of Public Health (ref. National Health Service Act 2006, s. 73A(1); and
- Director of Adult Social Services (ref. Local Authority Social Services Act 1970, s. 6(A1).

Some of these posts may be filled by the same person, the latter three being a case in point, whereas the others may not.

Member–officer relationship

Officer role

5.4 The traditional approach to decision-making meant that the role of officers in the past was limited to giving professional advice and procedural guidance although, in the one-time 'secrecy' of committee deliberations, officers could exercise considerable influence up to the point at which a decision was made. Indeed, it was often said that the officers were the non-voting partners in the conduct of local authority business. How effective in practice this input from officers was depended largely on the relationship between councillors and their chief officers; but where, as was not uncommon, there was real partnership in the sense of mutual trust and confidence, the influence of officers often meant that councillors accepted – sometimes perhaps too unquestioningly – what the officers proposed.

5.5 The practical effect of having meetings open to the public (see Chapter 3) has meant that officers are more inhibited in making a contribution to member deliberations at meetings – for example, full council. Some councils allow officers to speak at cabinet or senior committee meetings, while others do not. On the other hand, it could be argued that the role of the chief executive as the council's principal policy adviser enables them to take a bigger role in decision-making at top level in their contact with the leader of the council; the chief executive's role is to give effect to the political aspirations of the majority group.

5.6 The difficulty in setting out clearly the relationship between members and officers has been the cause of friction in many local authorities in recent times. Increased political emphasis in the functioning of local government has often led to senior officers becoming identified with one or other political groups and this inevitably raises problems when political control changes. In an attempt to cure this, s. 7(2) of the LG&HA 1989 required all appointments of officers to be made on merit (see 13.34). The Nolan Committee recommended that every local authority should have a written code or protocol that would govern the relationship between members and officers. This approach was repeated in the Local Government Act 2000: Guidance to English Local Authorities issued by the Secretary of State, which stated that local authorities should develop appropriate conventions setting out the roles, responsibilities and rights of officers and members and establishing the key principles governing officer/member relationships. A model Protocol on Member/Officer relations issued by ACSeS was adopted by a number of authorities, and, although this may have required review in the light of the adoption of new Member Codes of Conduct in 2012, most authorities do now have a written protocol in place.

5.7 Officers owe a duty both in legal and managerial terms to the council as a corporate whole, which overrides allegiance to whichever group, political or otherwise, is in control of the authority. This approach was endorsed in the 2000 Act Guidance, which confirmed that in relation to those authorities operating executive arrangements, officers should be responsible for day-to-day managerial and operational decisions within the local authority and should provide support both to the executive and all councillors in their several roles. Moreover, the Guidance emphasised that it is a key principle that all officers are employed by and accountable to the local authority as a whole.

5.8 However, relationships have had to take account of the political climate and the sensitivity demanded; and legislative changes have been introduced to strengthen the perceptions of political neutrality. Legislation has defined statutory duties given to officers and in particular to ensure that these officers are given an element of protection by virtue of their statutory roles. The 'triumvirate' of those officers designated as the head of paid service (in practice nearly always the chief executive or managing director), the chief finance officer and the monitoring officer have statutory protection against dismissal on the whim of members, and any disciplinary action can only be undertaken by an independent investigator (Local Authority Standing Orders Regulations 2001 (SI 2001/3384) reg. 7).

Responsibility for committee work

5.9 An authority's committee work used to be the responsibility of the county, borough or district secretary, sometimes designated the solicitor – and now often re-titled as director or assistant director for legal and democratic services or governance or law and governance, depending on the fashion of the moment. It is this officer who, whatever the title of the job, generally discharges the statutory responsibilities imposed upon the proper officer.[4] That role of proper officer will, more often than not, be allied to the responsibilities of the monitoring officer, whatever the substantive post is titled, although a few authorities do retain the post of 'clerk and chief executive to the council' where the proper officer remains attached to the most senior post of the council (harking back to the days when the clerk was almost exclusively a lawyer and was seen to be a first among equals of chief officer posts allied to each committee, rather than a head of paid service).

5.10 As a general principle, it is important that the work carried out by democratic services officers should be wholly centralised. There are patent disadvantages in any practice that allows some committee work to be performed by or within a service directorate for which the committee is responsible. For example, it was once common in local education authorities for education committee work to be discharged within the education department because of the particular character of the service and elsewhere for personnel committee work, to be under the control of the Head of HR on the grounds that there was a high degree of confidentiality in the proceedings. The executive changes have meant that authorities have tended to bring together and centralise all democratic services functions and this fits with the general theme throughout local government of achieving efficiencies through consolidation. In any event, there would be practical management issues of ensuring quality control across the whole of the council's democratic services arrangements and ensuring a consistent standard approach, and (particularly in the smaller authorities) of providing back-up if officers are away. There would also be a potential risk that officers with a professional or sectional interest in a committee's proceedings might consciously or unconsciously allow this interest to affect their recording of proceedings. Impartiality may be thought more likely to exist and be seen to exist where committee work is wholly independent of service interests. See below in regard to agenda control and as to what should be included or excluded from minutes.

Delegation to officers

5.11 The delegation of functions to an officer may be either to an individual officer by name or, preferably, to a post-holder (it is the obligation of the local authority to publicise officer delegations of more than six months' duration). The effect of delegation to an officer is that the act of the officer becomes the act of the local authority: see *Battelley v Finsbury Borough Council* (1958). Delegation in this sense means conferring authority on an officer to make decisions within the parameters of the delegation arrangements; hence the officer cannot pass on the decision-making authority to another officer, for otherwise the maxim 'delegatus non potest delegare' would be infringed, unless the sub-delegation is either expressly or impliedly authorised. It is evident, however, that the courts will not ordinarily upset a decision taken by a subordinate officer in the name of the chief officer to whom power has been delegated, particularly where what has been done was an administrative act. See a range of cases including *Provident Mutual Life Assurance Associates v Derby City Council* (1981) and *R v Southwark London Borough Council ex parte Bannerman* (1990).

5.12 A distinction needs to be made, however, between real delegation, which connotes the exercise of discretion, and mere executive tasks that officers can perform without formal delegation.[5] The delegation must not be fettered in such a way that, in effect, the decision in a particular instance is really made by an individual councillor; as explained earlier, this would be unlawful and if the action is really to be taken by the councillor, then it should be in accordance with powers delegated to them. Action taken under delegated powers does not have to be confirmed: it is immediately effective. Local authorities will, however, as a rule require officers to report what they have done under delegated power and particular rules apply if an officer has made a key decision. In the case of *R v St Edmundsbury Borough Council, ex parte Walton* (1999), it was held that if the local planning authority wished to delegate to an officer the making of a decision as to whether an environmental statement was required, they were obliged to do so formally. As they had not done so, the officer's decision had to be quashed.

Can there be delegation to a group of officers?

5.13 The statutory provisions governing the carrying out of functions by officers clearly refer to 'an officer';[6] and although the general rule of interpretation is that 'words in the singular include the plural and words in the plural include the singular', it is submitted that delegation is not permissible to a group of officers. The matter is a practical one rather than one of legality. An individual can be made accountable for what they do under delegated authority, but if a group of officers were collectively entrusted with the discharge of functions, both the powers so delegated and accountability would be diffused. Who in officer group decisions of this kind would decide what course to pursue if there was disagreement? If the decision were to be settled by majority vote, this would undermine the position of the chief executive in the management team. In practice, a committee minute or delegation requiring a number of officers to be involved in the exercise of a delegated power is likely to authorise a chief officer to exercise the delegation 'in consultation with' one or more colleagues.

Liability of officers

Immunity from personal liability

5.14 Local authorities, as corporate bodies, are separate and distinct from the persons who comprise an authority for the time being; and this means that individual councillors are not personally liable for the consequences of what is done in good faith and lawfully by the local authority. The position of officers, as servants of the corporate authority, is somewhat different but statutory provisions provide immunity against personal liability for both members and officers. The Local Government (Miscellaneous Provisions) Act 1976, s. 39, extends to local authorities in the execution of their statutory powers and duties the following provisions of the Public Health Act 1875, s. 265:

> 'No matter or thing done, and no contract entered into by any local authority . . . and no matter or thing done by any member... or by any officer of such authority or other person whomsoever acting under the direction of such authority shall if the matter or other thing were done or the contract were entered into bona fide for the purposes of executing this Act subject them or any of them personally to any action liability or claim or demand whatsoever; and any expense incurred by any such authority member or officer or other person acting as last aforesaid shall be borne and repaid out of the fund or rate applicable by such authority to the general purposes of this Act.'

This Act provides that councillors and local authority officers, when acting in the course of their duties and in good faith, have statutory immunity and are not personally liable for the actions they take. The Act provides for an indemnity in relation to potential liabilities and also costs.

Carrying out unlawful decisions

5.15 When officers, in advising members, find themselves called upon to implement decisions that are legally questionable, they need to act with care and should advise the monitoring officer of their concerns with regard to the legality of a decision. When a decision is challengeable on grounds of unreasonable exercise of the council's discretion, the officers can act to implement the decision without fear, because such decisions are legal until successfully challenged: see *Associated Provincial Picture Houses Ltd v Wednesbury Corporation* (1948).

Indemnity of officers acting as council representatives

5.16 An officer who becomes liable to damages as the result of carrying out an unlawful decision could only rely on any indemnity given by the council. The limitation on this was graphically shown in *Burgoine and Cooke v Waltham Borough Council and McWhirr* (1996), where action taken on behalf of an outside body on which the officers concerned represented the council was not covered by the specific terms of the indemnity given.

5.17 The situation relating to indemnities has been clarified further over recent years and the courts confirmed that an indemnity can be granted by virtue of ss. 111 and 112 of the Local Government Act 1972 Act both to defend and to instigate proceedings in appropriate cases. In *R v DPP ex parte Duckenfield* (2000), the South Yorkshire Police Authority was able to pay the costs of an officer prosecuted following the Hillsborough disaster. In *R v Westminster City Council ex parte* UMPO (2000), the court upheld the legality of an indemnity granted by the council to councillors and officers involved in the 'homes for votes' issue as being within the scope of s. 111 of the 1972 Act. In that instance, the indemnity was conditional on their being exonerated from any misconduct. Finally, in *R v Bedford BC ex parte Comninos* (2003), Sullivan J held that s. 111 empowered a local authority to indemnify officers for their legal costs when instigating libel proceedings arising out of their conduct of an election.

5.18 The position on indemnities further changed in November 2004, as a direct result of *Burgoine*, when the Local Authorities (Indemnities for Members and Officers) Order 2004 came into force. The powers under those Regulations are in addition to the existing powers that local authorities already have, including those under s. 111 of the 1972 Act. The Regulations make it clear that a council can provide an indemnity and take out insurance. Under the Regulations, a council (including principal councils and parish councils) can indemnify an officer or member in relation to any action that is authorised by the council or the exercise of any function at the request of, with the approval of, or for the purpose of the authority. The Regulations also allow an indemnity to be given where, when exercising the function in question, the officer or member does so in a capacity other than that of officer or member. This would permit an indemnity, for example, to cover the case where the officer or member acts as the director of a company at the request of his authority, and thus is acting in their capacity as a director. The council can also provide an indemnity where the action complained of is outside the powers of the council, or of the officer or member, provided they were acting under a reasonable belief that it was within those powers at the time it was taken.

5.19 Where an indemnity has been given or insurance provided under the Regulations, it cannot cover a member or officer in relation to criminal proceedings where a member/officer is found guilty, or liability arising from fraud, deliberate wrongdoing, or the cost of pursuing a defamation claim. In such cases any costs incurred under an indemnity would normally have to be repaid to the council or insurer. The terms of any indemnity must require the local authority or insurer to be reimbursed should there be a criminal conviction. Except for the limited circumstances set out in this paragraph, indemnities cannot be given under the Regulations in relation to criminal acts or intentional wrongdoing, fraud, recklessness, or in relation to the bringing of (but not the defence of) any action in defamation. Accordingly, in the circumstances outlined in *Comninos*, the authority would not be able to rely on the powers set out in the Regulations but would have to rely on its s. 111 powers.

Proper officer

Appointment by designation

5.20 A proper officer must be appointed by every local authority. Section 270(3) of the LGA 1972 provides that:

> 'Any reference in this Act to a proper officer and any reference which by virtue of this Act is to be construed as such a reference shall, in relation to any purpose and any local authority or other body or any area, be construed as a reference to an officer appointed for that purpose by that body or for that area, as the case may be.'

General principles

The choice of proper officer is entirely at the discretion of the local authority and obviously depends upon local circumstances. It would be prudent for an authority to appoint another officer to act as such in the event of his incapacity in a vacancy in the office.

5.21 The term 'proper officer' is peculiar to local government. It is a phrase used to identify a person designated as being responsible for a particular function or range of functions. Thus it is used in a variety of contexts, e.g. as the officer responsible for administering the local registration scheme for births, marriages and deaths, and in connection with committees as the officer responsible for issuing the summons to a council meeting.

Scrutiny officers

5.22 Section 31 of the Local Democracy, Economic Development and Construction Act 2009 had required local authorities, with the exception of district councils in areas where there is a county council, to designate one of their officers as a scrutiny officer to support the work of the authority's overview and scrutiny committee(s). This is repeated in the current provision, Section 9FB of the Local Government Act 2000 (inserted by the Localism Act 2011), with effect from 4 May 2012.

> **2.2** The statutory duties of the scrutiny officer are to:
>
> - promote the role of the authority's overview and scrutiny committee(s);
> - provide support to the authority's overview and scrutiny committee(s) and the members of those committee(s);
> - provide support and guidance to members of the authority, members of the executive of the authority and officers of the authority,
>
> in relation to the functions of the authority's overview and scrutiny committee(s).
>
> **2.3** A council may not designate any of the following officers as the scrutiny officer:
>
> - the head of paid service;
> - the monitoring officer; or
> - the chief finance officer.

In the original Local Authorities (Overview and Scrutiny) Bill 2010, there was a provision that the local authority must provide the scrutiny officer with such staff, accommodation and other resources as are, in the officer's opinion, sufficient to allow the officer to discharge their functions, which is similar to the provision for monitoring officers. However, this was not included in the Localism Act 2011.

Committee officers

Democratic services officers

5.23 The officers primarily concerned with committee practice are those who were at one time always termed democratic services officers: throughout this book we have tried to use the term 'democratic services officers', as most are commonly referred to, or committee manager. Whatever the title, all will be concerned with the preparation of agenda and drafting minutes and reports, and many have duties such as advising the committee on procedural matters and taking limited or full responsibility for ensuring action is undertaken on a cabinet's/committee's decisions.
5.24 The status of democratic services officers depended in the past upon the ability of individual officers and the inclination or disinclination of the former town clerk/ clerk of the council to entrust them with effective tasks. Often, too, the role democratic services officer has varied according to the size of the authority and the extent to which their work has been dominated by legal rather than administrative considerations. Thus, for example, Herbert Morrison felt able to say of the one-time largest local authority:[7]

> 'There is an important officer attached to committees called the democratic services officer . . . These men are of high standing, and they have substantial salaries. They are the eyes and ears of the chief officers concerned.'

Flatteringly, too, in a manual published some years ago under the auspices of the former Society of Clerks of Urban District Councils:

> 'The perfect democratic services officer requires to possess the foresight of Old Moore, the accuracy of an adding machine; the judgement of Solomon; the patience of Job; the memory of an elephant; the coolness and tact of a high ranking diplomat; and the literary skill of Bernard Shaw!'[8]

5.25 The democratic services officer is no longer a relatively junior officer – sometimes no more than a record taker – with predominantly clerical duties whose principal accomplishment was that of an efficient shorthand writer, with the ability to draft 'agendas, minutes and reports in a clear, well-written, grammatically correct style'. There has been a notable improvement of status in the case of most authorities, particularly the larger ones, encouraged, it is suspected, not only by the difficulty nowadays in retaining officers of high standard but also by the trend towards requiring legal representation at some committees or overview and scrutiny meetings only when legal issues arise. Officers have responsibility for handling the work of a major committee or a group of related smaller ones.
5.26 Today, as already indicated, responsibility for committees often rests with the

director of law and administration or the director of governance or corporate services, who has inherited most of the duties relinquished by chief executives over the years. Due to the trend to consolidate legal and democratic services in most authorities, the majority of senior posts in this area are held by lawyers, as the monitoring officer generally (although not always) holds this qualification.

Training

5.27 Little attention was given in the past to training staff for committee work. Most obtained their knowledge and expertise by practical experience on the job and thus competence depended on the environment in which they worked. It is for this reason that the old NALGO residential course in committee administration was so valued.

Qualifications

5.28 Local authorities, in advertising democratic services officer posts, rarely specify any particular qualifications but increasingly ask for education to degree standard.

5.29 In the past, the Diploma in Municipal Administration provided the recognised professional qualification for administrative staff in local government: a qualification that no longer exists. Without recanting the history, the similarities seen between the role of the local authority district or county secretary and that of a company secretary in a limited company or plc, as referred to earlier in this book, led to the incorporation of suitably qualified local government officers into the Institute of Chartered Secretaries, thereby becoming the Institute of Chartered Secretaries and Administrators (ICSA). As such, the Institute ran a set of public service stream examinations leading to graduate and member status for some years. Subsequently, however, this specialist stream was removed in favour of the examinations becoming once again generic, to a single international standard, across all governance sectors, including company, utilities, charity, local government NHS and central government. As well as that shift to the generic, this was due in part to the ending of certain funding agreements and in part lower take-up numbers than expected. The nature of the ICSA examinations, often run in combination with an associated master's degree in corporate governance, accounting, management or law, did not sufficiently suit or indeed interest all those who wished to become students of local government administration or who were existing democratic services officers. Since then, ICSA has become the qualification of choice for NHS management training, as a coordinated and promoted programme, but the Local Government Association graduate entry programme and the associated university schools of government tend now to lean towards the postgraduate diploma in public administration, master's in public administration or the even more generic master's in business administration. We shall see where future changes may take us.

5.30 Into this gap the Association of Democratic Services Officers (ADSO) have established (with some establishing support from ICSA) two recognised qualifications for democratic services officers: the Certificate in Democratic Practice and the newly developed Diploma in Local Democracy.

The Certificate in Democratic Practice is aimed at learners who already work in the democratic services area. The Certificate gives a learner the opportunity to show that they have the relevant knowledge and understanding for their role and that they can apply it in a work setting. This includes all democratic functions such as meetings support, scrutiny, member support and civic support, and is practice based.

The new, higher-level Diploma is an NVQ set at level 6 (Degree level) and it focuses on underpinning legislative knowledge within a democratic context, in conjunction with the requirement to demonstrate research skills and awareness of professional development, and undertake a dissertation based on a specialist pathway.

ADSO has been set up as the national body representing professionals working across all areas of democratic support within local authorities, joint authorities and employers' organisations. With over 900 members, it is rapidly achieving its vision of becoming a nationally recognised professional association.

Officers at meetings

General

5.31 With the exception of the oddity of the health and well-being board (see below), officers are not part of the membership of the local authority;[9] and so they cannot be a party to the decisions made by the full council, cabinet or in committee or sub-committee, even though they may have delegated powers enabling them to make decisions of sometimes greater significance than those made by members collectively in council or cabinet. Nevertheless, officers do participate in discussion at committee and sub-committee meetings (although cabinet is often treated differently) and may influence the decisions made by reason of the facts that they lay before the members or of the advice that they tender. In many authorities the relationship between members and officers is one of mutual trust and confidence, and in these cases the officers act virtually as non-voting partners in the business of local government. In other words, the officers join in the debate whenever they think fit, speak more than once if need be, sway members deliberately towards one course of action rather than another until the point when a decision is about to be made, when they must hold their silence – and, of course, accept unquestionably the decision when it is made, whether it is to their liking or not.

Council meetings

5.32 At council meetings, however, it is the tradition that officers shall not speak unless, exceptionally, any one of them may be called upon to do so. The chief executive may have announcements to make, the monitoring officer (council secretary or solicitor) will be responsible for advising the chair/mayor, and occasionally the full council, on procedure and, very rarely, the chief finance officer may have to fulfil his or her duties in advising on budget or expenditure proposal.

Committees

5.33 An officer should be scrupulous in ensuring, particularly if wishing to influence members to take the course that officer favours that all the relevant facts are before the relevant cabinet or committee including the pros and cons of alternative courses of action. Where an officer's report is not comprehensive enough to cover all the issues, the cabinet or committee runs the risk of having its decision declared invalid, as in *R v Isle of Wight ex parte O'Keefe* (1990). The officer must take care, too, not to dominate the meeting so as to impose their will upon the members, particularly nowadays with members of the public present, and if they find in the course of debate that the majority of members are against them, they must not then press their view unduly.[10]

5.34 If, on the other hand, officers are discouraged from speaking at meetings, then they must rely on the written material prepared for the cabinet or committee. There are times, however, when it is the duty of an officer to speak out even if forbidden to do so. No officer should sit silently by and allow members to embark on a course of action that is *ultra vires* or may have consequences that the members have clearly overlooked. As has been said elsewhere:[11]

> 'It is often a matter of judgement, not easy to exercise in practice, when discursive discussion in committee takes an unexpected turn, whether the officer should speak or hold his tongue. He must be careful to distinguish between, for example, errors of fact and errors of judgement. The officer ought to stand up – and persist in standing up and speaking even if ordered to sit down – if he sees his committee about to make a decision of consequence on a misunderstanding of fact. To remain silent would be a gross dereliction of duty. But it may be wise for him to remain unmoved and unspeaking if the committee in full possession of the facts is about to make a decision which is wayward, capricious, imprudent or manifestly wrong.'

Of course, this must now be read in the light of a specific legal duty imposed upon the monitoring officer (and a somewhat analogous duty on the chief finance officer) to report in writing on proposals or courses of action likely to involve breach of the law.

5.35 It needs to be borne in mind that some officers will not be regular participants in committee business and may attend only very exceptionally, perhaps merely to listen to discussion on a particular issue (when they might conveniently sit in the seats reserved for the public) or to advise on a matter that they have been handling personally or to support their director if detailed information is asked for. For such officers, attendance will be an unusual experience and they may need to be briefed to ensure they understand the conventions of procedure, know where to sit, when to speak (and whether to stand or remain seated when speaking), when to leave and so on. Such briefings should be part of the routine of pre-committee work.

Attendance at party groups

5.36 The ability of officers to act as effective advisers to councillors will, in some local authorities, depend on whether they attend, or are prepared to attend, meetings of the party groups. Widdicombe's research showed that attendance was the exception rather than the rule, possibly because of this specific clause sometimes found in officers' terms and conditions of service:

> 'The officer should not be called upon to advise any political group of the employing authority either as to the work of the groups or as to the work of the authority, neither shall he or she be required to attend any meetings of any political group.'

Widdicombe felt that this makes unnecessarily heavy weather of the subject. It recommended that no special inhibition should be placed on attendance at party groups subject to the following safeguards:

- all requests for attendance should be addressed to the chief executive who should decide which officers should attend; and
- the chief executive should notify the other parties and offer a similar facility.

These safeguards, it was said, should be included in the list of conventions that Widdicombe recommended that all local authorities should prepare, and, later in 1997, repeated in the protocol advocated by the Nolan Committee (see 1.59). In addition, it is suggested that where there are non-councillors present at party group meetings, the officer should be specifically informed of this in order to ensure that confidentiality is not breached.

Membership of health and well-being boards

5.37 The distinction between the roles of members and officers has been blurred in the case of health and well-being boards, established by the Health and Social Care Act 2012 (the 2012 Act). Significantly, the 2012 Act requires an authority's director of adult social services, director of children's services and director of public health to be members of its health and well-being board. While a health and well-being board is to be treated as a committee of the local authority, and as if established under s. 102 of the LGA 1972, it is clear that it is a different type of committee and the 2012 Act allows regulations to be made disapplying or modifying legislation normally applying to local authority committees. To facilitate the membership of the specified officers, regulations[12] disapply s. 104(1) of the LGA 1972 (which prohibits officers from being members of local authority committees). Concern has been raised about the blurring of the primary role of an officer at committee, to give impartial professional advice to councillors, particularly with regard to the prospect of officers voting in opposition to councillors, especially senior executive members. The regulations[13] permit an authority, in consultation with the health and well-being board itself, to determine which members of the health and well-being board should be voting members. Some authorities have used this flexibility to designate officers as non-voting members of the board.

5.38 Officers who are members of the health and well-being board and who are entitled to vote at the board meetings will be subject to the authority's member code of conduct, as such officers will (where they are able to vote) be regarded as co-opted members (Localism Act 2011, s. 27(4)).

Notes

1 As to the power of employing the generality of local authority employees: see LGA 1972, s. 112(1). Certain other categories of staff are employed under specific legislation.

2 There are several books on the local government service including various encyclopaedic loose-leaf works.

3 LG&HA 1989, s. 9.

4 Bains Report, para. 7.34.

5 There are several cases where the courts have considered the implications of, for example, unauthorised action by an officer: *Warwick Rural District Council v Miller-Mead* (1962), where it was held that a local authority can regularise the action by subsequent ratification; *Lever Finance Ltd v Westminster (City) London Borough Council* (1971), where it was held that an authority may be bound by the doctrine of estoppel when it is not prepared to ratify what has been done by an officer. In *Lever*, Lord Denning MR said at p. 231: 'An applicant cannot himself know, of course, whether such a delegation has taken place: that is a matter for the "indoor management" of the planning authority. It depends on the internal resolutions which it has made. Any person dealing with it is entitled to assume that all necessary resolutions have been passed.' Now, of course, an applicant could inspect the authority's statutory list of delegations to officers: LGA 1972, s. 100G(2).

6 LGA 1972, s. 101(1).

7 Herbert Morrison, *How Greater London is Governed* (1932).

8 *The Clerk of the Council and his Department* (1951).

9 For this reason it is not good practice to include the names of officers among those recorded as present at a council, committee or sub-committee meeting. Nevertheless, a record might usefully be made that a named officer, having declared an interest, withdrew from the meeting, and must necessarily be made where an officer – where charged with a specific duty to report, as, for example, in the case of the monitoring officer, or otherwise – has advised the meeting that a projected course of action is unlawful.

10 When an officer is speaking in council or committee, they must take care to ensure that they can be heard and understood by everyone in the room. Roland Freeman in *Becoming a Councillor* (2nd edn, 1975), p. 85, tells the story of a new member of a small district council who rose somewhat nervously after a meeting had been in progress for an hour to say, 'On a point of order, I can't hear what the clerk is saying and could he possibly speak up a little.' As the new councillor sat down an older member leant across to him and said, 'I'm so glad you did that. I haven't heard a word he's said for the past seven and a half years!'

11 Raymond Knowles, *Effective Management in Local Government*.

12 Local Authority (Public Health, Health and Well-being Boards and Health Scrutiny) Regulations 2013 (SI2013/218), reg. 5.

13 Ibid., Regulation 6 (modifying s. 13 of the Local Government and Housing Act 1989).

Part 2
Council Meetings

Chapter 6
Preliminaries

Notice and summons

Essential prerequisites

6.1 There are two essential preliminaries to holding a council meeting, i.e. the meeting in full assembly of a principal, parish or community council, and usually called 'full council'. These are the giving of notice and the service of a summons: the former is a public intimation, published in prescribed manner, to the community at large, not merely to local government electors; the latter is directed privately to the council members who are entitled to attend. Notice is general while the summons is individual.

6.2 If there is failure to comply with statutory requirements as to notice and summons, then the meeting itself may not be properly convened and the business transacted of no effect: see more particularly below. In certain circumstances the notice, and in every case the summons, must specify the business to be transacted. In this sense the agenda (a term not used in any of the statutes regulating local authority meetings until introduced by the LG(AI)A 1985: see 6.22) may be said to be part of the notice and summons. In the case of parish and community meetings the obligation at law is to give public notice only.[1]

Initiation of a meeting

6.3 As indicated earlier, a council meeting will be held:

- as directed by statute, e.g. the annual meeting;
- in accordance with the timetable of meetings fixed by the council, usually at the annual meeting, i.e. the cycle of ordinary meetings;
- for a special purpose required by statute or on the decision of the council; or
- upon the requisition of the chairman or the prescribed number of members, i.e. an extraordinary meeting.

Requisitioned meetings

6.4 It is expressly provided that if the chairman of a principal, parish or community council refuses to call an extraordinary meeting after a requisition for that purpose, signed by five members (in the case of a principal council: three in the case of a joint authority or two in the case of a parish or community council), has been presented to them; or if, without so refusing, the chairman does not call the meeting within seven days after the requisition has been presented, then, in the case of a principal council any five members (or in the case of a joint authority any three members and parish or community council any two members) may on that refusal or on the expiration of the seven days, as the case may be, themselves call an extraordinary meeting of the council forthwith. For a suggested standing order, see 6.14; and as to the subsequent withdrawal of a councillor who signed the requisition, see 6.19. There is provision also for the calling of parish and community meetings in similar circumstances, but the term 'extraordinary' is not used. The NALC (National Association of Local Councils) model standing orders do not cover this area, however.

What is meant by 'presented'?

6.5 The use of the word 'presented' in the statute suggests an act more formal than, say, serving the requisition by post or other method of delivery, and it may be that the requisition should be handed personally to the chairman by one of the signatories to the requisition. If, of course, the chairman cannot be contacted because of absence from the area and is thus unable to receive the requisition, it may be, strictly, that the requisition should be handed physically to the vice-chairman, who is empowered generally to act in the absence of the chairman, but it is submitted that the presenter must make reasonable attempts to present the requisition to the chairman before going to the vice-chairman. Compliance with the requirement to present the requisition is important because if an extraordinary meeting was called on the false claim that the chairman had refused or had neglected to call the meeting, the extraordinary meeting subsequently called by individual councillors might be held invalid.

What is meant by 'call a meeting'?

6.6 The obligation on the chairman to call an extraordinary meeting in the foregoing circumstances is to ensure that the notice and summons to the meeting are given within the prescribed seven days. It does not mean that the meeting itself must take place within that period (*Mallon v Armstrong* (1982)). The requisition could ask that the meeting be held on a particular date but the chairman has discretion and is not bound to comply with such a request. Upon the chairman's refusal or neglect, the extraordinary meeting called by the prescribed number of members – these do not necessarily have to be the members who signed the requisition – can be held whenever the members themselves determine: there is no time limit. In exercising discretion as to date, the chairman ought not to delay unduly in calling the meeting.

Notice

6.7 In the case of every meeting of the full council, public notice must be given:

- five clear days at least before a meeting of a principal council (and of its committees and sub-committees) and published at the council's offices; or, if the meeting is convened at shorter notice, then at the time it is convened; or
- three clear days at least before a meeting of a parish or community council 'fixed

in some conspicuous place'[2] in the parish or the community as the case may be; or

- not less than seven clear days beforehand (14 days in certain cases) in the case of a parish or community meeting by posting the notice in some place or places in the parish or the community as the case may be.

Although there is no statutory requirement to such effect, the notice at least of an ordinary or annual meeting is often signed by the chief executive[3] or the chairman: as to who signs in the case of an extraordinary meeting. Public notice must be given:

- by posting the notice in some conspicuous place or places within the area of the local authority; and
- in such other manner, if any, as appears to the authority to be desirable for giving publicity to the notice.

6.8 The LGA 2000 (s. 98) amended the LGA 1972, by the addition of a provision allowing the Secretary of State by Order to amend the three clear days set out in sch. 12 para. 4 to such greater number of days as they may specify. The Local Authorities (Access to Meetings and Documents) (Period of Notice) (England) Order 2002 came into force on 1 October 2002, and amended the period of three clear days to five clear days in relation to England, in relation to principal councils.

'Clear days' has long been interpreted in practice, on the basis of a ruling in *R v Herefordshire Justices* (1820), as meaning weekdays excluding the day a document becomes available and the day on which the meeting is held. This decision was supported by *R v Swansea City Council ex parte Elitestone Ltd* (1993). More specifically the period means five periods of 24 hours running from midnight to midnight and should not include Saturdays or Sundays (unless in its application to the inspection of agenda and reports council offices are open on those days (see 6.28).

6.9 There is an assumption in s. 100A(6) of the LGA 1972 (added by the LG(AI) 1985) that the power exists for the summoning of a principal council on less than five clear days' notice and provision is made for notices to be posted (and agenda to be deposited) in these circumstances. The only power to call meetings, and the formalities to be complied with, is in the LGA 1972 and this makes no mention of less than five clear days. In view of the doubtful legal basis for giving less than the five clear days' notice it would seem prudent that meetings of the full council should only be called in these circumstances in truly exceptional cases, if at all.

6.10 The notice of an ordinary meeting of a principal, parish or community council and of a parish or community meeting may take any form so long as it includes the time and place of the intended meeting. The notice must be reasonable and effective with sufficient information to enable an interested person to attend: thus the time must be precise as to date and time and the place of meeting clearly described. The notice must be prominently displayed, even in the case of a principal council where the requirement is merely to publish the notice at the council's offices rather than in some conspicuous place: it should, therefore, be displayed near the main entrance to the council's offices or on its notice boards (and, if there is more than one town or county hall or council offices in the area the notice should, it is suggested, be displayed at each); in the other cases the notice should be conspicuously displayed on official notice boards throughout the parish or community.

6.11 At least 28 days before a private meeting of the Executive, the Council must publish a notice, on its website and at its offices, of its intention to hold the meeting in private (reg. 5 of the Local Authorities (Executive Arrangements) (Meetings and Access to Information) (England) Regulations 2012 (SI 2089/2012)). The notice must also include a statement of the reasons for the meeting to be held in private.

6.12 The statutory requirements as to notice are contained in two places in the LGA 1972: first, in Sch. 12 as originally enacted, and secondly in s. 100A(6), which was added by the LG(AI)A 1985. Additional notice is required of meetings at which resolutions are to be considered to promote or oppose a Bill in Parliament (see 7.143).

Extraordinary meetings

6.13 In the case of an extraordinary meeting of a principal or parish or community council, there are two additional requirements as to form. In addition to the time and place, the notice must specify the business proposed to be transacted at the meeting, and must be signed by the members of the council who have called the meeting. This can be in general terms as long as the purpose of the business is fairly indicated (see 6.30). In any case the requirement that an agenda and accompanying reports must be open to public inspection (see 6.27 et seq.) reduces the need for the business to be spelled out in detail in the notice. If the chairman of the council calls a meeting of a principal, parish or community council, it is not clear whether they should sign the notice; but in the case of a parish or community meeting the notice must be signed by the person or persons convening the meeting.[4]

6.14 The model standing order in the Modular Constitution sets out the following:

> **3.1** Calling extraordinary meetings
> Those listed below may request the proper officer to call council meetings in addition to ordinary meetings:
>
> (i) the council by resolution;
> (ii) the chairman of the council/the mayor;
> (iii) [in mayor and council manager forms, the council manager];
> (iv) the monitoring officer; and
> (v) any five members of the council if they have signed a requisition presented to the chairman of the council and the chairman has refused to call a meeting or has failed to call a meeting within seven days of the presentation of the requisition.
>
> **3.2** Business
>
> (i) elect a person to preside if the chairman and vice chairman are not present;
> (ii) approve the minutes of the last meeting;

(iii) receive any declarations of interest from members;
(iv) [in mayor and cabinet forms receive any announcements from the chairman, the mayor, members of the cabinet or the head of the paid service];
[in mayor and council manager forms receive any announcements from the chairman, the mayor or the council manager];
[in leader and cabinet forms receive any announcements from the chairman, leader, members of the cabinet or the head of paid service];
(v) receive questions from, and provide answers to, the public in relation to matters which in the opinion of the person presiding at the meeting are relevant to the business of the meeting;
(vi) deal with any business from the last council meeting;
(vii) receive reports from the executive and the council's committees and receive questions and answers on any of those reports;
(viii) receive reports about and receive questions and answers on the business of joint arrangements and external organisations;
(ix) consider motions; and
(x) consider any other business specified in the summons to the meeting including consideration of proposals from the executive in relation to the council's budget and policy framework and reports of the overview and scrutiny committees for debate.

Summons generally

6.15 A summons to attend a council meeting must be sent to every member of the principal, parish or community council as the case may be:

- at least five clear days beforehand (three in the case of a parish council – see 6.7 above);
- specifying the business to be transacted at the meeting;
- signed by the proper officer of the council (see 6.17); and
- left at or sent by post to the usual place of residence of the member, and, of course, giving date, time and place of meeting.

This means that the document sent to councillors should strictly be phrased literally in the manner of a summons, e.g. 'You are hereby summoned to attend a meeting . . .' or words to like effect. There is no similar statutory obligation to summon members to attend executive, committee or sub-committee meetings. These statutory requirements apply whatever the type of meeting concerned: ordinary, annual or extraordinary or one called for a special purpose, e.g. to consider the promotion of a private bill in Parliament. There is no statutory requirement for members to be sent an agenda, but in practice this will form part of the summons. Delivery can be either personally by hand or by post; if the latter, then first-class post should be used wherever possible and timetables will usually make this necessary. Members of principal councils may give notice to the proper officer of their wish for the summons to be sent to an address specified in their notice rather than their normal residence; any such notice should be in writing and the effect is to make delivery to the specified address a valid service of the summons. As of 30 January 2015, the Local Government (Electronic Communications) (England) Order 2015 (SI 2015/5) amended Sched. 12 to the LGA 1972, so that a member may also give consent for the summons to be transmitted to them in electronic form to a particular electronic address.

6.16 There is no obligation to summon individual electors to a parish or community meeting; those entitled to attend must rely on the public notice. It may be thought appropriate to notify individually parish or community councillors as the case may be. The chairman of a parish or community council is specifically entitled to attend a parish or community council as the case may be (or, where a grouping order is in force, for any meeting of the parishes or communities within the group), whether or not he is an elector for the parish or community, and it may be that he should be individually notified.

Signature on the summons

6.17 As indicated above, a summons must be signed by the proper officer, i.e. the officer appointed for that purpose by the local authority, and, strictly, any document bearing the signature of an officer not so appointed will be invalid (see *West Ham Corporation v Benabo* (1934), and other cases that concern notices under the Housing Acts). But a signature purporting to be that of the proper officer may be a scanned copy. There may seem in practice little need for anyone to sign on behalf of the proper officer, but it may be that such a summons would not be effectively challenged under the analogy of *Tennant v London County Council* (1957), where it was held that this was permissible in respect of the authentication of the documents under s. 184 of the London Government Act (LoGA) 1939.

6.18 There may be some instances where, for a historical or other reason, the summons will be signed by an officer not needing to do so as the proper officer.

Member's withdrawal from requisition

6.19 What is the position if a councillor, having signed a requisition for an extraordinary meeting, indicates before the summons is issued that they wish to withdraw their signature? Does this invalidate the requisition? Where a course of action is prescribed by statute, those who exercise an entitlement to initiate that action cannot withdraw. The steps laid down should be started the moment the requisition is presented and thereafter not stopped by anything that may intervene before the issue of the summons (and certainly not between the summons and the holding of the meeting because under common law a meeting once convened cannot properly be postponed.

6.20 Of course the statutory provisions do envisage that the chairman of the council might refuse or neglect to call a meeting following the requisition, notwithstanding the clear duty to call it. It therefore seems reasonable to assume that if, before the summons is issued, a councillor who has signed the requisition withdraws, with the result that fewer than the number of councillors prescribed are, in effect, left seeking the meeting, the chairman will probably be judged to have acted reasonably if they refuse to call the meeting. There is the fall-back position whereby a similar number, who do not need to be the same councillors, can call the meeting themselves.

Want of service

6.21 By common law, failure to serve a summons upon everyone entitled to attend a corporate assembly invalidates the meeting.[5] However, so far as a meeting of a principal, parish or community council is concerned, there is express statutory provision to this important effect, i.e. that 'want of service of any . . . summons . . . on any member of the... council concerned shall not affect the validity of the meeting'.

Nevertheless, care should be taken to ensure there is no defect of service. The courts could be expected to construe this provision strictly and want of service on a substantial number of councillors or wilful failure or neglect to summon members could affect the validity of the meeting. It is recognised as good practice that any request from a member that they do not wish to receive a summons over a specified period (because, for example, of their absence overseas on holiday or business) should be ignored, although of course the reasons for this should be explained to the councillor. A record should be kept of the service of the summons to support evidence that the law has been complied with.

If a member of a principal council gives notice in writing to the proper officer that they desire summonses to attend meetings of the council to be sent to them at some address specified in the notice other than their place of residence, any summons addressed to them and left at or sent by post to that address shall be deemed sufficient service of the summons: see the Local Government Act 1972 Sch. 12, Pt I, para. 4(3).

Council meeting agenda

Business must be specified

6.22 The agenda for a meeting is the list of items of business to be transacted. There has always been a statutory prohibition against the transaction of business not on an agenda in the case of principal councils, although the statutory provisions were at one time differently worded in this respect for no apparent reason: Vaisey J called it 'a strange discrepancy' in *Ayles v Romsey and Stockbridge RDC* (1944). The position is now clear beyond doubt.

6.23 The prohibition against the transaction of business not specified in the agenda is now reinforced by the following provision in s. 100B(4) of the LGA 1972, which was added by the LG(AI)A 1985:

> 'An item of business may not be considered at a meeting of a principal council unless either:
>
> (a) a copy of the agenda including the item (or a copy of the item) is open to inspection by members of the public . . . for at least five clear days before the

> meeting or, where the meeting is convened at shorter notice, from the time the meeting is convened; or
>
> (b) by reason of special circumstances, which shall be specified in the minutes, the chairman of the meeting is of the opinion that the item should be considered as a matter of urgency.'

The obligation to make the agenda available for public inspection is dealt with below. The power conferred upon the chairman of the meeting represents an unusual, if not unique, statutory provision and it raises the question whether it is correct to include in any council agenda a concluding item: any other business. It may be that, at least in the case of committee meetings, it would not be improper to provide for any other business that the chairman decides is urgent. The discretion given to the chairman probably could not be challenged, though presumably it might, if the chairman exercised this power on so regular a basis that the justification becomes suspect.[6]

Urgent business

6.24 The power enabling the chairman of a meeting to permit the transaction of urgent business confers power with statutory authority on an individual member. The way in which this is handled in committees and sub-committees is dealt with in Part 3 of this book, but the problem arises as to whether urgent business of any kind is appropriate, or indeed lawful, at meetings of the full council.

6.25 A number of problems associated with the LG(AI)A 1985 stem from the failure to repeal or amend provisions in the LGA 1972, which are completely incompatible. Calling meetings at less than five clear days' notice is one example of the resulting confusion (see 6.9); urgent business at council meetings is another. The LGA 1972 in para. 4(5) of Sch. 12 provides:

> 'Except in the case of business required by or under this or any other Act to be transacted at the annual meeting of a principal council and other business brought before that meeting as a matter of urgency in accordance with the council's standing orders, no business shall be transacted at a meeting of the council other than that specified in the summons.'

The literal interpretation of this paragraph means that urgent business can only be considered at the annual meeting of a council, and then only if the authority's standing orders allow for it. The effect of the 1985 Act is to restrict this still further by requiring the chair to be of the opinion that the business is urgent before it can be considered. It does not extend the facility to consider urgent business to ordinary or extraordinary meetings of the council. Placing an item such as 'To consider such other business as the chairman considers urgent' does not satisfy the requirement that the business should be specified. The only exception to this would be where business required by law to be done was inadvertently omitted from an agenda. In these circumstances it would be permissible to deal with the business even though it was not specified on the agenda.

Urgent business at adjourned meeting

6.26 Nothing can be dealt with at an adjourned meeting except the unfinished business of the original meeting. Urgent business could properly be dealt with if the chairman considers it urgent under the statutory discretion accorded to them but only if the adjourned meeting is the annual meeting of the council and provision for dealing with urgent business is included in standing orders.

Public access to agenda

6.27 There is an obligation upon principal authorities, but not others, to make copies of the agenda for a meeting and copies of any report for the meeting open to inspection by members of the public for five clear days before the date of the meeting except that:

- where the meeting is convened at shorter notice, then the documents must be open to inspection from the time the meeting is convened; and
- where an item is added to an agenda afterwards, copies of any report relating to the item must be available for inspection from the time the item is added to the agenda.

Regulations (SI 2002/715) came into force on 1 October 2002, which required the three-clear-day period set out in ss. 100A to 100K LGA 1972 to be amended to five clear days in respect of England.

6.28 The precise terms of the statutory obligation require the agenda and reports to be open for inspection at the offices of the council for at least five clear days. The phrase 'offices of the council' would appear not to cover premises such as libraries unless they form part of the council's administrative headquarters. The meaning of 'clear days' has already been discussed (see above) and in this context should not include a Saturday or Sunday unless the offices happen to be open on those days and inspection is possible. It is also laid down that there is no obligation to make documents available for public inspection before copies have been made available to members, although the precise effect of this proviso is unclear and of no real effect. Unless these requirements have been complied with, the business concerned cannot lawfully be dealt with at the meeting: the judge in *Swansea* (see 6.8) had no doubt that the strict statutory requirements had to be complied with in every case, even in the absence of proof of damage by a third party.

6.29 Any part of a report may be excluded if it relates to items that, in the opinion of the proper officer, will be dealt with in part of the meeting which is not likely to be open to the public. In such cases the copy report or the relevant part of it must be marked '*Not for publication*' and a statement put on the report indicating, in the prescribed terms, under which item of exempt information the council is likely to exclude the public from that part of the meeting. The proper officer should act reasonably, i.e. take careful account of the circumstances and the public interest test, in forming their opinion. If the meeting then decides that the business is, in fact, dealt with in open session, the relevant papers should be handed out to the press representatives and the public present at the meeting.

With what detail should business be specified?

6.30 It is not necessary that the items for consideration at a meeting are set out in absolute detail, so long as the business is fairly stated. This means that those who are summoned to the meeting or are entitled to be present can judge whether the business warrants their attendance or not: it is especially important that the business to be transacted should be specifically stated if it is important and not merely a matter of routine or common occurrence and where the meeting has been specially convened. For example, in *R v The Corporation of Dublin* (1911), a special meeting of the corporation was summoned on a requisition of seven ratepayers to consider the question of unemployment in the city and ways and means of alleviating it. At the meeting a resolution was passed authorising the city treasurer to arrange payment of £10,000 on useful works for the alleviation of unemployment. It was held that the notice of the meeting was insufficient to enable the meeting to pass such a resolution. In a later case, *Longfield Parish Council v Wright* (1918), Peterson J said:

> 'It may be that a very important question is going to be considered at the meeting; it may be on the other hand that the only business is purely formal, paying some tradesman or something of that description. In the one case the members would attend in force and in the other case it was a mere matter of form, the members would not attend beyond the necessary quorum. Accordingly, the notice convening the meeting should contain sufficient description of the important business which the meeting is to transact, and the meeting cannot in ordinary circumstances go outside the business mentioned in that notice.'

6.31 The position as regards oral reporting by officers or of indicating that a report will be tabled is more appropriately dealt with in a later chapter.

6.32 It is not sufficient to include an item on the agenda that, for example, says in effect, 'To receive the report of the overview and scrutiny committee', unless the report itself is circulated to councillors and made available for public inspection for the five clear days preceding the meeting; nor an item, 'The chief executive will report', unless the subject matter and the purpose of the oral report are fairly summarised on the agenda.

Defamatory matter in documents

6.33 There is statutory protection as regards defamatory matter in published documents that are required to be accessible to members of the public. It is expressly provided by s. 100H(5) of the 1972 Act that where any such document:

- is supplied to, or open to inspection by, a member of the public; or
- is supplied for the benefit of any newspaper under s. 100B(7),

the publication of any defamatory matter contained in the document is privileged unless the publication is proved to be made with malice. This is also the case in respect of reports of the executive (reg. 21(5), SI 2012/2089).

Regulation of order of business

6.34 The agenda will not only specify the business to be transacted but will also determine the order in which that business is dealt with at the meeting. Usually this order, so far as it is not determined by statute, will be prescribed in standing orders, and the standing orders will invariably provide that the council may on grounds of urgency, possibly of convenience, vary that order on particular occasions.

6.35 There is other business dealt with at the annual meeting, i.e. invariably to appoint committees for the ensuing year and, where the authority is divided into different political groups, provision will be made to review their representation on committees and on other bodies.[7] There may also be an item to receive a report on the appointment of leader of the council and leader of the opposition, chief whip and opposition chief whip and their deputies. There may also be an item dealing with the appointment of political assistants – following an election the entitlement to political assistants may change (s. 9 LG&HA 1989). As to the allocation of time to the several items of business, see 7.33.

Notification of questions

6.36 Although questions proposed to be asked by members are not always specified in the agenda, there have to be arrangements to ensure that prior notice is given in order that answers can be prepared in advance of the meeting. The standing order in the Modular Constitution is as follows:

> **11.2 Questions on notice at full Council**
> Subject to Rule 11.4, a member of the Council may ask:
>
> - the chairman;
> - [a member of the executive in executive arrangements];
> - [the leader in alternative arrangements]; or
> - the chairman of any committee or sub-committee
>
> a question on any matter in relation to which the Council has powers or duties or which affects [the area].
>
> **11.3 Questions on notice at committees and sub-committees**
> Subject to Rule 11.4, a member of a committee or sub-committee may ask the chairman of it a question on any matter in relation to which the Council has powers or duties or which affect [the area] and which falls within the terms of reference of that committee or sub-committee.

10.7 Asking the question at the meeting
The chair will invite the questioner to put the question to the member named in the notice. If a questioner who has submitted a written question is unable to be present, they may ask the chairman to put the question on their behalf. The chairman may ask the question on the questioner's behalf, indicate that a written reply will be given, or decide, in the absence of the questioner, that the question will not be dealt with.

10.8 Supplemental question
A questioner who has put a question in person may also put one supplementary question without notice to the member who has replied to their original question. A supplementary question must arise directly out of the original question or the reply. The chairman may reject a supplementary question on any of the grounds in Rule 10.5 above relating to urgent business, of which such notice has not been given; but a copy of any such question shall, if possible, be delivered to the town clerk/clerk of the council not later than . . . o'clock in the morning of the day of the meeting.'

Question time at council meetings is dealt with in the following chapter.

6.37 In practice, officers will provide the leader of the council, executive members or committee chairman, as the case may be, with the basic facts and material for answering questions, or may provide them with a model answer. Care must be taken not to provide factual replies only and to ensure that members themselves put in whatever political take on the matter they wish. Questions are often put as a device to make a political point. Those asked of executive members are more likely to relate to the local authority's functions than any put to the leader of the council, but the comments on relevance in the case of original motions apply equally to questions.

Postponement and adjournment

Postponement

6.38 It is doubtful whether a council meeting, once convened, may properly be postponed in any circumstances: see *Smith v Paringa Mines Ltd* (1906), in which it was held in a company case that the postponement of a general meeting of shareholders was inoperative without special power to postpone being given by the regulations governing the meeting and therefore resolutions passed at a gathering of shareholders held in pursuance of the notice were valid and effective. It is unquestionably bad practice to cancel or abandon or postpone any meeting once it has been validly convened, and unlawful in any case to purport to postpone an annual council meeting to a date outside the prescribed statutory period for its convention. If circumstances make it impossible for the meeting to be held as convened (for example, the last-minute destruction of the council chamber or other meeting place), the proper course would seem to be to hold the meeting as nearly as possible in accordance with the notice and summons and then adjourn it. The purported postponement of a meeting is to be distinguished from failure to make a meeting.

Failure to make a meeting

6.39 Until a quorum is present, no council meeting can commence. In practice it is usual to wait a reasonable time to allow latecomers to assemble but, strictly, if a quorum does not exist at the time fixed for the commencement of the meeting, the meeting fails and those present are not competent to resolve upon its adjournment. It is therefore desirable (though in practice rare) for there to be a standing order to the effect that if a quorum is not present within, say, half an hour from the time appointed for the meeting, it shall stand adjourned. Alternatively, the meeting must be reconvened.

Effect of adjournment on convention

6.40 An adjourned meeting is part of the original meeting that it continues (*Scadding v Lorant* (1851)). It is not essential for notice of an adjourned meeting to be given (*Kerr v Wilkie* (1860)), but there is advantage in doing so. Nothing can be transacted at the adjourned meeting except the unfinished business of the original meeting (*R v Grimshaw* (1847)). Nevertheless, of course, there is nothing to stop a local authority from convening a separate meeting of the council to take place on the same day as the adjourned meeting – logically after the end of the adjourned meeting rather than before it – to conduct new business.
6.41 Because the rules of debate continue to apply to an adjourned meeting, a careful note needs to be kept of the names of members who have spoken already in a particular debate since under standing orders those members may not be entitled to speak again. This could cause considerable difficulty in adjourned budget meetings where the adjournment may come midway through the debate rather than at the end of a particular item of business. In such circumstances it is advisable to supply members with a note of the proceedings so far, who has spoken, and the procedure to be followed at the adjourned meeting. In practice, as most local authorities now record their meetings, a transcript can be supplied.

Meetings of the executive

6.42 Meetings of the executive are to be held in public or private under s. 22 LGA 2000 (as amended by the Localism Act 2011 Sch. 2), and subject to regulations made, it is for the executive to decide which meetings are to be public and which are to be private. A meeting must be held in public except where confidential information may be disclosed to the public in breach of confidence, or exempt information would be disclosed. The Local Authorities (Executive Arrangements) (Access to Information) (England) Regulations 2012 (SI 2012/2089) replaced the previous regulations (SI 2000/3272), and make provisions relating to public access to meetings. These regulations are now comparable to those made in Wales: see Local Authorities (Executive Arrangements) (Decisions, Documents and Meetings) (Wales) Regulations 2001, SI 2001/2290 (amended by SI 2002/1385, SI 2007/951).

The Regulations were changed in 2012 because the government believed that the previous Regulations did not provide maximum transparency, as the executive was only required to hold its meetings in public in limited circumstances, and could, in the main, choose whether to have a meeting in private or public. More information is contained in 'Your Council's cabinet – going to its meetings, seeing how it works', published by the DCLG in June 2013. The new rules also strengthened the rights of councillors outside the executive to access information.

Procedures prior to private meetings

6.43 The 2000 Regulations made provisions for a meeting to be held in private if it was likely that the advice of a political adviser or assistant would be disclosed, but this provision was left out of the 2012 Regulations. Exempt information has the same definition as previously; i.e. see s. 100I of the Local Government Act 1972 and Sch. 12A. The public may also be excluded for disruptive or unruly behaviour. Under reg. 5, the executive must make the public aware of the decision to hold a private meeting at least 28 clear days before the meeting, and publish notice on its website to that effect. The notice must include the reasons for holding the meeting in private. At least five clear days before a private meeting, a further notice must be published, and it must again include the reasons for the meeting being held in private, but should also include details of any representations made about why the meeting should not be held in private, and its response to those representations.

If the executive is not able to comply with the Regulations, then it must obtain agreement from the chairman of the relevant overview and scrutiny committee or chairman/mayor or, in their absence, the vice chairman/deputy mayor, that the meeting is urgent and cannot reasonably be deferred, Notice of the agreement must also be published, including on the website.

Procedures prior to public meetings

6.44 An item of business may only be considered if it has been available for inspection by the public for at least five clear days before the meeting, or from the time the meeting was convened (if shorter).

Under reg. 10, if it is impracticable for information regarding a key decision to be published, the proper officer must inform the chairman of the relevant overview and scrutiny committee that the executive wish to make a decision about the particular matter. If there is no chairman, then each and every member must be informed. The decision cannot be taken until five days have elapsed since the written notice given to the chairman or members was made publicly available. As soon as is reasonably practicable after informing the chairman, or members, the proper office must make available at the offices and publish on the website a notice setting out the reasons why it was impracticable for the information to be published. For matters of special urgency, see 6.51.

For the purposes of the Regulations, an officer briefing meeting for members is not to be treated as a meeting (SI 2002/716).

Exclusion of the public

6.45 The public may be excluded from any part of an executive meeting where:

1 it is likely that confidential information would be disclosed in breach of confidence;
2 it is likely that exempt information (as defined in Sch. 12A LGA 1972) would be disclosed; and
3 a lawful power is used to exclude a member or the public in order to maintain order or prevent misbehaviour at the meeting.

The Regulations set out that a resolution must be passed under (2) above, but in practice it is advisable to pass a resolution for all the above circumstances, and the resolution must set out the description of the exempt information, if applicable. The public may only be excluded for that part of the meeting during which it is likely that confidential or exempt information would be disclosed. For application, see Chapter 3.

Public access to agenda

6.46 There is an obligation to make copies of the agenda for a meeting and copies of any report for the meeting open to inspection by members of the public at its offices or on its website when they are made available to the executive or decision-making body, for five clear days before the date of the meeting, except that:

- where the meeting is convened at shorter notice, then the documents must be open to inspection from the time the meeting is convened; and
- where an item is added to an agenda afterwards, copies of any report relating to the item must be available for inspection from the time the item is added to the agenda.

This is very similar to the obligations under the LGA 1972; see 6.7 for a discussion of clear days and council offices.

6.47 Regulations (SI 2002/716) came into force on 1 October 2002 which required the three-clear-days period set out in SI 2000/3272 to be amended to five clear days in respect of England. The provisions for full council were brought into line on the same day (see 6.4).

6.48 There may be excluded from the copies of reports the whole or any part that relates only to items during which, in the opinion of the proper officer, the meeting is not likely to be open to the public. In such cases the copy report or the relevant part of it must be marked 'Not for publication' and a statement put on the report indicating either that it contains confidential information or, in the prescribed terms, the item of exempt information (LGA 1972, Sch. 12A) by virtue of which the council is likely to exclude the public during the item to which the report relates. The proper officer should act reasonably, i.e. take careful account of the circumstances, in forming their opinion. If the business is, in fact, dealt with in open session, the relevant papers should be handed out to the press representatives and the public present at the meeting.

6.49 A list of any background papers should be included in every report, and at least one copy must be available for inspection by members of the public at the council offices and on the website (reg. 15). A meeting must be held in public except where confidential information may be disclosed to the public in breach of confidence, or exempt information would be disclosed. Copies of the agenda and reports must be provided to the public or newspapers, if required, and the regulations provide that a reasonable fee can be charged for postage and copying. However, it would seem that a request could be made under the FOIA, and under that Act the council would not be able to charge (unless of course it met the statutory limits). But in practice, if requested under the FOIA, it is unlikely to arrive before the meeting!
6.50 The refusal or obstruction of access to the agenda and reports may be treated as an offence under reg. 23, for which a fine at level 1 can be imposed on summary conviction. There is no equivalent provision in the LGA 1972 in respect of council agendas and reports.

Urgent business

6.51 Unlike full council, the legislation provides that urgent business may be dealt with by the executive, provided certain criteria are fulfilled. If the business to be dealt with is a key decision, then agreement that the decision is urgent and cannot reasonably be deferred needs to obtained from the chairman of the relevant overview and scrutiny committee or, if there is no such person, the chairman of the authority, or, if there is no such person, the vice-chairman of the local authority (reg. 11 SI 2012/2089). Again, a notice must be published by the proper officer at its offices and on the website, setting out the reasons that the meeting cannot reasonably be deferred.
6.52 A report of urgent executive decisions should be made to the full council by the leader/mayor at such intervals as the council shall determine, and at least annually (reg. 19). Each report should set out the particulars of each decision and a summary.

Additional rights of access for members

6.53 In addition to the usual 'need to know' principles set out in 4.11, any member of a local authority has a right to inspect the agenda and reports of executive meetings.
6.54 Members are also entitled to inspect any document that relates to business transacted at a private meeting, or any decision made by an individual member with delegated authority, or any key decision made by an officer with delegated authority, at the end of the meeting or after the decision has been taken, as appropriate (reg. 16). However, this does not apply where this would involve the disclosure of exempt information (Sch. 12A LGA 1972). The exception to this is information of the type contained in para. 3 (except where this relates to contract negotiations) and para. 6, or the advice of a political adviser or assistant.
6.55 Members of overview and scrutiny committees have additional rights of access. A member is entitled to a copy of any document in the possession of the executive and that contains material relating to any business or decisions made by officers or the executive. If the document contains exempt or confidential information, then a

member is not entitled to a copy unless the information is relevant to any action or decision that is being reviewed or scrutinised in the work programme. Members are not entitled to any documentation that contains the advice of political advisers/assistants. Copies must be provided within ten days or else the executive must give written reasons for the decision to withhold.

In practice, this provision of inspection can be satisfied by making agendas and reports available at the council offices; they do not have to be sent to each member.

6.56 It is a criminal offence if a person, without reasonable excuse, refuses to supply the whole or part of a document which is required to be publicly available, or intentionally obstructs another. This is a level one offence, with a fine of up to £200 (reg. 22 2012/2089).

Notes

1 LGA 1972, Sch. 12, paras. 15(2), 30(2).
2 What is a conspicuous place is a question of fact: *West Hero Corporation v Thomas* (1908).
3 The 'proper officer' could sign the notice under s. 234 of the 1972 Act; and thereunder 'signature' includes a facsimile of a signature by whatever process reproduced. As to the proper officer, see 5.18.
4 LGA 1972, Sch. 12: Pt III, para. 15(2); Pt V, para. 30(2). See also as to public notice of a parish meeting: s. 233(2).
5 *Kynaston v Shrewsbury Corporation* (1736); *sub nom. R v Shrewsbury Corporation*, Lee *temp.* Hard 147; *Smyth v Varley* (1849); even though dispensed with by a particular member: *R v Langborn* (1836); see also *Mayor, Constables and Company of Merchants of the Staple of England v Governor and Company of the Bank of England* (1887).
6 It may be thought prudent for the chairman's consent to the transaction of urgent business to be put into writing and signed with the reason why the business is regarded by the chairman as urgent. There is nothing to stop the chairman consulting whomsoever they wish in arriving at their decision.
7 Although this may be done 'as soon as practicable after the meeting': LG&HA 1989, s. 15.

Chapter 7
Conduct

General character of proceedings

Introduction

7.1 Proceedings and the business transacted at a meeting of a principal, parish or community council, i.e. of the full council, must:

- take place in public except to the extent that the public is required to be excluded; (i) in the case of a principal council either during an item of business whenever it is likely that confidential information (see 3.4) would be disclosed in breach of the obligation of confidence or by resolution whenever there would otherwise be disclosure of exempt information (see 3.11); (ii) in the case of any other authority when the council by resolution excludes the public because publicity would be prejudicial to the public interest (see 3.22);
- follow any order prescribed by statute and standing orders or as set out in the agenda: the order of business is regulated by statute only in the case of the annual meeting of a principal council which prescribes that the election of chairman must be the first item (see 6.34);
- have been set out in the notice where the meeting has been convened by councillors (see 6.2) and in every case in the summons and in the case of principal councils in the agenda and accompanying reports (see 6.22): the transaction of business that is outside the scope of a notice convening a meeting will not render the whole meeting irregular: *Re British Sugar Refining Co.* (1857); and
- be *intra vires*, i.e. within the scope of the authority's powers and duties. In practice, local authorities sometimes pass resolutions on matters over which they have no jurisdiction but in which the local community may have an interest. There is no reason why they should not do so, but a resolution to act in defiance of the law is clearly *ultra vires*.

In addition, the meeting itself must be properly constituted, i.e. it must have been lawfully convened by public notice and individual summons to councillors entitled to attend (see above), the proper person must be in the chair, and a quorum must be present.

Insignia

7.2 The civic mayor, in the case of a borough (or lord mayor in the case of a city with charter), will wear the robes and chain of office at a council meeting, and the chair, in other cases, a badge of office. Robes may also be worn by the deputy mayor, and ex-mayor's badges by councillors who have held the mayoralty; but it is in comparatively few boroughs that they wear robes. Most important of the insignia at council meetings is the mace, which is the emblem of power and dignity of the mayor and the symbol of authority. All boroughs, except new boroughs created under the LGA 1972 and unitaries under the LGA 1992, have at least one mace and many have two or more; and in every case the mace (or maces) is (or are) carried by the mace-bearer into the council chamber preceding the mayor and placed in position horizontally before the mayor (with the crown to the right or in the more important direction) to remain there while the council is in session, and then carried in procession in front of the mayor on leaving. The deputy mayor, when acting on the mayor's behalf at council meetings (but no one else), is entitled to have the mace precede them.

Opening ceremony

7.3 Most local authorities open proceedings in the full assembly with a modicum of ceremony, adding to the dignity of council proceedings. In the case of a borough it is usual, after council members have assembled, for the mayor and chief executive (preceded by the mace-bearer) to enter the council chamber in procession; and for the members and public to stand on their entry either as a matter of course or upon the announcement of the mace-bearer: 'Ladies and gentlemen: Be upstanding for His Worship the Mayor.' In many instances the meeting is closed in somewhat similar manner.

Prayers

7.4 In some authorities it is the custom for proceedings to begin with prayers. Where the practice is followed, prayers are usually led by the mayor or chairman's chaplain (ordinarily an honorary post to which an appointment is made personally by the mayor or chairman) or in some cases by local preachers or as custom may dictate. A number of authorities have a standard council prayer specifically drafted for the purpose, often by representatives of local churches. In the event that the chaplain is unable to attend, the prayer is generally led by the chief executive. In 2012, in the case of *R (on the application of the National Secular Society and another) v Bideford Town Council* (2012), Ousely J held that local authorities had no power to hold prayers as part a formal council meeting or to summon councillors to a meeting at which prayers were on the agenda, and therefore that such actions were *ultra vires*. It has been stated that the general power of competence contained in s. 1 of the Localism Act 2011 (which came into force for all local authorities other than parish councils on 18 February 2012) provides the statutory authority for holding prayers during formal meetings of local authorities. There are, however, contrary views. In practice, many councils have avoided the issue by not including prayers as part of the formal agenda and holding them prior to the start of the meeting.

Council meetings

Business generally

7.5 The nature of the proceedings will vary according to the purpose of the meeting. Thus an annual meeting, apart from essential business (such as the election of a chairman and the appointment of committees for the ensuing year), is largely of a ceremonial character (particularly in the case of mayor-making); and an extraordinary meeting will be concerned as a rule with one item of business alone. Ordinary meetings will follow a fairly uniform pattern and the greater part of the business will be the consideration of committee/cabinet reports. So long, however, as an authority observes statutory requirements and does not violate the common law rules governing meetings procedure (including its own standing orders), the conduct of proceedings is for each authority to decide.

7.6 Business is ordinarily conducted in a formal manner and this means that for the greater part, discussion takes place upon a motion before the full council. It is a convention that officers do not participate in any way (although the chief executive or monitoring officer may be called upon to advise on procedure or they or any other chief officer may exceptionally be invited to speak). This means, as a general rule, that the officers' influence over proceedings and the efficient and effective dispatch of business is limited to preparatory work beforehand, i.e. in the preparation of council papers, the careful briefing of the chairman and the leader of the council, portfolio holders and committee chairmen, the stage-managing of procedure, and attention to the several matters relating to the physical conditions of the council chamber or other accommodation in which the meeting is to be held.

7.7 There is no reason in law why officers should not be invited to participate in council meetings just as they do in committee or cabinet: it is usually a matter of convention and practicality. With very large meetings it can be difficult to control proceedings where there is constant reference to officers whose views are then interpreted by members for purposes of the debate. On balance, therefore, it is better to restrict discussion to members themselves, particularly since in many authorities – certainly the larger ones – items will already have been discussed by the cabinet and/or in committees. However, it is important to ensure that decisions are not taken based on incorrect or misunderstood facts; and if this possibility arises, then officers should be given the opportunity to correct them or provide an accurate interpretation.

Confirmation of minutes

7.8 The confirmation of the minutes of the previous meeting is always placed as an early item on the agenda. The standing order in the modular Constitution is to this effect:

> **'18. Minutes**
> **18.1 Signing the minutes**
> The chairman will sign the minutes of the proceedings at the next suitable meeting. The chairman will move that the minutes of the previous meeting be signed as a correct record. The only part of the minutes that can be discussed is their accuracy.'

7.9 The minutes of an extraordinary meeting of the council can be confirmed at the next following ordinary meeting. One of the mandatory standing orders[1] is to this effect:

> 'Where in relation to any meeting of the authority the next such meeting is a meeting called under paragraph 3 (extraordinary meetings) or Schedule 12 to the Local Government Act 1972, the next following meeting of the authority (being a meeting called otherwise than under that paragraph) shall be treated as a suitable meeting for the purposes of paragraph 41(1) and (2) (signing of minutes) of that Schedule.'[2]

Behaviour of members

7.10 Although there are some forms of behaviour that are not expected of members present at a council meeting, e.g. conduct that is so disorderly as to interrupt business, there are no widely accepted conventions otherwise governing councillors' behaviour (although often members are expected to show respect to the chair when entering or leaving the council chamber and in some councils to stand when addressing the chair) and few other instances where behaviour is regulated by standing orders. One reason for this may be that it would be difficult to require members to comply, because in the final resort there is no power to exclude a councillor – probably not even temporarily – from a council meeting at which they are lawfully entitled to be present.

7.11 The standing orders of the House of Commons do contain several restrictions on the conduct of Members of Parliament in the House and the Speaker is endowed with formidable authority to secure compliance. MPs are required to keep in their places and not rove around the chamber; they must not read any book, newspaper or letter in their places except in connection with the business of the House; they are not permitted to wear decorations or uniforms and it is the custom for Members to wear jackets and ties; they may not smoke during any of the proceedings of the House, nor may refreshments be brought into or consumed in the chamber. It may seem strange, in view of the noisy behaviour often heard when proceedings in the Commons are broadcast, that members are expected to maintain silence or converse only in undertones, that members must not disturb a member who is speaking by hissing or interruption and that cries of 'Shame!' are strongly condemned. The Lords is directed by standing orders to maintain dignity and order. It may be thought that a council standing order to similar effect might be of advantage and there is no reason why an authority should not introduce one if it so wished.

Addressing the chair

7.12 Councillors are often expected (and standing orders will often so provide) to stand when speaking at a council meeting and always to address the chair. Whether the term 'Sir' or 'Chair', 'Chairman or Madam-Chairman' or 'Mr or Madam Mayor' is employed is a matter of local custom (but 'Mr or Madam Mayor' can never properly be shortened to 'Mayor'). Shortly after the Sex Discrimination Act 1975 came into effect, the term 'Chairperson' was favoured in some quarters but has not been widely adopted, if at all. The practice has grown up in the majority of local authorities now of referring to a committee chairman (as it is described in the LGA 1972) as 'Chair'. Some councillors, in occupying the chair, object to being addressed as a piece of furniture or as a verb. However, this is a matter of local taste and most councillors and certainly most officers would now more usually use the term 'chair' first and amend their term of address only if required to do so afterwards.

The chairman or chair

Electing the chair of the council

7.13 The chairman (see above) of a principal, parish or community council must be elected annually from among the councillors and the election must be the first business transacted at the council's annual meeting. It was decided in *R v McGowan* (1840) that any business carried out before the election of the chairman – in that case the election of aldermen – was void, but the election of the chairman was valid: see also *R v Parkyns* (1828). Anyone so elected cannot act in the office until the prescribed declaration of acceptance of the office has been made, which usually follows on immediately after the election.

Procedure on election

7.14 No procedure for the election is prescribed by statute and it is rare for standing orders to do so. In practice, councillors often agree upon a nominee beforehand (in the majority party group where the authority is run on party political lines with or without informal agreement with minority parties) so that at the annual meeting there is usually only one nomination proposed and seconded: a prior arrangement of this kind enables someone other than the nominee to preside at their. Most standing orders provide for appointments, and an elimination vote can be used where there are more than two nominees (which does not often occur). A succession of votes are taken, on each of which the nominee receiving the fewest votes is excluded from the next vote. This position, as with the leader in leader and cabinet executive forms, is rare in specifying it is an election and a direct ballot is the means by which the election is held, unless standing orders specify otherwise.

7.15 Voting at the election proceeds in the normal way, i.e. the election is decided by a majority of the councillors present and voting. The person presiding at the meeting must give a casting vote in the case of an equality of votes;[3] but where the person presiding only remains a member because of the saving provisions for chairman and vice-chairman, they are not entitled to any other vote.[4] Most authorities try to avoid contested elections for the chair or mayor, particularly in the case of boroughs where mayor-making is regarded as an important civic and ceremonial event and lack of unanimity is hardly conducive to the dignity of the occasion. One authority claims to have avoided the repetition of an earlier disaster where the chairman-elect failed to be elected to the annoyance of the majority group and the embarrassment of relatives who were present to see him installed: it holds what is in effect a 'shadow' annual meeting, which recommends a nominee for election and although there still remains the possibility of unexpected challenge, this has not occurred.

Failure to elect

7.16 If a council fails to elect a chairman the council is not properly constituted[5] and (except in the case of the chairmanship of a parish or community council or meeting) the High Court may direct the election to be held at a time fixed by the court. Despite the mandatory terms of the law as to election annually, it would not seem improper for a council to elect a chairman pro tem, but the term of office should be clearly stated.

Adjournment of election

7.17 A council may for a specific reason wish to adjourn the election for a short period, either until later in the proceedings (perhaps because of the absence of a particular councillor who is a candidate or of the proposer of a candidate) or to a later meeting (e.g. for political reasons). It would seem, on a strict interpretation of the terms of the statute, that this cannot be done: the election must be the first item of business. It may be, however, that an adjournment of the meeting could meet the circumstances, although other difficulties might be created.

7.18 On the other hand, it is arguable that the law does not require that someone shall necessarily be elected but only that the first business shall be the election. Therefore, so long as the question of election is considered as the first item of business, the decision on that consideration could be to adjourn the election. This is probably not a persuasive argument: indeed, the fact that the person presiding at the election is compelled to give a second or casting vote in the event of an equality of votes, seems additional support for the view that Parliament's intention was that the election must take place so that the council can be properly constituted.

Election of disqualified councillor

7.19 If the person elected as chairman is disqualified from being a councillor, it would seem that the election is nevertheless valid by the terms of s. 82 of the LGA 1972 (as amended), which provides that:

> '[(1)] The acts and proceedings of any person elected to an office under this Act [or elected or appointed to an office under Part . . . IV of the Local Government Act 1985] [or elected as elected mayor or executive leader] and acting in that office shall, notwithstanding his disqualification or want of qualification, be as valid and effectual as if he had been qualified.'

In *Forrester v Norton* (1911), it was held that since the election of the councillor had not been challenged by an election petition, they were a councillor de facto whose election as chairman was rendered valid by s. 73 of the Municipal Corporations Act 1882 (now s. 82 of the LGA 1972). This would not extend, it is submitted, to validate the election to the chairmanship of a person who is not de facto a councillor.

Presiding at one's own election

7.20 It is well established that a person who presides at an election is disqualified from being a candidate. In *R v Owens* (1858), the mayor of a borough had presided over the election of councillors and, as returning officer, had returned himself as one of the persons elected; the validity of this election was successfully impeached. Local practice, no matter how long established, cannot justify disregard of this rule: see *R v Reynolds* (1896).

Vacation of chair before election

7.21 However, if an outgoing chairman wishes to be re-elected, they can provide a substitute to perform their functions temporarily (see *R v White* (1867)). This in practice is what is ordinarily done, though it means that a person must be proposed as a candidate before the election. If, while presiding, their name is put forward as a candidate, they cannot then vacate the chair because the proposal made while they occupy the chair would be void. It means also that an outgoing chairman wishing to be re-elected must not preside and further must not be in the meeting,[6] because if they are present, they must preside.

Failure to give notice of election

7.22 There is authority for the view that the election of a chairman at a meeting for which notice has not been given is invalid. In *R v Langborn* (1836), in an action impeaching the validity of a mayoral election, the jury found that one of the burgesses (all of whom were entitled to vote) had not been served with a notice of the meeting at which the mayor was elected, and it was held that the mayor was not duly elected. The statutory provision that stipulates that want of service of a summons on any member shall not affect the validity of a meeting of a principal, parish or community council would seem to avoid challenge on these grounds. It might be, however, that the election of a chairman of a parish or community meeting would be held invalid if the requisite notices of such a meeting were not given.

The vice-chair

Appointment

7.23 A principal council must[7] and a parish and community council may[8] appoint a member of the council to be vice-chairman of the council. The LGA 1972 follows the wording of the former 1933 Act and refers to the appointment and not the election of a vice-chairman, but the difference in term is of no significance. The vice-chairman, unless they resign or become disqualified, holds office until immediately after the election of a chairman at the next annual meeting.[9] During that time they continue to be a member of the council notwithstanding the statutory provisions relating to the retirement of councillors.[10] Where a parish or community council decides always to have a vice-chairman, it may be convenient to adopt old model standing order no. 2, which is to the effect that: 'The council shall at the annual meeting appoint a vice-chairman'.

7.24 What has been said earlier about the procedure for the election of a chairman applies equally to the appointment of a vice-chairman.

7.25 Subject to standing orders, anything authorised or required to be done by, to or before the chairman may be done by, to or before the vice-chairman.[11] Standing orders can place such restrictions upon the vice-chairman's powers as the council thinks appropriate, except that it would not be lawful for standing orders to prohibit the vice-chairman from presiding at a meeting of the full council in the absence of the chairman, because the law expressly requires them if present to take the chair.

Who presides?

Principal councils

7.26 The chairman of the council (or the mayor) if present at a meeting of the full assembly of a principal council must preside. If, for any reason, they vacate the chair, they must leave the meeting so as not to contravene this specific statutory direction that they must preside if present. In *Re Wolverhampton Borough Council's Aldermanic Election* (1961), which concerned an election of aldermen for which the mayor was a candidate, the mayor vacated the chair just before the council proceeded to the election of aldermen but he delivered a voting paper and remained in the council chamber. Glyn-Jones J said:

> 'In my opinion it was Parliament's intention that at a meeting of the council the mayor's place, and his only place, should be in the chair. Seated in the mayoral chair he can exercise all his one and indivisible functions . . . When he is not in the mayoral chair . . . then, since his functions are one and indivisible, he has lost his right to exercise any of them so far as taking part in the meeting is concerned.'

7.27 If the chairman is absent from the meeting of a principal council, then:[12]

- the vice-chairman of the council, if present, must preside; and
- in the case of a London borough council (other than one that operates executive arrangements involving a mayor and cabinet executive), the deputy mayor, if at that time they remain a councillor and are chosen for that purpose by the members of the council then present, must preside.

if:

- in the case of a principal council, both the chairman and vice-chairman of the council are absent from a meeting of the council, another member of the council chosen by the members of the council present must preside. However, a member of the executive of a principal council may not be chosen; and
- in the case of a London borough council (other than one that operates executive arrangements involving a mayor and cabinet executive), the mayor and deputy mayor are so absent or the deputy mayor being present is not chosen, another member of the council chosen by the members of the council present must preside. Again, a member of the executive may not be chosen.

Parish and community councils

7.28 The chairman of the council must preside at a meeting of a parish council or a community council as the case may be if present at the meeting.[13] If the chairman is absent from the meeting, the vice-chairman, if present, must preside.[14] If both the chairman and the vice-chairman are absent from the meeting, then such councillor as the members of the council present shall choose must preside.[15]

Parish and community meetings

7.29 In a parish having a separate parish council, the chairman of the parish council, if present, must preside at a parish meeting; and if they are absent the vice-chairman, if any, must, if present, preside. In a parish that does not have a separate parish council, the chairman chosen for the year in question must, if present, preside. If the chairman and the vice-chairman of the parish council or the chairman of the parish meeting, as the case may be, is absent from an assembly of the parish meeting, the parish meeting may appoint a person to take the chair and that person has, for the purposes of that meeting, the powers and authority of the chairman. In a community for which there is a community council, the chairman of the council, if present, must preside at the community meeting (LGA 1972, Sch. 12).

In any other case, a community meeting must appoint a person to be chairman at that meeting (LGA 1972, Sch. 12, para. 33(1)).

Powers and duties of person presiding

Generally

7.30 Upon taking the chair at a meeting, the chairman (or whoever may be presiding) becomes invested with authority to regulate and control proceedings for the purposes of the meeting. The powers and duties of the chairman are not prescribed by statute (except in certain limited respects: they have conferred upon them, for example, the power to give a second or casting vote in the case of an equality of votes (see 7.115)), but derive from standing orders and common law. They collect their authority from the meeting.

7. Conduct

7.31 So long as the chairman acts bona fide and remains in the chair, they have virtually absolute rule. Admittedly the full council could by majority decision dislodge the person presiding (see *Booth v Arnold* (1895)), but not if they are the chairman of the council or the vice-chairman of the council, because the duly elected chairman of a principal or parish or community council remains in office until they resign of their own accord, or becomes disqualified, and if present at a council meeting must preside, as must a vice-chairman if present in the absence of the chairman. While acting in good faith the chairman's decisions, even if not strictly correct, will be upheld by the court, provided no substantial injustice has arisen as a result. It strengthens a chairman's position if a local authority adopts a standing order on the lines of the model standing order in the Modular Constitution, which is to this effect:

> 'The ruling of the [chairman of council] [mayor in boroughs and cities with leader and cabinet executive or alternative arrangements] as to the construction or application of this Constitution or as to any proceedings of the Council shall not be challenged at any meeting of the Council. Such an interpretation shall have regard to the purposes of this Constitution contained in Article 1.
>
> If, however, the chairman acts improperly or mala fide his decisions are not binding, and in a proper case the court will intervene. The proper course for anyone who considers that a ruling of a chairman is erroneous is to seek an order of the court compelling the chairman to convene a fresh meeting: the court will not ordinarily interfere unless the complaint of irregularity comes from a representative majority of the meeting, but if a specific individual right is infringed action could be taken by the party aggrieved.'

Specific functions

7.32 From judicial decisions there has emerged a widely recognised catalogue of powers and duties of a chairman. Thus it is the duty and function of the chairman (see *National Dwellings Society v Sykes* (1894)): to preserve order, and to take care that the proceedings are conducted in a proper manner, and that the sense of the meeting is properly ascertained with regard to any question which is properly before the meeting.

More specifically it is the chairman's responsibility, at council meetings, to:

(a) determine that the meeting is properly constituted and that a quorum is present;
(b) inform themselves as to the business and objects of the meeting;
(c) preserve order in the conduct of those present;
(d) confine discussion within the scope of the meeting and reasonable limits to time;
(e) decide whether proposed motions and amendments are in order;
(f) formulate for discussion and decision questions that have been moved for the consideration of the meeting;
(g) decide points of order and other incidental questions that require decision at the time (see *Re Indian Zoedone Co.* (1884));

(h) ascertain the sense of the meeting by:

- putting relevant questions to the meeting and taking a vote thereon (and if so minded, giving a casting vote):
- declaring the result; and
- causing a ballot to be taken if duly demanded;

(i) approve the draft of the minutes or other record of proceedings;
(j) adjourn the meeting when circumstances justify or require that course; and
(k) declare the meeting closed when its business has been completed.

The chairman's responsibility under (j) to adjourn the meeting must not be taken to mean that the power of adjournment vests solely in the chairman. A chairman cannot adjourn a meeting without the consent, express or implied, of those present. There could be implied consent in exceptional circumstances when, for example, a member may have collapsed and died in the course of proceedings. The right of adjournment is vested in the assembly but in practice, of course, only the person presiding can declare the assembly's decision to adjourn. As to the effect of an improper adjournment by a chairman, see below.

Allocation of time

7.33 Although it is in general the responsibility of the person presiding to ensure the orderly and efficient despatch of business and so to conduct proceedings that a requisite amount of time is allotted to the several items of business, those present can properly seek to influence the progress of business.

Quorum

General considerations

7.34 A quorum is the minimum number of members whose presence is necessary at a meeting for the valid transaction of business. In the absence of special custom or particular regulation, by statute or otherwise, a majority of the members of a body must be present at a duly convened assembly in order that an effective meeting should exist (*Mayor, Constables and Company of Merchants of the Staple of England v Governor and Company of the Bank of England* (1887). In the case of local authorities, a quorum is prescribed by statute for meetings of a principal, parish and community council but not for meetings of committees and sub-committees (LGA 1972, Sch. 12, paras. 6, 12, 18).
7.35 If a quorum is not present at a council meeting, any business transacted is (generally speaking) invalid. The mere fortuitous assembly of the requisite minimum number of councillors can never constitute a meeting for the purpose of transacting valid business, because there must be an intention to meet known to all members entitled to attend – i.e. there are, as already indicated, statutory formalities in regard to notice and summons which must be observed before a meeting may properly be held.

Statutory regulation

7.36 Subject to what is said below, no business may be transacted at a meeting of:

- a principal council, unless at least one-quarter of the whole number of members of the council are present (LGA 1972, Sch. 12, para. 6); and
- a parish or community council, unless at least one-third of the whole number of members of the council are present but in no case is the quorum to be less than three (LGA 1972, Sch. 12, paras. 12, 28).

The old model standing order reads:

> 'The quorum of a meeting will be one quarter of the whole number of members. During any meeting if the chairman counts the number of members present and declares there is not a quorum present, then the meeting will adjourn immediately. Remaining business will be considered at a time and date fixed by the chairman. If he/she does not fix a date, the remaining business will be considered at the next ordinary meeting.'

There is no statutory regulation in respect of meetings of the executive, and it is for them to set their own quorum (LGA 2000 Sch. A1, para. 3 (in England) and Sch. 1 para. 4 (in Wales)). However, the ordinary meaning of the word 'meeting' indicates that there must be a coming together of two or more people (see 1.8) and so a quorum cannot be fewer than two.

Calculation of quorum

7.37 The quorum is ordinarily calculated in relation to 'the whole number of members of the council', and this means the total number of seats: *Newhaven Local Board v Newhaven School Board* (1885). If, however, more than one-third of the members of the authority become disqualified at the same time, then – until the number of members in office is increased to not less than two-thirds of the whole number of members of the authority, i.e. seats – the quorum must be determined by reference to the number of members remaining qualified instead of by reference to the whole number of members. This provision is intended to meet the situation where a considerable number of members, i.e. more than one-third, are disqualified. If seats are vacant for other reasons, e.g. by reason of death or resignation, then these can be taken into account in calculating the total number of members. Members who have died or resigned clearly must not be counted with members who are disqualified.

Duration of quorum

7.38 Is it necessary, once a meeting has commenced with the requisite quorum present, for that quorum to be present throughout the meeting or at least present at the time a vote is taken? This can indeed pose a difficulty with the increasing length of meetings and the trend towards informality. The legal position appears to vary between company meetings, parliamentary business and council meetings. There seems to be a widespread perception that the local government position is similar to the parliamentary one, i.e. that proceedings should continue until attention is drawn to the absence of a quorum. While this may be a reasonable and practical course to adopt, particularly during lengthy debates, the legal position is clear and somewhat different: any business transacted at a council meeting in the absence of a quorum is invalid. So care should be taken to ensure that the requisite number of members is present whenever a decision is taken.

7.39 An old draft core standing order put forward by the working party is set out below:

> ‘0–1 If, during any meeting of the council, the person presiding, after causing the number of members present to be counted, declares that there is not a quorum present, the meeting shall stand adjourned for fifteen minutes.
>
> 2 If, after fifteen minutes, the person presiding, after again causing the number of members present to be counted, declares that there is still no quorum present, the meeting shall end.
>
> 3 Notwithstanding any provision in these standing orders that notices of questions or motions shall lapse, the consideration of all business which is on the agenda of a meeting brought to an end under the previous paragraph and which has not been completed before the meeting is brought to an end shall be postponed to the next meeting of the council, whether ordinary or extraordinary.’

This goes further than the standing order in the modular constitution, presumably to provide an opportunity to continue with the meeting if members have left the room for a period of time on other business.

Question time

Types of question

7.40 Many local authorities devote an allotted time to questions at every council meeting. Widdicombe attached importance to question time ‘as a means by which minority parties and “backbench” councillors may not only obtain information but also call the majority party to account’. There are, therefore, in effect two types of question: the spontaneous question, which may be asked at any time without notice; and the deliberate question, which, because of its character and the need usually for some research or verification of facts before an answer can be prepared, requires advance written notice. Questions can be set out in the agenda and this is a matter of preference, and many authorities record both questions and answers in council minutes.

Spontaneous questions

7.41 The model standing order in the Modular Constitution provides, in part, the following:

> **'11.1 On reports of [the executive or] committees**
> A member of the Council may ask [*in leader form of executive the leader*] [*in mayoral forms of executive* the mayor or the] chairman of a committee any question without notice upon an item of the report of [the executive or] a committee when that item is being received or under consideration by the Council.'

In some authorities, portfolio holders now also make a report to the full council and this standing order should be amended accordingly. Whether or not the committee chairman/portfolio holder answers will depend upon the question. If necessary, the chairman can always ask the member concerned to give notice or offer to provide the answer later.

Deliberate questions

7.42 The model standing order in the Modular Constitution relating to questions is set out in 6.36.

7.43 There are many ways in which question time can be regulated. If the authority sets a time limit for question time then it might permit members to ballot for a specified number to be answered orally and the remainder dealt with by written answer, much in the manner of parliamentary procedure. It is also a matter for consideration whether a councillor's question should be answered if they are absent when the question is called or, alternatively, provision made by standing orders that:

> 'If a member who has submitted a question is not present when the question is called, the question may, with the consent of the council, be asked by any other member.'

Widdicombe proposed that it should be obligatory on all local authorities to provide for question time at council meetings. 'The precise form of the requirement,' it said, 'would need further consideration but it should be limited to questions from councillors as opposed to questions from the public gallery,' and the arrangement should provide for:

- a reasonable time limit (at least 30 minutes);
- questions to be handed to the chief executive and addressed to the leader or the chairman of the responsible committee;
- a reply to be given unless there is good reason to the contrary (e.g. confidentiality); and

- a right to at least one supplementary question, with the questioner having priority.

This substantially reflects common practice, but with the complexity and range of council activities question time can sometimes still take up a disproportionate share of time at council meetings. Some authorities limit the length of the question to two minutes and one minute for a supplementary question, to try to shorten the time taken. Time can be shortened by arranging for questions and answers to be circulated prior to or at the beginning of the meeting. Setting up a procedure for question time at committees/cabinet also helps relieve pressure on time at meetings of the full council.

Petitions and deputations

Petitions

7.44 The Local Democracy, Economic Development and Construction Act 2009 briefly required a principal local authority to create a petitions scheme. The provisions of the 2009 Act regarding petitions came into force on 15 June 2010 and were repealed by the Localism Act 2011 with effect from 1 April 2012. For the majority of local authorities, processes for dealing with petitions were already in place and petitions submitted to a local authority by a body of its citizens were usually presented to the full council by one of the council members. Some councils have removed or amended the provisions regarding petitions from their constitutions following the repeal of the statutory requirements, while others have retained the schemes introduced under the 2009 Act. Practice varies, but as a rule, no speech or debate is permitted on the petition that, either on the motion of the member presenting it or of the chairman or automatically under standing orders, is referred to the appropriate committee or cabinet for consideration.

Deputations

7.45 A local authority may also receive a deputation at a council meeting when the issue is thought sufficiently important to justify that course rather than refer the deputation to an appropriate committee or the cabinet.

Public participation

7.46 One of the old draft model standing orders prepared by the Association of Council Secretaries and Solicitors (see 2.3) was to this effect:

> 'The chairman [of the council] will indicate the time at which questions may be put to him by individual members of the public. If the chairman rules a question to be proper (particularly in that it refers to a matter of general concern and not the affairs of an individual named or not), the chairman may ask a

member or an officer to respond. The time allowed for questions and answers shall not, without the consent of the council, exceed fifteen minutes, or in the case of one questioner, five minutes. Written questions may be entertained and written response may be used. Questions and responses shall not be matters for debate.'

Motions

Discussion out of order otherwise

7.47 Discussion and debate at a council meeting will ordinarily only be permitted on a motion properly before the full council: that is to say, any matter before the meeting for consideration must be expressed as a motion in positive terms to adopt a certain course of action or to do some act or declare a particular attitude. When passed by a majority of the members present and voting, with or without amendment, the motion becomes a resolution.

Types of motion

7.48 Motions are broadly of two types: original and procedural. The first, defined more explicitly below in the local government context, is one propounding a substantial issue for consideration and action; a procedural motion (see 7.70), sometimes called a formal motion, and which includes a dilatory motion, is one affecting matters of procedure or form. An amendment is a motion to amend the main proposition before the meeting.

Original motions

7.49 An original motion may not be moved at a council meeting unless prior notice has been given so that its terms may be included in the agenda. This is necessary so as to comply with the statutory requirement that the summons to attend (and, sometimes, the notice of) the meeting must specify the business to be transacted (see 6.1). The procedure for giving notice and the consequential steps are usually prescribed in standing orders. Only one original motion can be before the council at any one time.
7.50 The model standing order from the Modular Constitution on notices of motion is set out below:

'12.1 Notice
Except for motions which can be moved without notice under Rule 12, written notice of every motion, signed by at least [n] members, must be delivered to the [proper officer] not later than [*time*] before the date of the meeting. These will be entered into a book open to public inspection.

12.2 Motions set out in agenda

Motions for which notice has been given will be listed on the agenda in the order in which the notice was received, unless the member giving notice states, in writing, that they propose to move it to a later meeting or withdraw it.

12.3 Scope

Motions must be about matters for which the Council has a responsibility or which affect [*the area*].'

7.51 There are in practice countless variations of the foregoing in use, but the general effect is much the same in every case. What is important is that the arrangements for giving notice to the proper officer are clearly set out and well understood by members. Standing orders usually require notice to be in the hands of the proper officer at least seven working days before the date of the meeting. Arguments about when and where a notice was sent by post can be embarrassing: if possible, a standing order requiring personal delivery is to be preferred and officers should ensure that the date and time received are clearly recorded.

Motions that stand referred

7.52 Where a motion stands referred without discussion to a committee when proposed and seconded, the proposer has no right to a speech, introductory or otherwise. It is submitted that the proposer could, under standing orders, with the consent of the council and without seeking to explain the reason, alter the wording of the motion. The term 'without discussion' means precisely that. No one may speak and there can be no discussion unless the chairman allows the motion to be dealt with at the meeting at which it is brought forward, i.e. it does not stand referred. Nor, if it stands referred, is any amendment permissible. This is because the council, in referring the motion to a committee for consideration and report, is neither accepting nor rejecting it. If a councillor wishes to make a point essential to the motion, they can do so in one or both of two ways: they can ask to be allowed to attend and speak at the committee meeting at which the motion is to be considered (indeed they may be so entitled under standing orders); and they will in any case ultimately have an opportunity of participating in the debate when the committee's report comes before the full council.

Rejected notices of motion

7.53 The proper officer must consider whether the motion of which notice has been given is one that may properly be accepted. If it is and notice has been given in time, then they must proceed to place it on the agenda for the next council meeting. If they consider the terms of the motion out of order, illegal, irregular or improper, they should consult the chairman and/or the leader, or take such other action as may be laid down in standing orders. In any case, if a motion is rejected, the member giving notice should be advised. A standing order covering these matters might be framed in these words:

> If notice is given of any original motion that, in the opinion of the proper officer, is out of order, illegal, irregular or improper, the proper officer shall immediately submit such notice to the chairman and it shall not be accepted and placed on the agenda without his sanction. In the event of non-acceptance, the proper officer shall inform the member giving notice.

7.54 A motion that seeks to require the local authority to do something that it patently cannot would be out of order and one that sought action that was *ultra vires* or otherwise illegal would similarly be out of order. One that was defamatory or offensive could be ruled out as improper. But a motion ought not to be rejected merely because it refers to matters that are not within the scope of the authority's powers and duties. What may be relevant for the council's consideration is a difficult question to determine. A motion protesting against the raising of railway fares, for example, may be considered relevant, in that it may affect the council's housing tenants or employees and have an impact on staff recruitment or the letting of houses. There are some topics of general interest to the local citizens on behalf of whom the council may deem itself the proper representative body to express opinion; but there are limits to this. Expressions of opinion on foreign affairs, for example, are not the concern of local government and are not appropriate for debate by a local council.
7.55 A motion that is rejected must nevertheless be recorded in the book kept for that purpose and a note made to the effect that it was rejected.
7.56 A motion may also be rejected on the grounds that it is vague and equivocal in its terms: and in such circumstances it may properly be returned to the member with an indication to that effect and need not, it is submitted, be recorded in any way until it has been resubmitted in acceptable form. Whether a motion that is ungrammatical or otherwise imperfectly expressed but whose purport is clear should be corrected by officers is a matter of judgement: if the grammatical error is a simple one it might be corrected, but if the changes that ought to be made are extensive, it would be wise for the officers tactfully to seek the member's prior approval before making corrections. In any event it is advisable for there to be an 'early warning system' in existence so that the form of a notice of motion can be considered by officers before being placed on the council agenda.

Debate on a motion

7.57 The meeting is not bound to pursue consideration of a motion in the form in which it is originally proposed or to come to any decision upon it at all. Original motions may be passed with or without amendment or may be thrown out, and the debate may at any time be interrupted either by the moving of a procedural (or dilatory) motion (see 7.70) or by a member raising a point of order (see 7.82).

Need a motion be seconded?

7.58 Notwithstanding that notice of motion has been duly given the motion must still be moved at the meeting. By common law it is not necessary that a motion should be seconded: in *Re Horbury Bridge Coal, Iron and Wagon Co.* (1879), James LJ said:

> 'There is no law of the land which says that a motion cannot be put without a seconder and the objection that the amendment was not seconded cannot prevail.'

In practice, most local authorities require by standing orders that every motion – whether one of which notice has been given or otherwise – shall be seconded as a prerequisite to its being open to discussion. Where standing orders require a seconder and a motion is moved but not seconded, it drops as a matter of course and the next business can be proceeded with. In certain circumstances, however, there is a convention whereby the chair/mayor at full council will formally second a motion submitted by a single member in order to allow the motion to be debated (see Chapter 11).

7.59 Model standing order no. 14 from the Modular Constitution (which deals fairly comprehensively with the rules of debate at council meetings (see 7.68)) includes the following provision:

> '**14.1 No speeches until motion seconded**
> No speeches may be made after the mover has moved a proposal and explained the purpose of it until the motion has been seconded.
> **14.2 Right to require motion in writing**
> Unless notice of the motion has already been given, the chairman may require it to be written down and handed to him/her before it is discussed.
> **14.3 Seconders speech**
> When seconding a motion or amendment, a member may reserve their speech until later in the debate.'

Alteration of motion

7.60 In the course of discussion on a motion – or even before discussion commences the proposer may wish to make an alteration that he thinks might make the motion more acceptable to members. Old model standing order 9 provides that:

> '9 A member may with the consent of the council signified without discussion:
> (a) alter a motion of which he has given notice; or
> (b) with the further consent of his seconder alter a motion which he has moved if (in either case) the alteration is one which could be made as an amendment thereto.'

See below for the model standing order (para. 14.6) regarding amendment included within the Modular Constitution.

Withdrawal of motion

7.61 Old model standing order no. 10, giving effect to the common law rule, provides for the withdrawal of a motion in these terms:

> '10 A motion or amendment may be withdrawn by the mover with the consent of his seconder and of the council, which shall be signified without discussion, and no member may speak upon it after the mover has asked permission for its withdrawal, unless such permission shall have been refused.'

See 7.63 for the model standing order (para. 14.10) regarding withdrawal included within the Modular Constitution.

Problems can arise where a member who has given notice of motion decides at the meeting not to move it or to withdraw it, possibly because, suspecting that it will not secure the council's backing, they may not wish to see it defeated for political reasons. Should the chairman assume that the member's silence is tantamount to withdrawal of the motion? But what if the council refuses to give consent to its withdrawal? The better course probably is for the chairman to rule that the motion falls for not having been moved.

Amendments

Definition

7.62 An amendment is a formal proposal to vary the terms of a motion before the latter is adopted by the meeting. The motion in its original form, before amendment, is called 'the original motion'. The original motion, altered by the incorporation of any amendments passed, is known as the main motion or substantive motion; and this substantive motion may be further amended. If amendments fail the motion should still be referred to as the original motion: it becomes a substantive motion only if amendments have succeeded.

Motions and amendments that may be moved without notice

7.63 Some motions and amendments may be moved without notice, as per the following model standing order from the Modular Constitution.

> **14.10 Motions which may be moved during debate**
> When a motion is under debate, no other motion may be moved except the following procedural motions:

(a) to withdraw a motion;
(b) to amend a motion;
(c) to proceed to the next business;
(d) that the question be now put;
(e) to adjourn a debate;
(f) to adjourn a meeting;
(g) [that the meeting continue beyond [n] hours in duration . . .] (*if a guillotine rule is used*);
(h) to exclude the public and press in accordance with the Access to Information Rules; and
(i) to not hear further a member named under Rule 21.3 or to exclude them from the meeting under Rule 21.4.

7.64 An amendment must not negate the motion that it seeks to alter, because the same effect can be achieved by voting against the motion. It must be pertinent and relevant to the original motion, or otherwise a question may be brought before the council of which the requisite notice has not been given. It must also be within the scope of the meeting, for the same reason.

7.65 There are circumstances during the discussion of contentious business when the chairman may have difficulty in interpreting the rules governing amendments. For example, an amendment may be moved that, otherwise consistent with the rules outlined above, virtually displaces the original motion. It is a matter of judgement for the chairman whether such an amendment is acceptable, although in practice they will probably ask for advice from officers. The chairman would probably be wise to allow rather than disallow amendments if the sense of the meeting can finally be determined on the issue before it. After all, the purpose of the rules of debate (and of standing orders) is to help members to do what they want to do, so far as it is consistent with the law.

Amendments must be put to meeting

7.66 The chairman must put an amendment that has been moved (and, if standing orders so require, seconded) unless:

- it is *ultra vires*, i.e. it is outside the scope of the meeting or beyond the council's powers;
- it is irrelevant, where it bears no relation to the original motion or subject matter;
- it is inconsistent, where it is incompatible with a decision previously taken at the same meeting;
- it is vexatious and intended only to impede the transaction of business; or
- in bona fide exercise of their discretion as chairman they have grounds for excluding it by standing orders or resolution of the meeting itself.

An improper refusal to put an amendment will vitiate the decision to which the proposed amendment relates: *Henderson v Bank of Australasia* (1890).

Series of amendments

7.67 Each amendment must be voted separately. There can be no amendments of an amendment and if notice is given of several amendments these should be taken in due succession: the chairman should examine the amendments and determine the order in which they should be put to the meeting. No amendment can be considered that is inconsistent with an amendment already adopted or that reproduces an amendment previously rejected. There are circumstances when a motion cannot be amended, e.g. in the case of a special meeting of the council to pass a resolution in specific form to meeting statutory requirements.

Order of debate

General considerations

7.68 There are various procedural matters that are often referred to collectively as the 'order of debate'. Again, it is relevant to quote the following model standing order

14. Rules of debate
14.1 No speeches until motion seconded
No speeches may be made after the mover has moved a proposal and explained the purpose of it until the motion has been seconded.
14.2 Right to require motion in writing
Unless notice of the motion has already been given, the chairman may require it to be written down and handed to him/her before it is discussed.
14.3 Seconder's speech
When seconding a motion or amendment, a member may reserve their speech until later in the debate.
14.4 Content and length of speeches
Speeches must be directed to the question under discussion or to a personal explanation or point of order. No speech may exceed [n] minutes without the consent of the chairman.
14.5 When a member may speak again
A member who has spoken on a motion may not speak again while it is the subject of debate, except:

(a) to speak once an amendment has been moved by another member;
(b) to move a further amendment if the motion has been amended since he/she last spoke;
(c) if his/her last speech was on an amendment moved by another member, to speak on the main issue (whether or not the amendment on which he/she spoke was carried);
(d) in exercise of a right of reply;
(e) on a point of order; and
(f) by way of personal explanation.

14.6 Amendment to motions

(a) An amendment to a motion must be relevant to the motion and will either be:
  i) to refer the matter to an appropriate body or individual for consideration or reconsideration;
  ii) to leave out words;
  iii) to leave out words and insert or add others; or
  iv) to insert or add words

as long as the effect of (ii) to (iv) is not to negate the motion.

(b) Only one amendment may be moved and discussed at any one time. No further amendment may be moved until the amendment under discussion has been disposed of.
(c) If an amendment is not carried, other amendments to the original motion may be moved.
(d) If an amendment is carried, the motion as amended takes the place of the original motion. This becomes the substantive motion to which further amendments are moved.
(e) After an amendment has been carried, the chairman will read out the amended motion before accepting any further amendments, or if there are none, put it to the vote.

14.7 Alteration of motion

(a) A member may alter a motion of which he/she has given notice with the consent of the meeting. The meeting's consent will be signified without discussion.
(b) A member may alter a motion which he/she has given notice with the consent of both the meeting and the seconder. The meeting's consent will be signified without discussion.
(c) Only alterations which could be made as an amendment may be made.

As to content of speeches: see next paragraph; and as to points of order, see below.

Content of speeches

7.69 The power vested in a chair by common law to regulate the conduct of a meeting and to preserve order may be assumed to include power to direct a member to cease making unseemly remarks in the course of a speech. This is also supported by a standing order to that effect in the modular constitution and current model standing orders.

As to defamatory statements, see above.

Procedural motions

7.70 Procedural or formal motions are designed to close the debate, either by forcing an immediate vote on the motion or amendment before the meeting or by postponing a decision on the motion or amendment: hence they are sometimes termed 'closure' (as in model standing order 14.11 from the Modular Constitution), 'dilatory' (this being best used to describe a motion that obstructs or frustrates the transaction of business) or 'interruptive' motions. They cannot be moved by anyone who has moved or seconded or spoken on the original motion being debated, and no person may intervene in discussion on a particular motion by moving more than one formal motion.

7.71 The procedural motions include:

(a) the motion to proceed to next business;
(b) the motion 'that the question be now put';
(c) the motion to adjourn the debate; and
(d) the motion to adjourn the meeting.

To proceed to the next business

7.72 The procedural motion 'that the council proceed to the next business', or in the alternative at some authorities 'that the motion be not now put', means quite simply that the debate is stopped where it is, with no outcome, and the meeting moves on to its next item of business. (This used also to be referred to as 'the previous question', and was often used in the meeting as 'I move the previous question', because it proposes an independent issue that must be decided previously to the main issue. Thankfully for plain English users everywhere, this phrasing is no longer used.) Once accepted by the chair or mayor and seconded, the procedural motion may be discussed but cannot be amended, and if carried, the original question is removed from the scope of the meeting and can only be revived by a motion at a subsequent meeting. If, however, the motion is lost, then the implication is that the meeting desires the substantive question to be put to the vote forthwith and thus further discussion cannot be permitted. The mover of this procedural motion has no right of comment on the reply of the mover of the original motion.

'That the question be now put'

7.73 This motion, which is a form of closure, must be voted upon without debate after it has been moved and seconded, unless the chairman refuses to accept it on the grounds that the matter before the meeting has been insufficiently discussed. If carried, the main question must be put immediately after the mover of the original motion has been given their right of reply. If the matter under discussion is an amendment, the closure affects only that amendment.

7.74 There is nothing to prevent the chair applying the closure, with the consent of the meeting, if they are of opinion that the views of the minority have been reasonably heard (*Wall v Exchange & Northern Assets Corporation* (1981)). This they can do simply by calling on the mover of the motion to reply to the debate.

Adjournment of debate

7.75 This motion, which may seek to delay discussion on the question before the meeting either for a specified time or indefinitely, may be moved by any member other than the mover or seconder of the main question or the mover or seconder of any amendment or formal motion in reference to it. No amendment is possible except as regards the period of suspension or the time to which discussion is to be postponed or the place to which adjournment is proposed. If the motion is not explicit as to this, then, depending on standing orders, the discussion on the main question will be resumed at the next ordinary meeting of the council. Such a standing order may be to this effect:

> 'When a motion that the debate be now adjourned is carried the discussion shall be resumed at the next meeting of the council, when the member who moved its adjournment shall be entitled to speak first.'

If the motion is rejected, a second motion for adjournment may be moved during the same meeting after the lapse of a reasonable time or such period as may be prescribed in standing orders.

Adjournment of meeting

7.76 A motion to adjourn the meeting (a suspensive motion) is a more drastic proposition than any of the procedural motions so far considered, for it operates if carried to bring about a suspension of the entire proceedings either for a particular period or indefinitely. An adjournment may be:

- *sine die*, i.e. for an unspecified period of indefinite duration;
- for an unspecified period not exceeding a given maximum;
- until a date specified, or for a fixed interval of time;
- to another place; or
- for a given time and to a named place.

There is no statutory power to adjourn a council meeting but by common law an assembly is deemed to be invested with the power to adjourn its proceedings of its own volition (*Stoughton v Reynolds* (1737)).
7.77 It seems that, even where certain matters must be transacted on a particular day, a local authority has an implied power to adjourn so as to enable business that could not be finished for lack of time on the day fixed to be brought to its conclusion (*Rex v Carmarthen Corpn* (1813)); this inherent power exists also where it is not possible to transact the whole of the business for which a meeting has been called (*Kerr v Wilkie* (1860)).
7.78 The motion to adjourn may be proposed at the close of any speech but cannot be moved by a person who has already spoken on the question then before the meeting or who has moved or seconded an amendment or formal motion in relation to it. When moved and seconded the motion creates an independent question for the immediate consideration of the meeting, and discussion on the substantive question (and on the previous question if it has been moved) must give way to the motion to adjourn the meeting.

7.79 Discussion on the motion is governed by the ordinary rules of debate (except insofar as they may be altered by standing orders) but the mover has no right of reply nor has the owner of the original motion;

- no amendment is permissible other than alteration of the time or place of adjournment (or both); and
- subject to standing orders, the motion to adjourn may be renewed after the lapse of a reasonable time in the course of the same meeting.

Standing orders sometimes limit the effect of the motion – for example, when a motion 'that the council now adjourn' is carried, the council, before adjourning, may take the remaining business on the agenda that is unopposed, and the question under debate, if any, shall stand adjourned to the next meeting.

In cases where such a standing order applies, the chairman after the motion has been carried should seek the view of the meeting as to the unopposed business.

Adjournment by chairman

7.80 The power of adjournment vests in the full assembly: it arises from 'the common right, which is in the whole assembly, where all are upon an equal foot' (*Stoughton v Reynolds* (1736)). This means that only in exceptional circumstances, e.g. in the case of persistent disorder, can the chairman order an adjournment.

7.81 If a chairman illegally declares a meeting to be adjourned, e.g. in circumstances where it is patently not the wish of the majority of those present, then after the chairman has left the members may elect someone to preside over the transaction of the remainder of the business, and their act and the business transacted are valid (*R v Doris* (1908)). In *National Dwellings Society v Sykes*, above, Chitty J said:

> '. . . in my opinion, the power which has been contended for is not within the scope of the authority of the chairman: namely, to stop the meeting at his own will and pleasure. The meeting is called for the particular purposes . . . According to the constitution . . . a certain officer has to preside. He presides with reference to the business which is then to be transacted. In my opinion, he cannot say, after that business has been opened, "I will have no more to do with it; I will not let this meeting proceed; I will stop it; I declare the meeting dissolved and I leave the chair." In my opinion, that is not within his power. The meeting by itself can resolve to go on with the business which the other chairman forgetful of his duty or violating his duty, has tried to stop because the proceedings have taken a turn which he himself does not like.'

What if the chair of the council/mayor, who must preside if present at the council meeting, having improperly declared the meeting adjourned, remains in the council chamber? If they do remain they cannot be deemed to be 'in the meeting' and the council could elect someone else to preside.

Points of order

7.82 A point of order is an objection submitted to the chairman for decision claiming some irregularity in the constitution or conduct of the meeting. The more usual irregularities include:

- the use of irrelevant or improper language;
- that a quorum is not present;
- that an amendment is a simple negative of the motion before the meeting;
- that the motion is *ultra vires* or not within the scope of the notice given;
- that no question is before the meeting, e.g. where a motion has not been seconded (if this is required by standing orders); and
- any non-compliance with standing orders.

7.83 A member may raise a point of order at any time without notice. It must, however, be raised immediately the alleged irregularity or impropriety becomes apparent. The member who is speaking must stop, sit down and allow the chair to make a decision: and the chair's decision is conclusive and final. Ordinarily no debate is permitted on a point of order; but some authorities do allow a short discussion of the point raised, but this does encourage others to express views as to whether the point of order should or should not be upheld and that is a decision better left for the chair.

7.84 A point of order relates to procedure. It is not concerned with the arguments or the principles or the political views put forward in debate or with the truth or falsehood, correctness or incorrectness of statements made in the course of debate. A difference of opinion is not a point of order. Nor may a member making a point of order abuse it by making a speech.

7.85 When a point of order is raised, it is a common occurrence for the member raising it not to specify the standing order or rule of debate alleged to have been infringed. The chair should be rigorous in asking for this information since a 'point of order' is often used to clothe a simple disagreement and give the member a second opportunity to speak when not entitled to do so. Thus a useful standing order is as follows:

> 'On any member indicating a desire to raise a point of order s/he shall state at the outset the standing order or rule of debate considered to have been infringed. Every point of order shall be decided by the chairman before the debate proceeds and his/her decision shall be final and cannot be discussed.'

Personal explanation

7.86 A member may find that they have made a misstatement that is being quoted by a later speaker or that the latter has misunderstood or misquoted them. In such circumstances the member is allowed to rise on a point of explanation and to interrupt the speaker for a few moments while they (the member) makes the desired correction. This prevents the speaker developing their argument on wrong facts or figures or a misunderstanding and so wasting the time of the meeting. The concession is one that should be carefully controlled by the chair to avoid misuse similar to that which afflicts points of order.

Consideration of committee reports

General approach

7.87 The consideration of committee/cabinet reports is ordinarily the main item of business of the full council. These reports, whose style will depend upon local practice:

- record matters dealt with by committees under delegated powers and submitted to the council for information; and
- submit recommendations for the council's approval with or without amendment or rejection or reference back.

It is the practice of some local authorities to require the submission of the full minutes of committees, or an edited version or a selection of those minutes containing recommendations for the council's consideration. This gives rise to procedural problems because the minutes of committee proceedings are a record of business already transacted and thus cannot be altered in the full assembly. For this, and other persuasive reasons discussed later (see 12.40), most authorities make use of the report system, which requires committees to submit a report of their proceedings, with any necessary recommendations, instead of the minutes.

Motion 'that the report be received'

7.88 The motion 'that the report be received' or 'the report be noted' is wholly appropriate and can be resolved upon in those terms where the whole of the report records action taken under delegated powers or otherwise contains no recommendations for action by the council. The use of the word 'received' indicates that the council has had the report before it but does not necessarily approve or disapprove it. There are variants, useful in distinguishing the 'reception' of the report for procedural purposes and its 'reception' in another sense: thus the motion could be 'that the report be accepted' or 'that the report be noted'. As to the minuting of the consideration of committee reports, see 8.10.

Amendments by leave of the council

7.89 If the committee chair, or someone on their behalf, wishes to make an amendment to the report (which, strictly, may only be done with the leave of the council) or proposes to speak themselves in explanation or elaboration of a particular paragraph in the report, it is usual for an indication to that effect to be given in moving the report. The committee chair may say, 'I move the report and' – as the case may be – 'with the leave of the council wish to make a correction on paragraph . . .' or 'I would like to say something on paragraph . . .' The committee chair will then make their correction or statement when the paragraph concerned is called from the chair. Where the report is the approved minutes from a previous committee, then the chair cannot propose a correction.

Adoption of report

7.90 Where a committee/cabinet report contains recommendations on which there is no dissent, the motion at the conclusion of the report, moved either by the committee chair or the leader or portfolio holder, is to the effect 'that the report be approved and adopted' or, alternatively, 'that the report and the recommendations contained therein be approved'.

Reference back

7.91 It is in order, upon the reception of a report or later in the course of debate, for a motion (not an amendment, for the motion for reception is procedural only) to be moved 'that the report be referred back to the committee/cabinet' either 'for further information' or 'for further consideration' or with an instruction that some specified action be taken. Additionally, there can be a reference back to a particular paragraph of a report.

Withdrawal of report

7.92 Alternatively, the committee/cabinet chair might decide, with the leave of the council, to withdraw a report or a paragraph within that report, either in the light of the debate that has taken place or because circumstances have arisen since the committee's meeting that make such a course desirable. The withdrawal of a report or one of its paragraphs should be regarded as exceptional. It may be a tactical move politically to avoid defeat on a proposal of importance but, as a general rule, proceedings placed before the full council with the object patently of being acted upon should not ordinarily be withdrawn.

Regulation by standing orders

7.93 The particular procedure favoured by a local authority in dealing with reports at a council meeting should be laid down in standing orders.

Rescission of resolutions

Not at meeting at which passed

7.94 It is a widely accepted rule and a matter of common sense that a resolution cannot be rescinded at the meeting at which it is passed or adopted, even though all present are prepared to consent to such a proposition. Different considerations might apply in the case of a committee meeting.

If passed at earlier meeting

7.95 A resolution passed at one meeting may be rescinded at a subsequent meeting provided there are no practical obstacles, e.g. where action taken under the original resolution would make its rescission a nullity or the rights of third parties who have acted on the earlier decision need to be taken into account and safeguarded. A proposal to rescind a resolution must be treated as an original motion unless it arises out of a committee report. Local authorities normally make provision in standing orders to control the rescission of resolutions (and to restrict the frequency with which unsuccessful motions can be revived). This is provided in the current model of standing orders, but a good example is actually old model standing order no. 14:

> 'No motion to rescind any resolution passed within the preceding six months, and no motion or amendment to the same effect as one which has been rejected within the preceding six months, shall be proposed unless the notice thereof given in pursuance of standing order . . . bears the names of at least . . . members of the council. When any such motion or amendment has been disposed of by the council, it shall not be open to any member to propose a similar motion within a further period of six months.'

This is provided that this standing order shall not apply to motions moved in pursuance of a recommendation of a committee.

The kind of decisions that can be rescinded are, generally speaking, those that have determined the authority's policy or that otherwise are of continuing effect. There is a category of decisions that can be rescinded only in special circumstances – revoked is a more appropriate term. This is most commonly used in respect of development control decisions and, as a matter of good practice, it is based around the principles of judicial review, thereby hopefully avoiding a real one in the eyes of the mover of such a motion. It is also best practice that the matter is referred back rather than the whole of full council being turned into a very large development control committee, with all the risk that entails, and a new decision made. Some councils have put in place a planning review committee especially for that purpose rather than allowing the matter to go to full council, but the principles remain the same. Those and other councils have added further to the standing orders defining and controlling the use of the rescission motion, an example of which is as follows:

> N.3 Rule [N.1] does not apply to a Committee or Sub-Committee acting under delegated powers, which may rescind, replace, amend, or defer action upon any of its previous resolutions, whenever passed, after receiving and considering an Officer's report recommending departure from a previous resolution, where it considers such departure to be justified in all the circumstances.

N.4 No resolution will be rescinded, no action will be deferred, and no matter referred back, where it has already been acted upon, if the rescission or deferment would disadvantage a third party who has become entitled to a right as a result of the resolution.

N.5 A resolution of a Committee or a Sub-Committee passed under delegated powers is deemed to have been passed by the whole Council.

N.6 When a Member intends to submit a motion to rescind a decision, notice must be given to the Monitoring Officer within 24 hours of the decision of the Member's intention to submit a rescinding motion, in order to prevent the decision being implemented. The actual motion must be signed by at least five Members, and be submitted within five working days of the decision being taken.

N.7 The motion must state the grounds on which the motion is made. The motion must be expressed in terms of the principles of judicial review, that is, that the decision is flawed on the grounds of one or more of;

(a) illegality (the Committee misdirected itself in law);
(b) irrationality (the Committee took into account irrelevant matters or failed to take into account relevant matters); or
(c) procedural impropriety (the Committee failed to follow its own procedures, including rules of natural justice).

Rescission of a rescission

7.96 Where a resolution is rescinded and later the rescinding resolution is itself rescinded then, in the absence of any clear indication to contrary effect, the original resolution is revived (see *Weir v Fermanagh County Council* (1913)): but it is bad practice to leave in doubt, or leave to be implied, the true intention of a decision. As a general rule, the purported rescission of a resolution is of no effect if executive action has been taken under the original resolution and the intention is to invalidate what has properly been done under such resolution.

Voting

General considerations

7.97 As indicated in Chapter 1, in all ordinary instances questions coming or arising before a local authority are required to be decided by a majority of the members present and voting thereon at a properly constituted meeting of the authority.[16] In the case of principal councils the method of voting is not prescribed by statute; in the case of parish and community councils the voting is by show of hands unless standing orders otherwise provide,[17] and any member may 'on requisition' require that the voting shall be recorded so as to show whether each member present and voting gave a vote for or against the question.[18] In the case of parish and community meetings a question is similarly decided as a rule by show of hands in the first instance (although the statute does not expressly so stipulate), and the decision of the person presiding as to the result of the voting is final 'unless a poll is demanded'.[19]

7.98 The following draft core standing order was proposed by the standing orders working party on which the mandatory standing order specified in the next paragraph impinges:

'00–1 Except where a requisition is made under the next paragraph, the method of voting at meetings of the council, committees and sub-committees shall be by show of hands.

2 If a requisition is made by the specified number of members, the voting on any question shall be recorded so as to show whether each member present gave his vote for or against the question or abstained from voting.

3 The specified number of members is:

(a) one-fifth of the members entitled to vote at the meeting; or

(b) where the council is divided into political groups, in a case of a meeting of the largest political group, and in the case of a meeting of a committee or a sub-committee, the number of seats on that body allocated to the second largest political group among the members of the council, whichever is the less.

Variation: A smaller number than specified may be adopted.

4 If a vote is taken by show of hands, any member who is present when the vote was taken may require that his/her vote or abstention shall be recorded in the minutes by notifying forthwith the proper officer of his/her wish.

5 Where a vote is required on a motion to appoint or elect a member of the council to a position to be filled by the authority, and there are two or more members nominated for that position, the names of all those nominated shall be put to the meeting in alphabetical order of surname. Those entitled to vote shall each vote for only one person. If there is not a majority of those voting in favour of one person, the name of the person having the least number of votes shall be struck off the list and a fresh vote shall be taken, and so on until a majority of votes is given in favour of one person.'

7.99 A mandatory standing order[20] relating to the recording of votes is set out below:

'1 Where immediately after a vote is taken at a meeting of a relevant body any member of that body so requires, there shall be recorded in the minutes of the proceedings of that meeting whether that person cast his/her vote for the question or against the question or whether he/she abstained from voting.

> 2 In this paragraph, "relevant body" means the authority, a committee or sub-committee of the authority or relevant joint committee or sub-committee of such a committee.'

The importance of this entitlement for the individual councillor is discussed later. Members who are present and do not vote may, in certain circumstances, be regarded as having acquiesced in the decision taken. There are instances, however, in which a member may well wish their abstention to be recorded: where, for example, they are a member of Parliament and they feel the vote may be against parliamentary policy and do not want their vote to be recorded.

Meaning of 'present and voting'

7.100 Members present at a meeting who do not vote or are prohibited from voting on the particular question before the meeting are nevertheless present for purposes of forming the necessary quorum; and a bare majority of those who in fact vote is sufficient to pass a resolution even if that number is less than the quorum. If, however, members under a disability are excluded from the meeting by standing orders or themselves voluntarily leave the council chamber until the particular matter is dealt with, they are not 'present'; as would be the case with a member who is not able to take part, but who has not actually been excluded, or voluntarily left (e.g. members of an overview and scrutiny committee who are not able to vote on non-education matters).

Who may vote

7.101 Council members at a council meeting, if 'present' in the sense just referred to – i.e. are under no legal disability from voting – are entitled to vote. It has been held that persons who are de facto councillors may vote until such time as they are in fact unseated: *Holden v Southwark Corpn* (1921).

7.102 What if a member who is clearly under a disability persists in speaking and voting? As indicated above, such a member is probably technically not present and therefore the chair of the meeting would be justified in refusing to count their vote 'for the "vote" has been cast illegally and . . . can be said not to be a vote at all'. As to a vote cast by a councillor having an interest in an issue of a quasi-judicial nature, see 11.37.

7.103 The position is more difficult where the member concerned, thought to be under a disability (e.g. having a disclosable pecuniary interest), has chosen not to declare it and takes part in the debate and votes. In these circumstances it is, perhaps, better for the vote to be counted since the only person who can decide whether a disability of this kind exists is the member themselves. A further difficulty that can arise from these circumstances is the possibility that the decision itself might be challengeable as illegal, certainly if it depended on the vote of the member who was subsequently shown to have a disabling interest. Any chair finding themselves faced with this situation would be well advised to persuade the meeting to adjourn for a short period so that the question could be discussed with the member concerned.

Methods of voting

7.104 Despite differences in the words of the statute, most local authorities proceed by taking most votes by show of hands and the chair will ordinarily make their decision on the evidence of the show of hands without taking a count. There is no reason, however (at least in the case of principal councils), why a vote should not be taken in some other way, e.g. by voice or by conduct (such as nodding the head or 'is that agreed?'): and it is well established that there can be an implied vote in favour by silent assent.

In *R v Highbury Corner Magistrates' Court and another, ex parte Ewing* (1991) 3 All ER 192, it was held that a resolution by a local authority may be validly passed even though there is no ballot or show of hands of members, as for example where a non-controversial resolution recommended by a committee of the authority is passed 'on the nod', i.e. without dissent. This confirmed the long-held position that where no formal vote is taken, any member present may be held to have voted in favour if he or she does not clearly indicate his or her dissent: *R. v Hendon Rural DC, Ex p. Chorley* (1993). However, this is not good practice. Similarly, where an interested person was present at a meeting at which a resolution was carried unanimously and so entered on the minutes and the defendant did not dissent or abstain from voting though they did not expressly indicate assent, it was held that they had voted for the resolution: *Everett v Griffiths* (1924) (see also 7.112).

7.105 In some authorities, electronic voting systems are in use, but these would not be permitted in the case of parish and community meetings. These are not without difficulties – for example, former Suffolk County Councillor Jane Hore was disqualified for one year on 16 September 2009, following a Standards for England investigation into allegations that she voted twice at a full council meeting. The Adjudication Panel for England found that Ms Hore, who lost her seat in the council elections in June 2009, had brought her office and authority into disrepute by misusing the council's electronic voting system.

7.106 There are circumstances where it is impracticable to reach what might be termed a fairly representative decision by simple majority vote, e.g. in the case of the election of persons to various offices where there are several nominations, or in the selection of an individual from a shortlist of candidates for a staff appointment when the interviewing panel cannot agree. Local authorities as a rule adopt some kind of balloting system that provides for the choice of nominee who secures the greatest number of individual votes, but this can be an imperfect mechanism because it can produce a perverse result, e.g. the choice may fall on someone with fewer votes than the aggregate of votes for other candidates. Model standing order no. 17 of the Modular Constitution makes this provision:

> **'17.7 Voting on appointments**
> If there are more than two people nominated for any position to be filled and there is not a clear majority of votes in favour of one person, then the name of the person with the least number of votes will be taken off the list and a new vote taken. The process will continue until there is a majority of votes for one person.'

7.107 Some local authorities have experimented with the single transferable vote system[21] in circumstances where there are more nominees than places available, e.g. on the election of the mayor, committee chairmen and vice-chairmen, and in choosing councillors to serve on committees and sub-committees, and as representatives on outside bodies. A standing order that has been used by one such authority provides:

> 'If the number of nominations exceeds the number of vacancies there shall be a secret ballot of the members present at the meeting in which each member of the council shall vote for as many candidates as there are vacancies to be filled. Vacancies shall thereupon be filled using the single transferable vote system. Any ballot shall be conducted by the secretary whose return shall be final and conclusive.'

The Electoral Reform Society (whose principal object is to promote the adoption of proportional representation for elections in the British Isles and elsewhere) states:

> 'At the moment the voting system used in local elections (First Past The Post), means too many people's votes simply do not count. The main way in which people can influence local policy is by choosing the councillors they want to represent them but under First Past the Post (FPTP) we often end up with councillors who more of us voted against than for.'

Challenge to chair's ruling

7.108 Any challenge to a chair's ruling, including their decision on a vote on a show of hands, must be made promptly at the time (*Anthony v Seger* (1789)). A show of hands, convenient though it is at both council and committee meetings, is 'only a rude and imperfect declaration of . . . sentiments'. Where it is believed that the chairman's declaration of the result of a show of hands is in error, the proper course is for the meeting to call for the voting to be determined more accurately in some such manner as described in the foregoing paragraphs. In *Cornwall v Woods* (1846), the court refused to upset a decision of a meeting of parishioners at which a rate was fixed because, if the chair was in error, the correct procedure should have been to call for a division or a poll.

Taking a poll

7.109 Exceptionally, in the case of parish and community meetings there is provision in law for the taking of a poll in certain circumstances (LGA 1972, Sch. 12, paras. 18–34). A poll may be demanded before the conclusion of a meeting on any question arising and must be taken if the person presiding consents or the poll is demanded by not less than 10, or one-third, of the electors present at the meeting, whichever is the less. A poll so demanded is a poll of the local government electors and is conducted substantially as for the election of parish or community councillors as the case may be.

Abstention

7.110 It may be convenient here to discuss more fully a point referred to earlier. There is a presumption that councillors who merely abstain from voting assent to the resolution and where no formal vote is taken, all those present are presumed to have assented. A record of abstentions from voting has the added advantage of accounting for all members present at the time the vote was taken.

7.111 The principles involved are drawn from common law, mostly in cases which concern appeals against the old regime of 'surcharge' by the district auditor. If a councillor votes against a proposal and their vote is not recorded in the minutes, other evidence could be used to show they have abstained or dissented: see *Attorney-General v Tottenham Local Board* (1872). In the classic case of *Roberts v Hopwood* (1925), four councillors who had initially been surcharged were able to show to the satisfaction of the court that they dissented from the motion to incur unlawful expenditure; and in another case, *Rothnie v Dearne UDC* (1951), Devlin J said:

> 'No one should suppose that the mere failure to vote against an illegal resolution necessarily entails the consequences which have followed in this case.'

The principle that abstention may amount to acquiescence is at least partly based on the duty that a councillor undertakes in making their declaration of acceptance of office (see *Asher v Secretary of State* (1974); and as to acceptance of office: see 4.3).

Special consideration was given to the position of certain individual members. Two members of the old council had not been present at council meetings at which resolutions had been passed authorising expenditure held to be illegal. They had been present at earlier committee meetings when the proposals had been discussed and officers had advised of their illegality. The district auditor found that they were aware that the proposals were to be considered by the council at the meetings from which they were absent, and that they knew or ought to have known that the proposals were illegal. He held that they were therefore under a duty to attend the council meetings and to oppose the proposals or, if they were unable to attend the council meetings, to take such steps as they would to make known their opposition. Since they failed in this duty he held that they shared responsibility for authorising or incurring the expenditure and also that loss was caused by their negligence and misconduct.

One person, one vote

7.112 The practice of voting by show of hands means that each person present at a meeting must, in order to vote, put up one hand only and so exercise one vote. It is, in any case, a common law rule that every person voting at a meeting is reckoned as one vote (*Rex v Rector of Birmingham* (1837) pp. 259, 260); that each voter is accorded one vote unless there exists, in some form, a specific provision to the contract (*Re Horbury Bridge Coal, Iron & Wagon Co.* (1879)), as in the case, of course, of a chairman's second or casting vote.

7.113 The principle of one person one vote means that on each issue on which a vote is taken a person may vote once only, either for or against. A person cannot properly vote both for and against even though this could be said to have the same effect as an abstention because the vote for and the vote against cancel each other out; nor even, it would seem, to correct an error made in voting in the first place or to suggest by the record that a quorum was present when it was not.[22]

No authoritative decision exists as to whether an error on the part of a voter in giving their vote can be corrected. When the result has been declared the voting is regarded as closed: before the declaration the chair could presumably exercise a discretion to allow a voter to correct an error.

Chair's casting vote

7.114 The chairman of every local authority meeting has a second or casting vote that may be exercised where there is an equality of votes under the Local Government Act 1972 Sch. 2, s. 39(2).

7.115 There are differing opinions as to what precisely is meant by the term a second or casting vote. It has been argued that it means that whoever presides may only vote to avoid a deadlock on an equality of votes if they have already exercised their right to vote as a councillor. The preferred view, and the one generally accepted, is that the true intention of the statute is that the person presiding may vote to avoid a deadlock no matter how it arises, i.e. whether they had already voted or not. Cave J said in *Nell v Longbottom* (1984):

> 'The justification of a second or casting vote, as it is called, is the creature of the statute law introduced for the purpose of avoiding the deadlock which would otherwise ensure.'

Thus the position therefore seems to be as follows: if there is an equality of votes, whether or not the voting includes a vote by the chairman, the chairman may 'break the deadlock' by then using the casting vote. If the chairman does not elect to use their second or casting vote in this way the proposition falls, i.e. it is not carried. In the case of a controversial question or in other instances where an affirmative vote is not required as a matter of urgency, the chairman may choose not to exercise their second or casting vote on the grounds (though they are not bound to explain their action) that in their impartial capacity as chairman they ought not to determine an issue on which opinion is equally divided or where the matter can be raised again at a later date. Of course a chairman may not regard their role as impartial where they had been put into the chair by the ruling group's control of the vote or where there is a hung council, and this was so in recent cases before the courts.

7.116 Examples may help clarify what a chairman may or may not do. Suppose, after a motion has been moved and seconded and the chairman asks those present to signify, first those in favour and three members so signify, and then those against and three members so signify, the chairman may use their casting vote. If, however, when the proposition has been put, three members, including the chairman, vote in favour and three members vote against, the chairman may use their second vote in favour. The preferred opinion seems to be (although there is some doubt as to whether it could be sustained) that the chairman cannot withhold their ordinary vote and then purport to give two votes when it is evident how the voting is going, i.e. they cannot properly say when there are, for example, two votes for and three against a proposition: 'I'm in favour of the motion so it's a tie and I'll use my casting and second vote to carry the motion.' They can, however, give a contingent casting vote in certain circumstances.

7.117 In the late 1980s, the Lord Mayor of Bradford's use of his second or casting vote in a hung council in favour of his own party's policies was challenged before the courts. The Lord Mayor had consistently used his second or casting vote to secure the passage through the council of proposals of his fellow councillors which in a hung situation might not otherwise have secured approval. In *R v Bradford Metropolitan City Council ex parte Wilson* (1989), the Divisional Court held that the purpose of a chairman's second or casting vote was to break deadlocks that would otherwise arise in view of the lack of such a vote by common law. If a chairman always used that vote in such a way as to preserve the status quo, the effect would be to maintain the deadlock rather than break it. The court decided not to interfere in such a case as this, where the Lord Mayor had used his second or casting vote honestly and according to his own perception of what was best in the public interest. In *R v Bradford Metropolitan City Council ex parte Corris* (1989), the Court of Appeal took a similar view when upholding a refusal to grant judicial review in respect of another instance where the Lord Mayor's second or casting vote had again been used in favour of the implementation of his own party's policies. The court said it did not think that the power to give a second or casting vote was fettered by any implied restriction that it should be exercised without regard to any party political considerations, nor by an interparty agreement on the rotation of the lord mayoralty that it would not be used politically.

Contingent casting vote

7.118 A casting vote may be given contingently in circumstances where the chairman has good reason for believing that one of the votes cast may be invalid. Thus in *Bland v Buchanan* (1901), both petitioner and respondent were candidates for the office of mayor of a borough. The mayor in office presided at the election. Sixteen votes, including the mayor's first vote, were cast for the respondent and 15 for the petitioner. The mayor, with good reason for believing that one of the votes cast for the respondent might be impeached, purported to give a casting vote for the respondent. The casting vote was held valid in these circumstances.

7.119 The extent to which the above principle can be stretched appears uncertain. In *Bland*, above, the mayor was simply reinforcing a decision that a majority of councillors had supported. The more interesting question is whether a contingent casting vote could be used to reverse a decision that had been dependent upon a vote that was subsequently impeached. The principle appears to be the same, but the implications suggest that a contingent vote in these circumstances should be used only in exceptional circumstances, e.g. where a decision of the council is required to comply with a timetable.

The moment of decision

7.120 It has been considered earlier when a resolution becomes effective. But when, precisely, does a meeting commit itself to a decision on a vote? Suppose, after a show of hands on a motion but before a requisition, i.e. a recording of the vote, is demanded (either under standing orders or, in the case of a parish or community council, under statutory provisions), a late-arriving member turns up and demands to be included in the voting. Is this permissible or is the requisition a clarification of the voting already under way, i.e. merely machinery for ascertaining accurately what the sense of the meeting was on the discussion that has preceded it?

7.121 The answer is that a member present at a meeting is entitled to vote at any time before the chairman declares the outcome of the voting in a final way. Thus, where a requisition is demanded after a show of hands (and, as indicated above, it must be demanded immediately), a decision has not yet been made and there is nothing to stop a member who was not present at the show of hands from voting on the requisition or to prevent a member who voted one way at the show of hands changing their mind and voting differently. Just when a vote has finally been settled is a question of fact, which must rest with the chairman. These rules are also subject to any particular requirements imposed by standing orders. Some authorities have adopted a standing order that provides that members must be in the council chamber 'when the question is put' in order to be able to vote. Putting the question means asking for those in favour of a motion, and it would not be in order, under such a standing order, for a member to arrive in the chamber after that point had been reached and expect their vote to be counted. See the discussion at 11.38 on when a committee decision has been finalised.

Voting under misapprehension

7.122 It is not good practice to allow a member to alter their vote after they have cast it. Except, therefore, where a member changed their mind before the final declaration by the chairman of the outcome of the vote (see above), a member who has voted under a misapprehension ought not to be allowed subsequently to alter their vote.

7.123 Voting in meetings, particularly in large meetings, can be difficult to manage and is one of those activities where there is room for error. To have a vote challenged can be embarrassing and confusing, and whoever is in charge of the counting, be it chairman or officer, needs to get it right first time and ensure that members know exactly what it is they are voting on, and when the voting for or against is called. A moment or two devoted to this is time well spent and could avoid possible allegations of illegality later on. A good chairman will also insist that all members are in their seats when formal votes are counted. This not only ensures that a check can be kept on who votes, but also avoids the problem of members entering the chamber and voting after the question has been put if standing orders preclude this.

Preservation of order

Chairman's powers and duties

7.124 The chairman of a meeting is entitled to call upon any disorderly person, whether councillor or stranger, to behave properly. If that person continues to misbehave then, if the person is a stranger (i.e. a member of the public or, conceivably, an officer) they should be asked to withdraw from the meeting; and if they refuse the chairman may direct their removal by such force as may be reasonably necessary for the disorderly person's expulsion. If the person is a councillor, they should be asked to withdraw voluntarily; and if they refuse, the chairman's most practical course is to suspend or adjourn the meeting temporarily (see 7.80). The distinction between councillor and the public is important because a member of the public is present by licence on what are private premises (and this is the case even though there is a statutory right for the public to have access to local authority meetings), whereas a councillor is present by right of their office and cannot be excluded from attending. See *Marshall v Tinnelly* (1937), as to ejection of a disorderly councillor from the meeting of an urban district council.

7.125 Where there is unruly behaviour by several persons, whether councillors or strangers or both, so that the continued transaction of business is impracticable, the chairman may (and in practice ought to) suspend the meeting temporarily until order can be restored: suspend is a more appropriate term than adjourn in such circumstances, although the terms are interchangeable. Thus, in *John v Rees* (1969), Megarry J said this (and the learned judge's views merit quoting at length now that, regrettably, violent disorder at council meetings has become common):

> 'The first duty of the chairman of a meeting is to keep order if he can. If there is disorder his duty, I think, is to make earnest and sustained efforts to restore order, and for this purpose to summon to his aid any officers or others whose assistance is available. If all his efforts are in vain, he should endeavour to put into operation whatever provisions for adjournment there are in the rules, as by obtaining a resolution to adjourn. If this proves impossible, he should exercise his inherent power to adjourn the meeting for a short time, such as 15 minutes, taking due steps to ensure so far as possible that all present know of this adjournment. If instead of mere disorder there is violence, I think that he should take similar steps, save that the greater the violence the less prolonged should be his efforts to restore order before adjourning. In my judgement, he has not merely a power but a duty to adjourn in this way, in the interests of those who fear for their safety. I am not suggesting that there is a power and a duty to adjourn if the violence consists of no more than a few technical assaults and batteries. Mere pushing and jostling is one thing; it is another when people

are put in fear, where there is heavy punching, or the knives are out, so that blood may flow, and there are prospects, or more, of grievous bodily harm. In the latter case the sooner the chairman adjourns the meeting the better. At meetings, as elsewhere, the Queen's Peace must be kept. If then, the chairman has this inherent power and duty, what limitations, if any, are there upon its exercise? First, I think that the power and duty must be exercised bona fide for the purpose of forwarding and facilitating the meeting, and not for the purpose of interruption or procrastination. Second, I think that the adjournment must be for no longer than the necessities appear to dictate. If the adjournment is merely for such period as the chairman considers to be reasonably necessary for the restoration of order, it would be within his "power and his duty"; a longer adjournment would not. One must remember that to attend a meeting may for some mean travelling far and giving up much leisure. An adjournment to another day when a mere 15 minutes might suffice to restore order may well impose an unjustifiable burden on many; for they must either once more travel far and give up their leisure, or else remain away and lose their chance to speak and vote at the meeting.'

Disorderly conduct by members

7.126 Standing orders will usually set out a procedure seeking first to stop the individual member from engaging in disorderly conduct, and if they do not stop when requested by the chairman, for the temporary suspension of the meeting. The model standing order in the Modular Constitution is as follows:

21.3 Member not to be heard further
If a member persistently disregards the ruling of the chairman by behaving improperly or offensively or deliberately obstructs business, the chairman may move that the member be not heard further. If seconded, the motion will be voted on without discussion.
21.4 Member to leave the meeting
If the member continues to behave improperly after such a motion is carried, the chairman may move that either the member leaves the meeting or that the meeting is adjourned for a specified period. If seconded, the motion will be voted on without discussion.

7.127 The terms of this standing order would not preclude the chairman themselves from calling the offending councillor to order because of the chairman's common law duty to preserve order; but the chairman would be wise – because of the member's statutory right to be present in the council chamber – not to ask the councillor to leave, even temporarily, without positive assurance that it is the wish of the meeting. There is no power (unlike in the case of Parliament) to suspend a member. The power of the House of Commons to expel a Member of Parliament derives from the ancient usages of Parliament. The Speaker is nowadays armed by standing orders with precisely defined powers. The Commons can, if so minded, expel an MP for any reason whatsoever, even though in so doing it effectively disenfranchises the electors who voted the member into office. This extreme power is rarely exercised in full measure. What is more usual is for a Member of Parliament, having been named by the Speaker for, say, gross disorderly conduct, to be suspended under the Commons standing order no. 45 for five sitting days of the House including the day of suspension, and then to be escorted from the precincts of the House by the sergeant at arms using such force as may be necessary. It is interesting that the model standing order does not provide for a councillor's removal by force, nor did the previous old standing orders. See *R v St Mary's, Lambeth* (1832), as to the adjournment of a meeting by the chairman of his own volition when general uproar arose.

7.128 The Nolan Committee was concerned about the absence of sanctions available against members who flout standing orders or otherwise fall short of acceptable behaviour in meetings. Previously, the standards committee of a local authority could deal with any such matter if it was the subject of a complaint to the standards committee, e.g. by imposing disciplinary sanctions, including suspension from meetings for up to three months. The new standards regime for England introduced by the Localism Act 2011 has, however, removed the ability to apply such sanctions (see chapter 4).

Disorderly conduct by the public

7.129 Disorderly conduct by an individual other than a councillor is best dealt with if practicable by their removal after they have been given the opportunity, and refuse, of leaving quietly of their own accord. If the disorder is committed by a number of persons, a short adjournment is preferable either to give the offending persons the opportunity of behaving properly or to facilitate their removal from the meeting. No more force should be used than is reasonably necessary for the purpose of securing the offenders' removal (see *Hawkins v Muff* (1911)). If unnecessary violence is used in ejecting a person, damages may be awarded against the chairman (but only if the chairman personally authorised the removal beforehand (*Doyle v Falconer* (1866)) or subsequently ratified the ejection (*Lucas v Mason* (1875)). If public disorder is likely, then it may be wise to request that the police attend the meeting to ensure that no public order offences are committed, or to exclude the public.

7.130 If a person expelled by order of the chairman resists his removal and lays hand on the chairman or other person who is removing them, it is an unjustifiable assault amounting to a breach of the peace. Such resistance would justify their being given or taken into custody. But mere disorderly conduct short of a breach of the peace, though it may justify ejection, would not justify a person's being given into custody: see *Wooding v Oxley* (1839).

7.131 Model standing order no. 22 of the Modular Constitution is to the following effect:

22. Disturbance by public
22.1 Removal of member of the public
If a member of the public interrupts proceedings, the chairman will warn the person concerned. If they continue to interrupt, the chairman will order their removal from the meeting room.
22.2 Clearance of part of meeting room
If there is a general disturbance in any part of the meeting room open to the public, the chairman may call for that part to be cleared. Widdicombe felt it was important that there should be this express duty: on a chairman to bring disturbance to a halt because of 'suspicion of connivance by the chair' in disorder at council meetings.

Anticipation of disorder

7.132 It appears that a local authority could properly on reasonable grounds anticipate the probability of disorder and so exclude the public in advance. In *R v Brent Health Authority ex parte Francis and Another* (1985), it was held that it was lawful for a body to which at that time the Public Bodies (Admission to Meetings) Act 1960 (PB(AM)A 1960) applied to exclude members of the public from attending a meeting in view of the likelihood that members of the public would disrupt proceedings. Forbes J said:

> 'Exclusion did not only have the meaning of excluding people already at a meeting but also . . . of preventing people coming at all.'

Mass demonstrations

7.133 Mass lobbying of councillors attending council meetings and the presence of large numbers of demonstrators in the public gallery are ever-present possibilities that need to be anticipated and appropriately regulated so as to permit orderly and effective representations without disruption of council proceedings and breach of public order. It will rarely be practicable to accommodate all those who may wish to enter the council chamber (and there is no obligation on the local authority to go beyond making reasonable provision in this respect (see 3.17)), but much can be done to avoid trouble and misunderstandings if simple precautionary measures are taken in advance, for example:

- When the presence of large numbers of demonstrators is expected, invite the organisers to attend beforehand for a discussion as to how best to meet their reasonable and lawful wishes.
- Offer to provide assembly points for demonstrators outside the council offices, an opportunity for their leaders to meet the chairman or leader of the council before

the meeting begins, and the reservation of an agreed number of seats in the public gallery for representatives of the demonstrators. It may be thought desirable to publicise the likelihood of an abnormal attendance and explain that the general public will be admitted up to the limit of accommodation on a 'first come first served' basis.

- Review security measures to prevent unauthorised access to the council's offices and restrict entry to the public gallery by one door only.
- Alert the police and enlist their help and cooperation: see next paragraph.
- Consult the fire officer on means of escape and maximum numbers that can safely be admitted to the meeting place.
- Consider relaying the proceedings into another room/alternative building so that a larger number can listen.
- Consider relaying the proceedings over the internet by webcast.

Powers of the police

7.134 The police have no power to enter upon council premises, except by leave of the council or its officers, unless they have reason to believe that a breach of the peace is being committed or they have reasonable grounds for believing that an offence is imminent or likely to be committed (*Thomas v Sawkins* (1935)). It is a wise precaution therefore for the local authority to ask for the police to be present when disorder is anticipated.

7.135 Where the police are present they should not be called upon to intervene unless there is a breach of the peace or a breach is imminent. The chairman should ask any disorderly person to leave and if this proves ineffectual, they should direct the council's own employees to eject the offending person in the first place and only if they violently resist would the police be justified in intervening. The police, indeed, must intervene if there is breach of the peace and may arrest without warrant anyone they believe responsible for such breach. It is useful to ensure that any attending police officers are aware of which officer will try to eject the public and when they will be expected to intervene, prior to the commencement of the meeting.

Duration of council meeting

7.136 Unless standing orders provide to the contrary or the members at a meeting decide otherwise, proceedings must continue until all business on the agenda has been dealt with. However, many authorities provide by standing orders for a break in proceedings after a specified period of time, particularly as most meetings of the full council are held in the evening.

7.137 The model standing orders suggested alternatives to allow for a 'guillotine' when a particular time limit was reached. Some councils had already sought to improve the quality of decision-making by restricting the length of meetings to, say, two and a half or three hours on the basis that an adequate level of concentration cannot be maintained for extensive periods.

In the following model standing orders from the Modular Constitution, Option 1 forces the meeting to end by a certain time but avoids matters being talked out deliberately to block them. Option 2 is not an absolute guillotine, but the majority of the meeting must want to continue after a set period.

9. Duration of meeting

Option 1 – guillotine

9.1 Interruption of the meeting

If the business of the meeting has not been concluded by [time], a bell will be rung and the member speaking must immediately sit down. The chairman must interrupt the meeting and call for the vote immediately on the item under discussion. The vote will then be taken in the usual way without any further discussion.

9.2 Motions and recommendations not dealt with

If there are other motions or recommendations on the agenda that have not been dealt with by [time], they are deemed formally moved and seconded (together with any amendments). No speeches will be allowed on these items and the vote will be taken in the usual way.

9.3 Recorded vote

If a recorded vote is called for during this process it will be taken immediately.

9.4 Motions which may be moved

During the process set out in Rules 9.19.3 above, the only other motions which may be moved are that a matter be withdrawn or that a matter be delegated or referred to an appropriate body or individual for decision or report.

9.5 Close of the meeting

When all motions and recommendations have been dealt with, the chairman will declare the meeting closed.

Option 2 – majority vote to continue

Unless the majority of members present vote for the meeting to continue, any meeting that has lasted for [n] hours will adjourn immediately. Remaining business will be considered at a time and date fixed by the chairman. If he/she does not fix a date, the remaining business will be considered at the next ordinary meeting.

Transaction of special business

Honorary aldermen and freemen

7.138 A principal council may, by resolution passed by not less than two-thirds of the members voting thereon at a meeting of the council specially convened for the purpose with notice of the object[23] (no other business can be transacted at such a meeting, but the specially convened meeting could either precede or follow an annual or ordinary or extraordinary meeting of the council), confer the title of honorary alderman or honorary alderwoman on persons who have, in the opinion of the council, rendered eminent services to the council as past members of that council but who are not then councillors of the council.

7.139 An honorary alderman/alderwoman may attend and take part in such civic ceremonies as the council may from time to time decide but, as such, has no right:

- to attend meetings of the council, cabinet or a committee other than as a member of the public (including a joint committee upon which the council is represented); or
- to receive any of the allowances or other payments to which councillors are entitled.

7.140 Section 249(4A) of the LGA 1972 provides that principal councils:

> '. . . may spend such reasonable sum as it thinks fit for the purpose of presenting an address, or a casket containing an address, to a person upon whom it has conferred the title of honorary alderman or honorary alderwoman.'

7.141 It may also, by resolution passed by not less than two-thirds of the members voting thereon at a meeting of the council specially convened for the purpose with notice of the object, admit to be honorary freemen or honorary freewomen of the city, borough or royal borough, persons of distinction and persons who have, in the council's opinion, rendered eminent services to the city, borough or royal borough, but the admission of a person to be an honorary freeman/freewoman does not confer on them the rights granted to be honorary aldermen/alderwomen. The council may spend such reasonable sum as it thinks fit for the same purposes as in the case of an honorary alderman/alderwoman.

7.142 In most cases the proposal to confer the title of honorary alderman/alderwoman or to admit a person to be an honorary freeman/freewoman will be submitted to the specially convened meeting of the council as a recommendation from the cabinet. Appropriate recommendations would be that:

> '1 That . . . be admitted as an honorary alderman/freeman [alderwoman/freewoman] of the... under s. 249 of the Local Government Act 1972 in recognition of [the eminent services which s/he has rendered to...] [his/her distinguished . . .] [and that his/her name be enrolled on the freemen's roll].
> 2 That the common seal of the council be affixed to the [enrolment of . . . on the said freemen's roll and to the certificate to be presented to him/her on his/ her admission as an honorary freeman [freewoman] of . . .] [certificate conferring upon . . . the title of honorary alderman [alderwoman]].
> 3 That an estimated expenditure of . . . be approved for purposes associated with the appointment and that the leader be authorised to agree any consequential matters.'

Promoting or opposing a bill in Parliament

7.143 A local authority, other than a parish or community council, if satisfied that it is expedient so to do, may promote a local or personal bill in Parliament; and any local authority – again, if satisfied that it is expedient so to do – may oppose any local or personal bill.[24] In either case, however, it may only do so in accordance with the procedure laid down.

7.144 This procedure requires that a resolution of the council to promote or oppose a bill shall be:

- passed by a majority of the whole number of the members of the authority at a meeting of the authority held after the requisite notice of the meeting and of its purpose has been given by advertisement in one or more local newspapers circulating in the area of the authority, such notice being given in addition to the ordinary notice required to be given for the convening of a meeting of the authority; and
- in the case of the promotion of a bill, confirmed by a like majority at a further meeting convened in accordance with the paragraph above and held as soon as may be after the expiration of 14 days after the bill has been deposited in Parliament and, if the resolution is not confirmed, the local authority shall take all necessary steps to withdraw the bill.

For this purpose, the requisite notice is 30 clear days' notice in the case of promotion of a bill and 10 clear days' notice in the case of opposition to a bill.

7.145 This procedure overrules that by which questions before the local authority are ordinarily decided, i.e. by a majority of the members merely present and voting at a meeting, and, further, requires additional notice. Exceptionally, too, in the case of the promotion of a bill there has to be a confirmatory resolution at a further meeting convened after special additional notice. The terms of the statute imply (though they do not expressly state) that the meeting must be specially convened and exclusively for the purpose. Any doubt there may be in this respect could be overcome by arranging for such a meeting to be held immediately before an ordinary meeting of the council.

Political organisation of council business

Acknowledgement in standing orders

7.146 It is generally the practice, apart from the statutory provisions providing for political balance in the membership of committees, etc., for authorities to acknowledge the existence and the role of party politics in the provision made in standing orders. There is much to commend this: for example, the chief executive will ordinarily turn to the leader of the council, i.e. the leader of the majority political group on the council rather than as in the past to the chairman of the council or the mayor when wishing in circumstances of urgency to take the council's collective view of a matter; and, as circumstances may dictate, consult also the leader of the opposition group. The major parties invariably appoint whips for the organisation of group business, and certain nominal duties associated with the membership of the council may well fall upon them: settling, for example, the seating arrangements in the council chamber.

7.147 With the development of hung or balanced councils, where no one party has overall control, has come the practice of consulting spokespersons of all the main parties. This practice is part of the list of conventions for dealing with political arrangements adopted by authorities, such as hung councils, with little if any experience of dealing with such a council. Where spokespersons of several parties are involved in consultations between meetings, it is often the case that no action can be taken by officers unless there is unanimity between the politicians.

Party group business

7.148 Standing orders may properly be drawn up to require the party groups to notify certain information to the council officially, to place nominal duties of a political nature upon the party whips, and such like. However, standing orders must not, for example, by recognising decisions taken in party groups, override the formal decision-making procedure prescribed by law as that would be *ultra vires*.

Standing orders

7.149 With regard to whips, standing orders might provide that:

> 'Two members of the council elected from time to time as whips by the members forming the party in office on the council and by those forming the largest party in opposition on the council respectively shall be known as the chief whip and opposition whip respectively.
>
> The whips shall, as far as possible, jointly and in consultation with the chief executive, consider as necessary the despatch of the business at meetings of the council and its committtees and the appointment to membership of committees and other bodies.
>
> The party in office on the council may appoint junior whips.'

7.150 Certain other consequential matters may need to be included in standing orders, e.g. in the standing order dealing with the order of business at the annual meeting, the following item:

> 'To receive a report as to the appointment of leader of the council and leader of the opposition, chief whip and opposition whip, and their deputies as necessary.'

Notes

1 See Local Authorities (Standing Orders) Regulations 1993, Sch. 2, para. 2.
2 Para.41 is amended by the LG&HA 1989, Sch. 11, para. 30.
3 LGA 1972, ss. 4(3), 8 (Sch. 2, paras. 3(3), 23(3).
4 Ibid., s. 4(2), 8 (Sch. 2, para. 3(2)), 15(3), 23(2).
5 Ibid., ss. 2(1), 2(2), 2(2a), 14(1), 8 (Sch. 2, para. 1), 2 1(1), 33(1).
6 Ibid., ss. 3(2), 15(4), 22(2), which provide that the chairman shall continue in office until his successor becomes entitled to act as chairman; and Sch. 12, paras. 5(1), 11(1), 27(1), which provide that the chairman, if present, shall preside.
7 Ibid., s. 5(1).
8 Ibid., ss. 15(6), 34(6).
9 Ibid., ss. 5(2), 15(7), 34(7). Strictly interpreted this provision might seem to deny a vice-chairman, unless they resign first, the opportunity of being elected as chairman in the event of a vacancy in the office of chairman before the next annual meeting!
10 Ibid., ss. 5(2), 15(8), 34(8), and Sch. 2, para. 4(2).
11 Ibid., ss. 5(3), 15(9), 34(9), and Sch. 2, para. 4(3).
12 Ibid., Sch. 12, para. 5(1).
13 Ibid., Sch. 12, paras. 11(1), 27(1).
14 Ibid., Sch. 12, paras. 11(2), 27(2).
15 Ibid., Sch. 12, paras. 11(3), 27(3).
16 Ibid., Sch. 12, para. 49(1).
17 Ibid., Sch. 12, paras. 13(1), 29(1).
18 Ibid., Sch. 12, paras. 13(2), 29(2) and see 7.102.
19 Ibid., Sch. 12, paras. 34(2), 18(2). It is expressly provided that each elector eligible to attend may give one vote and no more on any question, whether at a meeting or at a poll consequent thereon: paras. 18(1), 34(1).
20 Local Authorities (Standing Orders) Regulations 1993, Sch. 2, para. l.
21 The single transferable vote system has long been used in Northern Ireland. In the Electoral Law (Northern Ireland) Order 1972 it is defined thus: ' "Transferable vote" means a vote:

(a) capable of being given so as to indicate the voter's preference for the candidates in order; and
(b) capable of being transferred to the next choice when the vote is not required to give a prior choice the necessary quota of votes or when, owing to the deficiency in the number of votes given for a prior choice, that choice is eliminated from the list of candidates.'

22 In July 1975 in the House of Commons, three MPs cast their vote twice, i.e. both for and against a motion in an attempt, unsuccessfully as it happened, and not seriously it was said, to achieve a quorum on the record and so enable a resolution to be passed to which it was known the majority was not opposed. The ruse was discovered and the Whips concerned had to apologise.
23 Notice would need to be given in accordance with LGA 1972, Sch. 12, para. 4(2), apart from the specific obligation in this case.
24 LGA 1972, s. 239.

Chapter 8
Council minutes

General considerations

Introduction

8.1 This chapter is concerned with the law and practice relating to the keeping of local authority minutes of proceedings and their authentication, and the obligation to make them available for public inspection. Many of the statutory provisions apply also to minutes of committees and sub-committees, and to executive meetings; where there are differences these will be referred to later in Chapter 12. Also considered here is the form that council and cabinet minutes take, invariably differing from that adopted for committee and sub-committee minutes. For reasons that defy logical explanation, the formality of meetings of the full council is generally reflected in a corresponding formality of style in minuting the proceedings.

What are minutes?

8.2 Minutes, in the sense commonly understood, are brief notes of the proceedings at a meeting that in particular record the decisions made. There is, however, no statutory definition of minutes and by common law there is no obligation that a permanent or any written record of matters transacted at a meeting should be kept. Clearly it is expedient and convenient, apart from any legal requirement, that minutes should be kept in some permanent form. However, if the record is to have greater weight than mere recollection, the minutes must be made within a reasonable time after the meeting to which they relate (*Toms v Cinema Trust* (1915)). Even where, as in the case of local authority minutes, the law requires that minutes shall be kept, the minute book may be written up from rough notes taken at the time of the meeting (*Re Jennings* (1851)).

8.3 There is justification for the view that minutes can mean two things: the narrative record of all business transacted at a meeting, and a copy of the resolutions passed by those present. The law permits evidence to explain the narrative, e.g. to show reasons for a decision and the basis upon which it was taken;[1] but not to explain a resolution, and there is a view that resolutions must be framed so as to be self-explanatory, and wholly intelligible without reference to any other document or evidence. In *Re Fireproof Doors Ltd* (1916), evidence was held to be admissible to show that a resolution that was not recorded had in fact been passed.

The minute book

Keeping the minutes

8.4 The law requires that the minutes of proceedings of council and committee (and sub-committee) meetings, when drawn up, shall be 'entered in a book kept for that purpose'. This requirement,[2] formerly enacted in the LGA 1933 and earlier legislation, was rigidly construed, so that it was the practice of many local authorities at one time to insist that the minutes were written up by hand in the numbered pages of a bound book; later that they were entered in such a book either by typing direct on the pages (by means of a special typewriter, probably no longer manufactured, called a book-writer) or by pasting in to the book sheets of paper on which the minutes had been typed. Then later still, before the law was changed, authorities began to defy the strict letter of the law and kept their minutes temporarily in a loose-leaf system until there were sufficient sheets to warrant binding.

Loose-leaf minutes

8.5 Minutes may lawfully be 'recorded on loose leaves consecutively numbered, provided each sheet is initialled by the person who signs the minutes to which the leaves relate' (Local Government Act 1972 Sch. 12, para. 41). This initialling must be done at the time the minutes are signed.

Preservation in perpetuity

8.6 Minutes must be kept in perpetuity. For this reason they must be prepared on durable paper and, if kept initially in loose-leaf form, bound up ultimately in order to preserve them. The arrangements should be made the specific responsibility of an identified officer and systematically planned in advance, i.e. it should be decided how frequently the loose leaves are to be bound together (because this will determine the consecutive numbering of pages and the make-up of the index) and whether documents incorporated by reference are to be bound in the minute book itself as appendices or preserved separately and, if separately, in what manner.

Safe custody

8.7 The safe custody of minutes is important, and it is the responsibility of each principal council:

> '. . . to give directions as to the documents of any council and to make proper arrangements with respect to any documents which belong to or are in the custody of the council or any of its officers.[3] Minutes must be kept under lock and key and ordinarily in fire-resistant safes (although not so inaccessibly stored away as not to be readily available for purposes of inspection): and these precautions are especially needed in the case of minutes kept in a loose-leaf system pending binding.'

Council minutes form

General

8.8 Council minutes can take whatever form is preferred by the individual authority or relevant officer concerned. There are certain general principles governing the drafting of minutes that should be observed (and these are set out later in Chapter 12 in regard to committee and executive minutes), but the principles are flexible and what matters primarily is that the minutes record clearly and concisely all decisions taken at the meeting and of the other proceedings as is necessary to give reasons to the decision-making. To quote one example only of the wide variation in practice: some authorities meticulously minute all questions asked and the replies given at question time in the council chamber, but most authorities do not.

General style

8.9 As indicated above, council minutes traditionally reflect the formality of council proceedings and are generally different in style to committee minutes. Resolutions can be recorded showing the names of the proposer and seconder, e.g.:

> 'Moved [or proposed] by Councillor Jones. Seconded by Councillor Smith, and Resolved: That the report of the Cabinet . . . be approved and adopted by the Council.'

Or, as an alternative style:

> 'It was moved by Councillor Jones and seconded by Councillor Robinson that the report of the Cabinet be approved and adopted by the Council.
>
> An amendment was moved by Councillor Smith and seconded by Councillor Brown that the following words be added to the motion: "except that para. A be referred back to the Cabinet for reconsideration".
>
> After debate the amendment was voted upon and declared not carried, 15 members voting "for" and 25 "against".
>
> A further amendment was moved by Councillor White and seconded by Councillor Black that the following words be added to the motion: "except that para. A be approved in principle only and that the Cabinet be instructed to report further on the detailed implementation of the recommendations".
>
> After debate the amendment was voted upon and declared carried by 25 votes to 15. It was RESOLVED that the report of the Cabinet dated . . . be approved and adopted as amended.'

Or, where the local authority has adopted the practice of using a motion to receive cabinet reports, i.e. the procedural motion to bring a report before the council for consideration (see 7.42), the style reflecting this could be to the effect, e.g.:

> **'00 Report of the Cabinet**
> Moved (or proposed) by Councillor Jones, Seconded by Councillor Robinson; and Resolved: That the report of the Cabinet of . . . be received. Amendment Moved (or proposed) by Councillor Smith, Seconded by Councillor Brown: That para. A be referred back to the Cabinet for reconsideration.
> After debate,
> Amendment put to the vote and declared not carried. Further amendment Moved (or proposed) by Councillor White, Seconded by Councillor Black: That para. A be approved in principle only and that the Cabinet be instructed to report further on the detailed implementation of the corporate plan.
> After debate,
> Amendment put to the vote and declared carried.
> Resolved: That the report of the Cabinet of . . . be approved and adopted as amended.'

8.10 There could be almost endless variations in this style. However, there are some basic principles to be followed in all minuting, particularly the formal minuting of meetings of the full council, and the recording of key decisions of the executive. The final resolution should be clear and ideally capable of being understood without extensive cross-referencing because the more this is necessary, the greater the chance of some future researcher being misled or confused, and the more pieces of paper and research that has to be carried out if a public request is made for a copy. Where a number of amendments have been carried relating to the same motion it is helpful to set out in full the final substantive motion, e.g. as in the example in 8.9. Also, it is important that there is consistency within each authority so as to avoid the use of different phrases meaning the same thing, i.e. there should be an agreed standardisation of layout and commonly occurring phrases and terms to avoid any ambiguity.

8.11 There are occasions, i.e. whenever there is a division or a request for a recorded vote, when the names of members present must be recorded to show how each voted – for or against – or abstained from voting. No particular form of minute is required, so long as the manner in which each member voted or abstained from voting is clearly recorded.

Minuting and receiving committee reports

8.12 Each local authority has its own practice in the way in which a committee or cabinet report to be submitted to the meetings of full council for decision are incorporated in the council minutes and the debate thereon recorded. This is not the regular standard practice it once was – under the old committee system, some authorities went to the extreme of insisting that full council ratified the decision of each committee before that decision could be implemented. Where such referrals to councils are more common than not, however, the practice most widely adopted was for committee/cabinet reports to be incorporated by reference. For example, the adoption of a cabinet report will be minuted in this manner (and the report itself will have to be sought elsewhere by those who do not have access to the signed minutes):

> 'Moved by Councillor Jones, Seconded by Councillor Robinson; and Resolved: That the recommendations of the Committee/Cabinet . . . (set out [specify where]) be approved.'

Generally the particular report will be identifiable by reference to the council meeting agenda. Where the recommendation in a report is amended or there is debate to be recorded, the minuting will be as indicated above.

8.13 As reports for adoption by council from the executive or a committee are now more seldom and limited to major policy documents and the budget, it is more normal to include each cabinet/committee report, together with that body's minutes and recommendations where available in time, along with the council agenda and minutes.

Minuting question time

8.14 Some local authorities minute verbatim the questions that are asked at council meetings, and the answers provided by cabinet members. Where this practice is adopted then both question and answer should be recorded. Some authorities merely record the question with a note to the effect that the portfolio holder/cabinet member replied without specifying the terms of the answer.

Indexing

8.15 What is said later in Chapter 12 about indexing committee minutes applies substantially to the indexing of council minutes.

Authorising the common seal

General considerations

8.16 Because the use of the local authority's common seal on a deed binds the authority (and provides unimpeachable authenticity to any other document to which it is affixed),[4] the seal must be kept in safe custody and used only in pursuance of a resolution of the council or cabinet, or an officer to whom the council has delegated its power in that respect. Model standing orders deal with both matters.

Safe custody

8.17 The old model standing order provided that the common seal of the council would be kept in a safe place in the custody of the town clerk/clerk of the council and would be secured by two different locks, the keys of which shall be kept respectively by the mayor/chairman and the town clerk/clerk of the council (provided that the mayor/chairman may entrust their key temporarily to another member of the council, and the town clerk/clerk of the council may entrust their key temporarily to any deputy appointed by the council).

In practice now, it is more likely that the common seal will only have one lock on it, if any, and that the keys are kept by officers.

Sealing of documents

8.18 The model standing order is to this effect:

> **14.05 Common Seal of the Council**
> The Common Seal of the Council will be kept in a safe place in the custody of the [chief legal officer]. A decision of the Council, or of any part of it, will be sufficient authority for sealing any document necessary to give effect to the decision. The Common Seal will be affixed to those documents which in the opinion of the [chief legal officer] should be sealed. The affixing of the Common Seal will be attested by the [chief legal officer] or some other person authorised by him/her.

8.19 The previous model standing orders provided for the mayor or chairman to attest the seal but of course this could cause practical difficulties in getting documents sealed on a regular basis, and also involved members in operational details of the council's business.

Date of sealing operative date of document

8.20 A resolution to make, for example, a compulsory purchase order that must be sealed does not itself 'make' the order: the resolution is no more than an expression of intention or instruction to those who have the duty of affixing the seal. A local authority can, subject to exceptions not here relevant, act only by seal for certain purposes, e.g. a compulsory purchase order is not 'made' until sealed.

Council minutes as reference documents

8.21 Where the council minutes set out in full the cabinet or principal committee reports before the full council, this single document (the minutes for a particular meeting) can be referred to in the confident knowledge that the minutes are wholly self-contained. Where, as in the majority of cases, the cabinet reports are not reprinted direct into the minutes, a reader must necessarily look at two documents: the council minutes and the cabinet/committee reports referred to; and although this may not be an onerous task, it is often not difficult to misread or misunderstand the reasons for a decision in the council minutes.

Authentication of minutes

Confirmation

8.22 Council minutes, when written up, and entered in the minute book, are submitted for confirmation to the next succeeding meeting. This means that minutes of the full council, whether of an annual or extraordinary meeting, are properly submitted at the next meeting of the council whatever its character, i.e. the minutes of, say, an annual meeting do not have to wait for confirmation until the next annual meeting.

8.23 There is a mandatory standing order as regards the minutes of an extraordinary meeting to this effect:

> 'Where in relation to any meeting of the full council the next such meeting is a meeting called under paragraph 3 (extraordinary meetings) of Schedule 12 to the Local Government Act 1972, the next following meeting of the authority (being a meeting called otherwise than under that paragraph) shall be treated as a suitable meeting for the purposes of paragraphs 41(1) and (2) (signing of minutes) of that schedule.' [Local Authorities (Standing Orders) Regulations 1993, SI 1993/202, Sch. 2 para. 2; and the Local Authorities (Standing Orders) (Wales) Regulations 2006, SI 2006/1275, Sch. 2 para. 2.]

8.24 The term 'confirmation' is misleading. Minutes do not require confirmation in the ordinary sense of that word: the decisions taken at a meeting are of immediate effect (but note the decisions of the executive) and do not depend upon their first being written up and subsequently approved and signed at the next succeeding meeting. The minutes are merely a record of what has already actually taken place but their confirmation – in the manner referred to below – has important legal consequences.

8.25 The act of confirmation does not require the minutes to be read nor need a copy have been circulated beforehand to members. Minutes of the previous council meeting are nevertheless often circulated with the summons and agenda. If the unsigned minutes are circulated it makes it difficult for any person to challenge their accuracy after confirmation. If they are not circulated the minute book should be kept available for inspection by any member who may wish to check the minutes before agreeing to their confirmation and the minute book should be laid on the table for, say, half an hour before commencement of the meeting at which the minutes are to be confirmed.

8.26 The only question that can properly arise on the confirmation of minutes is that of their accuracy. Model standing order no. 18.1, for example, provides that:

> **'18. Minutes**
> **18.1 Signing the minutes**
> The chairman will sign the minutes of the proceedings at the next suitable meeting. The chairman will move that the minutes of the previous meeting be signed as a correct record. The only part of the minutes that can be discussed is their accuracy.'

The occasion is not one for a resumption of debate on items recorded in the minutes (see *Mawley v Barber* (1803) and *R v Mayor of York* (1853)), nor, strictly, should the minutes be used as the basis for reporting subsequent action. The inclusion on an agenda of an item to the effect: '00. Matters arising on the minutes', is bad practice and of doubtful legality.[5] If any item dealt with at a previous meeting needs to be discussed further, a separate item should appear on the agenda.

8.27 Within the model standing order, it is a convenient arrangement that the chairman moves the minutes. The motion to confirm the minutes of the previous meeting can be moved and seconded by members who were not present at that meeting, although it is preferable that those who were not present should abstain from voting and comment on the motion. Ordinarily, of course, there will be no formal motion: the chairman, will merely ask whether they may sign the minutes as a correct record and will proceed to place their signature in the minute book upon murmurs of assent. Where, however, a member does vote in favour of the signing of the minutes, they vote not for the decisions recorded but only for the accuracy of the record and they do not incur any liability or responsibility for the proceedings at such a meeting if they were not present at such meeting (*Re Lands Allotment Co.* (1894)).

8.28 The chairman who signs the minutes does so in pursuance of the requirement that they must do so and they need not have been present at the meeting of which the minutes are a record. If, however, for any reason, e.g. that the chairman suspects an inaccuracy in the minutes but has no support for this contention, and refuses to sign the minutes, the proper course is to record the circumstances by a minute to this effect:

> **'00 Minutes**
> The minutes of the meeting of . . . were confirmed as a correct record of the proceedings at that meeting but the chairman refused to sign them on the grounds that he believed them to be inaccurate in the following particular . . . but his view was not upheld by the council/committee/sub-committee.'

Evidence without further proof

8.29 Minutes that have been drawn up and entered in the minute book and signed at the same or next following meeting by the person presiding, i.e. at the meeting at which confirmation takes place, are prima facie good evidence of the proceedings:

the law prescribes that any minute purporting to be so signed 'shall be received in evidence without further proof'.[6] It is a common law rule that where minutes have been properly kept they shall be admissible as evidence. The effect of the provisions in the LGA 1972 Sch. 12 para. 41(1) and LGA 2000 s. 22 is that the minutes are inadmissible unless signed. Furthermore, until the contrary is proved, under LGA 1972 Sch. 12 para. 41(3), the meeting is deemed to have been duly convened and held and all the members present are deemed to have been duly qualified. There is no corresponding provision for meetings of the executive.

8.30 Under the LG (Miscellaneous Provisions) Act 1976 s. 41, a document that purports to be a copy of: (i) a resolution, order or report of a local authority or its committee or sub-committees; or (ii) the minutes thereof, and bears a certificate purporting to be signed by the proper officer or someone authorised by the proper officer or the council and stating that the resolution was passed or the order or report was made by the council (or its committees or sub-committees), is evidence in any proceedings of the matters stated in the certificate and of the terms of the resolution, order, report or minute in question. Section 41(2A) provides for similar provisions to the above in respect of decisions made by the executive (cabinet).

The effect of the above is that if an officer of the local authority goes into a witness box in court and produces the relevant certified minutes, there is no need to prove that the minutes were actually signed at the meeting or that the signature on them is actually the signature of the person presiding.[7] These provisions do not, however, mean that a signed minute is unchallengeable proof of the events recorded in the minutes. It is open to anyone who wishes to do so, for good reason, to try to prove in court that the minutes are not a true record of what took place at the meeting. But the onus of proof to the contrary is on the person challenging the signed minute.[8]

8.31 The case of *R v South Somerset District Council ex parte DJB (Group) Ltd* (1989) shows that the court will not lightly set aside properly authenticated minutes. The company had contended that the minutes of the council's policy and resources committee did not reflect what had actually happened at a meeting and that either the item of business in which it, the company, was interested was not really discussed or the discussion was merely by way of simply rubber-stamping an earlier decision taken between officers and the committee chairman without applying any, or any proper, thought to the item. The court refused to accept that there was anything irregular about the minutes. Saville J said:

> 'The allegations in respect of these minutes are of an extremely serious nature. They necessarily involve the assertion that those responsible for drawing them up and those who support them as an accurate account of what transpired have deliberately set out to adopt a course of dishonest conduct designed to deceive those who read the minutes without full notice or knowledge of what in fact transpired.'

The judge went on to refer to a minute of the next meeting of the committee recording that the minutes of the previous meeting had been approved as a correct record and signed by the chairman. The challenge to the authenticity of the minute, said the judge, necessarily involves the proposition that those present at this later meeting and who had been present at the earlier meeting (and there was a considerable number) were themselves either in the conspiracy to produce wholly inaccurate minutes for the purpose of deception or, at the lowest, had wholly failed in their duty to satisfy themselves that the minutes were an accurate record.

South Somerset is of interest for another reason. In the course of the judgement, the court commented on the principle that observations made by individual councillors in debate cannot be accepted necessarily as the grounds on which the collective decision was taken.

Alteration of minutes

8.32 Once the minutes have been confirmed, they must not be altered in any circumstances whatsoever.[9] However, if when a meeting is being asked to confirm the minutes of the preceding meeting and it is agreed – either on a member's representation or that of the chairman – that there is an inaccuracy that needs to be corrected, it is advisable for the fact to be duly noted in the minute recording the signing of the minutes, e.g.:

> 'Resolved: That the minutes of the meeting of . . . were approved and signed by the chairman subject to correction of . . .'

If an inaccuracy is discovered after the minutes have been signed then, again, the inaccuracy should be corrected by resolution, e.g.:

> 'Resolved: That the minutes of the meeting on . . . approved and signed by the chairman at the meeting on . . . be amended in the following respect to correct an inaccuracy subsequently discovered.

The particular minute challenged and agreed to be inaccurate should never be altered although a pencilled note could properly be made against the disputed minute by the proper officer indicating its subsequent correction.

Inspection of minutes

Statutory provisions

8.33 The public right of inspection of council minutes depends on the type of local authority and the date of the council meeting. Prior to the LG(AI)A 1985, the minutes of the proceedings of every local authority full council meeting were required to be open to inspection by any local government elector for the area and any such elector was entitled to take a copy or extract from the minutes. That is still the position as regards the minutes of parish and community councils. Now, by virtue of the 1985 Act, the minutes of the council meetings of principal councils are open to inspection by the public generally, but strictly for a period of six years, beginning with the date of the meeting. The position is substantially the same as regards the committee and sub-committee minutes of principal councils.

The minutes of the executive are also open to inspection by the public generally, these provisions being the Local Authorities (Executive Arrangements) (Access to Information) (England) Regulations 2012, made under s. 22 of the Local Government Act 2000. While generally referred to as 'minutes', this provision is actually better described by the Regulations as the 'recording of executive decisions made at meetings'. Regulation 14 provides that the minutes of an executive decision shall be made available for inspection by members of the public as soon as is reasonably practicable, at the offices of the local authority and on its website. Regulation 21 reflects the provisions under the LGA 1972 concerning time limits for retention.

Who may inspect

8.34 The simplification of the law by extending the right of inspection of council minutes of principal councils to the public and not just electors alone has eliminated some of the problems that had arisen in the past over who may in fact exercise the right to inspect. Nevertheless, as regards the council minutes of a local authority meeting held prior to 1 April 1986 (and still as regards those of parish and community councils and a parish meeting), the right of inspection vests strictly only in electors, although the right can be exercised through an agent: see *R v Gloucestershire County Council* (1936). However, see Chapter 3 for the provisions on Freedom of Information.

8.35 A member of every local authority has always possessed, as a councillor, a common law right to production of documents, including council minutes, which they need to see to carry out their council duties, but not for any other purpose (see *R v Wimbledon UDC* (1897) and *Stevens v Berwick-upon-Tweed Corporation* (1835)), although as there is now a public right of inspection and also the Freedom of Information Act 2000 provisions, the motive of the person inspecting is now immaterial.

8.36 Strictly speaking, the officer who has custody of the minutes of a parish or community council or parish or community meeting ought to check upon a person's credentials before making the minute book available for inspection. This may rarely be done in practice either because the council or the meeting makes its minutes freely available (e.g. by depositing copies in public libraries in the area or on its website) or because it decides that anyone may inspect as a matter of policy.

What may be inspected

8.37 The distinction between council minutes and committee, sub-committee and executive minutes is, for the purposes of inspection, no longer as important as it was prior to the LG(AI)A 1985 because, at least in the case of principal councils, all must equally be available for public inspection. In the case, however, of the minutes of parish and community councils and of all other council minutes of meetings prior to 1 April 1986, the minutes that must be open to inspection by electors include the minutes of a committee if submitted to the council for approval (*Williams v Manchester Corporation* (1897)).[10] Such committee minutes are inseparable from the council minutes because, it has been held, 'one could not understand the approval without seeing the recommendations'.

8.38 The law provides that after meetings of the full council, or committees and sub-committees, the following documents must be open to public inspection at the offices of the council until the expiration of a period of six years beginning with the date of the meeting:[11]

- the minutes, or a copy of the minutes,[12] of the meeting excluding so much of the minutes of proceedings during which the meeting was not open to the public as discloses exempt information;
- where applicable, a summary of the whole or part of the proceedings;
- a copy of the agenda for the meeting;[13] and
- a copy of so much of any report for the meeting as relates to any item during which the meeting was open to the public.

The summary must be prepared by the proper officer where, as a result of excluding exempt minutes, the document open to inspection does not provide the public 'with a reasonably fair and coherent report' of the whole or part of the proceedings without disclosing any exempt information.

Background papers

8.39 In addition, if and so long as copies of the whole or part of a report for a meeting of a principal council are required to be open to inspection by members of the public, there must be open to inspection at the council's offices for up to four years afterwards beginning with the date of the meeting:

- copies of a list,[14] compiled by the proper officer, of the background papers for the report or the part of the report; and
- at least one copy of each of the documents included in that list. However, there is no obligation to include any document that discloses exempt information or 'any document that, if open to inspection, would disclose confidential information in breach of the obligation of confidence'. A member of the public cannot demand the instant production of the papers: it will be sufficient to produce them on request at a suitable time and place; a clause in the original bill enabling the public to have immediate and largely unrestricted access was modified.

In reality, the majority of papers are now available for inspection on the local authority's website and clearly, where background papers are available, it is helpful if they are similarly held on the website.

8.40 Background papers are defined as those documents relating to the subject matter of the report:

- disclose any facts or matters on which, in the opinion of the proper officer, the report or an important part of the report is based;

- have, in their opinion, been relied on to a material extent in preparing the report;[15]

but do not include any published works.[16]

8.41 There are several questions that arise as a result of the above. Why, for example, was six years fixed as the period for inspection of minutes, agenda and reports when, at least in the case of council minutes, a local authority would ordinarily allow inspection virtually in perpetuity? Does it mean that inspection could be refused to a member of the public who wished to see minutes and other supporting papers for meetings (other than the executive) that are more than six years old? Why the difference between the six years for minutes, agenda and reports and four years only for background papers? It may be that s. 9 of the Limitation Act 1980 was in mind when a claim must be brought within six years. However, since the introduction of the Freedom of Information Act 2000, the time limits have become largely irrelevant, as requests can be made at any time. One kind of document likely to be caught by these provisions is a draft report, e.g. one prepared by officers and changed by the portfolio holder, with perhaps even recommendations altered. Such a report would almost certainly be caught by the statutory provisions, making it open to public inspection. Officers should be aware of this and consider destroying drafts once a final version has been settled.

8.42 Committee clerks' notes taken at a meeting, and on which the minutes are subsequently drafted, do not fall within the documents that must be made available for inspection; they are clearly not minutes, nor are they background papers. It is, however, good practice in any case, to destroy notes taken at a meeting as soon as the relevant minutes have been approved and signed. Otherwise they are of course subject to the provisions of the FOIA.

When minutes may be inspected

8.43 Documents, including minutes, open to public inspection, must be made available at all reasonable hours and:

- in the case of background papers, upon payment of such reasonable fee as may be required for the facility; and
- in any other case, i.e. including minutes, without payment.

Where a document is open to inspection then any person may, subject to what is said below as to copyright:

- make copies of or extracts from the document; or
- require the person having custody of the document to supply a photocopy of or
- extracts from the document; upon payment of such reasonable fee as may be required for the facility.

In practice, as said before, minutes are now available on most local authorities' websites and, in respect of executive decisions, must be so available.[17]

Copyright

8.44 There is, however, protection for copyright. Nothing above requires or authorises the doing of anything that infringes the copyright in any work except that, where the owner of the copyright is a principal council, the above does not constitute an infringement of copyright. This means that, although members of the public may inspect copyright documents, they must not be allowed to copy them; for example, deposited plans and drawings for planning and building regulations approval may not be copied without the author's consent, but the application forms and the usual sort of site plan could be. Consent to reproduce written material can be implied from the circumstances and a number of authorities have a standard form of reply to the senders of plans, etc., covered by copyright indicating that where there is an obligation to disclose it will be assumed that a waiver from copyright protection has been given. It is arguable, however, how far this would protect an authority against an action for breach of copyright. There might certainly be problems if the communication or plan had been annotated in a way that rebutted any implied consent to waiver, e.g. by marking the plan 'Confidential'.

Obstruction of the right to inspect

8.45 Anyone having custody of the documents of a principal council required to be open to public inspection, who without reasonable excuse:

- intentionally obstructs anyone exercising the right of inspection or of making a copy of or extracts from the document; or
- refuses to furnish copies to any person entitled to obtain them,

is liable on summary conviction to a fine not exceeding level l on the standard scale Local Government Act 1972 s. 100H(4) (as amended) and SI 2012/2089 reg. 22. The absence of the person having custody of the documents is no excuse for the failure to produce the documents for inspection: see *R v Andover RDC* (1913), where it was said that when the clerk to a council goes away, some person with authority should be left available to produce the minute book to anyone entitled to see it.

8.46 In the case of parish and community councils and parish meetings, obstruction of the right of inspection and of making a copy of or extract from documents required to be open to inspection by electors renders the person with custody of the documents liable on summary conviction to a fine not exceeding level 1. The right to take copies is not a right to be furnished with copies (see *Russell-Walker v Gimblett* (1985)).

8. Council minutes

Notes

1 Evidence was allowed to explain minutes, as distinct from resolutions, in *Westminster Corporation v London and North Western Rail Co.* (1905), where a chairman of the works committee was allowed to prove that the primary object of a committee in providing certain conveniences was for sanitary purposes and not as an underground passage from one side of a street to the other, that being the point of substance in the case and one on which the recorded resolution was silent; and in *Clanricarde (Marquess) v Congested Districts Board for Ireland* (1914), where the resolution was definitely ambiguous, even if – as was disputed – it amounted to a resolution at all.

2 In *Hearts of Oak Assurance Co. Ltd. v James Flower & Sons* (1935), it was held that, under similar provision in the Companies Act 1929, a number of loose leaves fastened together in two covers in such a way that anyone could take a leaf out and substitute another was not 'a book' within the meaning of that Act.

3 In practice, responsibility for the safe custody of council documents will be placed upon the proper officer (LGA 1972, s. 270(3)).

4 Certain documents require by law the affixing of the common seal of the authority, e.g. bylaws: LGA 1972, s. 236(3), which however, in the case of bylaws made by a parish or community council not having a seal, permits the authentication by the hands and seals of two members of the council.

5 LGA 1972, s. 100(B)(4).

6 It is a common law rule that where minutes have been properly kept, they shall be admissible as evidence. The effect of the provisions in the LGA 1972, Sch. 12, para. 41(1)(2), is that the minutes are inadmissible unless signed as prescribed.

7 Under the LG(MP)A 1976, s. 41, a document which (a) purports to be a copy of (i) a resolution, order or report of a local authority or precursor of a local authority, or a committee or sub-committee or the executive (including any individual member), or (ii) the minutes of the proceedings at a meeting of a local authority or precursor of a local authority or the executive, a committee or sub-committee thereof, and (b) bears a certificate purporting to be signed by the proper officer or someone authorised on that behalf by themselves or the authority and stating that the resolution was passed or the order or report was made by the authority or precursor or committee or sub-committee thereof on a date specified in accordance with para. 41 of Sch. 12 to the LGA 1972 or the corresponding earlier provisions, is evidence in any proceedings of the matters stated in the certificate and of the terms of the resolution, order, report or minute in question.

8 See *Re Indian Zoedone Co.* (1884). In this case the chairman made an entry in the minute book that a resolution had been confirmed and the court declined, in the absence of evidence that votes were improperly disallowed, to question the decision of the chairman.

9 *Re Cawley & Co.* (1889). In this case the directors at a board meeting passed a resolution making a call on shares, but omitted to state the date of payment. After the minutes had been signed, the secretary repaired the omission by adding a date. Esher MR said: 'I trust I shall never again see or hear of the secretary of a company, whether under superior direction or otherwise, altering minutes of meetings, either by striking out anything or adding anything.'

10 Even though in s. 228(1) of the LGA 1972, as originally enacted, the term 'local authority minutes', rather than 'council minutes', was used, the minutes of a committee exercising delegated powers were not open to inspection notwithstanding that the decisions of the committee had in all respects the force and validity of decisions of the local authority itself: *Wilson v Evans* (1962).

11 LGA 1972, s. 100C, added by LG(AI)A 1985.

12 It may be convenient ordinarily to make a copy available so as to make it easier not to disclose excluded minutes.

13 Except for the statutory requirement to preserve a copy of the agenda it would be common practice, as in the past, to dispose of the agenda because it has no practical or legal significance after a meeting. Presumably the obligation to preserve the agenda or a copy of it for

inspection is to enable a member of the public to check that an item of business was or was not transacted and if it was that the item was duly minuted. See 12.19.

14 The fact that a list must be prepared with copies of the documents on the list means that, conveniently, the originals can be retained in the appropriate files.

15 LGA 1972, s. 100D(5). It is probable that the proper officer need not list, or otherwise disclose, papers which have been looked at and rejected as not relevant to the issue reported upon.

16 There is no definition of published works, but presumably the term would cover publications of HMSO and therefore most government departmental circulars and guidance.

17 The Local Authorities (Executive Arrangements) (Meetings and Access to Information) (England) Regulations 2012 (SI 2012/2089).

Part 3
Committee Practice

Chapter 9
The committee system

Introduction

9.1 As indicated earlier in Chapter 1, the framework of decision-making for the majority of principal councils (county/metropolitan/unitary/district) has undergone drastic changes in recent years with the introduction of the executive/scrutiny split. Notwithstanding the fact that the executive models have their own specific legal regime, the essential elements of the traditional committee system are still very much alive in terms of practice and procedure in the executive, overview and scrutiny, and the regulatory committees.

What is a committee?

Importance of definition

9.2 There is no statutory definition of a committee for purposes of local government, nor of a sub-committee for that matter. Yet it can be important to be able to say what is a committee or sub-committee and what is not. For example, committee and sub-committee meetings, and meetings of an authority's executive under the LGA 2000 when it is considering certain matters, are required to be open to the public, which is not the case of meetings that are not meetings of committees or sub-committees.

9.3 According to the Concise Oxford Dictionary, a committee is 'a body of persons appointed for a special function by, and normally out of, a normally larger body', and in the Chambers Twentieth Century Dictionary it is defined as 'a portion selected from a more numerous body, or the whole body, to which some special business is committed'. But these definitions are not satisfactory for local government purposes, although it is interesting that they imply a plurality of persons. There are groupings of councillors that might seem to satisfy the dictionary definitions of a committee but which are not local authority committees in a statutory or even common law sense. A working party (now more likely to be known as a task and finish group or some other such term) composed both of councillors and officers is not a committee or a sub-committee because the inclusion of officers within its constitution takes it out of the definition of a committee or sub-committee. It cannot have functions delegated to it and does not need to reach decisions on the basis of a majority of those present and voting. For somewhat similar reasons, so-called committees for consultative purposes (e.g. a joint staff committee or a committee for health and safety purposes) are not local authority committees; and there are within local government committees of a special character that fall outside the generality of committees within the terms of the LGA 1972.

Plurality of membership

9.4 Although delegation to an elected mayor or individual councillor on the executive is authorised under the LGA 2000, for general local government purposes a committee or sub-committee must comprise a plurality of persons. There cannot be a committee (or a sub-committee) consisting only of one person, any more than there could conceivably be a meeting of one person alone (see Chapter 1). In *R v Secretary of State for the Environment ex parte Hillingdon London Borough Council* (1986), referred to earlier in connection with the earlier practice of committee chairman's action (see Chapter 4), the local authority had argued unsuccessfully that it could delegate functions to a committee chairman if it had constituted that single councillor as a committee of one person. The court would have none of it. Having dismissed the argument that there could be delegation to an individual councillor under s. 101 of the LGA 1972, Woolf J went on to rule that there could not be a committee of one member alone:

> 'The 1972 Act . . . must, in my view, be taken to use the word "committee" in the sense that that word is now used [i.e. in ordinary parlance] and if this approach to the interpretation of the section [i.e. s. 101] is correct, then the only permissible interpretation is one which involves rejecting the concept of a committee of one'

and, quoting from the Secretary of State's decision letter in the case:

> '. . . had it been the intention that the terms "committee" and "sub-committee" in s. 101(1) should include a committee or sub-committee of one, it is considered that this would expressly have been provided for.'

9.5 It is indeed clear that the LGA 1972 supports plurality of membership in, for example, Sch. 12, para. 39, where it lays down the cardinal principle that all questions coming before the local authority are to be decided by a majority of members present and voting. It would be impossible, of course, to secure a majority in a committee of one. What has been said earlier (see 1.9 and *R v Swansea City Council ex parte Elitestone Ltd* (1993)) about the minimum number of persons who may constitute a meeting for local government purposes applies equally to the minimum number of persons who may constitute a committee or sub-committee. Accordingly, although the LGA 2000 allows delegation to an individual councillor in specific executive arrangements, the basic 1972 Act position still applies in all other instances of decision-making.

Definition for local government purposes

9.6 It is possible, by collecting together the several references to committees in the relevant statutes, to build up a definition of a committee or sub-committee for purposes of local government. In this way, it can be said that a local authority committee or sub-committee is a body that the council, in the case of a committee, or a committee, in the case of a sub-committee, has formally constituted by resolution to act as a unit forming part of the hierarchy of legal power, and which:

- has functions of the local authority referred or delegated to it (LGA 1972, s. 101);
- has a fixed and not a fluctuating membership (LGA 1972, s. 102(2));
- may include persons who are not councillors (s. 102(3) and LG&HA 1989, s. 13)
- has its proceedings regulated by the local authority's standing orders and/or Sch. 12 of the 1972 Act;
- must admit the public and the press to all or part of its meetings;
- cannot (with one exception)[1] wholly comprise or include paid officers of the council;[2]
- must comprise at least two and preferably three members (on the basis that there can be no fewer number to constitute a meeting: see 1.8);
- has a limited term of office and prescribed area of authority (LGA 1972, s. 102(2));
- can, in the case of a committee, delegate its functions to a sub-committee (which it alone can appoint) or, equally with a sub-committee, to an officer unless the terms of its appointment forbid it (LGA 1972, s. 101);
- must reach decisions by a majority of members present and voting in prescribed manner (LGA 1972, Sch. 12, para. 39);
- must keep formal minutes of its proceedings in prescribed manner (LGA 1972, Sch. 12, para. 41);
- will ordinarily be required to report its decisions direct to the council in the case of a committee and to a committee in the case of a sub-committee and not through any intermediary (as standing orders will generally provide); and
- may exclude from participation in the business of its meetings any person, including councillors (save for the exercise of their common law right to be present on the basis of a 'need to know': see 4.6), who is not among the number of members of the committee appointed by the council, or in the case of a sub-committee, appointed by the committee.

9.7 There are, however, committees that fall outside this definition and are not therefore local authority committees under the LGA 1972. There are, for example, consultative committees set up by local authorities comprised of equal numbers of council and trade union or other employee representatives whose decisions must be reached by a majority vote of those on each side; and committees of a special category altogether: school admission appeal committees of local education authorities whose powers and functions are conferred direct by statute and whose decisions are binding on the local authority.

Committee structure

General principles

9.8 Committees are not just separate groupings of councillors each operating in isolation and independently of one another: committees can have no greater powers than those conferred on them by the authority as a whole and cannot themselves amend their terms of reference or shelve the business committed to them, and can never dissolve themselves. Committees are part of a unified system and have long been an integral feature of the internal organisation of local authorities in this country. The committee system, it has been said, is engrained in British life and democratic control of local government services would, in the past, have been thought impracticable without it. In addition, the law has obliged local authorities from earliest times to set up particular committees for the discharge of specific functions. The committee in English local government exists to administer, a function that a committee is peculiarly unsuited to perform. Yet this is what, traditionally, the local authority committee has attempted to do: and, against the balance of probability, has performed passably well. It has been the task of committees to administer a number of related services by exercising oversight of the chief officer and department (and later the executive member(s)) responsible for the executive work, to contribute to policy by making recommendations to the full council for the development of existing and new services, and under delegated authority to make such decisions as may need to be made for the implementation of policy.
9.9 Because local authority committees must reach decisions in accordance with the cardinal principle referred to earlier, i.e. by a majority of members present and voting (see Chapter 1), there was no scope for minority reports from councillors who disagreed with the majority view. Their objection could only be expressed by voting against a proposition in committee and in the full council; and any members who felt particularly strongly about the issue could have their votes recorded in the minutes. However, some local authorities operate a system whereby opposition members can bring forward minority reports to overview and scrutiny committees.

Flexibility

9.10 An important feature of the traditional committee system as an instrument of administration has been its flexibility. New committees can be set up permanently or temporarily as need dictates. Existing committees whose tasks have been completed can be dissolved. Committees whose duties have diminished or lost their former importance may be amalgamated with others. There can, in short, be continual arrangement and rearrangement in this way to meet altered circumstances. Standing committees can be increased or reduced in membership to meet changes in the interests to be represented and the sub-committee organisation can be adjusted accordingly. Special ad hoc committees can be set up to examine and report upon particular matters of topical concern or special importance. Joint committees may be set up to deal with matters which concern more than one committee or to deliberate or act upon matters of common interest to two or more local authorities. The elasticity of the committee system can be stretched, indeed, to the extreme without the necessity of altering, amending or adapting the parent body. This is true, of course, of the committee system of any association but it is of paramount importance to the local authority, which has to resolve into a workable, manageable whole a complexity of related and sometimes unrelated functions, many of a highly specialised nature and all possessing individual technicalities.

9.11 There are necessarily physical limitations to this flexibility. The size of membership of the authority and its resources in revenue and staff are limiting factors, not of the quality of flexibility but of the stretch of elasticity. Unless there is a limit to the number of committees and task groups set up, there will not only be disintegration but also too heavy a call on members' time, and too burdensome a responsibility for imaginative or sustained good work and for the creation of that quasi-specialisation that inevitably emerges from committee experience. For the present it need only be pointed out that the flexibility of the system can be misused either by deploying available resources beyond a certain point or, less common, by not making sufficient use of it. The problems of committee work closely bound up with all this will be considered later.

Durability of the system

9.12 It came to a point where the disadvantages of the committee system were thought to outweigh the advantages and, in its consultation paper 'Modernising Local Government: In Touch with the People', the government of the day considered the traditional committee structure of local government to be 'inefficient and opaque'. Accordingly, to increase the efficiency, transparency and accountability of local authorities, the LGA 2000 introduced new executive arrangements. Nevertheless, notwithstanding the particular procedural rules relating to meetings of the executive, the tripartite split of the executive/scrutiny/regulatory bodies set out in the LGA 2000 still offered recognisable variants of the committee system and emphasises its flexibility and durability.

9.13 Subsequently, the disadvantages of that system also became increasingly apparent and the Localism Act 2011 introduced the option for most local authorities to revert to the committee system. In 'A Plain English Guide to the Localism Act', the Department of Communities and Local Government expressed the view that:

> '. . . the Act also offers real choice for councils and local people to decide how their council should be governed. This includes allowing councils, where they wish, to move away from an executive form of governance (i.e. a leader or a mayor) to a committee system.'

By virtue of s. 9B of the LGA 2000 (inserted by the Localism Act 2011), the committee system is now one of three systems of governance a local authority can adopt (the other two being variants of executive arrangements). Chapter 3 of Part 1A of the LGA 2000 makes specific provisions regarding the committee system, additional to the provisions in the LGA 1972. For example, the Secretary of State may, by regulation, specify that a particular function may not be delegated to a committee (i.e. that decisions in relation to that function must only be made by the full council). Chapter 4 of Part 1A of the LGA 2000 makes provision for the manner in which a local authority may change its governance arrangements.

Legal basis

9.14 It needs to be said at this juncture that by common law and by statute the power of a local authority to appoint committees to discharge its functions is well recognised. There are wide powers in the LGA 1972 enabling an authority to appoint committees (recognising, too, that the authority is compelled for certain functions to appoint specific committees) and to refer and to delegate functions to them. Similarly the LGA 2000 provided that local authorities must set up overview and scrutiny committees, rather than it being a power.

9.15 The courts have placed considerable credence on the effectiveness of committees, even where powers have not been expressly delegated. Thus it has been held that action taken by an officer on the direction of a committee before the committee's act was confirmed by the council effectively ratified the officer's action. In *Firth v Staines* (1897), a health committee had directed a sanitary inspector to serve notice on an owner to abate a nuisance and after the failure of the owner to comply with it laid information against him and a summons was issued. After the issue of the summons, the committee's acts were confirmed. The court held, applying the principles of the doctrine of ratification, that the acts of the committee became valid as from the time when they were done. In *Firth v Staines*, however, the committee had had specific authority to act subject to subsequent ratification by the vestry: an unusual arrangement. Where there is express delegation there is, of course, no requirement upon the council to confirm or ratify or approve what has been done under delegated powers. Thus an act of the committee in such circumstances is the act of the local authority and what the committee does binds the council.

9.16 It is thus evident that a local authority's committee system is regulated by law, structure and procedure. It must be framed to meet the authority's objectives: the system is not an end in itself but an administrative instrument through which the authority can effectively, efficiently, lawfully and democratically discharge its several functions.

Structural considerations

9.17 The committee system (including the executive arrangements under the LGA 2000) must be arranged so that it contributes to the effective and efficient management of the local authority. It must ensure that ultimate direction and control lie with councillors; it must enable them to review progress and the performance of the services provided for the community; and it must assist in the identification of the authority's objectives and the formulation of plans to achieve those objectives.

9.18 If it is to meet these criteria, there should be no more standing committees (including overview and scrutiny committees) than are necessary, the membership of the committees should be small, their terms of reference should be clearly specified, and their relationship to the rest of the decision-making structure clearly defined. Each committee should be concerned with matters that can only be dealt with at member level, i.e. there should ordinarily be no involvement in matters of day-to-day administration and operational business that is properly the responsibility of officers.

Coordination

9.19 Maud[3] considered the absence of any kind of managing body within the organisation as one of the fundamental weaknesses of the committee system in English local government. Maud recognised that committees had been accepted axiomatically as 'practically essential as a means of conducting business' where executive authority is 'entrusted to a large body'; and it saw the committee system as 'a contrivance for decentralising the various functions of the council and for creating a number of microcosms of it to meet problems as they arise; it is not a means of establishing responsibilities of individual members or groups of members'.

9.20 This 'disunity in the whole' persuaded Maud to draw up the outline of a management structure based on the following principles:

- effective and efficient management under the direction and control of the members;
- clear leadership and responsibility among both members and officers;
- an organisation that presents to the public an intelligible system of government; and
- responsiveness to the needs of the public.

Maud felt that the existing committee system made it difficult to identify major issues and to isolate them from routine matters. It considered it necessary to establish more clearly the functions and responsibility of members and officers. To remedy these defects, Maud recommended the establishment of a management board, an idea that had little support at the time although it prepared the way for Bains's policy committee and the same reasoning led to the executive arrangements set out in the LGA 2000.

9.21 Not only is it necessary to coordinate executive functions, but it is also necessary to coordinate the exercise of the overview and scrutiny function, particularly where those committees are cross-cutting and cover a number of service areas and departmental responsibilities. To that end, a number of authorities have formed an Overview and Scrutiny Management Board, or such other named group or committee made up of overview and scrutiny committee chairs and group spokespersons, to coordinate the work programmes and activities of the overview and scrutiny committees.

Types of committees

Broad classification

9.22 There are several ways of classifying committees. The broadest classification is between committees with power only to consider and report upon matters within their terms of reference and those with delegated powers to make the final decision on all or some of the matters within their terms of reference. A committee's terms of reference are its remit: they specify, precisely or broadly (preferably always the former), the matters with which the committee is concerned; and they may go further and specify the delegated powers of the committee on matters within the terms of reference. It is crucial that the council is clear exactly what powers it wishes to delegate and that the members of the committee are clear exactly what they have the power to decide. So far as the remit of a committee is concerned, it can be formed to deal with specific programme areas, or can cover more than one service or programme area. The advice at para. 3.21 of Chapter 3 of *Local Government Act 2000: Guidance to English Local Authorities* in relation to overview and scrutiny committees is that:

> 'Overview and scrutiny committees should take a cross-cutting rather than narrow service-based view of the conduct of the local authority's business and therefore the aim should be for local authorities to have, at any given point in time, a relatively small number of such committees.'

Statutory and discretionary committees

9.23 Committees may be statutory or discretionary, i.e. there are committees that a local authority is compelled to set up by express statutory enactment, and others that it is not bound to set up but may do so if it wishes. Committees set up year after year are often referred to as 'standing committees'.

Statutory committees

9.24 There are a number of statutory committees that must be established by a local authority, such as a standards committee (in Wales) and a licensing committee in respect of the functions under the Licensing Act 2003. For those authorities operating executive arrangements, it is also a statutory requirement under s. 9F (for England) and s. 21 (for Wales) of the LGA 2000 to appoint one or more overview and scrutiny committees. Other statutory committees have become fewer in number over the years. The requirement to set up an education committee was removed by the Education Act 1993, and the Police and Magistrates' Courts Act 1994, Sch. 9 saw the end of the local authority police committees. So far as a social services committee is concerned, s. 102 of the LGA 2000 provides that an authority operating executive arrangements is no longer required to have a social services committee to discharge social services functions as these will be the responsibility of the executive. There is no statutory requirement for a local authority to have an audit committee but CIPFA estimate that about 90% of local authorities have an audit committee or a committee which fulfils the functions of an audit committee. There is now a statutory requirement under s. 194 of the Health and Social Care Act 2012 for single-tier authorities to establish Health and Well-Being Boards, which are, strictly speaking, ordinary committees under the LGA 1972, but with a number of additions and restrictions tacked on.

9.25 The LGA 1972, s. 101(8), provides that any enactment (except those relating to the statutory committees set out in s. 101(9) (which have now all been repealed)) that contains provisions empowering or requiring local authorities singly, or in collaboration with other authorities, to establish committees, including joint committees, for any purpose, or enabling a minister to make an instrument to such effect, shall, to the extent that it makes such provision, cease to have effect. This blanket provision means that any statutory provision (other than, as just indicated, the statutory committees that were continued in operation by the 1972 Act) in force prior to the coming into effect of the 1972 Act need not be followed.

Overview and scrutiny committees

9.26 As stated earlier, it is a statutory requirement for those authorities operating executive arrangements to appoint one or more overview and scrutiny committees. Authorities operating the committee system style of governance may, by resolution, in accordance with s. 9JA of the LGA 2000, appoint one or more of their committees as overview and scrutiny committees. Overview and scrutiny committees should be cross-cutting and few in number. So far as membership of those committees is concerned, it may include anyone who is not a member of the local authority but they are not entitled to vote, with the exception of church and parent governor representatives on the committee dealing with education matters who are allowed to vote on those issues.

9.27 The LGA 2000 specifically provides in s. 9FA(6) (in relation to England) and s. 21(11) (in relation to Wales) that an overview and scrutiny committee is to be treated as a committee or sub-committee of a principal council for the purposes of the LGA 1972 and it is to be politically balanced. As noted in Chapter 1, the LGA 2000 gives overview and scrutiny committees a very specific remit to review or scrutinise decisions taken by the executive or any other part of the council, and make reports to the council or to the executive. They can also report on any matters that affect the authority's area or its inhabitants. Their role includes developing and reviewing policy and holding the executive to account. The committee may require executive members and officers to attend before it to answer questions and may also invite other people to attend meetings. Members and officers have a statutory duty to comply with the requirement to attend and answer questions. Section 9F(5) (England) and s. 21(4) (Wales) of the LGA 2000 prohibits an overview and scrutiny committee from discharging any functions other than those listed in the relevant section (which are, in England, functions under s. 9F to 9FI of the LGA 2000, functions under the Police and Justice Act 2006 (scrutiny of crime and disorder matters) and functions conferred by regulations made under the National Health Service Act 2006 (scrutiny of health matters) and in Wales, functions under ss. 21, 21A and 21B of the LGA 2000 and under the Police and Justice Act 2006).

9.28 The key question is how the committee is to discharge its functions. A number of councils have produced a scrutiny 'tool kit' setting out how overview and scrutiny committees will operate. The Guidance issued by the Secretary of State made it clear that overview and scrutiny committees should consider different approaches and formats for their meetings, and it gives a number of examples of good practice, including: holding time-limited inquiries; having 'new style meetings' outside the town hall; and co-opting from a wide range of community and voluntary groups. An example of a 'new-style meeting' by one local authority was to set up a stall in Mothercare during a review of maternity services, which enabled the committee to benefit from the first-hand accounts of new mothers and fathers and others have scrutiny days, which allow in-depth evidence gathering and analysis on a topic by the committee and its members.

9.29 The role of overview and scrutiny committees is still evolving, with additional statutory requirements having been introduced since 2000, in particular requirements to scrutinise external services/organisations, such as crime and disorder partnerships and health bodies. Overview and scrutiny committees do give a tremendous opportunity for councillors to develop and review policy, and contribute to the decision-making process by that means. In addition, they allow the executive to be held to account in a more formal way. The Centre for Public Scrutiny (CfPS) carried out a survey in 2004 into the operation of overview and scrutiny in local authorities. At that time, on average, an authority had four scrutiny committees supported by 1.2 full time equivalent (fte) dedicated scrutiny officers, rising to 2.9 fte among county and single-tier authorities. So far as the perception of overview and scrutiny is concerned, the survey indicated that while only 11% gave scrutiny parity of esteem with the executive, 69% of responses stated that scrutiny is valued by the organisation and 89% agreed that scrutiny adds value to the council. The end of the 2005–10 Labour government saw some attempts to strengthen the role of overview and scrutiny committees, through the Green Paper 'Communities in Control' and the Local Authorities (Overview and Scrutiny) Bill 2009–10. However, the Bill was not passed by Parliament. A more recent survey by the CfPS of scrutiny activity in 2012/13 showed that budgets for scrutiny were being squeezed and that the number of dedicated scrutiny officers were in decline, with an increased trend in supporting scrutiny through 'twin-hatted' or generic posts, where the officers have other duties alongside their support for the scrutiny function.

9.30 The Local Government and Public Involvement in Health Act 2007 and the Local Democracy, Economic Development and Construction Act 2009 gave general powers for overview and scrutiny committees to look at the work of partners, provided it related to a target under a Local Area Agreement. When the Localism Bill was first published, it retained the link to LAA targets, but as these were subsequently abolished, the Act now contains provisions to encompass scrutiny of any activities carried out by a named partner (LG&PIH Act s. 104). This should mean that local authorities are able to carry out a wider scrutiny role over the whole of their locality, and a potentially broader scrutiny work programme.

It may also call for more dialogue with those s. 104 partners to ensure that they have a better understanding of scrutiny, rather than viewing it as an adversarial process, and ensuring that members similarly have an improved understanding of their broader role in scrutiny.

Discretionary committees

9.31 The law confers upon local authorities a general power[4] to appoint a committee (or a joint committee in the case of two or more authorities) for purposes of discharging any of their functions (except functions for which a statutory committee must be established), and to appoint area committees for the purpose of discharging functions delegated by the executive. Even without this express statutory power, a local authority could conceivably set up any number of discretionary (non-statutory, or permissive) committees so long as the committees' functions were deliberative and not executive, i.e. limited to considering and reporting. However, without the express statutory power that exists, the authority would not be able to delegate to any such committee because of the maxim *delegatus non potest delegare* (see 9.76).

9.32 This general enabling but not unrestricted power extends to permit expressly any such discretionary committee to appoint one or more sub-committees and the authority or authorities or, in the case of a sub-committee, the appointing committee to fix the number of members, their term of office and the area (if restricted) within which the committee (or sub-committees) is (or are) to operate (LGA 1972, s. 102(2)).

9.33 The restrictions upon this general enabling power are that:

- in the case of a committee for regulating and controlling the finance of the authority, the members must be members of the appointing authority or authorities or, in the case of a sub-committee, of the authority or authorities of which it is a sub-committee (see 9.38);
- in the case of other committees the members may include co-opted, i.e. non-voting persons; and
- in the case of any committee, every member who at the time of their appointment to the committee was a member of the appointing authority or one of the appointing authorities ceases to be a member of the committee when they cease to be a member of the appointing authority or one of them.

Advisory committees

9.34 A power, first conferred by the LGA 1972, s. 102(4), enables an authority either by itself or jointly with another or other authorities to appoint a committee to advise the appointing authority or authorities or executive on any matter relating to the discharge of their functions. An advisory committee may comprise members or non-members[5] of the authority or authorities, appointed for whatever term may be determined; and the committee may appoint one or more sub-committees to advise the committee. The consultative committees that authorities set up for certain personnel functions are not advisory committees under s. 102(4).

Special committees

9.35 A special committee is one appointed for a short-term purpose, e.g. to deal with a specific matter that does not fall within the terms of reference of any standing committee or that otherwise is considered to merit particular attention by a committee of members, perhaps selected for their knowledge or experience. Sometimes such a committee is referred to as an ad hoc committee, for obvious reasons. The late J. H. Warren considered that a committee 'regularly appointed from time to time for recurring purposes' should be regarded as a special committee.[6]

9.36 An example of such a special committee is the selection committee appointed to recommend the personnel for standing committees, and often invested with the duty of revising standing orders and the terms of reference to standing committees.

9.37 However, if an authority's standing orders provide for the appointment of a selection committee, or a committee of this kind is in practice regularly appointed year after year, there is justification for considering it a standing committee, even though, as may be the case, the committee is constituted somewhat differently from other standing committees. A second example from Warren is, perhaps, a better one, i.e. a committee appointed by some local authorities to consider the choice of mayor.

Finance committee

9.38 Any committee set up specifically for purposes of regulating and controlling the finance of the local authority or of its area or charged with that responsibility as part of other functions must be composed solely of councillors (LGA 1972, s. 102(3)). The majority of authorities have audit committees to help ensure that the council's financial systems are systematically appraised, obtain assurance that the prevention and detection of fraud and corruption are promoted, and give confidence that the findings of internal and external audit reports are properly considered, implemented and monitored. In authorities with executive arrangements, this has often been either a sub-committee of the executive, or a function of overview and scrutiny. Increasingly, however, authorities are being encouraged to appoint an audit committee as a full committee of the council, independent of the executive and scrutiny functions and indeed this is a specific recommendation of the CIPFA/SOLACE publication, *Delivering Good Governance in Local Government*, which was published in 2007.

Committees of parish meetings

9.39 A parish meeting in a parish where there is no separate parish council may set up a committee of local government electors for the parish to discharge any of the functions of the parish meeting. Express power to do this, conferred by the LGA 1972, s. 108, was no doubt thought necessary because a parish meeting is not a local authority and therefore the general powers enabling local authorities to set up committees do not apply. Apart from the statutory provision there would appear to be no reason why a parish meeting should not set up a committee of electors for purposes of considering any matter of concern to the parish and reporting back to the parish meeting. Most of the statutory provisions relating to local authority committees apply also to the committees of a parish meeting (s. 99).

Committees of community meetings

9.40 There is no express statutory power conferred upon a community meeting to establish a committee of local government electors for the community.

Joint committees

9.41 There are two kinds of joint committee:

1 those set up by a single local authority to consider a matter which falls within the terms of reference of two or more standing committees; and
2 those set up by two or more local authorities or by a combination of one or more local authorities and another body or bodies for purposes in respect of which they are jointly interested.

The first of these is dealt with below (see 9.42); the other, which is of the character of a committee for a special purpose, is examined in Chapter 13. The term 'joint committee' is also commonly used for committees of council and employee representatives but these are of an entirely different character.

9.42 A joint committee set up by a local authority will be established under its general enabling power to appoint a committee for any purpose it thinks fit. Therefore its membership, term of office, terms of reference and so on can all be determined by the council at its discretion.

Constitution of committees

Membership

9.43 A local authority has discretion over whom it appoints to serve on its committees subject, however, to prescription in respect of statutory committees (see 9.3) and, generally, to the statutory requirements as to political balance (see 9.46).

Membership of committees may, with some exceptions, comprise both councillors on the one hand and non-councillors on the other who are ordinarily co-opted members, although the term 'non-voting members' is now more usually employed in relation to co-option, even though (see 4.51) some co-opted members enjoy voting rights. According to *R v Brent London Borough Council ex parte Gladbaum* (1989), only the council itself has the power of appointment to and removal of members from a committee. It is a power that cannot be delegated, a decision that sits uneasily with the power over appointments to committees by political groups (see 9.47). So far as membership of any committee of the executive in those authorities operating executive arrangements is concerned, it is clear that only members of the executive itself can be members of any committee of the executive (see Chapter 4 of the Guidance).

Appointment

9.44 Members are selected for committee membership at the council's annual meeting or as soon as practicable thereafter: indeed, there is a statutory requirement substantially to that effect where the local authority is divided into political groups and political balance is to be provided for in the membership of committees (see 9.48). This means that it is helpful to settle in advance of the council's annual meeting, so far as possible, the names of councillors who are to be nominated as members of the various committees. Previously this was done in an informal manner, with councillors meeting collectively in private or in party groups. Just how the nominations emerged depended on local practice, but it is now common for the process to be formally coordinated by the political leadership of each group where the members are divided into political groups.

9.45 Each local authority will still have its own arrangements, but it may be appropriate here to set out the relevant draft standing order among those initially proposed (see 2.4) as part of a set of core standing orders to be prescribed under the LG&HA 1989, Pt. I:

'*Appointment of committees and subcommittees*

00–1 Subject to sections 101 and 102 of the 1972 Act . . . at their annual meeting [after each ordinary election of councillors],[A] the council:

(a) shall resolve what committees shall be appointed, and what shall be the terms of reference of each of those committees, and of how many voting members each committee shall consist;

(b) may resolve that non-voting members, assessors and advisers shall also be appointed to any such committee;

(c) if they resolve to make appointments under sub-paragraph (b), shall specify what number of appointments are to be made and what functions in relation to the committee each person so appointed may exercise; and

(d) may resolve what limitations shall be placed on the powers of any such committee to arrange for the discharge by a subcommittee of any functions which they may discharge.

Variation:

Authorities other than county councils may omit reference to the Police Act 1964; authorities with no coastline may omit reference to the Sea Fisheries Act 1966; authorities whose area does not include part of a national park other than the Peak District or Lake District may omit reference to schedule 17 of the 1972 Act; and non-metropolitan district councils may omit reference to the enactments other than sections 101 and 102 of the 1972 Act.

2 The council may at any time amend resolutions under the previous paragraph.

3 Every committee set up under this standing order, and every subcommittee set up by such a committee, shall continue to discharge the

functions committed to them until the council or committee, as the case may be, resolve otherwise.

4 Subject to section 102(5) of the 1972 Act (councillor not re-elected to cease to be a member of a committee) and paragraph (7), every person appointed as a voting member of such a committee or subcommittee and every person appointed to exercise other functions in relation to a committee shall continue as such until the appointment is terminated by the authority.

5 Whenever:

(a) the council is required to review the allocation of seats on committees between political groups; or
(b) the council resolves to carry out such a review; or
(c) a committee is required to review the allocation of seats on a subcommittee between political groups; or
(d) a committee resolves to carry out such a review,

the proper officer shall submit a report to the council or committee (as the case may be), showing what allocation of seats would, in his/her opinion, best meet the requirements of section 15(4) of the 1989 Act.

6 In the light of such a report, the council or committee, as the case may be, shall determine the allocation of seats to political groups.

7 Whenever an appointment of a voting member of a committee or subcommittee fails to be made in accordance with the wishes of a political group to whom the seat has been allocated, and whenever such an appointment fails to be terminated in accordance with such wishes, then the proper officer shall make or terminate the appointment accordingly.
Variation:
In place of the words "then the proper officer shall make or terminate the appointment accordingly" may be substituted:

"then, where membership of a committee is concerned, the [Policy and Resources Committee] or their subcommittee appointed to deal with urgent matters and, where membership of a subcommittee is concerned, the committee which appointed them, or their subcommittee appointed to deal with urgent matters, shall make or terminate the appointment accordingly' or 'then the council or the committee, as the case may be, at a meeting at which the wishes of the political group are expressed, or at the next meeting after those wishes are expressed, shall make or terminate the appointment accordingly".[B]

8 Subject to any resolutions by the council under this standing order, every committee may appoint subcommittees for such purposes as they think fit, and may make arrangements for a subcommittee to discharge any of the functions of the authority which the committee may discharge.

9 The chairman and vice-chairman of the council, and the leader of the council (if any), may attend and speak [and move and second motions] (but may not vote) at a meeting of a committee or subcommittee of which they are not voting members.

10 The persons appointed to preside at the meetings of a committee and his/her deputy, may attend and speak [and move or second motions] at a meeting of any subcommittee appointed by that committee, but may not vote unless appointed as a voting member.

11 A member of the council who is not otherwise entitled to attend and speak at a committee or subcommittee shall be entitled to do so (but not to vote) at a meeting of the committee or subcommittee:

(a) during the consideration of any motion of which notice has been given which he/she has moved or seconded at a meeting of the council and which has been referred to that committee or subcommittee; or

(b) with the agreement of the person presiding at the meeting of the committee or subcommittee.

Variation:

Add:

"(c) during the consideration of any matter which affects his/her ward/electoral division differently from all other wards/electoral divisions."

Notes:

A The draft standing order had these two footnotes appended, i.e.

1. Authorities which are elected by thirds (metropolitan district councils and some non-metropolitan district councils) may prefer to review committee arrangements every year. They should delete the passage in square brackets. Councils which are elected in whole council elections may prefer to set up arrangements for the whole of an electoral period: they should include the passage in square brackets.
2. Section 102(1) of the 1972 Act provides that members of subcommittees are appointed by a committee. However, a council which wishes to appoint the members of subcommittees directly may do so by resolving themselves into a committee of the whole council and as such appointing all the subcommittees.

B The draft standing order had these two footnotes appended, i.e.:

1. The effect of the 1989 Act is that, where a seat is allocated to a political group, the decision on which member of the council is to fill that seat rests with that political group.
2. A member of the council has rights by common law (whether or not this standing order is adopted) to attend, but not speak or vote, at meetings of any committee or subcommittee where the acquisition of information in this way is necessary for his work as a councillor.'

No similar model standing order was contained in the Guidance on Modular Constitutions.

Political balance

9.46 The requirements as to political proportionality in the membership of committees, embodied in the LG&HA 1989, have their origin in the recommendations of the

Widdicombe Report. The committee felt that the discretion enabling a local authority to appoint whoever it liked to its committees should be conditional upon there being an appropriate political balance in membership. It is a statutory requirement[7] that where a relevant authority (see Chapter 1) has a membership divided into different political groups (and members are to be treated as so divided when there is at least one political group in existence constituted as prescribed) then, unless there is a decision to the contrary taken with no members voting against, it must ensure that appointments to fill seats on:

- an ordinary committee or sub-committee of the authority;
- an advisory committee and any sub-committee appointed by an advisory committee; and
- a number of prescribed bodies[8] where at least three seats have to be filled by the relevant authority,

are allocated in the same proportion as that in which the council as a whole is divided. There is in that case a duty to review the representation of political groups and to determine the allocation of seats to be filled to 'the different political groups into which the members of the authority are divided' and in so doing ensure, as far as reasonably practicable, to make decisions that conform with prescribed principles. These principles are:

(a) that not all the seats are allocated to the same political group;
(b) that a political group with an overall council majority gets a majority of seats allocated;
(c) subject to (a) and (b), that the total number of seats each political group has on all ordinary committees is in proportion to that group's share of the total council elected membership; and
(d) subject to (a) and (c), that each political group has the same proportion of seats as it holds on the council as a whole.

Any seats that are or may be filled by people who are not elected members must be taken into account in calculating a majority of all the seats, though not for any other purpose; and an advisory committee seat 'shall not be treated as one which may be so filled unless the authority have determined that it must be so filled'. These principles apply to a relevant authority's representation on outside bodies where at least three of the appointments fall to be made by the authority.

9.47 Once the allocation of seats has been decided upon, there is a duty to give effect to the allocation by making appointments thereto in accordance with the wishes of the political groups. The detailed rules, somewhat complex, are prescribed by regulations.[9] The main purport, however, is as follows. It is for the council formally to resolve, i.e. to comply with the *Gladbaum* dictum,[10] members that are to be appointed to serve on committees in accordance with group wishes. Technically, it might be legal to allow this to be done by a committee since no discretion is involved, but the initial appointment should be made by the council itself to be on the safe side! The wishes of a properly constituted political group for this purpose are taken to be those expressed to the proper officer either orally or in writing by the leader or other representative of the group or in a written statement signed by the majority of the members of the group and, if different wishes of a group are expressed, the proper officer must accept that expressed in the written statement by a majority of the members. To help each group to express its wishes the proper officer is required to notify the leader or other representative of each group of the allocation of the seats to the group or the vacancy in the allocations. If a group fails to express its wishes within a period of three weeks of being notified of the allocation or vacancy, the council may make such appointment as it thinks fit. Any defect in the procedure of a technical or inadvertent nature will not invalidate the proceedings but, obviously, one that renders ineffective the duty imposed will not be excused.

9.48 The foregoing statutory requirements mean that, where the rules as to political proportionality apply, there can be no one-party committees or sub-committees, but, of course, policies may still be formulated on a single party basis – in a working party that falls outside the definition of a committee (see 9.3) or outside the formal decision-making structure of the authority (see 5.30) – for translation through the legal hierarchy of committees. Where a relevant authority or any other local authority has decided not to adopt the prescribed political balance arrangements for its committee, it can still appoint committees of one, i.e. the majority, party only: see *R v Rushmoor Borough Council ex parte Crawford* (1981); *R v Newham London Borough Council ex parte Haggerty* (1986).

When considering a directly elected mayor, it seems that, while the mayor is a member of the council for the purposes of the LGA 1972 that does not seem to be the case for the LG&HA 1989. As a result, the appointment of the mayor to a committee would seem to be within the gift of the council, but outside the political balance rules. It may have been envisaged that the mayor would not wish to be on an ordinary 1972 Act committee or it may either not have been permitted or have been undesirable (as in the case of overview and scrutiny and the audit committees), but the exception is the HR or personnel committee, where a member of the executive is required to be a member. One approach of some mayoral authorities is build that appointment directly into standing orders so that the terms of reference of the HR committee are 'the mayor plus n members of the council'.

Revocation of committee membership

9.49 It is clear that a local authority is entitled to put an end to a councillor's membership of a committee at any time. It can do this either by dissolving the committee altogether or by terminating the membership of an individual councillor, i.e. even before the expiration of the term for which they had been appointed. This general concept can be traced back to *Manton v Brighton Corporation* (1951), where it was held that as the council had power to revoke the authority of a committee as a whole, it also had power to revoke the authority of a single member before the end of their prescribed period of office. This assertion needs now to be regarded as subject generally to rationality (on the Wednesbury principle (see 1.46)), to the political proportionality regulations (see 9.44) and to compliance with standing orders (see *R v Rushmoor Borough Council ex parte Crawford* (1981)) provided any relevant standing order is itself reasonable (see *R v Newham London Borough Council ex parte Haggerty*

(1986), where the local authority was held entitled to formulate criteria as to who should be appointed to its committee subject to rationality).

9.50 There have been cases where the court has had to consider the legality of specific reasons for the removal of a councillor from a committee, but these do not run counter to what has been said in the previous section.

9.51 A local authority cannot properly deprive a councillor from committee membership purely as a punishment for doing what the councillor is lawfully entitled to do: e.g. if the purpose was to fetter the exercise of discretion: see *R v Greenwich London Borough Council ex parte Lovelace* (1990)). In the circumstances of today, however, a local authority can properly remove councillors from committee membership who obstruct the council's policy and replace them. The distinction here is a fine one. In Lovelace, above, Neill LJ said:

> 'It seems to me . . . that at the present day, when local government is organised on party lines, some additional constraints [on committees] resulting from the existence of a party line or strategy on particular issues are inevitable. Penalties by way of punishment must clearly be avoided or any action which is vindictive or malicious. But a political party is entitled to take steps to ensure its cohesion and I can see nothing intrinsically wrong in a decision to change a party's representation on a committee or sub-committee so as to advance the policies which the party considers desirable. In this sense "group discipline" does not connote punishment but an attempt to keep the party group together.'

9.52 The requirements for fairly suspending councillors from committee membership were also examined in *R v Portsmouth City Council ex parte Gregory* (1990), which concerned a recommendation to suspend that was beyond a specially appointed sub-committee's powers. There is nothing in the rules governing political balance or committees (see 9.46) to prevent a political group – clearly the majority group in the circumstances just referred to – from changing its representation on a committee.

9.53 These principles relating to the removal of a member from a committee have to be interpreted in the light of the proportionality regulations, which effectively give the power of appointment, and, by implication, the power of removal to the political groups (see 9.47). It appears that if a particular political group were to insist on one of its members remaining on a committee, the council itself could not require that member's removal, even if a significant majority of the council wished this to happen. This also has the effect of reducing the impact, if not in these particular circumstances negating altogether, the decision in *R v Brent London Borough Council ex parte Gladbaum* (1989) (see 9.43).

Ex-officio members

9.54 Ex-officio members of a committee are those councillors, such as opposition spokespersons on particular subjects or the elected mayor, whose appointment to a committee or sub-committee is by virtue of the office held and not by their selection as individuals. Unless the council determines otherwise, ex-officio members are full members of the committee, able to speak and vote. There appears to be no reason, however, why a local authority should not, if so minded, restrict the right of ex-officio members to that of mere attendance at committees and sub-committees, i.e. with no voting rights; the view has been expressed that it would equally be in order for the authority to permit an ex-officio member to propose or second a motion but not to vote (if voting, however, the appointment will need to be in accord with political balance rules). Whatever the local arrangement it should, of course, be regulated by formal standing orders, indeed, this was envisaged in the draft of the proposed core standing orders.

Substitute members

9.55 Many local authorities operate a substitute system, which provides for the attendance at a committee or sub-committee meeting of a substitute member whenever a regularly appointed member cannot be present. It is a common practice due to the political proportionality rules, and clearly there is much to be said in preserving the political balance of committees when one or more of its ordinary members are unable to attend a particular meeting. It avoids decisions being taken that are not the wish of the majority of the council and ones likely to be overturned at a higher level or a subsequent meeting. The problem is particularly acute in authorities where the political majority is small or where there is no overall majority. The development of the substitute system is the practical expression of the way in which the needs of parties has usurped the role and responsibilities of individual councillors as committee members.

9.56 There have been conflicting views in the past as to the legality of substitution and some councils that have accepted its legality have from time to time doubted its desirability. There are at least two opinions from leading counsel in support of the legality of such a system and many lingering doubts now appear to have been overridden and the majority of councils have a substitute scheme in place. This does not apply to meetings of the cabinet, where substitutes are prohibited under the Local Government Act 2000.

9.57 The main issues now appear to be how to achieve a sensible and workable arrangement that ensures that the membership of every committee is known at any given time and that the right people are present and participating in each meeting. This is generally achieved in one of two ways: either by allowing the mechanics of appointing to a committee to be carried out by an officer on the instructions of the groups concerned or by nominating a prescribed list of substitute members for each committee. Either method would seem to be lawful, but there are advantages and disadvantages attached to each.

9.58 Leaving matters to an officer (usually the monitoring officer or head of democratic services) has the advantage of flexibility but needs to be sanctioned by a specific resolution of the council. One way to handle this is to ensure that at each annual meeting a resolution is passed authorising the officer chosen to make changes in the standing appointments to committee and sub-committees on the instructions of the political groups. This ensures that the power to appoint remains with the groups as required by the Local Government (Committees and Political Groups) Regulations 1990 (as amended), but the administrative action is carried out by the officer concerned. Councils that follow this practice usually specify a time prior to the meetings when nominations have to be made. This should be at least the day before the meeting and preferably longer to allow time for papers to be sent to the substitute with adequate time for them to be read. Technically, this procedure operates as a formal change to the membership of the committee and lasts for as long as is determined by the instructing group. The disadvantages of this method is that it operates against the principle of fixed membership of a committee and encourages last-minute changes, with members being appointed who have no prior knowledge of the work of the committee concerned but who just happen to be available. It is not unknown for some members to be elevated to the status of 'professional substitutes' for no better reason than their lack of regular employment.

9.59 The alternative method, and one that is perhaps to be preferred, is for the council to appoint substitute members itself for each committee and sub-committee. The members will be named and appointed, usually at the same time as the regular committee membership is decided, at the annual meeting of the council. This method has the advantage of certainty in that the substitute membership is well publicised in advance so that the members concerned can build up some knowledge and expertise in the subject area of their particular committee and attend relevant training, but it is not always liked by the political groups because of the lack of flexibility. It does, however, measure up more closely to the principles of committee appointment laid down in the *Gladbaum* case. It also enables the council to maintain an accurate register of committee and sub-committee membership as required by the LGA 1972, s. 100G. Where the council is not divided into political groups, this is the only way that substitution can be properly authorised.

9.60 Whichever procedure is used, it is important that it is clearly understood by the members and accurately applied to avoid confusion, embarrassment or even possible illegality. The period covered by the substitution must be clearly set out and so, too, must the position, if the original member and the substitute both turn up at the same meeting (see 9.61). Certainty of membership is vital to the successful operation of any substitute system and only another formal change can revoke the original change. Ideally the practical arrangements should be set out in standing orders and most authorities do make formal provision.

9.61 If a substitute member is present at a meeting at which the member whom they are replacing turns up during the course of proceedings, the original member should be required to withdraw from further participation in the business. A substitute member attending a meeting speaks and votes in their own capacity: they do not, as it were, relinquish their own personal responsibilities or take on the mantle of the other member. The substitute is personally under the same obligations as any other councillor to disclose any disclosable pecuniary interests (and other interests as required by the authority's Code of Conduct) before the committee or sub-committee, and must follow the usual rules set out under the Code of Conduct.

9.62 So far as executive arrangements are concerned, an executive is not able to have formal substitute or deputy members who are not themselves members of the executive. Also, the executive has no powers to co-opt other councillors or anyone else on to the executive. However, some local authorities have adopted the practice of 'portfolio holders assistants' for which special responsibility allowances are paid, although the assistant has no decision-making responsibility.

Non-members of a committee

9.63 As to the attendance of non-members of a committee at a meeting of a committee, see Chapter 5.

Size

9.64 The number of members on a committee or sub-committee is a matter to be decided by the local authority or, in the case of a joint committee, the authorities that set it up (LGA 1972, s. 102). Several considerations affect the size of membership. One, of course, is to provide for a requisite political balance. In any case, just as there must be more than one person present to constitute a meeting, so too must there be more than one person to constitute a committee or sub-committee. There is a limit to the size of a committee because a committee that consists of all members of the council (or perhaps more than that if co-opted members were brought in) cannot by definition be a committee of the parent body.

9.65 There are very strong grounds for the view that a local authority committee ought not to comprise fewer than three persons. It cannot comprise one member alone for the reason just given, nor is it desirable that it should comprise two only because the power of the person presiding to give a second or casting vote would mean that the committee could become a dictatorship of the chairman.[11] It could be argued also that even a committee of three members gives considerable power to the chairman insofar as they can cast an original vote or a casting vote if the other two are divided in their views, so as to decide any matter in the chairman's favour. These are, possibly, theoretical objections: an authority that constitutes a committee of two or three members must be presumed to know what it is doing (and, in any case, the potential danger is not very real even if the committee is entrusted with executive powers because of the authority's freedom to dissolve the committee at any time), and, of course, it is a convention that a committee chairman should not be too freely disposed to exercise their second or casting vote.

9.66 Taking account of the foregoing and of the advantages of a small rather than a large committee, an optimum size could be four or five members including the chairman, preferably an odd number so as to eliminate the possibility of too frequent an equality of votes. A small committee is more likely to reach a decision speedily and is less costly to convene, but it may not be fairly representative of political or other opinion or of electoral wards or divisions.

Can there be a committee of the full council?

9.67 If, as indicated above, there is a minimum number of members that may validly constitute a committee or sub-committee, can there be a maximum number? Or, put another way, can there be a committee of the whole membership of the local authority? As a matter of historical fact, before local authorities were compelled to throw open their committees to the public, councils sometimes resolved to go into committee so as to exclude the public and press. No one challenged their right to do so. However, there is now no need for the expedient of going into committee, at least to exclude the public, because such a move would be purposeless.

9.68 There seems, nevertheless, to be no lawful reason why a local authority should still not decide to go into committee if it wishes, or otherwise set up a committee composed of all members of the council. After all the House of Lords and the House of Commons each resolves itself into a committee of the whole house on occasions (each is itself 'in a less formal guise', says Erskine May)[12] and there is no reason why a local authority cannot do the same, despite the cogency of a contrary view that what purports to be a committee of the whole council cannot by definition be a committee of the parent body. In any case, there is no longer today the former justification of the whole assembly going into committee to avoid the obligation to admit the press and public to a meeting: a committee of the whole council cannot evade the obligation to meet in public. Further, that the terms of the 1972 Act, looked at as a whole, presuppose that a committee will comprise fewer members than the whole council membership, and that in the case of delegation of functions to a committee, which the law permits, it would be nonsense to contemplate the delegating body delegating functions to itself, albeit in another guise. Further still, the statutory arrangements for the discharge of functions by committees can be likened to the relation of principal (the council) and agent (the committees), and for the council to appoint itself as agent for itself is nonsensical.

9.69 What if the local authority does set up a committee of the whole membership? It must mean that the formalities required to be observed in the case of council meetings need not be followed, e.g. the chairman of the council does not automatically take the chair (indeed, it would be inappropriate for them to do so) and a committee chairman would need to be elected; and, further, non-voting persons from outside the council's membership could be co-opted.

Terms of reference

Definition

9.70 A committee's terms of reference, its remit, specify the functions with which the committee is charged and define the limits of its authority. Precision is important in framing terms of reference so as to avoid doubt about the scope of a committee's tasks. If the terms are narrowly drawn, the committee's powers and duties may be unduly restrictive; if widely drawn there is risk that the terms may overlap those of another committee or committees.

9.71 Terms of reference should be collectively all-embracing and mutually exclusive. By this is meant that the terms of reference of all committees should cover the whole of the council's area of operations, but should be so drawn that one set of terms does not overlap another. However skilfully the terms are drafted, it is impossible to foresee every eventuality and thus most authorities provide for the terms of reference of an appropriate committee, e.g. one of the overview and scrutiny committees, to include responsibility for 'Any matter not delegated or referred to or coming under the remit of any other overview and scrutiny committee'.

Form

9.72 It is common practice but not essential for terms of reference to be framed in imperative words, e.g.:

> 'To fulfil all the functions of an overview and scrutiny committee as they relate to . . .'

or:

> 'To perform the overview and scrutiny role in relation to . . .'

or, for other committees:

> 'The committee will have the following roles: . . .'

Delegation to committees

General power to delegate

9.73 Every local authority has power to delegate, within limitations,[13] any of its functions (other than functions with respect to levying or issuing a precept for a rate),[14] or executive functions under the Local Government Act 2000), including any functions it may be discharging on behalf of another local authority, to a committee or sub-committee (or, indeed, to an officer).

9.74 The LGA 1972 does not use the term 'delegate' as did the LGA 1933. It provides that 'a local authority may arrange for the discharge of any of their functions' and this difference in wording is necessary no doubt because of the wider power available enabling an authority to arrange for the discharge of functions by any other local authority (LGA 1972, s. 101). This could not properly be described as delegation, because delegation implies the existence of a principal and a subordinate, whereas the use of another local authority in this way is a matter between a principal and an agent.

Specific power to delegate

9.75 Specific power is conferred upon local authorities required to set up statutory committees to delegate functions to the statutory committee. Subject to the precise executive model adopted, the LGA 2000 allows delegation of executive functions to a committee of the executive. The statutory Guidance makes it clear that the membership of that committee can only include members of the executive (see Chapter 4 of the Guidance).

9.76 Without express statutory power to do so, a local authority would be unable to delegate its decision-making powers because of the common-law maxim *delegatus non potest delegare* that a delegate cannot delegate: this is one of the pivotal principles of administrative law. In other words, an agent to whom an authority or decision-making power has been delegated by a principal or higher authority may not delegate this power to a sub-agent unless the original delegator expressly authorises it, or there is an implied authority to do so. Parliament entrusts functions to local authorities as such, not directly to their committees and sub-committees or officers, and any delegate entrusted with a task cannot lawfully pass that task on to another without the concurrence of the delegator. Indeed, the earliest of the modern local authorities were expressly denied the power to delegate: s. 22(2) of the Municipal Corporations Act 1882 read as follows (although, of course, the concluding words were not italicised in the official text):

> 'The council may from time to time appoint out of their own body such and so many committees, either of a general or special nature and consisting of such number of persons as they think fit for any purposes which, in the opinion of the council, would be better regulated and managed by means of such committees; *but the acts of every such committee shall be submitted to the council for their approval.*'

9.77 County councils when set up under the LGA 1888 were, however, wholly relieved of this disability. Section 8 2(2) of the 1888 Act provided:

> 'Every committee shall report its proceedings to the council by whom it was appointed, but to the extent to which the council so direct, the acts and proceedings of the committee shall not be required by the provisions of the Municipal Corporations Act 1882, to be submitted to the council for their approval.'

Effect of delegation

9.78 A local authority does not abdicate its responsibility by delegating functions to committees: this was so decided in *Huth v Clarke* (1890), but now, in any case, the LGA 1972 expressly provides in s. 101(4) that:

> 'Any arrangement made by a local authority . . . for the discharge of any functions by a committee, sub-committee (officer or local authority) shall not prevent the authority or committee by whom the arrangements are made from exercising those functions.'

This means two things: first, that the local authority remains responsible (and this, of course, is so of any principal who delegates because it is authority that is delegated and not responsibility) and the committee when it acts does so for and in the name of the local authority; second, that the council can continue to perform the functions that it has delegated.

9.79 In *Goddard v Minister of Housing and Local Government* (1958), the plaintiff challenged the validity of a compulsory purchase order made by a committee under delegated powers and put forward two contentions: one was that the council itself had never applied its mind to the issue, for the resolutions of the council's committees were merely 'rubber-stamped', whereas the council was obliged by statute to 'satisfy' itself. The court held that the council, acting through its committee, was satisfied.

9.80 The principle that an authority can continue to exercise the functions it has delegated could in practice lead to difficulties and possible confusion. The council must take care not to act in a matter which is also being dealt with by a committee under delegated powers, or at least not to act without close consultation with the committee. If it wishes to do so, it ought first to withdraw the delegated powers from the committee in respect of the particular matter on which it proposes to act itself. What it cannot properly do is to purport to put an end to delegated powers retrospectively so as to invalidate what a committee has done already in exercise of those powers where third-party interests are affected: see *Battelley v Finsbury Borough Council* (1958).

9.81 In the model standing orders, retained in the updated model, there is the provision to rescind a previous decision. It is this standing order that is commonly used (if an explicit standing order has not been introduced for the purpose) to allow a meeting of full council to consider a decision made by a committee under delegated authority and, in effect, remove that delegation and either replace it with a new decision by council or send it back to be remade (see Chapter 7).

Method of delegation

9.82 There are two ways in which the terms of delegation can be expressed. An authority can either:

- list the particular matters that a committee has the power to do without reference to the full council, or
- give each committee the power to take action on everything within its respective terms of reference except those matters specifically excluded.

The former is usual where the scope of a committee's delegated power is intended to be limited to a few specific functions and the other where delegation is extensive: the latter is to be preferred because it is easier to put down in writing and interpret in practice, and the exclusions would mean that the full council would have to address itself to the exclusions and therefore avoid doubt.

Handling urgent business

Regulation by standing order

9.83 Every authority makes arrangements to enable urgent business to be dealt with when the matter cannot wait until the next meeting of the appropriate committee.

9.84 Arrangements for handling urgent business at committee or sub-committee meetings are now governed by statute, which requires the chairman's approval before an urgent item can be considered and for the reason for the urgency to be recorded in the minutes. In practice this has often resulted in the former agenda item of 'Urgent business' being replaced by 'Any business the chairman regards as urgent' or to similar effect, although many councils do not include the item at all, in the view that it encourages members to raise items. The reasons given by the chairman for accepting urgent business should be legitimate ones: political expediency or forgetfulness on the part of reporting officers do not accord with the spirit of the legislation.

9.85 So far as those authorities operating executive arrangements are concerned, an urgent decision that is contrary to the policy framework may be taken by the executive if the chair of the relevant overview and scrutiny committee agrees that the decision may reasonably be regarded as urgent in the circumstances. Otherwise, the matter must be referred to the full council for decision. Where a key decision needs to be made in relation to a matter not in the forward plan, there will need to be five clear days' notice given to the chair of the relevant overview and scrutiny committee (or, if there is no chair, to each member of the committee) and to the public before the decision is taken. If the matter is urgent and cannot wait for five clear days' notice to be given, the agreement of the chair of the relevant overview and scrutiny committee that the making of the decision is urgent and cannot reasonably be deferred is needed to enable the decision to be made otherwise, it will have to wait for the expiry of the five clear days' notice. It is, however, important to ensure that financial regulations do not conflict with standing orders on urgent business where a decision to be taken is outside the budgetary framework.

Sub-committees

Power to appoint

9.86 A discretionary committee appointed by a local authority individually or by two or more authorities under the LGA 1972 may by that same Act appoint 'one or more sub-committees' (s. 102(1),(4)), constituted as the committee concerned may determine (see 9.94).

9.87 The decision in *R v Brent London Borough Council ex parte Gladbaum* (1989) (see

9.43) gave added force to the ordinarily accepted principle that sub-committee membership should not be decided by the full council. Because of the difficulty that could arise in practice, particularly for councils that prefer to settle all their committee and sub-committee structure at the annual council meeting, an appropriate legislative amendment negating the effect of *Gladbaum* was inserted into the LG&HA 1989, but has never been brought into force, probably because the effect would have been to remove sub-committees from the political balance rules, since a sub-committee so appointed would not be an 'ordinary' sub-committee. One practical way of avoiding the problems of appointing sub-committees direct by the full council would be for the parent committee at its first meeting to confirm the membership of its sub-committees.

Constitution

9.88 A committee may determine the number of members of each of its sub-committees, the term of office and the area (if restricted) within which the sub-committee is to exercise its authority,[15] and the sub-committees may include non-voting persons. Most of the statutory provisions relating to committees are applicable also to sub-committees (as to the manner in which decisions shall be made, the casting vote of a chairman, the recording of names of members present, the keeping and signing of minutes, the applicability of standing orders, and the validity of proceedings despite defects in its constitution or in the election or qualification of members).

Delegation to sub-committees

9.89 A local authority has a general power in respect of discretionary committees to delegate any of its functions (except with respect to levying, or issuing a precept for, a rate) to a sub-committee; and a discretionary committee may, unless the authority otherwise directs, itself delegate any of its functions to its sub-committees; and, in turn, a sub-committee may unless otherwise directed delegate any of its functions to an officer. No longer is a committee bound by the maxim *delegatus non potest delegare* in delegating to sub-committees, as was formerly the case.[16]

9.90 Where an authority has made arrangements for another authority to discharge the functions of the former then, subject to the terms of the arrangements, that other authority may delegate in the same way as an authority in respect of its own functions.

Advantages and disadvantages of sub-committees

9.91 Sub-committees should not be set up unless such a course is unavoidable. Professor K. C. Wheare said:[17]

> 'Difficulties are avoided, decisions postponed, discussion shortened or prevented by the use of sub-committees. And the process of referring matters to smaller and smaller bodies seems at times to have no limits – sub-committees

have their sections, sections their subsections; there are panels and working parties and informal groups and drafting sectors and segments. There is a sort of law of gravity in committee work by which things are referred farther and farther back and down. Along with this tendency there goes the tendency for each small group to feel a sense of its own importance and to conspire against the body to which it is nominally subordinate.'

9.92 Sub-committees can, however, assist positively in advancing the work of a committee: a smaller group of members can often more effectively examine a matter requiring detailed consideration, or more efficiently and effectively constitute an officer appointments panel; and there is the advantage that a small number of members can be called together more easily than the membership of a full committee. Sub-committees should never be set up, as Professor Wheare implies, to postpone an unpalatable decision or as a device to shelve an item of business. Ideally, a committee should decide at the outset of its term of office whether there is need for any standing sub-committees and to accept as a near immutable principle that it shall not set up any ad hoc sub-committee during the council year. If the disadvantages of sub-committees are recognised, there is less risk of appointing them needlessly or of misusing those that are unavoidable.

9.93 Nevertheless, it is preferable for a local authority to allow a committee with substantial responsibilities to appoint sub-committees for each identifiably different part of its totality of functions rather than for the authority to divide the responsibilities between two or more committees.

Working parties

Devolution of decision-making

9.94 Bains favoured the setting up of working groups, without the constraints of formal sub-committees, in order to provide members with the opportunity to identify themselves with areas of activity in which they have a particular interest and to provide officers with an immediate point of reference to opinion of elected members. In practice, now, most authorities set up 'task groups' to take forward particular items of business and to make recommendations to overview and scrutiny committees.

When a working party is not a committee

9.95 The question of whether or not a working party could exist within a local authority outside the committee system was raised by the provisions of the LG(AI)A 1985. Proponents of the Act maintained that any gathering of members dealing with council business must be either a committee or a sub-committee and the public access and notice provisions must therefore apply in all cases. The issue became clearer with the case of *R v Eden District Council ex parte Moffat* (1989), where the court at first instance and the Court of Appeal both accepted that the concept of a working party was acceptable in law. The facts on which this case was brought related to events that occurred before the 1985 Act, but the principles remain valid. The conclusion reached by Webster J was that there was no reason why a local authority should not create a working party 'to have a think about the best way of doing things'. The body of members at the centre of the dispute was a working party, said the judge, and Eden District Council's standing orders, which allowed access by members to committees and sub-committees, could not be invoked by a councillor who wanted to attend a particular meeting of a working party. The working party in this case also contained officer representation that was regarded as evidence of the intention by the council to establish an informal body.

9.96 The importance of the intention of the council was emphasised again in *R v Warwickshire District Council ex parte Bailey* (1991). This case involved a working party established to consider the reorganisation of secondary education in the county and to make recommendations as it thought fit. Public access to the meetings was denied and opponents of the working party's proposals maintained that the meetings were unlawful. The court took the view, however, that the critical factor was the manifest intention of the council so long as there was nothing inherently unlawful behind that intention: the council had quite properly intended the body to be a working party and therefore that was what it was.

9.97 A local authority often seeks to set up working parties or task groups as a way of considering matters in private, i.e. without the need to give public notice and so be able to exclude the public and press without the formality of giving adequate reasons. The position appears to be that it is permissible to set up a working party, provided the council makes clear its intention to follow that course and there is no conferment of delegated powers. Simply calling a body a working party or a task group may not be good enough, particularly if there is any suggestion or likelihood of decision-making because this is clearly an exercise of the functions of the council which, under the LGA 1972, s. 101, can only be carried out by a committee or sub-committee (or officer): any attempt to do so through a working party is inherently unlawful and fails the test in the case of *Bailey*.

Notes

1 Health and Well-being Boards – Regulation 5(1) of the Local Authority (Public Health, Health and Well-being Boards and Health Scrutiny) Regulations 2013.
2 LGA 1972, s. 80 and s. 104(1)
3 Maud Report, vol. 1, paras. 93–96.
4 LGA 1972, s. 102(1).
5 Non-members in this case are voting members: LG&HA 1989, s. 13(4).
6 J. H. Warren, *The English Local Government System*.
7 LG&HA 1989, s. 15 and Sch. l, and the Local Government (Committees and Political Groups) Regulations 1990. The Local Government (Committees and Political Groups) (Amendment) Regulations 1998 exclude from the voting regulations a number of joint committees exercising specific functions.
8 These bodies are prescribed by LG&HA 1989, Sch. 1, para. 2, and include a fire authority, a waste disposal authority, a joint authority, any successor to residuary bodies, an economic prosperity board or a combined authority established under the Local Democracy Economic Development and Construction Act 2009, the Broads Authority, a National Park authority, an inshore fisheries and conservation authority, a conservation board

establishment under the Countryside and Rights of Way Act 2000, a superannuation committee, a board or committee appointed under a local Act and a joint committee appointed under the LGA 1972, s. 102(1)(b).

9 Local Government (Committees and Political Groups) Regulations 1990 as amended.

10 See the decision in *R v Brent London Borough Council ex parte Gladbaum* (1989) that only the council in full assembly can appoint members to its committees. There is a view, however, that the political proportionality provisions of the LG&HA 1989 must be regarded as having overruled *Gladbaum* where political groups effectively make appointments to committees. In the circumstances, it may be thought prudent, to secure nominal compliance with the ordinarily accepted practice that only a parent body can constitute its own committees, for the full council's formal endorsement (albeit it that it has no discretion) to be sought to the names of members put forward by the political groups.

11 See nevertheless *R v Swansea City Council ex parte Elitestone Ltd* (1993), where it was held that a local authority committee of two members was lawful.

12 Erskine May's *Parliamentary Practice*, 20th edition.

13 LGA 1972, s. 101. The limitations are those contained within the 1972 Act (e.g. the election of chairman of a principal council must be conducted by the full assembly) or by any statute passed subsequently. Among other business that cannot be delegated are, e.g. consideration of a s. 114 report by the chief financial officer under the LGA 1988, s. 115(4), consideration of a s. 4 report by the head of the paid service under the LG&HA 1989, s. 4(5), consideration of a s. 5 report by the monitoring officer under the 1989 Act, s. 5(5). Further limitations in respect of local authorities operating the committee system of governance are contained in the Local Authorities (Committee System) (England) Regulations 2012 (SI 2012/1020).

14 Ibid, s. 101(6). The former reference to borrowing in this section was removed by the LG&HA 1989, s. 45(5).

15 LGA 1972, s. 102(2).

16 Ibid, but note that the phrase 'may arrange for the discharge' of any of its functions is used instead of the word 'delegate'.

17 *Government by Committee* (1955), p. 194.

Chapter 10
Work before meetings

General considerations

Timetable of meetings

10.1 Most local authorities fix their timetable of meetings for a period of one year in advance (at or about the time of the annual council meeting), compiled as a rule by an updating of the programme for the previous year. The modular constitution provided that the programme of ordinary meetings would be agreed at the annual meeting of the council. There is much to commend this widely adopted practice: councillors and officers can enter the dates in their diaries before other commitments arise and it sets the pattern for the organisation and transaction of council business at member level.

10.2 Considerations to note in drawing up the timetable include the following:

- There should be no more meetings than the volume of business demands: not all committees need meet in each cycle, while some may need to meet more than once.
- The actual dates of meetings should be related to the dates of council meetings, particularly where recommendations may need to be submitted to the full council.
- The order of meetings within the cycle should be related to the character of business: committees that regularly or periodically have to consider the recommendations of other committees must meet at the end of the cycle but in sufficient time before the council meeting to enable reports to be prepared and incorporated within the council agenda. In the case of executive meetings, this is not so crucial as the executive in most councils meet on a more regular basis than committees.
- Administrative considerations must not be overlooked: time needs to be allowed for reports to be drafted and for member briefings, and the preparation and despatch of the summons and agenda, ensuring that the five clear days are observed.
- Indeed, the timetable of meetings can form the basis of a committee programme for administrative purposes, showing the various deadlines that democratic services officers will need to observe, including, for example, the last date for the receipt of items for an agenda (see 10.23).

10.3 In particular cases it may not be practicable to prepare a programme for a committee or cabinet (because, for example, of an irregular and unpredictable flow of business). Even then, however, it is good practice at each meeting to fix the date and time of the next meeting (which can be cancelled if need be) rather than wait until there is enough business to warrant calling another meeting.

10.4 A prearranged timetable of meetings still means that you must give separate notice of each meeting at the proper time: notification of a committee or cabinet meeting merely by means of the circulation annually of a timetable is unlikely to be held to be proper notice because by common law, a summons must be served upon members with an agenda of the business to be transacted. Some authorities prepare a weekly bulletin of meetings, which is circulated for the information of members generally and this serves not only as a reminder to members of particular committee or cabinet meetings in advance of the summons and agenda, but as notification to members who may wish to attend committees or the cabinet if they are not members.

Time of meeting

10.5 The time at which committee meetings are held must be related to the convenience and availability of members. Generally, county councils arrange committee meetings during the day, because of the distance many have to travel and the consequent difficulty of returning home after a late evening meeting. Most district councils opt in the main for evening meetings. It may be that the pattern of timing is being materially affected by the payments available to members.

Convening committee meetings

Notice, summons and agenda

10.6 There is now less difference than formerly between the legal requirements as to the notice and summons in the case of committees and sub-committees, and those of the full council. Public notice of the meeting of every committee and sub-committee of a principal council must be given and the agenda and accompanying reports (excluding any reports or parts of reports for items of business during which the meeting is likely to be closed to the public) made available for public inspection at least five clear days before a meeting. The process is regulated (see above) by the LGA 1972, ss. 99, 100 and Sched. 12 as well as Part VA (Access to Meetings and Documents of Certain Authorities, Committees and Sub-Committees).

10.7 This also applies to meetings of the executive (cabinet), which is regulated by the Local Authorities (Executive Arrangements) (Meetings and Access to Information) (England) Regulations 2012. Business not specified on the agenda may not be considered unless the chair agrees that it is urgent, and in the case of key decisions to be made at meetings of the executive, if approval of the chair of the relevant O&S committee has been obtained.

10.8 In short, all that has been said earlier (see Chapter 6) about the giving of public notice of a council meeting and its agenda and the making available of agenda papers and reports applies equally to committees and sub-committees of principal councils.

10.9 However, in the case of the meetings of committees and sub-committees of parish and community councils, the rules governing the summons and agenda will be those set out in the standing orders of the council concerned or, where standing orders are silent, then as prescribed by common law.

10.10 There is no common form of summons or agenda for a committee or sub-committee meeting. Many authorities omit any formal words of summons, e.g. an agenda is despatched to those entitled to attend headed merely with the name of the committee or sub-committee and the date, time and place of meeting.

10.11 The agenda may also need to be sent to certain councillors other than those appointed to the committee or sub-committee according to local practice, e.g. to ward members with an interest in certain of the items on the agenda or to councillors claiming a 'need to know' (see Chapter 4) or to substitute members where such an arrangement exists. Any document that contains material relating to any business to be transacted at a public meeting of the executive (cabinet) must be available for inspection by any member of the local authority as required by reg. 16 of the Local Authorities (Executive Arrangements) (Meetings and Access to Information) (England) Regulations 2012. In practice, most authorities make agendas for all meetings available for members to view in the members' room, and some authorities send copies of cabinet agendas to all members. In addition, most authorities publish agendas on their website for ease of access by both members and the public.

If a councillor is wrongly summoned because, for example, their surname is the same as that of another member entitled to be present, that person cannot claim a right to be present. If, nevertheless, the wrong councillor does attend a meeting that they are not entitled to attend and actually votes, their vote is invalid (see Chapter 7). It is, of course, good practice for the democratic services officers to check that the correct members are in attendance to ensure that this does not happen. Errors in service of the summons do not affect the validity of proceedings.

Regulation by standing orders

10.12 Not many authorities think it necessary to regulate the agenda of committee meetings, but the working party on standing orders (see Chapter 2) nevertheless drafted this possible core standing order:

'00–1 At least [five] clear days before every meeting of a committee or sub-committee,
or as soon as the meeting is called, whichever is later, the proper officer shall send to every voting member and to every other person entitled to receive the papers of the committee or sub-committee a copy of the agenda for the meeting.

2 The agenda shall include:

(a) all items of business which have been, or are deemed to have been, referred to the committee or sub-committee by the council or by another committee or sub-committee, as the case may be;

(b) all reports submitted to the committee or sub-committee by the head of the paid service or any chief officer;
(c) any item of business directed to be included by the person appointed to preside at the meetings of the committee or sub-committee; and
(d) any other item of business of which the requisite notice has been given to the proper officer by a member of the committee or sub-committee (whether voting or not); provided that no member (other than the person appointed to preside at meetings of the committee or sub-committee) may give notice of more than one item of business for any one meeting.

3 The requisite notice is [five] clear days' notice in writing before the date fixed for the meeting of the committee or sub-committee.
4 Subject to any directions given by the person appointed to preside at the meetings of the committee or sub-committee, the items of business shall be arranged in such order as the proper officer thinks will best ensure the effective despatch of business.'

Notice of meetings one after the other

10.13 It is not unusual, particularly in the case of smaller authorities, for committee meetings to follow one another on the same day or evening; each to begin upon the conclusion of another. Because a notice must be clear, explicit and unconditional, it is never satisfactory for a committee (or any other body for that matter) to be convened to meet at an indeterminate time 'immediately upon the rising' of an earlier committee: even though it may be felt to be justified in circumstances where the two committees comprise the same membership. For certainty an estimate of the likely starting time should be made and the summons can then clearly state, for example, that the meeting will commence:

'. . . at 7 p.m. or upon the rising of the . . . committee, whichever is the later.'

This is useful where the council has a concurrent meeting of the statutory committee under s. 6 of the Licensing Act 2003, covering alcohol, gambling and so forth, and a regulatory or licensing committee under s. 101 of the LGA 1972, covering taxis and so on, which usually consist of the same members for consistency, convenience and as a means to ensure that the licensing committee adheres to political balance rules.

Notice to officers and others

10.14 Officers must also be notified of meetings where they are expected to be present, especially, of course, where an officer not usually in attendance (or, indeed, an outside adviser) is being invited to attend for a particular item of business. Such an officer, or other person, may need to be briefed in certain respects before the actual meeting.

Who may convene

10.15 The proper officer will normally convene committee or executive meetings in accordance with the prearranged timetable and, in consultation with the committee chairman or leader, convene special meetings as circumstances may warrant. There is no provision in law, as in the case of council meetings, for members to requisition a meeting of a committee or the executive, but old model standing order no. 32 is to the following effect:

> 'The chairman of a committee or the mayor/chairman of the council may call a special meeting of the committee at any time. A special meeting shall also be called on the requisition of a quarter of the whole number of the committee, delivered in writing to the town clerk/clerk of the council but in no case shall less than [three] members requisition a special meeting. The summons to the special meeting shall set out the business to be considered thereat, and no business other than set out in the summons shall be considered at that meeting.'

10.16 If there is no standing order to this effect and a number of members demand a special meeting, the committee chair should agree to one being convened. If the chair is not prepared to agree, the chief executive would no doubt advise them to do so if the number of members asking was substantial; and if the number comprised the majority of members the chief executive, or proper officer in practice, might well feel obliged to convene a meeting irrespective of the wishes of the committee chair. However, in respect of executive meetings, it is unlikely that the leader would be in a position whereby his or her own group were requesting an additional meeting of the cabinet – this type of debate is more likely to take place at group meetings. If neither committee nor chief executive will act, the members could always, of course, make use of their power to call a special council meeting to deal with the situation (see Chapter 1). However, if the decision to be made related to executive functions, then a meeting of the council could not deal with these.

Committee agenda

General principles

10.17 The purpose of an agenda is to:

- provide advance notification of the business to be transacted at a particular meeting; and
- facilitate the transaction of business at the meeting itself.

The document may have practical purposes in addition (it may often provide the basis for the minutes of the meeting and, indeed, is sometimes written in a form that will help officers prepare the minutes), but an agenda's objective must always be to advance the purposes for which the committee/cabinet has been set up in an efficient manner. It should be regarded as a document framed to secure or at least encourage decision-making, and it can only do this effectively if councillors understand what is being put before them. It should not ordinarily be used merely to inform, i.e. items for noting; and the items placed before the committee should be those that unavoidably demand the committee/cabinet's consideration. The Maud report critically observed[1] that it saw the growth of business adding to the agenda of committees and squeezing out major issues that need time for consideration, with the result that members are misled into the belief that they are controlling and directing the authority when often they are only deliberating on things that are unimportant and making decisions on matters that do not merit their attention. This comment is hopefully less valid now due to the cabinet system, under which members should be controlling the direction of the authority. Item 'for noting' should therefore be limited to those that are strictly necessary, to ensure that members can focus on strategic issues and are not bogged down with triviality.

Agenda setting

10.18 The build-up of cabinet and committee agendas is virtually a continuous process: as soon as one meeting has been held, reports start accumulating for the next. Democratic services officers should maintain a list of items which need consideration. How this list is kept is a matter of choice, but clearly should be accessible to others if the officer is absent. The material for the draft agenda will come to democratic services from various sources; it will comprise:

- items that democratic services officers will themselves have 'noted':
  - (a) matters deferred or retained from previous meetings;
  - (b) periodically recurring items or reports: it is common practice for officers to look back at the committee agenda for the corresponding meeting in the previous council year to ensure that matters which arise annually are not overlooked;
  - (c) references from other committees, the council, or other bodies.
- other items:
  - (a) initiated by other officers or the corporate management team;
  - (b) that individual councillors may ask to be included;
- forward plan (cabinet only):
  - (a) those items that are set out in the forward plan to bring forward to cabinet.

The extent to which councillors are permitted to call for items to be placed before the executive or committees depends upon the practice and procedure rules of individual local authorities. However, it would seem reasonable to take the view that cabinet membership confers some rights in relation to the agenda. With regard to O&S and other committees, officers might be on difficult ground in refusing to accept an item as long as the matter concerned is within the terms of reference. It would, of course, remain open to the committee to refuse to discuss the matter. The position would conceivably be different where the member concerned does not serve on the committee since they have the option of raising the issue by way of notice of motion at a council meeting. It is useful for there to be a working arrangement or provision in standing orders' permitting, for example, individual councillors to initiate agenda items only after consultation with the committee chairman or leader of the council, a 'members items,' and some authorities provide for this. Often, however, it can be left for the democratic services officer to advise a committee chairman that another member has put forward an item onto the agenda; this may not always be welcome news, particularly where it is from an opposition member.

Control of agenda

10.19 It will be evident that whoever prepares an agenda has a significant, even possibly decisive, influence on the business conducted at the meeting. Items are likely to be initiated by the leader or portfolio holder in respect of cabinet meetings, in discussion with their officers. Widdicombe refers in one of its research volumes to practice in highly politicised local authorities whereby committee chairmen exercised considerable influence over agenda setting. A chairman may demand the right to add items of their own (which generally reflect pressure from their party group) or to postpone, occasionally delete, items that officers intended to include, possibly ask for a change in the order of items and in extreme instances seek to bring about changes in the content of officers' reports (as opposed to officers' advice). Indeed, where it is an agenda of the cabinet, it can be expected that there will be significant influence by the leader over agenda setting.

10.20 Where there is pressure from councillors for an agenda item to be delayed or amended solely for political purposes, the issue can be more contentious. If delay involves no legal problems or perceived disadvantage to third parties, then there would be no objection. Officers should always aim to meet the legitimate wishes of councillors. However, where the delay is inspired by motives of political advantage (Widdicombe's research, for example, discloses instances of the avoidance of 'bad news' prior to a local election) or the item in dispute is one that the officer concerned has, or believes they have, a duty to report at that particular time, then there can be a problem. In such a delicate circumstance the chief executive or monitoring officer should discuss with the leader of the council and an acceptable solution can hopefully be reached. Similar difficulties can arise where members demand that the terms of an officer's report should be altered. Again it is probable that a compromise can be reached. Officers are likely always to prepare material for the executive or committees in such a way as to acknowledge the political goals of the majority group and this clearly requires skills of political sensitivity and of drafting. What is important, however, is that officers must insist on their own right to have their own professional or technical viewpoint known, recorded and not significantly amended by members in its published form, and this is normally part of any member–officer protocol.

10.21 Problems of the above are becoming more common, and that they do happen at all is indicative of the growing importance of local politics. Closely linked is the parallel issue of the authorship of cabinet reports. Instances of members writing their own reports are not unknown and, at cabinet meetings at least, many executive members will present reports on matters within their own portfolio.

Drafting the agenda

10.22 At an early stage, preferably at a prescribed date prior to the committee/cabinet meeting, the democratic services officer will prepare the agenda in draft. In some authorities this may be circulated to all officers concerned, or at least to the management team, so that they may see what is already on the draft and add matters that they themselves wish the cabinet or committee to know about or decide upon. Where this is the practice, the draft should state the date by which amendments or alterations should be given to democratic services together with any additional items; and this date must be rigidly stuck to if the agenda is to be finalised and despatched on time.

10.23 Because an agenda is often compiled from material submitted from several sources, some editing may be necessary on the part of the democratic services officer, otherwise the final document will lack uniformity and can look like it has had many 'fingers in the pie'. Many problems can be reduced or avoided if the prescribed deadline for receipt of agenda items is enforced and, of great importance, if there are prescribed rules and guidelines regulating the manner in which material is to be prepared.

10.24 It should be accepted that the agenda is the responsibility of the proper officer and that they are the final arbiter of what goes on the agenda and in what form. An officer should be consulted if their report is held back, substantially amended or rewritten.

Agenda planning meetings

10.25 In some authorities an agenda planning meeting is held at which all officers concerned in the work of a particular committee meet together, discuss items on the draft agenda, and agree whether a matter is to be submitted as drafted, modified or taken to a future meeting. In the case of executive meetings, the agenda is likely to be discussed at the management team meetings.

Consultation with chair

10.26 It is comparatively uncommon for the committee chair to be consulted on the draft agenda in detail. Such a course might be justified in certain circumstances, e.g. where an item of political sensitivity or major importance is concerned or where a particular member has asked for a matter to be brought before the committee. In respect of cabinet meetings, however, it is common for leader/elected mayor or members of the cabinet to agree items to be included on a cabinet agenda and in any event, agenda items for key decisions will be included on the forward plan.

10.27 A committee chair will, however, expect to be briefed before the meeting (possibly with the vice chair and group spokespersons) and a cabinet briefing will normally involve all members of the cabinet.

What should be included

10.28 Local practice must determine what kind of items are included on the agenda. As a general guide, however, it may be said that a matter should be placed before the executive or a committee only if:

- it is within their terms of reference;
- it cannot be dealt with at officer level either because it:
  a) raises an issue of policy or principle of major importance not already decided; or demands a decision beyond an officer's delegated authority; or
  b) is politically contentious;
- it will eventually require a resolution of the full council, e.g. to meet the requirements of the law or of standing orders; and
- the committee/cabinet has itself requested the information.

10.29 It should be a principle in the conduct of local authority business that everything that needs a decision should be decided at the lowest level at which it may competently be taken. Unfortunately, it frequently happens in local government that decision-making is pushed upwards unnecessarily and councillors are called on to decide matters that could be dealt with at officer level. Of course, there may be occasions when an officer decides that it might be politic to bring before the cabinet/committee a matter on which they have delegated authority. The fact that an officer can be called to account is safeguard enough as a rule against arbitrary decisions at officer level. In addition, members sometimes ask that matters come before the cabinet or committees, even if they could be dealt with by members, because it is politically expedient for greater publicity to be given to a matter. While this is not good practice, nonetheless officers will generally agree to this course of action unless there is a legal or procedural reason for not doing so.

10.30 Among matters that do not justify inclusion on a committee agenda are reports confirming that an officer has carried out the committee's instructions (though the committee may be expected to want to know if an officer has been unable to execute a decision!), and information items (e.g. statistical material or trivia) that do not call for action.

10.31 Items that should be included for noting on the agenda are those where an officer has taken a key decision under their delegated authority, or where a cabinet member has taken an executive decision. Also, exemptions from standing orders relating to contracts should be included under items for noting, either to the cabinet or full council.

Form

10.32 A committee/cabinet agenda normally consists of a fully documented paper where all relevant information on each item of business is provided on the agenda itself or incorporated in appendices attached to the main document.

Clearly the amount of material produced for members can vary considerably, more often, it seems, because of the practice of the authority rather than the weight or significance of the issue to be decided. Maud reported:

> 'Behind . . . quite startling variations in the quantity of paper circulated lies a wide divergence of practice in the amount of written information submitted to sub-committees and committees and also in the methods of referring information and recommendations from sub-committees to committees and from committees to council. These differences in practice may in some places arise merely from a persistent adherence, for one reason or another, to different long-established traditions. On the other hand, they may well reflect elsewhere completely different philosophies.'

Some officers feel that the amount of written material should be kept to a minimum so that members can concentrate on a few major issues, but there are others who believe with equal conviction that it is their duty to provide members with the fullest and most detailed information possible so that they can make their own decisions as to what they feel to be significant, rather than having the selection determined for them.

Verbal reporting is not permissible unless related to an item already on the agenda or can be justified under the urgency provisions. An item on an agenda that merely states that a report will be made verbally is out of order if it gives no indication whatsoever of the subject matter or purport of the report to be made. There is no reason, however, why an officer cannot update verbally at a meeting a report that has been properly circulated in advance, although it may be advisable for the likelihood of an updating to be referred to on the agenda and, if significant new material is introduced, for the chair to take the update as an urgent item (subject to meeting the requirements for that action, depending on whether it is a committee or a public meeting of the executive).

10.33 Apart from variations in the amount of paper produced, there are also differences of a more fundamental character. Some authorities incorporate a formal summons as part of the agenda paper; others do not. Some make it a practice to set out the names of all members of the committee at the top of the first page or at the bottom of the formal summons; other authorities restrict this to the first meeting of a new committee.

Order of business

10.34 It is usual for the order of items to be standardised. Certain business must necessarily be dealt with first, e.g. the election of a chairman where this is called for, and confirmation of minutes; and if a petition is to be received or question time held, these are matters conveniently dealt with soon after the commencement of proceedings so that persons concerned can be given a definite time to attend. Some authorities prefer to deal with relatively routine or non-controversial matters first and more important business afterwards. In some authorities the agenda is divided into two parts: first, items requiring decisions or special discussion including whether it is to be dealt with in private or not; then items submitted for information/noting. Sometimes the order is arranged so that officers are not required to sit through business that does not concern them, and this is gratefully appreciated! It is good practice to group associated matters together so that members do not find themselves dealing with a jumble of important items of policy and trivial detail. The amount of attention given to a particular item can often be affected by its position on the agenda and that the order of agenda items is a matter that needs careful consideration. For example, most authorities find that members do not pay sufficient attention to the work programme of the committee if it is the last item at an evening meeting, and some have moved this to the beginning of the agenda.

10.35 Procedural items are generally included at the beginning of an agenda. Many local authorities include an item early in the agenda to enable members to declare their interests or enable the chairman to indicate the existence of urgent business they are prepared to allow later on. This has the advantage not only of discouraging the submission of so-called urgent items during the meeting, but also of giving notice to any members of the public or press present that one or more items not specified on the agenda are to be discussed later.

First meeting of new committees

10.36 When an entirely new committee is set up or a standing committee is newly constituted with several new members, it may be considered desirable to:

- include on the agenda a statement of the names of the members, the committee's terms of reference and, possibly, a resume of the committee's functions; and
- despatch with the agenda all documents in current use relating to the work of the committee that could provide useful background or essential information for members.

Care should be taken in the selection so as to avoid including documents that soon become out of date: for example, it is questionable whether the members of a staffing committee should be given copies of national schemes of conditions of service because of the cost and difficulty of updating them as changes occur.

Papers for special committees

10.37 It is obvious, no doubt, that when a special committee or task group is set up to inquire into or investigate a particular matter or to consider a specific problem, the first meeting may need to be devoted to certain preliminaries: defining the area of inquiry, ascertaining the basic facts, planning a programme of work and so on. It will usually be helpful if a paper is circulated with the agenda for the first meeting setting out the terms of reference, reciting the circumstances in which the committee came into being and providing as much factual information as can be gathered that is relevant to the task before the members.

Agenda items – the reports

10.38 Every agenda item has at least five principal parts:

1 the heading;
2 the question to be decided, succinctly expressed;

3 the relevant facts, including – according to circumstances – a note of the authority's legal powers, of its policy on the subject matter or related topics, and of the financial considerations involved;
4 the options open and the consequences of pursuing each alternative posed; and
5 an indication of the particular course recommended, and reasons for the recommendation.

Reports to committees in most local authorities follow the same format although reports for some committees may not include suggested reasons for the decision. This same order should be followed in officers' reports to the cabinet, together with those extra elements that may be required for those executive decisions such as those viable alternatives considered and recommended to be rejected. The only exception is for those administrative committees considered to be quasi-judicial, such as development control but more particularly individual regulatory matters.

10.39 Of crucial importance is that the Members councillors are given all the relevant information in order that they may make an informed judgement and reasoned decision. In *R v Isle of Wight County Council ex parte O'Keefe* (1991), it was held that a decision of the local authority to make a modification order granting a public right of way should be reached only after a proper consideration of all the evidence and the legal problems involved: the court quashed the decision that had been taken because the officers had failed to present the evidence fully in that they did not include in their report necessary qualifications of the strength of witnesses' evidence on the public user of the path concerned, nor did they include a proper assessment of the submissions of the owner of the land. In an earlier case, *R v Rochdale Metropolitan Borough Council ex parte Cromer Ring Mill Ltd* (1982), the law was inaccurately summarised in an officer's report and the court found that the committee had taken into account an irrelevant consideration and its decision was bad.

More recently, there have been a number of judicial review cases where the courts have found that members have been given inadequate information to make a decision. In *R (on the application of JM & NT) v Isle of Wight* (2011) EWHC 2911 (Admin), it was held that the reports to the cabinet and council did not provide members with sufficient information to discharge their duty under s. 49A DDA 1995. See also *R (on the application of Sefton Care Association) and Sefton Council* (2011) EWHC 2676.

This reflects the role of the democratic services officer in being the last, although one would hope also the first, line of defence in helping report writers ensure that their reports provide all that is required by the Members, and no more, in order to come to a sound decision. One way of putting this, as a mantra, is that it is the officers' role to put all of the evidence before the Members, with a recommendation, and it is the Members' role to weigh up that evidence and come to a decision.

In essence, the legal and democratic services officers are there to help the member to positively answer those questions they need to ask themselves in order to reach a lawful decision. As a brief and summary crib-sheet, this might be boiled down to:

1. Do we have the authority from statute to make this decision?
2. Is the decision going to be in furtherance of the policy and objectives of the statute?
3. Do we have the authority from Council to make this decision?
4. Have we performed our duties as required?
   - Provisions on meetings, fiduciary duty, reduction of crime & disorder, public sector equality duties, the rules to apply when considering any consultation[2], etc.
5. Have we followed the correct procedures?
6. Have we taken into consideration all of the relevant factors?
7. Have we disregarded all of the irrelevant factors?
8. Have we followed the rules of natural justice (heard all sides and not been a judge in one's own cause)?
9. Is our likely decision a proportionate balance between the necessary objectives and the civil rights effected?
10. Have we exercised our discretion as required (and not fettered it)?

For example, *R (Galaxy Land Ltd) v Durham County Council* [2015] EWHC 16 (Admin) was the result of a substantially sized report butu one which nonetheless produced a failure to consider, explain or include viable alternative options for the cabinet to consider, a failure to include all relevant information, a failure to consult stakeholders as ought, a failure to follow statutory procedures and failure to follow their own financial procedures. The result, as in other such cases, is judicial comment including: *"This was the discharge of an executive power to dispose of public assets and the Cabinet did not have regard to material considerations in doing so . . ."*; *"In my judgment the Cabinet was not provided with the necessary information so that it could take into account obviously relevant considerations . . ."*; and *"The upshot is that the Cabinet decision is consequently flawed"*.

10.40 Competence in drafting will determine the brevity with which each item is covered. It is not, however, enough merely to use words economically. A sense of proportion is also necessary. Routine matters of minor importance, if they must be submitted for committee consideration, can often be dealt with in a single line. These can be severely pruned in appropriate circumstances: certain knowledge, for example, can be assumed on the part of councillors, and details that members can easily look up for themselves in past minutes, standing orders or other regulations need not necessarily be set out in full. Only local practice and sensible judgement can provide a guide. The order of material within an item can rarely be changed, however, without sacrifice of clarity and logical exposition: the question to be decided; the facts; the courses open and the consequences; and, often, a recommendation.

10.41 Quality control processes differ from authority to authority. A report will go through various stages before it results in a published paper before the members. This will often include departmental team meetings and the most senior management team, to ensure the report fits with other matters going on in the authority, makes sense, and is justifiable, lawful and affordable. That said, report authors will still, at some point or another, provide a draft that has slipped through the net or been rushed so that it results in last-minute matters being put in front of democratic services officers that are poorly written, verbose, in-cohesive and of generally sub-standard content. In such a case, the democratic services officers must either do their best to help correct matters or, as a last resort and where empowered to do so, refuse to publish and refer the matter back.

10.42 These situations can arise simply because of time pressure, but they can also be caused by a lack of knowledge of what is required; this is where training comes in. A common additional step in processes at many authorities is also what is traditionally known as a 'call-over board', where democratic services, policy, legal, finance and other officers from central services can provide a sense-check for report authors, a place to pitch the report before going to the strategic leadership team (or whatever the authority's most senior office grouping is called) and a form of quality control and advice.

10.43 The legalities of what should and should not be included in a report or prospective decision were discussed in Chapter 1. As a short-hand, however, a checklist of questions to ask oneself when looking at whether a decision (and thus the information, supporting evidence and recommendation in a report) is lawful is set out below.

> The decision-maker needs to ask themselves the following questions:
>
> - Do we have the authority from statute to make this decision?
> - Is the decision going to be in furtherance of the policy and objectives of the statute?
> - Do we have the authority from council to make this decision?
> - Have we performed our duties as required, covering provisions on meetings, fiduciary duty, reduction of crime and disorder, public sector equality duties, etc.?
> - Have we consulted those who hold a legitimate expectation or statutory right to be consulted?
> - Have all essential elements of consultation been met?
> - Have we followed the correct procedures, including statutory and our own standing orders and policies?
> - Have we taken into consideration all of the relevant factors?
> - Have we disregarded all of the irrelevant factors?

Routine items

10.44 Routine or regularly recurring items should be standardised in the minimum number of words consistent with clarity. For example, the item that deals with the submission of minutes of the previous meeting for confirmation could be dealt with in one line:

> 'MINUTES. Confirmation of minutes of . . . June, 20. .'

This would be better expressed, however, as, e.g.:

> 'MINUTES To confirm the minutes of the meeting of . . . June, 20. .'

Although councillors can be expected to know the purpose of the item, a reminder in express words could nevertheless be desirable.
There are several similar items that can be set out in summary fashion on the agenda: the election of a chair and vice-chair (never the appointment, unless, of course, the item has been placed on the agenda for the proper officer to report formally that the full council has appointed the committee chair); the appointment of representatives of the council to serve on other bodies; the submission of a sub-committee's report; and so on.
10.45 Apart from routine items as above (where the intention is self-evident), care should be taken to indicate clearly what action is expected of the committee. Briefly expressed items can be introduced in the style: To consider, To decide, To receive. A common error, however, where agenda items are prefixed by the word 'To' is to employ it carelessly and incorrectly:

> 'TOWN CENTRE REDEVELOPMENT To report that . . .'

when what was intended was:

> 'TOWN CENTRE REDEVELOPMENT Chief Executive to report that . . .'

It is good practice to indicate who is in fact reporting particular items.

Item or appendix?

10.46 It is not always easy in practice to determine whether particular business is better presented as an item on the agenda or in an accompanying document. Importance can be a matter of opinion and practice varies, in any case, as to the form of an agenda. Length may be more relevant. An item that can be dealt with in less than a page of type is generally more conveniently included on the main agenda, while one that extends beyond, say, a page in length is probably better dealt with as an appendix. In the majority of cases a committee agenda will contain items of varying length.

Appendices

10.47 Attaching papers to the agenda as appendices has the advantage of providing separate documents that can easily be incorporated in the subsequent minutes. It also helps preparation of the agenda because the printing and collating can be distributed among a number of officers, and it invariably makes for a tidier, more easily understood agenda paper.

10.48 Appendices should be identified by letter or number, e.g. as APPENDIX A or APPENDIX 1, whichever may be preferred, and it assists members in referring to several appendices if the documents are reproduced on different-coloured paper, if finances allow. For example, an item would appear on the agenda paper to this effect:

> '00 Provision of Temporary Accommodation Report of Task Group A (Yellow)'

And the document itself would be identified by this reference at the top right-hand corner of the first page (on coloured paper, if possible):

> APPENDIX A
> (see agenda item 00)

10.49 Sometimes it may be necessary for documents to be attached to appendices. These need to be distinguished from the appendices by, for example, referring to them as ENCLOSURE or STATEMENT or ANNEXE, according to choice, and if appendices are lettered A, B, C and so on, these further attachments can conveniently be numbered 1, 2, 3, etc., or, perhaps, I, II, III, etc. Whatever is favoured, it should be standard throughout the authority.

Any other business

10.50 It was once common practice for a committee agenda to conclude with an item 'Any other business'. Following the changes to the LGA 1972 introduced by the LG(AI)A 1985, the practice was properly discontinued because an item of business may not be considered at a meeting of a principal council unless requisite advance notice has been given (see Chapter 6). The same applies for executive decisions and cabinet agendas. Some authorities include as a matter of routine a final agenda item for committee meetings 'Any other business which the chairman considers to be urgent', to cover the possibility of urgent business arising, but most would now consider this to be bad practice.

Despatch of papers

Need for efficient arrangements

10.51 There must be an efficient arrangement for the issue of notices and despatch of papers to ensure that:

- appropriate notice is given to the press and public – available at the office(s) five clear days beforehand, not including the day of the meeting and the day of publication, means a copy must be physically available at the public office before they close on that day of publication (although 4.55pm, when closing at 5.00pm, would technically meet that requirement);
- the summons and agenda are in the hands of members by the time prescribed by regulations; and
- officers required to be present and any persons invited to attend on the particular occasion are appropriately notified and advised; and that the papers are complete and that no one entitled to receive them is omitted from the despatch.

This is achieved by:

- strict compliance with a checklist of members' names, press representatives and officers' names;
- double-checking that no one has been omitted either by:
  - (a) writing the names of addressees on the front sheet of the agenda paper and then, after separately selecting the appropriate preaddressed envelopes, putting the papers in the envelopes; or
  - (b) one officer calling out the names of the addressees and another putting the agenda papers in previously selected pre-addressed envelopes;
- ideally (but practicable only in the smaller authorities in compact areas) arranging for hand delivery; and
- recording the despatch.

A prescribed procedure and a record kept help to emphasise the importance of the despatch: failure to serve the summons and agenda correctly could affect the validity of the meeting.

Pre-committee/cabinet briefings

General considerations

10.52 The amount of briefing a committee chair or cabinet members may require before a meeting depends upon the type of meeting and the experience and/or knowledge of the members. It is usual, and desirable, for the chair or cabinet to discuss beforehand with the appropriate officers the items on the agenda.

10.53 There are arguably objections to the pre-committee/cabinet briefing on the grounds that the chair and officers could agree tactics to steamroller the committee/cabinet into agreeing a particular course of action. This should not be the purpose. There is nothing wrong in the officer making clear to the chair what is in their mind and their own preferences or recommendations, but there should be no conspiracy between chair and officers to force a particular decision upon the committee/cabinet. If the chair gains the advantage of knowing what is in the mind of the officers then the officers, for their part, become aware of the chair's feelings. The chair's views on a matter may well reflect the political opinion of the majority group and this, in turn, will alert the officers to the possible need to treat a matter with sensitivity and discretion.

It is equally important that cabinet briefings are not used as an opportunity for members to ask questions and decide the outcome, as this could make the meeting itself seem like a rubber-stamping exercise. As with committee briefings, they should be used as an opportunity for officers and members to receive each other's views and for issues to be clarified.

10.54 It is for the individual chair to determine whether there should be a briefing, what form it should take and what officers should be present. In some cases the chairman may prefer to read through the agenda and discuss with the officers concerned those items on which the chairman queries or needs further information; perhaps a telephone discussion may be sufficient. Other chairmen may think it sufficient to rely on the relevant officer contacting them if circumstances merit a briefing. But, as Maud pointed out:[3]

> 'Whether committee briefing takes place incidentally or on a specific occasion, there is no doubt that in many instances the initiative rests entirely with the officer, who has already prepared (and in some cases already circulated) the agenda and reports.'

Maud contains several paragraphs on the pros and cons of committee briefing, and Widdicombe produced evidence to show that pre-committee briefing was universal.

Committee clerk should be present

10.55 It is essential for the democratic services officer to be present at any pre-committee briefing. Sometimes they are not, and this will make their job unnecessarily difficult; indeed, it means that the chair and officers will not benefit from their advice in respect of procedural issues and their wider organisational knowledge in respect of matters which are being dealt with in other areas.

Officers and invitees

10.56 It may also be necessary, primarily in relation to procedure, to brief those invited to attend a particular committee meeting who are not usual attendees: an officer, for example, who is to present an item of business but has never attended a committee meeting before; or an independent adviser or consultants who have been invited to attend; or petitioners who will feel more comfortable if properly briefed beforehand as to what to expect when entering the room, where to sit, how to conduct themselves and so on. It is easy for officers who are familiar with council work to forget that, for an officer who rarely attends a members' meeting, it can be an uncomfortable or daunting experience to be asked to attend and speak at a meeting at short notice. It can also be a daunting experience for members of the public who may never have attended a local authority meeting before and may be confused by the way in which many meetings are conducted. A few preliminary words of explanation are always appreciated.

Final preparations for meeting

Availability of accommodation

10.57 Before committee/cabinet papers are finally despatched to council members and others, officers should check, even though the dates of meetings and accommodation have been prearranged, that:

- a suitable room is available with reasonable seating for the public, and table and seating for the press;
- waiting accommodation is conveniently situated for invitees to the meeting;
- no other committee or sub-committee with common membership has been subsequently arranged for the same time;
- nothing, such as noisy repair work in adjoining accommodation, is likely to interfere with the meeting; and
- any recording and public address and/or voting system is working and any hearing loops are working.

Then, on the day of the meeting, the officer should inspect the room beforehand to ensure that:

- tables are appropriately arranged[4] and there are sufficient chairs;
- the room is properly equipped, water or other refreshments are available, and with facilities for displaying maps, etc., or other visual aids;
- heating, ventilation and lighting are functioning;
- recording/video equipment has been checked and is working;
- emergency evacuation procedures are understood; and
- the meeting is shown on the notice board in the foyer or reception of the building concerned and that visitors are shown to a waiting area and escorted or appropriately signposted to any meeting room.

10.58 This last point is more important where the committee/cabinet is meeting in an unfamiliar venue, in which case a map of the venue might usefully be sent with the notice showing, for example, a convenient route of access and car parks available.

What should be taken to the meeting

10.59 The documents needed at a meeting will depend upon the type of committee and the character of business: for a staffing committee; for example, it would be prudent to have ready to hand a copy of the authority's authorised staff establishment, up-to-date handbooks on national conditions of service, staffing regulations, procedure agreements and so on. All papers should be assembled beforehand and, ideally, compared with a standard checklist of items so that nothing is overlooked. Care must be taken to anticipate what may be required: e.g. if a plan is to be referred to, it should be displayed prominently before members begin to assemble and it should be of a scale clearly visible from every seat. Sometimes it may be desirable to draft out alternative versions of likely resolutions.

10.60 The items likely to be on a checklist include:

- minutes of the previous meeting for signature after confirmation;
- current minute book;
- attendance book;
- spare copies of the agenda (now a statutory obligation: see Chapter 3) and other circulated papers; committee clerk's notebook and spare pencils (even if you are using a laptop!);
- standing orders and any rules or regulations (including earlier policy decisions);
- governing matters within the particular committee's terms of reference;
- current constitution of the committee: the list of members (and substitute members if any) of the committee and any associated sub-committees, its terms of reference, timetable of future meetings, etc.;
- forward plan, schemes, plans, files and other papers relating to the business to be transacted, assembled in agenda order, with particular documents flagged for easy reference; and
- standard reference books, yearbook, relevant statutes, etc.

Notes

1 Maud Report, vol. 1, para. 128. This was written, of course, before performance management became fashionable and the corporate performance assessment (CPA) came into being.

2 *R (Moseley) v Haringey London Borough Council* [2014] UKSC 56, [2014] 1 WLR 3947 gave guidance on 'a prescription for fairness' when a local authority conducts consultation. That is that the Supreme Court:

(1) formally endorsed the 'Sedley criteria' for a fair consultation, namely:

(i) Consultation must be at a time when proposals are still at a formative stage

(ii) The proposer must give sufficient reasons for any proposal to permit of intelligent consideration and response

(iii) Adequate time must be given for consideration and response

(iv) The product of consultation must be conscientiously taken into account; and.

(2) added that the degree and specificity of information which must be provided to consultees will depend on the context, including:

(v) the identity of the persons being consulted;

(vi) whether the proposal would deprive consultees of an existing benefit

3 Maud Report, vol. 5, para. 145.

4 'A long table, and a square table, or seats about the walls, seem things of form, but are things of substance; for a long table, a few at the upper end in effect sway all the business; but in the other form, there is more use of the counsellors' opinions that sit lower': Sir Francis Bacon, *Of Counsel*.

Chapter 11
Work at meetings

Introduction

Business must proceed

11.1 It is good practice to adopt the principle that business must proceed as planned once a committee meeting has been convened, provided there is no overriding reason why it should not. The general rule is that a meeting that has been properly convened cannot be postponed (see Chapter 6), although in practice this is often done; but there can be failure to make a meeting, e.g. where, for example, a quorum is not present when the meeting should begin. It is also a general rule that the proceedings of any meeting are invalid if the meeting has not been properly constituted. Strictly speaking, the chair of a committee should satisfy themselves that these requirements are fulfilled before the committee conducts its business. In practice, the chair assumes that the necessary formalities have been met unless they are advised to the contrary or it is self-evident that, for example, there is no quorum. It is submitted that this principle should be extended so that there shall be a presumption, until the contrary is shown to be the case, that a committee has been validly convened and is properly constituted, and that the meeting can properly proceed with the transaction of business. The business to be transacted can only lawfully be that of which notice has been given on the agenda unless:

- the chair accepts it as urgent (and the further council or executive legal requirements have been met); or
- whether written or presented orally, it merely updates an item already on the agenda without introducing wholly new matter.

An agenda item report 'to be tabled' is simply not permissible unless it comes under one or other of these headings.

Record of attendance

Attendance of members

11.2 The law provides that the names of council and co-opted members present at a local authority meeting must be recorded. In the case of many parish councils, this is done by providing an attendance book for signature by those present: the book can be passed round at the meeting (in which case the democratic services officer in attendance must be alert to ensure that the book is placed in front of latecomers) or, preferably in the case of large committees, placed at the entrance to the committee room so that those attending can sign before they enter the meeting.

11.3 The attendance book can be an ordinary hard-covered ruled book in which the democratic services officer writes as necessary the name of the committee and date of meeting at the top of the page on which members are required to sign. Or, preferably, it can be a prepared two-column loose-leaf sheet headed with the name of the committee and date of meeting, with the names of members typed in the left-hand column; each member is expected to sign on the appropriate line in the right-hand column. This helps in the case of illegible signatures and in determining quickly in the case of large committees who is present and who is absent.

11.4 The usual method for principal councils, however, is for the democratic services officer to have a list of the membership of the committee in the book used to take the notes of the meeting, and the democratic services officer then puts a tick alongside the names of those members who attend the meeting, or alternatively for this to be in the template, where a laptop is being used. The importance of an accurate record of attendance lies in the fact that this will be prima facie evidence for purposes of determining disqualification in the event of failure to attend for a consecutive period of six months (see 4.86) and may be used for other purposes: e.g. in checking council members' travel claims. Councillors may wish to check the record for political purposes, or for evidence that they were not at a meeting at which a particular decision had been taken.

11.5 Where an attendance book is still kept, standing orders will usually place upon members an obligation to sign it. The old model standing order no. 17 states:

> 'Every member of the council attending a meeting of the council, or of any of its committees of which he is a member, shall sign his name in the attendance book or sheet provided for that purpose. [And every member attending some other meeting, conference or inspection on approved duty shall sign his name in the register kept for that purpose.]'

The democratic services officer would be wise, however, to keep their own check on members' attendance by, for example, ticking against the list of members of the committee as each one enters.

11.6 Councillors who attend a meeting of a committee of which they are not members in exercise of a right conferred upon them by standing orders or of their common law 'need to know' will not ordinarily be credited with an attendance (nor may they take part in the proceedings unless expressly permitted to do so). A standing order governing the attendance of non-committee members might be to this effect:

> Any member of the council may be present during a meeting of any committee or sub-committee but unless he is a member of that committee or sub-committee shall not (except with the permission of the chairman) take part in the proceedings thereof, neither shall he be entitled to sign the register of attendance nor to have his attendance recorded for any purpose of these standing orders.

11.7 On the other hand, a non-committee member present at a meeting by express invitation ought to be credited with an attendance – for example, a cabinet member being held to account at a scrutiny committee.

Return of attendances

11.8 It is usual for a return of members' attendances to be prepared as soon as practicable after the end of the council year for circulation to members and the press and for the guidance of any selection committee in determining committee membership for the following year.

Appointment of committee chair

Procedure

11.9 It is for the local authority to decide whether the chair of a council committee should be appointed by the full council or elected by the committee itself, assuming it wishes to appoint a chair (see Chapter 1), but in either case the term of office is normally for the following year. The standing orders working party (see Chapter 2) produced this draft core standing order in terms obviously influenced by widespread practice ensuring that committee chairmen are nominees, or at least appointed with the consent of the majority party:

'00–1 The council may appoint, from among the voting members, a person to preside at the meetings of a committee or sub-committee, and a person to preside in the absence of the first person.

2 If any appointment possible under the previous paragraph is not made, a committee may appoint, from among the voting members, a person to preside at the meetings of any sub-committee appointed by them, or a person to preside in the absence of the first person, as the case may be.

3 If any appointment possible under the previous two paragraphs is not made, the committee or sub-committee at their first meeting after the annual meeting of the council shall, from among their voting members, appoint a person to preside at their meetings, and may, in the same way, appoint a person to preside in the absence of the first person.

4 If the persons appointed under the previous paragraphs of this standing order are absent, a meeting of a committee or sub-committee shall appoint, from among the voting members present, a person to preside at that meeting.

5 If it is necessary for the committee or sub-committee to appoint a person to preside, the proper officer shall call on a member of the committee or sub-committee to move that a voting member of the committee or sub-committee shall take the chair.

> 6 If discussion arises, the proper officer shall exercise the powers of the person presiding to regulate that discussion, and to maintain order at the meeting.
> 7 The motion, and any amendments, shall be put to the meeting in accordance with standing order 00(5) (voting on appointments).'

No special formalities are called for in the process. Some local authorities formerly provided in standing orders for the appointment to be by election and to be conducted by ballot and for members to nominate in advance of the meeting persons for the chairmanship and vice-chairmanship. Where committee chairs are not appointed by the council, it is sometimes the practice for the chair of the council or civic mayor to attend the first meetings of committees to preside over the appointment of chair and vice-chair. In terms of the executive, of course, it is the senior executive member, the leader or directly elected mayor, to choose to chair public meetings of the executive (cabinet) themselves or allow someone else to do so.

Who presides?

11.10 A person cannot preside at their own election or appointment and, therefore, it is necessary for someone other than the prospective chair to preside at the outset of the meeting. This may be prescribed by standing orders but it is more likely to be a matter of local practice. Thus the mayor/chairman of the council may attend the initial meeting of all committees each year expressly for the purpose of presiding over the election of a committee chair. However, it is more likely in practice that the first item of business will be the election of chairman, and that the democratic services officer, legal officer or other senior officer present will call for the nomination of the chair, particularly since it is now accepted that the appointment to the chair is not an essential prerequisite for a valid meeting. Where the council appoints the committee chairman, they assume the chair of the committee from the outset.

Eligibility for committee chairmanship

11.11 Some local authorities place restrictions on the eligibility of council and co-opted members (see Chapter 4 and below) for the chairmanship of committees. So, for example, see the two standing orders below adopted by a former county council:

> 'The chairman of the council shall not be appointed as the chairman of any committee of the council except of the selection committee or of any committee specially appointed from time to time.
>
> No member of the council shall be chairman of more than one committee at the same time, nor shall any chairman of a committee act as vice-chairman of another committee at the same time.'

11.12 A co-opted member who possesses voting rights could be elected as a committee chairman. There are, however, some disadvantages in this. A co-opted member chairman has not the political responsibility of a councillor chairman and this could be regarded as a reason for not choosing a co-opted member for that office. In practice, a committee chairman has responsibilities going far beyond their duty to preside at meetings of their committee. Further, unless standing orders specifically allow it, a co-opted member would not be able to present their committee's report or minutes at the full council meeting and steer through or defend the committee's proposals or answer questions on the committee's work; but a vice-chairman could, of course, perform these tasks on the chairman's behalf at the council meeting.

Vice-chair

11.13 It is good practice to appoint a vice-chairman of a committee because there can then be no doubt who should act in the chair's absence. It eliminates the need for a separate election of an acting chair whenever the chair is absent from a meeting (because the vice-chair automatically presides in the absence of the chair at a committee meeting) and it provides training for prospective chairs.

There should always be a chair

11.14 There is persuasive authority for the principle that a meeting, other than a council meeting, can lawfully proceed without someone in the chair (see 4.71). However, it is undesirable for a committee to proceed without a chair and the members should ordinarily seek to appoint one. In the event of there being no nominations or an equality of votes, the meeting should pass a resolution to the effect that it wishes to proceed without a chair. If a temporary chair is elected and if, later, the chair or vice-chair arrives it is usual, but not essential (as in the case of a meeting of the full council where the chair or mayor, if present, must preside) – for the acting chair to relinquish the chair in favour of the chair or vice-chair as the case may be. They will not do this immediately as a rule, but will wait until the conclusion of the item or business under discussion at the time.

Chair's casting vote

11.15 The chair or vice-chair, or whoever else may be presiding at a committee or sub-committee meeting, has a second or casting vote (LGA 1972, Sch. 12, para. 39(2)).

Quorum

None prescribed by statute

11.16 No quorum is prescribed by statute in the case of committee meetings, but the local authority has power to prescribe one by standing orders. If it does not do so, the committee may determine its quorum.

11.17 The relevant core standing order drafted by the working party on standing orders (2.3) was to this effect:

> '00–1 No business shall be transacted at any meeting of a committee or sub-committee unless at least one quarter of the whole number of voting members of the committee or sub-committee, as the case may be, are present: provided that in no case shall any business be transacted unless at least two voting members are present.
>
> 2 The provisions of standing order 0 shall apply to a meeting of a committee or sub-committee at which a quorum is not present as they would apply if it were a meeting of the council.'

Absence of quorum

11.18 On the principle put forward earlier (see 11.1) that committee business should proceed rather than not, that the objective always should be to deal with the business rather than delay it, then the following courses might be taken when there is no quorum present at the time of the meeting:

- If it is known for certain or there is reasonable cause to believe that additional members will be present later, the members present could proceed to discuss the business on the agenda on the understanding that, as soon as a quorum is present, the business already transacted will be affirmed by those then present and this would legitimise what had been done. However, this could cause difficulties if those members present would hold opposing views, as this would necessitate further debate when they arrive.
- If a committee has power merely to consider and report, there seems no reason why business should not proceed, provided it is made clear at the time of report to the parent body (the full council in the case of a committee; the committee in the case of a sub-committee) that any recommendations put forward are those of the members concerned and not of the fully constituted committee or sub-committee: the decision of the parent body if it chooses to adopt the recommendations thereby endorses and so validates what has been done.

If a committee has delegated power then, somewhat similarly, the members present could, notwithstanding the absence of a quorum, proceed to discuss business on the agenda and, instead of taking decisions, put forward recommendations for consideration on the same basis as outlined above.

As suggested above, the temporary absence of a quorum should be ignored unless the attention of the chair and, therefore, the committee is drawn to it expressly.

Confirmation of minutes of previous meeting

General

11.19 What has been said about confirmation at a council meeting of the minutes of the council's previous meeting applies for the most part in respect of confirmation of minutes at a committee or sub-committee meeting. The agenda should provide for this item to be taken as first business (except where there is need to elect a chairman) and the only matters that may properly be raised on the confirmation of minutes are questions as to their accuracy. It is good practice to cover this specifically in a standing order:

> 'No motion or discussion shall be allowed upon the confirmation of minutes, except as to their accuracy, and any questions upon this point shall be determined by a majority of the members of the committee present when the matter in question was decided.'

Although it is not unreasonable to expect only those members present at the meeting concerned to vote on the confirmation of the minutes, it may be that a standing order in these terms is invalid because it seeks to infringe a statutory rule that all questions coming before a local authority shall be decided by a majority of those present and voting (LGA 1972, Sch. 12, para. 39).

11.20 Whereas minutes of a council meeting are usually printed and circulated to council members, practice varies as to whether minutes of a committee meeting should be circulated to committee members (other than where the committee minutes have been submitted in their entirety to the council). If not, then some other arrangement may be thought desirable in order that members may be satisfied as to the accuracy of the minutes before agreeing to their confirmation. In some councils, it is the practice to obtain the chairman's approval to the draft committee minutes and to lay the minutes on the table before the commencement of a meeting, so that members who wish may have the opportunity of inspecting them. A standing order to the following effect is useful:

> 'At every committee meeting the minutes of the previous meeting shall be taken as read, but shall be read, either in part, or in their entirety, before signature, if a majority of members of the committee then present so require.'

The practice of obtaining a chairman's approval to draft minutes is a questionable procedure because the responsibility for minuting a correct record lies with the democratic services officer and in the event of disagreement it is the chairman's view that should ordinarily prevail. Clearly there may be an advantage in finding out whether or not a particular minute will be accepted as a correct record, but if the practice is for officers to do this by consulting the chairman, the arrangement should be clearly laid down.

Minutes must be of previous meeting

11.21 The law requires that minutes must be confirmed at the same or next following meeting. This was so also under the LGA 1933, Sch. 3, para. 3(1) of Part V, but there was a useful amendment made by the LoGA 1963, Sch. 4, para. 44 (not, unfortunately, carried forward into the 1972 Act) that permitted the minutes of committee meetings (but not of council meetings) to be lawfully confirmed at any subsequent meeting, i.e. not necessarily the same or next meeting.
11.22 A mandatory standing order, prescribed in the Local Authorities (Standing Orders) Regulations 1993 provides that the minutes of an extraordinary meeting of the council may be signed at the next ordinary meeting.

Matters arising

11.23 One of the potential problems arising out of the confirmation of minutes is the temptation for members to raise issues apart from simply confirming the minutes as a correct record. At its worst, this can lead to an attempt to change a decision taken at the previous meeting and any such discussion should be ruled out of order by the chair. Some authorities have had an item on the agenda 'Matters arising from the minutes' to allow, for example, members to be advised of the current position of items discussed at the previous meeting. However, this is not good practice and, unless the subject to be raised is related to a matter specifically referred to in the agenda, is likely to be unlawful as it infringes the statutory restriction that only business specified in the notice can be dealt with (LGA 1972, s. 100B). The model standing order provides the following:

> '**18.1 Signing the minutes**
> The chairman will sign the minutes of the proceedings at the next suitable meeting. The chairman will move that the minutes of the previous meeting be signed as a correct record. The only part of the minutes that can be discussed is their accuracy.'

Recording the proceedings

Introduction

11.24 Because of the informality of committee proceedings, where discussion is discursive and not always directed towards a specific proposition before the meeting, considerable skill is demanded from the democratic services officer whose task it is to grasp the collective sense of the committee and to record the decision that emerges out of the debate. Some chairs ask for a proposition to be moved: others, for example, say at a particular stage of the proceedings, 'We're agreed then', or words to that effect, and move on to the next business, in confident expectation that the democratic services officer will note down on paper a form of words that will fairly reflect the views of the majority. It is this that distinguishes committee meetings from proceedings of the full council and makes greater demands upon the competence of the democratic services officer.

Sense-taking

11.25 A democratic services officer is unlikely to be able to crystallise at any particular point the emerging view of the committee if they are engrossed in extensive note-taking, even less so if they are making a scrupulously accurate shorthand record of all that is being said. It is of little value to the chair if they turn to the democratic services officer for a recap of the committee's views, to be told that the only guidance available is a verbatim note of what was said by the last speaker. Admittedly it is the chairman's responsibility to 'hold the thread of the discussion, summing it up at intervals if necessary', but not all chairmen do so. The late Lord Normanbrook, who was a parliamentary Cabinet Secretary, is reported to have said:

> 'I used to take the Cabinet notes in longhand, just with an old-fashioned fountain pen. I rarely wanted to get down what was said, except perhaps when they were trying to formulate the wording of an announcement and various people had different versions. What I was trying to get was the sense of a Cabinet meeting.'

This is precisely what the effective democratic services officer should strive to do: to capture the sense of the meeting. It is all too easy sometimes for a democratic services officer to allow their knowledge of what a committee chairman was briefed to say or a chief officer intended to say – but in fact failed to say explicitly – to influence their view of the consensus reached at a meeting. This is less likely, admittedly, at a committee meeting but can happen when, for example, a committee chairman may be meeting representatives of an outside body.

Note-taking

11.26 Just how best to take notes at a committee meeting is very much a matter of personal preference. Some local authorities insist that the democratic services officer keeps their notes in a book; others leave the decision to the democratic services officer who may use a laptop to do this.
There are advantages and disadvantages of taking a laptop into a meeting. The advantages include:

- the minutes are already on the computer, so there isn't the time lag of typing up the handwritten notes;

- if you can touch-type, you can maintain better eye contact with members and keep a note of what is going on; and
- you can get the minutes nearly finished during the meeting, particularly if you use a template and are filling in the blank parts.

However, there are disadvantages, such as:

- you can probably type faster than you can write, which will simply result in more notes, not necessarily better ones; and
- typing can be a distraction and some keyboards (and typists) are more noisy than others.

If you use a laptop, you should always take a mains cable and ensure you are near a power point. Set the 'autosave' to one minute and save the document at the end of every point/paragraph.

In general terms, if taking written notes, officers should note down each possible decision as it begins to emerge and then cross it through as the discussion moves to some other proposition. Apart from keeping track of the discussion, the democratic services officer should carefully record:

- specific motions with the names of the mover and any seconder and, necessarily, any amendments similarly;[1]
- the name of any individual member who expressly asks that their vote be recorded;
- the names of members who vote for and against a motion and of those who abstain upon a requisition for the voting to be recorded; and
- any incidental happening, e.g. a member's declaration of interest, the chairman's vacation of the chair for a specific item, a temporary adjournment and so on.

11.27 If there is doubt in a democratic services officer's mind about a decision, they should ask for clarification immediately, from the chairman, i.e. before the committee proceeds to the next business. This is vital because it is useless, after the end of a meeting, to canvass opinion as to what the decision on a particular item of business might have been:[2] apart from the failure to carry out the task (because the recording of decisions is the democratic services officer's responsibility), there is unlikely to be unanimity of opinion among those whose views are sought! If a competent democratic services officer does not understand the committee's decision, it may safely be assumed that no one else does either. However, if the sense of the meeting is abundantly clear to the members, neither the chairman nor the majority on the committee will thank the democratic services officer in seeking clarification for providing an opportunity for discussion to be reopened on a matter already decided.
11.28 A somewhat different approach in note-taking is necessary if a committee is considering a long-term matter in the course of a series of meetings. Here the democratic services officer will not be concerned in minuting the proceedings but in collecting material from which to frame the committee's ultimate report, in delving for facts, in submitting papers on particular aspects of its terms of reference and so on.

Voting

Motions

11.29 It is often the case that such a motion, or sometimes a lengthy amendment, is proposed after quite some discussion and debate, and the chair will often ask – or occasionally the clerk will insist – that the motion is read back to the committee to ensure that the committee understands exactly what they are voting on. This can require some detailed drafting skills and quick thinking on the part of the democratic services officer. The process of motions and amendments itself is discussed in Chapters 1 and 2.

11.30 Almost all authorities' standing orders require motions and amendments to be proposed by both a mover and seconder to enable them to be debated or voted upon, even where the motion is simply to adopt the officer's written recommendation. With a motion or amendment raised in a committee meeting this is of no real concern, as it is then clear to both the member who moved the motion or amendment, and to the rest of the meeting, that going any further would be a waste of time. On occasion, however, such as full council where a written motion is placed on the agenda as an item for debate, the motion can be of significant importance to that member.

11.31 *R (Armstrong-Braun) v Flintshire* (2001) held that the council had failed to give adequate consideration to the implications of a new standing order requiring that notice of every motion to full council, other than motions that may be moved without notice, had to be given in writing and signed by both a proposer and a seconder. The case was brought by the only member of the Green Party on the council, who thereby felt disenfranchised as a councillor in terms of having matters debated. The Court of Appeal did not rule on the inherent implications of the standing order, however, only the process behind its introduction.

11.32 The effect of this has been that most local authorities made one or both of the following changes so that:

- motions to full council may be submitted by one councillor for inclusion on the council agenda; and
- where a member in that position moves such a motion or an amendment, and it is thereby clear that it is unlikely any member would act as seconder, the chair or civic mayor will by convention second the motion or amendment formally (without speaking on it) to allow the matter to be debated, in order to allow a member fulfil their role as a councillor.

Voting: ordinary mode

11.33 The law does not prescribe the method of voting at committee or sub-committee meetings but ordinarily it is by show of hands. The modular constitution provides the following:

'17.3 Show of hands
Unless a ballot or recorded vote is demanded under Rules 17.4 and 17.5, the chairman will take the vote by show of hands, or if there is no dissent, by the affirmation of the meeting.
17.4 Ballots
The vote will take place by ballot if [n] members present at the meeting demand it. The chairman will announce the numerical result of the ballot immediately the result is known.
17.5 Recorded vote
If [n] members present at the meeting demand it, the names for and against the motion or amendment or abstaining from voting will be taken down in writing and entered into the minutes. A demand for a recorded vote will override a demand for a ballot.'

As to entitlement to vote (see below) and on the recording of votes, including a mandatory standing order in this respect.

Counting a vote

11.34 In practice, the chair will call for a show of hands only if unsure of the collective sense of the meeting. When a show of hands is asked for, it is a wise precaution for the democratic services officer to count the raised hands both for and against, and to count aloud as they point to each member so that members can check the voting if they wish. It is, however, for the chair to declare the decision and thus the democratic services officer, after counting, should pause after voicing the total numbers and, even when the decision is obvious, leave it to the chair to say whether the motion or amendment is carried or lost. Thus the sequence should be:

- chair: Those in favour?
- democratic services officer: One, two, three, four, five: five, chair.
- chair: Those against?
- democratic services officer: One, two, three: three, chair.
- chair: The motion is carried.

11.35 The importance of this procedure is underlined where there is an equality of votes and the chair must decide whether to use their second or casting vote (see below):

- chair: Those in favour?
- democratic services officer: One, two, three, four, five: five, chair.
- chair: Those against?
- democratic services officer: One, two, three, four, five: five, chair.
- chair: The motion isn't carried. *[or]* I shall use my casting vote: the motion is carried.

11.36 Ensuring that a clear resolution is passed is even more important where, for example, a formal decision is needed to exclude the press and public on account of the likely disclosure of exempt information (see Chapter 3). This can be helped by printing on the agenda itself the terms of the motion to be moved so that all the chairman, or any other member, has to do is to move 'That the press and public be excluded as set out on the agenda'. Even when this is done, a clear decision has to be taken and minuted. Failure to do so could result in the kind of argument that erupted in North Wales in 1981 where Clwyd County Council's economic development sub-committee failed to ensure than an unequivocal decision to exclude was taken and found it necessary to repeat the meeting before matters could proceed. During subsequent court proceedings, Nolan J took the view that it was enough for a chairman 'to take the sense of the meeting' but this must be done 'in a clear and unambiguous way' and minuted accordingly: *R v Clwyd County Council ex parte Delyn Borough Council* (1987).

Eligibility to vote

11.37 Not all members present at a committee meeting are necessarily entitled to vote. There may be members present who are not members of the committee, who are attending by invitation or under a claim of a 'need to know' (see Chapter 4), or under the provisions of a standing order that permits non-members to be present at any committee but does not allow them to take part in the discussion, except by leave of the committee, or to vote. If a councillor under a disability persists in voting, their vote is likely to be void; and where a committee or sub-committee is acting in a quasi-judicial capacity, a vote cast by a member having an interest in the subject matter is likely to render the committee's or sub-committee's decision as contrary to natural justice on account of bias and therefore void (see *R v London County Council* (1982), *R v Hendon RDC ex parte Chorley* (1993) and *R (on the application of Richardson) v North Yorkshire County Council* (2003). As to conflict of interest of councillors with local authority employee and/or trade union associations: see Chapter 13. It is often difficult for the chair in a large committee to recognise whether those voting are all in fact entitled to vote, e.g. co-opted members who can only vote on education matters. The democratic services officer ought to draw attention to any vote by someone not entitled to vote but, of course, the difficulty may be no less for the officer. The chair might well be advised to remind the assembled gathering that only members of the committee may vote, particularly if the vote is on a crucial matter. Difficulties of this kind are usually overcome by requiring non-members to occupy seats set apart from the committee members.

Voting rights of non-members

11.38 As indicated in Chapter 4, persons present at a committee meeting who are not appointed members of the committee do not possess a right to vote. That, at least, is the position ordinarily. However, a councillor is able to be present with full voting powers when substituting for an appointed councillor who is absent from the particular meeting.

11.39 Suppose a councillor is summoned to a committee meeting in error (e.g.

because of a confusion over similar surnames) and that councillor attends and actually votes and the voting error is not detected at the time. What is the position? First, the proceedings are not invalidated solely on that account, nor can the constitution of the meeting be easily challenged subsequently because of the presumption that after the minutes have been confirmed the meeting was properly constituted.[3] But a vote that is an invalid vote is no vote at all and if such a vote was critical – e.g. if a proposition was carried by one vote – then the decision is open to challenge: see *Nell v Longbottom* (1894), in which it was held that an invalid vote could not be regarded as having been cast.

Co-opted and non-voting members

11.40 While, in general, co-opted members on a committee must be treated as nonvoting members under the LG&HA 1989, s. 13, there are exceptions to this rule by virtue of s. 13(4).

Chair's second or casting vote

11.41 The statutory power of a chairman of any local authority meeting, including that of a committee or sub-committee, to give a second or casting vote has already been discussed. The modular constitution, no doubt to avoid uncertainty, provides specifically a model standing order for a second or casting vote by the person presiding:

> **'17.2 Chairman's casting vote**
> If there are equal numbers of votes for and against, the chairman will have a second or casting vote. There will be no restriction on how the chairman chooses to exercise a casting vote.'

11.42 The ordinary rule is that when a meeting has resolved upon a certain issue, the resolution cannot at the same meeting be extinguished or changed by a second resolution purporting to rescind, reverse or vary the first resolution. The rule should be observed inflexibly in the case of council meetings. If specific procedure is made for the rescission of resolutions, the prescribed procedure must be stringently observed or the purported rescission will be ineffective: *R v Tralee UDC* (1913).

11.43 The view could be taken, however, that (subject necessarily to standing orders) in the case of committee deliberations, where procedure is informal and a strict order of debate is rarely observed or needs to be, the conclusions or decisions of the committee are not settled until the chairman declares the meeting at an end. Much depends upon the character of the committee and the business being transacted. In the case of a committee appointed for a specific or one very general purpose (as in the case of a committee of inquiry), the discussion may range over the whole terms of reference and such conclusions as may emerge during the course of the discussion are purely tentative ones that are not finally settled until the concluding stages of the proceedings. In such cases, there seems nothing to prevent the committee from changing its mind several times.

11.44 However, this view could hardly be sustained in the case of the ordinary local authority committee sitting to consider an agenda with quite separate items of business. It would not be logical to regard the committee meeting as sitting in continuous session to deal with the business *en bloc*, because in fact each item of business discussed and not deferred is settled there and then by a decision expressly stated or implied. Nevertheless, the wishes of committee members are paramount and, provided that the members present when the business was first dealt with are still present and no others have come into the room and no action has been taken on the resolution by an officer – i.e. the circumstances are precisely as they were at the time when the original decision was taken – it would not seem unlawful for the chairman to permit the matter to be reopened.

11.45 Where exceptionally an earlier decision is reversed or varied later, the minutes should record only the second resolution as being the properly considered decision of the committee. Where, however, it is the practice to prepare minutes to reflect precisely the order of business and the movement of members in and out of the committee, the minutes would misrepresent the proceedings if the first resolution was not recorded. The dilemma then is that the minutes themselves would record, if not an irregularity, at least a departure from conventional procedure, which might provide evidence upon which the validity of the second resolution could be challenged. This may be thought further justification for the generally accepted view that a question once settled cannot properly be reopened at the same meeting.

Duration of committee meetings

Setting a time limit

11.46 Although it is not uncommon for standing orders to set a limit upon the duration of council meetings (or at least set a time at which members must decide whether or not to continue the sitting) it is slightly more unusual for committee meetings to be so regulated. Nevertheless, there is much to be said for limiting the duration of committee meetings because long meetings are not conducive to good decision-making: members excuse themselves and leave if the meeting is long drawn out, the attention of others wavers as time goes by and concentration on business becomes difficult as members grow tired and possibly hungry, too. Some committee chairs (and a chairman's competence is usually critical) will set themselves or agree with members a target time for completion of business: there is widespread agreement that the efficiency of any meeting dwindles after an hour and a half, but nonetheless committee meetings can flounder on for three or four hours. In respect of committees arguably carrying out judicial functions, such as development control, a long meeting may be argued to be prejudicial to the interests of those heard only at the end of a long meeting.

11.47 The morning is no doubt the ideal time for business (though few meetings seem to take place then) and at least the need for lunch provides automatically for a break in proceedings if not for the termination of the meeting. Afternoon meetings suffer the disadvantage of there not being a natural break, and evening meetings (common particularly among district councils) suffer every possible disadvantage: they tend to go on far too long and often after members and officers have already worked for a full day beforehand. The overriding virtue of evening meetings, however, is that members of the public are normally more able to attend them, and working members do not need time off from their employment to attend.

Conclusion of meeting

'That concludes the business'

11.48 The chairman should always end the meeting by saying expressly, 'That concludes the business of the meeting' or words to like effect. There can then be no doubt that the meeting has ended and less likelihood that continuing discussion between members after the end of official business may be misinterpreted as part of the meeting.

Noting the time

11.49 The time at which the chairman declares the meeting at an end should be recorded as good practice, even though it is no longer needed as evidence of the period of attendance for purposes of members' allowances and it is unlikely in the case of officers that they would be entitled to overtime, although they may get time off in lieu for committee attendance.

Collection and disposal of committee papers

11.50 It should be the democratic services officer's responsibility to gather up committee papers left behind by members and officers after the meeting. This is particularly important in the case of papers relating to business conducted while proceedings were closed to the public and press; in the case of confidential papers the democratic services officer will be expected to dispose of them by shredding.

Notes

1 Not to be recorded necessarily in committee minutes but to jog the memory if the chairman suddenly asks, 'Was the motion formally proposed [or seconded]?'

2 Or, for that matter, for the democratic services officer to decide themselves what they believe was decided, on the analogy of the following, variously attributed, as the task of the Cabinet secretary:

> 'And so while the great ones repair to their dinner,
> The secretary stays, getting thinner and thinner,
> Racking his brains to record and report
> What he thinks they will think that they ought to have thought!'

3 Decisions of a committee not properly constituted are nevertheless deemed valid by the LGA 1972, Sch. 12, para. 44(2).

Chapter 12
Work after meetings

Introduction

12.1 At the conclusion of a meeting the clerk should do the following things, although the order of priority and urgency will depend upon circumstances:

- draft the minutes of the meeting;
- if necessary, prepare a report for submission to the full council, where the practice locally is to submit reports instead of full minutes to the council (see 12.42);
- advise other officers of any matter referred to another committee or meeting;
- notify other officers of actions that fall to them by the preparation and circulation of an action sheet, following the meeting;
- implement the decisions of the committee/cabinet that fall to the democratic services officer to carry out personally;
- record in a diary or bring forward system any matters that need to be followed up or reported to a later meeting of the committee;
- record each decision in the appropriate correspondence file; and
- update the index to the committee's proceedings in the minute book.

Matters requiring immediate action

Action sheets

12.2 In some authorities the democratic services officer prepares, as soon as practicable after each meeting, a brief summary of proceedings or action sheet (the description varies according to the purpose). The aim is to provide an immediately available guide to the decisions made and, in some instances, details of the officer expected to take action. It is for the democratic services officer to decide whether the minutes should be drafted prior to this.

12.3 An example of an action sheet is set out below:

'Medway Council
Children's Services Overview and Scrutiny Committee: 10 June 2013
Decision/Action Sheet

Agenda Item No	*Subject*	*Decision*	*For action by*
1	Minutes: Meeting of 1 April, 2013 . . .	Confirmed	–
2	Apologies		Chief Executive
3	Membership of Bishop of Chichester Academy: appointment of council representative	Cllr. Jones to be nominated	Head of Legal & Member Services
4	Closure of The Old Rectory Children's Home	Further report for next meeting	Director of Children's Services'

In some cases there is a fifth section that gives a target date by which action is expected to be taken. Items subject to council approval need to be clearly indicated.

References to other committees/cabinet

12.4 Where cabinet or another committee follows in quick succession to council or other committees, there is always the possibility of a referred item failing to reach the subsequent meeting in time if the democratic services officer is slow in providing the necessary information to the other officers concerned. Often the probability of a reference from a council/committee to cabinet/committee (or vice versa) can be foreseen, and in that event it is prudent to include an appropriate item on the agenda.

12.5 References from one committee to another or cabinet are of three types:

- those on which the views of another committee have been sought before the cabinet resumes or completes its consideration of the matter concerned;
- those that, as a matter of routine, stand referred to other committees, e.g. staffing matters to a personnel committee or constitutional matters to a governance committee, before consideration by the cabinet or the full council; and
- those that involve matters of policy or important principle, which either by law or standing order are thought to do so, are placed before cabinet (or policy committee in non-executive governance) or full council.

12.6 Unnecessary references between committees and cabinet can be avoided by careful arrangement of business. The general principle should be to place an item only before the committee that has the power to make a decision or frame a recommendation, unless the cabinet requests the committee to provide comments.

Urgent executive action

12.7 Next, after references to other committees/cabinet, attention should be given to matters of urgency where failure to take immediate action could frustrate the cabinet/committee's intention or otherwise prejudice the council's interests. These include:

- items of business on which the cabinet/committee has expressly instructed that action should be taken as a matter of urgency; and
- anticipatory action on recommendations to another committee or the full council where delay could nullify the eventual decision.

Minutes or reports?

12.8 If minutes are used as the means of reporting a committee's or the cabinet's proceedings to the full council, the preparation of these will be a matter of priority for the democratic services officer after conclusion of the cabinet meeting: the minutes will need to be drafted, approved by the officers concerned, submitted for the chair or leader's agreement, put on the website (as a draft) and printed for inclusion in the council meeting agenda. If, however, the authority has adopted the report system, it will be the democratic services officer's responsibility to prepare the report first and the minutes subsequently: the report will similarly need to be drafted, approved and printed. These differing methods of reporting upwards are discussed later.

Preparation of minutes and decision records

Objectives

12.9 The minutes of a meeting cannot be successfully written up without a clear understanding of the purpose of minutes. These include the need to:

- establish an accurate record of the decisions taken;
- comply with legal requirements; and, where minutes are used as the mechanism to bring proposals before the cabinet, other committee or full council for decision, the need also to:
    - ensure that the record is sufficiently self-explanatory to enable the council to make a decision in full possession of the relevant facts; and
    - provide adequate information about the authority's business for press and public.

12.10 In practice it is difficult, if not impossible, to meet these several and sometimes conflicting objectives satisfactorily. The obligation on local authorities to keep minutes of proceedings could be met by brief notes, as the law does not prescribe the form in which minutes should be written up: but the authority may need to substantiate its actions by production of the minutes authorising the action taken, and the minutes must be drawn up in terms that will satisfy legal requirements. However, although the law imposes constraints, administrative and public relations needs to provide scope for skilful and imaginative drafting.

12.11 As a result of the cabinet system, there is no longer a need to prepare two documents: the actual minutes in which are recorded the whole of the committee's proceedings; and a report that, in wholly different style, sets out only those items of business that must be submitted to the full council for information or approval. Only those matters requiring the approval of full council now need to be submitted. The advantages and disadvantages of the report system and the several ways in which it is operated in practice are referred to later.

Drafting minutes

12.12 There is no right or wrong way of preparing minutes: the form adopted by any particular local authority is a matter of individual choice or local custom. The obligation to keep minutes does not mean that the minutes must be written up during the course of the meeting. This could be done,[1] but is not likely to be practicable as the democratic services officer needs to be paying attention to the proceedings. However, in the case of the cabinet, democratic services officers often have a draft set of minutes prepared beforehand to save time, as there are unlikely to be any surprises at a cabinet meeting! It is usual and perfectly permissible for the minutes to be transcribed from rough notes taken at the meeting: see *Re Jennings* (1851).

In the course of time a number of cardinal principles of good practice have become widely accepted. Thus, for example, a minute should be:

- brief, i.e. precise and concise, recording exactly what was done and no more;
- self-contained, i.e. complete in itself and intelligible without reference to other documents (but see below); and
- decisive, i.e. there must be no ambiguity or doubt as to the intention; and thus clarity is an indispensable part of the accuracy of the record.

12.13 Minutes can be kept brief by being selective: a minute is not, and should never be, a verbatim record but a summary of the proceedings that includes only the essence of the discussion (if that) together with the decision and (where required but held as best practice) a sense of the reasons for coming to that decision. There is good reason for this: see below, *R v London County Council ex parte London and Provincial Electrical Theatres Ltd* (1915), and *R v City of Swansea ex parte Quietlynn Limited* (1986).

12.14 Minutes of executive decisions must be formulated in a way that includes the following:

(a) a record of the decision, including the date it was made;
(b) a record of the reasons for the decision;
(c) details of any alternative options considered and rejected by the decision-making body at the meeting at which the decision was made; and
(d) a record of any conflict of interest relating to the matter decided which is declared by any member of the decision-making body that made the decision, together with a note of any dispensation granted by the authority's head of paid service.

Minutes must also be numbered distinctively.

This could also be said to provide a good basis for the minimum content of any minuted decision.

12.15 It is rarely necessary to reproduce, however summarily, what a particular speaker said; but it is helpful, as a rule, to pick up the main threads of the discussion that led to the conclusion: indeed, there is danger in recording individual contributions since all members are likely to want the same treatment. To be self-contained does not mean that a minute cannot properly refer to supporting material, e.g. an officer's report incorporated as an appendix, a plan, deed or other significant document that cannot physically be made part of the minute book. But a minute must not rely on extraneous material for its understanding or interpretation; the actual resolution should always be understandable on its own. Some authorities choose to record their meetings, which means that the democratic services officer has an accurate record from which to draft the minutes.

12.16 Minutes collectively should be complete in the sense that they include at least a brief reference to every item of business dealt with, so that it may safely be assumed that any matter not mentioned was not discussed at the meeting.

Skill in drafting

12.17 Good drafting comes generally from practical experience; what is necessary is workmanlike competence. While is it helpful to use a template to follow (see e.g. the following paragraphs on form), this alone will not produce the clarity and precision necessary in good drafting. Constant attention to the construction of sentences is necessary. All adjectives must be eliminated. The simplest word rather than the unusual must be used, the active rather than the passive style, positive rather than negative construction. Every word must contribute something material to the meaning of the minute: the article 'the', for example, can almost always be omitted before dates and in many other instances, and there is always something additional to learn. With increased skill in drafting comes an appreciation of layout, and then importance begins to be attached to the visual appearance on paper, to the proper balance between long and short paragraphs.

Form

Minutes individually and collectively

12.18 In considering the structure of minutes, officers should examine both the form of the individual minute covering a particular item of business (which, as already indicated, must be complete and self-contained: see 12.13), and that of the set of minutes that collectively relates to the proceedings of a meeting as a whole.

Set of minutes

12.19 Each set of minutes, i.e. the minutes that collectively relate to a particular meeting, will ordinarily follow a prescribed pattern. It will first identify the committee/cabinet concerned and the date of the meeting, and also, possibly, the time of commencement and the place of meeting, e.g.:

> 'MINUTES of a meeting of the CHILDREN'S SERVICES OVERVIEW AND SCRUTINY COMMITTEE held at the Blanktown City Hall on 1st May, 2016 . . . at . . . pm.'

There will usually be recorded[2] after this the names of council members and, if any, co-opted members present, distinguishing between the two as a rule, with the chairman's name appearing first and the names of the others in alphabetical order, e.g.:

> 'Present: Councillor John White (Chair); Councillors Black, Green, Grey and White; and, Mrs Orange and Mr Pink.'

12.20 If someone other than the chair is presiding, that member's name will still appear first but followed with an appropriate description (in the chair), or (presiding), according to local practice. Whether or not members' initials are included is, again, a matter of custom. Some authorities prefer to list the names of all members of the committee and to indicate attendance by an asterisk. It is not good practice to include the names of officers who are in attendance because the officers are not part of the membership of the committee. However, some authorities do record officers who attend working groups or other meetings, and if so it should be clearly marked that these are officers attending, to avoid confusion.

12.21 The minutes should be prepared to reflect the order in which business was transacted. This is also a logical order because it is often convenient to record, for example, a change in chairmanship, e.g.:

> 'Councillor John Brown relinquished the chair at this point and Councillor Jack Smith assumed it.'

Or some other happening, e.g.:

> 'Councillor White declared a pecuniary interest in item 12 and left the meeting before the commencement of discussion.'

It would be difficult to insert these items in the minutes, unless the minutes followed the actual order of business. Some authorities follow the order of the agenda; but in doing so you should incorporate the agenda paper in the minute book in order to shorten the text of minutes by cross-referencing to material in the agenda. This is not necessarily good practice, even if convenient, as:

- the agenda has no legal significance, though it must be kept open for public inspection and a meeting can refuse to discuss or receive an item on the agenda; and
- it may encourage the drafting of resolutions that are understandable only when read with the agenda.

Individual minutes

12.22 Section 9G(3) of the Local Government Act 2000 provides that a written record must be kept of prescribed decisions made at cabinet meetings. An individual minute of the cabinet should consist of a heading and a preamble or narrative (if required). Under reg. 12 of SI 2012/2089, it must also contain:

- a record of the decision, together with the reasons for the decision;
- details of any alternative options considered and rejected by the cabinet at the meeting at which the decision was made; and
- a record of any conflict of interest in relation to the matter decided that is declared by any member of the cabinet, together with a note of any dispensation granted by the authorities' head of paid service,

and must be numbered distinctively.

12.23 There should be a uniform style adopted throughout the authority. For example, using in some instances: 'The committee decided to . . .' and at other times: 'Resolved: That . . .'

This may cause a reader to believe there is significance in a difference that is no more than an inconsistency.

Heading

12.24 A minute heading or title should be brief and explain the subject matter; once settled it should be retained unaltered to facilitate indexing, at least in its main wording, for all subsequent minutes on the same subject. There is advantage in referring immediately after the heading to previous minutes or the last minute on the same subject.

12.25 It is not always easy, however, to determine the wording of the heading. Take, for example, the following:

> '908. Flooding: Rochester Riverside (see Minute 866) The Director of Regeneration reported on the flooding which had occurred in . . .'

It is a matter of judgement in relation to the particular circumstances whether the heading might more appropriately be reversed so that it becomes:

> '908. Rochester Riverside: Flooding (see Minute 866).'

Or indeed, if it is more informal in style:

> '908. Flooding at Rochester Riverside.'

If the subject of flooding is a continuing problem before the committee, then this might fairly be chosen as the main part of the heading. If, however, the committee has a special interest in Rochester Riverside, it is preferable that this should form the main part. In either case, despite the merit of brevity, a heading of one or the other alone is not satisfactory; if flooding is used by itself, it implies that flooding in general is the subject matter of the minute; and if Rochester Riverside is used alone, the heading could mean anything.

12.26 A common error is to use a wholly inappropriate heading. An example is using an Act of Parliament as the heading to a minute that is not in any way concerned with the statute as such:

> '418. Food Safety Act 1990
> The Head of Legal Services reported that at xxchester Court on 1st January 20 . . . the firm of . . . had been fined for . . .'

12.27 There is some justification for the view that a heading is not really part of a minute and should, if it appears at all, be placed in the margin of the minute book as a head note in this fashion:

'Flooding: Rochester Riverside (see Preamble)	908.	The Director of Regeneration reported on the flooding that had occurred in . . . Minute 866.'

12.28 A summary or narrative should be included only if it serves a purpose, i.e. it contains the reasons for the decision and details of alternatives considered. It may be appropriate to indicate the officer who brought a particular matter before the committee/cabinet, but if the officer's act is no more than procedural, there is no need to recite it. An example of an entirely superfluous preamble is:

> '123 Local Government Association: Annual Conference, 20. . . The Chief Executive submitted an invitation to the Council to appoint delegates to the 20. . . annual conference of the Local Government Association to be held at Brighton from . . . to . . .
> Resolved: That Councillors Smith, Brown and Robinson be appointed as the Council's delegates to attend the 20. . . annual conference of the Local Government Association to be held at Brighton from . . . to . . .'

If, however, the officer is making a recommendation or giving advice, there is merit in including a reference to the recommendation or advice given, e.g.: 'The Chief Executive advised the Committee that...'; and it is vitally important that the advice should be minuted if an officer provides advice which they consider it their duty to give and the committee/cabinet chooses to disregard it:

> 'The Borough Solicitor advised the committee that in his view there was no legal authority for the expenditure which the committee wished to incur . . .'

There are particular circumstances, of course, where the law requires the calling of a special meeting to consider a report of the monitoring officer or the chief finance officer advising the local authority of the risk or certainty of legal or financial impropriety (see 13.17).

12.29 The summary can properly be used to record in narrative form the tenor of the discussion on the particular item of business but in an impersonal way, i.e. not attributing views to individual members. The main advantages of this form are that it makes for brevity. A point raised by one speaker will often be taken up and developed by others; in an impersonal minute the democratic services officer need record it only in its final form. The impersonal style tends to stop suggestions for amendments of the minutes, for members naturally look with special care at paragraphs that attribute statements to them personally, and tend to ask for additions and modifications that are not strictly necessary for the purpose of a minute. This can be done, for example, in this way, not necessarily following the order in which the points were made:

> 'The following points were raised in discussion: (a). . .; (b) . . .; and (c) . . .'

or, where there was broad agreement on the points raised:

> 'The committee had regard to/took account of the following points made in the course of discussion: (a)...; (b)...; and (c)...'

What must be avoided – at all costs! – is this form:

> 'Mr A. said . . .; Mr B. replied . . .: and Mr C. then pointed out that . . .'

Such a discursive description in conversational style obscures the thread of discussion and leaves the minute-writer open to charges that he has misinterpreted what Mr A. or Mr B. said, or unfairly summarised their contribution.

12.30 It is doubtful whether there is merit in recording that discussion preceded the decision without indicating the gist of it, e.g.:

> 'After discussion [it was] Resolved: That . . .'

Admittedly it conveys to a reader that at least the committee did not merely accept unquestioningly the advice of an officer or rubber-stamp a recommendation of a sub-committee, but it does little else. The presumption must be that councillors considered the question before them. In many instances, where the course of action is clear-cut, the chairman is likely to have said, as the particular item on the agenda was reached, 'Agreed?' and the members, in effect, replied 'Yes', and the meeting passed to the next item of business.

12.31 It is not usual to record in the narrative the procedural steps through which the members reached their decision. Thus, for example, the names of proposers and seconders of motions, whether passed or not, are not normally recorded; nor, ordinarily, is any record kept – as already indicated – of the contribution of particular members to the discussion.

Unsupported statements

12.32 Care needs to be taken, in drafting a narrative that goes to some length, not to include independent sentences that represent statements unidentified as to their source. This is permissible in a committee report because of the presumption that all that is included represents the collective view of the committee unless otherwise indicated. In the case of a minute this is not so. For example, a narrative may begin 'The Director of Children's Services explained that . . .' and continue at length. When, however, the Director's reported statement goes on to a new point, it is never sufficient just to begin a new paragraph but, in order to avoid an unsupported statement – i.e. one not clearly attributable to anyone in particular – it is necessary to write either 'The Director went on to say . . .' or 'The Director further reported that . . .', or words to that effect.

Reasons for decisions

12.33 This may be an appropriate point at which to examine the question whether the reasons for a decision of the council or one of its committees or sub-committees should be minuted as well as the resolution itself. There are some instances where the authority is bound to provide reasons for its decisions (executive decisions), and in the case of the rejection of a planning application, for example, and in such circumstances these reasons must be minuted. Also in respect of members' items under s. 21(A)(7) LGA 2000 (inserted by the LGPIHA 2007) where reasons must be given, and where reasons need to be given for actions taken under petition schemes which are debated. In all cases, if an authority can show the reasons why it reached a particular decision, the authority's act can be expected to have greater credibility in the minds of those affected by the decision. On the other hand, this provides evidence for those who may wish to dispute the decision to show that the decision was an unreasonable one in the light of the considerations that influenced the authority in reaching it. Nevertheless, it would seem a good principle that an authority should always be prepared to justify its action by giving a reason, unless there are overriding considerations to suggest it should not do so.

While there is no general duty to give reasons for a decision (other than a decision made under executive arrangements and other particular statutory requirements), nonetheless the courts have found that there was a duty in a large number of cases, on the facts of each case. The greater the interests of third parties, the more desirable it is to give reasons: see *R v Lambeth London Borough Council ex parte Walters* (1993) and *R v Bristol City Council ex parte Bailey* (1994). In the former, a decision on a housing tenancy allocation was held to be unlawful because no reasons were given, whereas in the latter the giving of reasons was not required because the hearing was in public.

In particular, an apparently aberrant decision might require reasons so that it could be seen whether it was challengeable. *R v Higher Education Funding Council, ex parte Institute of Dental Surgery* (1994). Halsbury's Laws considers that the rationale is:

> '. . . the obligation to provide a reasoned decision will exist when general considerations of procedural fairness require it, and factors such as the need for reasons to give substance to a right of appeal; to explain an otherwise aberrant outcome; to demonstrate that issues had been properly addressed; the nature of the interest affected by the decision and the extent to which the interest is affected by the decision; the need to promote transparency in the decision-making process; whether the duty would impose an undue burden on the decision-maker or otherwise frustrate the purpose to be achieved by the decision-maker; and the extent to which the judgements made were capable of being reasoned, or whether they were simply matters of academic or other evaluation. This list is not exhaustive. What is relevant will depend on the particular context concerned. The outcome of the application of this principle will differ from case to case depending on the circumstances; this simply reflects the fact that the weight to be attached to similar considerations will vary from context to context.'

12.34 It may be that in particular circumstances it would be against the council's interests (and, therefore, it may be presumed, against the public interest) for a reason to be disclosed; or it may be that the reason is far from certain: the fact that a decision has been reached even unanimously does not necessarily mean that all those who voted were similarly motivated or influenced by the same considerations. In *R v London County Council ex parte London and Provincial Electrical Theatres Ltd* (1915), Pickford LJ said, at pp. 490 and 866:

> 'With regard to the speeches of the members . . . I should imagine that probably hardly any decision of a body like the London County Council . . . could stand if every statement which a member made in debate were to be taken as a ground of the decision. I should think that there were probably few debates in which someone does not suggest as a ground for decision something which is not a proper ground; and to say that, because somebody in debate has put forward an improper ground, the decision ought to be set aside as being founded on that particular ground is wrong.'

Taylor J expressed himself thus in *R v City of Swansea ex parte Quietlynn Limited* (1986), reported in Lexis:

> 'If every observation made by a councillor in all frankness in the course of debate were to be regarded as some bar to his voting or an indication that he had, in the end, taken into account an irrelevant consideration, it is hard to see how local government could continue to function. One would either have people clamming up and avoiding saying those things which they felt it right to say, lest they later heard other views which persuaded them that what they had said ought to be discounted, or one would have an obligation on a councillor to abstain from voting or even to leave the committee whenever he had it pointed out to him that something he had said was outside the statutory criteria in that particular context.'

Two things emerge from the above. One is that the contribution of individual councillors to a debate should never be minuted: something already advised (see above). The other is that, wherever possible, councillors should be asked to agree on the terms of the reason for their collective decision; if a reason is not voiced, then an officer should not record their own interpretation of the grounds on which the authority or committee or sub-committee was influenced collectively.

12.35 Where there is no possibility of misinterpreting a committee's conclusions properly drawn or inferred from the facts before them that led finally to the decision, the following can be used:

> 'The committee [concluded] [took the view] [were of the opinion] that . . . and [accordingly] [for that reason] [on those grounds] Resolved: That . . .'

or, less positively:

> 'The committee [inclined to the view] [felt on balance that] [considered it prudent] that . . . and [accordingly] [for that reason] [on those grounds] Resolved: That . . .'

12.36 The decision should ordinarily be set out at the end of the individual minute in the form of a resolution. If, however, the minute falls naturally into different sections the resolutions may properly be interspersed appropriately at the end of each section rather than brought together at the end. In every case each resolution should commence with the word 'That', preferably indented from the margin of the text, and preceded in capital letters or underlined or in heavy type or some other distinctive manner by the word RESOLVED.

12.37 There are rules ordinarily to be observed in framing resolutions apart, of course, from what has been said about clarity and brevity:

- The introductory phrase RESOLVED: That governs all that follows. Therefore it is correct to write:
  'RESOLVED: That the Head of Human Resources be authorised:
  i) to make all appointments to vacant administrative staff posts within the council's authorised establishment;
  ii) to sign on behalf of the council contracts of employment in respect of such appointments; and be required to submit periodically to the cabinet a list of all such appointments made.'

  but not:
  'RESOLVED: That the Head of Human Resources be authorised:
  i) to make all appointments to vacant administrative staff posts within the council's authorised establishment;
  ii) that he be authorised to sign on behalf of the council contracts of employment in respect of such appointments; and a list of all such appointments be submitted to the cabinet periodically.'
- Because a resolution should be self-contained, it is bad practice to employ such phrases as:
  'RESOLVED: accordingly.'
  or:
  'RESOLVED: That the matter be dealt with accordingly.'
  or, where the decision cannot be fathomed without reference to an accompanying report:
  'RESOLVED: That the recommendations in the report of the Director of Corporate Services (a copy of which marked 'A' is attached to these minutes) be approved.'
  or, though with less objection, to make use of the heading:
  'Clerical and administrative staff
  RESOLVED: That the Head of Human Resources be authorised to make all appointments of this nature within the council's authorised establishment.'
- Resolutions can be numbered serially (at least through each set of minutes) as an additional safeguard against tampering with the minute book by deletion:
  'RESOLVED: 1. That . . .'

12.38 There are also matters of individual style. For example, the resolutions of a working party without delegated powers may be preceded by either:

> 'RESOLVED TO RECOMMEND: That . . .'

or:

> 'RECOMMENDED: That . . .'

or:

> RESOLVED: That the Committee be recommended to . . .'

or, preferably, because the resolution can then be identifiable as the council's resolution without alteration of the words:

> 'RESOLVED: That it be recommended to the committee that . . .'

And there is advantage often in clearly indicating which officer is to take action:

> 'RESOLVED: That . . . and that the Chief Executive be authorised to take all such steps as she considers necessary to comply with the Council's resolution . . .'

Some authorities favour the style: 'RESOLVED UNANIMOUSLY . . .' on particular occasions of formality or when they wish to indicate that the council is patently 'at one' – generally where the matter is not party political: for example, sympathy to be expressed over the death of a former councillor. On the other hand, the use of 'Resolved unanimously' might imply some lesser value of resolutions not so distinguished.

Procedural considerations

12.39 Where full minutes are submitted, it is good practice to bring to the attention of the council in the case of committee/cabinet minutes, and the attention of the committee in the case of sub-committee minutes, matters of significance. Where there is no delegation of powers, this may be sufficiently evident by the use of bold type to show recommendations, but there are other methods, e.g. by sidelining recommendations in the margin or (a practice not to recommended because it increases the volume of paper) by extracting and listing together separately all recommendations for the parent body's consideration. Even in the case of reports, as distinct from minutes, recommendations should be clearly distinguished from the main text.

12.40 Some local authorities divide each set of minutes (or reports) into two parts to distinguish between matters dealt with by the committee under its powers and those that are referred to another meeting respectively. Whether there is virtue in such an arrangement is a matter of opinion, but it can facilitate proceedings at the council meeting.

Reporting upwards

Minutes or reports

12.41 The minutes of the cabinet and committees can be used to report their proceedings to the full council. Similarly a sub-committee's minutes can be the mechanism by which the sub-committee reports to its parent committee. The view is taken by some local authorities that this is an efficient and economical arrangement: minutes must be prepared in any case as a matter of administrative and legal necessity and it is unnecessary and time-consuming for another, different document to be produced either to advise the parent body of action taken under delegated powers or to bring before it matters upon which the parent body alone can make the final decision. Other authorities prefer the report system as the method of bringing before the parent body the proceedings of the cabinet or sub-committees, as the case may be, for purposes of information or consideration. As to the advantages and disadvantages of the report system, see below.

12.42 Minutes record, in the past tense, the business actually transacted at a particular meeting: very often an individual minute (as distinct from a resolution) may be intelligible only by reference to preceding minutes on the same subject matter and they must, in the case of the cabinet, recite the reasons which influenced the meeting in reaching its decision or the alternative courses of action considered and rejected. A report, on the other hand, normally written in the present tense, need not limit itself to matters actually dealt with at a particular meeting: it can deal with an issue comprehensively, covering proceedings at several past meetings, and so present to the parent body a full account in readable, intelligible form. The style, too, is different, e.g. 'The cabinet has considered . . .' or 'We have considered . . . and now recommend'.

Challenge to committee or cabinet minutes at full council

12.43 It can happen, where a local authority submits committee or cabinet minutes rather than reports to the full council, that the minutes will be before the council in advance of their confirmation by the committee or cabinet. What, then, should happen if a councillor questions the accuracy of a cabinet minute and the question of accuracy is critical either to the council's understanding of what has been decided or could affect what is proposed? The minute, even if its inaccuracy is evident to the full council, cannot properly be corrected because that can only be done by the committee or cabinet when the minutes come before it for confirmation. The correct procedure would be for the member who is challenging the accuracy of the minute to move its reference back to the committee or cabinet. If the motion is approved, it will be for the committee or cabinet to consider the objection when it comes to confirm the minutes at the next meeting. In practice it seems unlikely that such a motion would be approved: after all, the minutes will have been drawn up by the officers and probably approved by the committee/cabinet chair; and the chair is likely to oppose the reference back and will conceivably be supported by the meeting's members present at the council meeting. If, of course, the report system is adopted, a procedural problem of this kind cannot arise (see below). It would be perfectly proper for the full council to debate a motion seeking to refer back a paragraph in the report or to amend a recommendation contained in it.

Advantages and disadvantages of the report system

12.44 The comparative advantages and disadvantages of the contrasting systems may seem self-evident: they have, in any case, been thoroughly discussed elsewhere. If business dealt with in committee or sub-committee is considerable, and does not involve questions of major policy, there may seem little advantage in submitting the full minutes of proceedings to the parent body: the sheer bulk may make it difficult for the parent body to distinguish between the important and the trivial, and to concentrate attention on matters of policy or principle. If, however, the position is otherwise – if the committee of sub-committee only discusses issues of important questions (i.e. where there is substantial delegation to officers or a sub-committee in a functional committee such as in a regulatory committee) – it can be fairly argued that the preparation of a report in a report in addition to (accordingly slimmed down) minutes is unnecessary. However, members often prefer to receive a full report with the council agenda, and clearly it would be impracticable to leave it to be decided in each instance whether the full council should sometimes be advised by minutes and sometimes by report. There must be one system laid down and properly regulated to ensure that the full council receives essential information whether advised by a report or by minutes. It is the content rather than form that matters in this respect. See *R v Brent London Borough Council ex parte Gunning* (1985) (and 12.48), where the decision of a local education authority was held to be *ultra vires* largely because the authority had not been provided with sufficient information in a committee minute on which to reach a decision.

12.45 Local authorities that adopt the report system may think it prudent to have arrangements to confirm any other committee decisions that require confirmation but that have not been included in the reports – either by accident or design!

Cabinet

12.46 In the case of cabinet in executive forms of governance arrangements, the norm is that minutes are reported to council, if at all, and matters that require approval of full council will require the submission of the originating report to cabinet to sit alongside that minute. This is for the reasons outlined above.

Overview and scrutiny

12.47 The conversation continues, however, in respect of the specific case of overview and scrutiny committees' work programmes. Such committees often wish to convey the considerable depth of discussion, evidence gathering and deliberation that has gone on. The weight of such a set (or sets) of minutes, where the committee and democratic services officers have given way to the temptation of including that bulk, can lead to the above-cited example of the need to sift those minutes to obtain useful information (and the obvious temptation not to bother) on the part of the receiving body. An alternative has been to slim down the minutes of such meetings in order to, instead, concentrate on the production of a report to be adopted by the committee for submission to cabinet or council. Such a report would collate their investigations, recommendations and supporting evidence in respect of the larger pieces of work undertaken and be presented in a concentrated (and rather harder to ignore) format.

Statutory committee reports to council

12.48 Cases that have come before the courts in relation to committee reports to the full council have done so because of a statutory obligation on the local authority to consider a report from the relevant committee before exercising obligatory functions. In *R v Kirklees Metropolitan Borough Council ex parte Molloy* (1987), on a judicial review of the education committee's decision to close a school, it was held that the decision must be quashed because the authority had not had before it 'a proper report' of the education committee. Mann J recognised that it was not easy to say what exactly was a report but quoted from the judgement of Forbes J in *R v Liverpool City Council ex parte Professional Association of Teachers* (1984):

> 'There is argument about what a report consists of... [in my view] a committee should either make some recommendation or should at least, if not making a recommendation, set out the arguments for and against a particular course of action. Otherwise I cannot see how . . . the authority are to inform themselves adequately of the views of the . . . committee before performing . . . their functions . . .'

Of *R v Brent London Borough Council ex parte Gunning and Others* (1986), Mann J said in Kirklees:

> '. . . a report must in my view involve an evaluation. It must be an account of the issues involved in a decision . . . A bland recommendation does not in my judgement satisfy the requirements of statute. An evaluation is essential . . .'

Although the foregoing cases concern reports from the education committee, the principles apply equally to other committees and cabinet (see above), i.e. the need that there should be a proper evaluation of the courses of action proposed is one that clearly should be followed as a precept in all instances of committee reports to the full council and, of course, of sub-committee reports to a parent committee.

12.49 It seems that the courts would regard the requirement upon a local authority to 'consider a report' as satisfied even if the authority had to take account of a document incorporated in the committee's minutes by reference. In *Nichol and Others v Gateshead Metropolitan Borough Council* (1988), it was held that the council had properly considered a report of its education committee when it had before it a minute of the committee that indicated that the committee had followed a recommendation in a report of the director of education, a copy of which had been sent to every member of the council, and had adopted one of the options put forward in the officer's report. It may be thought, nevertheless, that this is not good practice: the incorporation of documents in minutes by reference ought to be restricted to instances where the document cannot physically be included (see above).

Hybrid systems of reporting committee minutes/outcomes

12.50 Some authorities attempt, with varying degrees of success, to combine the advantages of the report system with the advantages of submitting full minutes to the parent body. Thus an authority will submit to the full council 'only certain sections of the minutes', the choice being made administratively, sometimes on the basis that only non-delegated business will be reported selectively or by the committee itself. Where the practice of submitting full minutes means the minutes on confidential matters must be drawn in general terms, only certain unreported minutes will be written up solely for recording in the committee minute book.

Other work involved

Implementation of decisions

12.51 It is ordinarily the democratic services officer's responsibility to see that decisions are implemented either by ensuring that the appropriate officer is advised of the action to be taken or by the democratic services officer themselves performing some of the tasks. Reference has already been made to the importance of taking urgent action immediately after a committee/cabinet meeting and to the practice of some authorities in circulating an action sheet (see 12.2 and Chapter 7). On many items, however, action will need to be delayed until the committee's/cabinet's recommendation has been accepted by the council or, prudently, until the minute has been written up, or in the case of cabinet decisions, once the call-in period has expired.

12.52 Practice varies widely in this respect. In some cases, a note is circulated to chief officers indicating the action that is expected of them; in others it is well established that officers will automatically take action on the minutes as soon as they are sent round and on the basis, say, of any action sheet already circulated. This latter is probably the ideal situation, provided the democratic services officer chases those items that may be required.

12.53 It is not the job of the democratic services officer to have to satisfy themselves that a particular officer has done what is expected of them, but there are generally a number of officers that democratic services staff will have concerns about, in terms of whether they have followed up on action. In that case, the conscientious democratic services officer may wish to chase them up!

Destruction of democratic services officer's notes

12.54 Once the minutes have been confirmed, the democratic services officer's notes should be destroyed. The reason for this is that there should be no other record, however informal, that might cast doubt upon the correctness of the official record. If the notes are known to be retained there is always the likelihood that they may be required to be produced, whether under the Freedom of Information Act 2000 or otherwise, and this has generally stamped out the practice of keeping the old notebooks for a number of years. If the notes constitute a verbatim shorthand record (which is unlikely, nowadays) there should, of course, be no possibility of their contradicting the minutes. Indeed, it could be argued that the notes are of value in supporting the minutes if challenged, but otherwise rough notes are capable of misinterpretation and could in that event be capable of proving the opposite. As a number of meetings are recorded, this makes it of less value to retain original notes for any period of time.

12.55 Though few authorities favour retention of the democratic services officer's note, opinion is divided on the issue. The benefit of retention might be thought to be demonstrated in *R v Hereford and Worcester County Council ex parte Wellington Parish Council* (1995), which concerned a gypsy site and questions of possible bias on the part of members of the county planning committee. The democratic services officer gave evidence on affidavit and produced their notebook to show the way in which the meeting had proceeded and the contributions made by individual members. In principal authorities, the practice of recording or web-casting the meeting would now render such a need superfluous in any event. Despite the usefulness of the notebook in that particular case, therefore, it seems more likely that the actual notebook would contain unhelpful information and destruction after confirmation of the minutes still seems the safest course.

Indexing

12.56 Minute books must be indexed, for self-evident reasons. Unless it is possible to trace the minute on a particular matter the decision, at least as a record, might as well not exist. It is good practice to record separately, possibly bound up as an addendum to standing orders, a copy of minutes on matters of policy or important principle that are of continuing effect.

12.57 The indexing should be carried out in a systematic manner in accordance with prescribed guidelines formulated by each local authority to meet particular needs and entrusted to someone with knowledge and understanding of the subject matter and the purposes for which the index is likely to be used. There are many minutes that do not merit indexing: the record of apologies for absence (if, indeed, these are minuted at all); the confirmation of minutes; matters of purely procedural or transitional interest. Where full committee minutes are submitted to the council, there seems no advantage in duplicating in the index to the council minute book the individual items in committee minutes that are more appropriately indexed in the minute books of the respective committees.

12.58 It is usual to bind up sets of minutes in volumes covering a year or half-year (perhaps multiples of a year for committees that seldom meet) according to the amount of business transacted. Each minute book should have an index relating exclusively to the minutes it contains. If you are using traditional minute books, the easiest way to build up an index is on a loose card system that can then be transcribed for incorporation in the binding. The task is facilitated if each minute has a standardised heading and explanatory subheading. However, the majority of authorities now, due to budget cuts, use some form of loose-leaf binding and indexing can therefore be updated easily.

Minute numbering

12.59 Each minute should be numbered consecutively. This facilitates indexing, reference and cross-reference from one minute to another, and makes more difficult any tampering with the minute book, i.e. it is impossible for a new page to be fraudulently substituted or a particular minute omitted altogether (although, of course, a spurious minute could be written in to replace the authentic one). In any case, each page of a minute book should be initialled by the person who signs the particular set of minutes to which the pages relate.

12.60 It is a matter of individual choice or local practice whether the numbering is recommenced for each set of minutes, i.e. the minutes relating to a particular meeting, or is continued throughout, say, the council year (of advantage if the minutes are bound annually). There is simplicity in beginning with 1 again for each set of minutes though cross-referencing is necessarily lengthier (assuming cross-referencing is favoured), as indeed it is if there is renumbering for each year. It means, for example, that the reference to a previous minute on the same subject will need to be 'See minute no. 10 of 1st May 20 . .' or 'See minute no. 00 of 20--' instead of merely 'See minute no. 1,000'. On the other hand, the reference to date may facilitate retrieval of the particular minute required.

Inspection of committee minutes

12.61 Since 1 April 1986, the minutes of committees (including cabinet) and sub-committees of principal councils have been open to public inspection on the same terms and subject to the same limitations as in the case of council minutes. Prior to that date only the minutes of the education committee were open to inspection and only by local government electors. The minutes of other committees and sub-committees were only open to inspection so far as they were laid before the council meeting for approval. Councillors have always possessed a common-law right to inspect committee and sub-committee minutes so far as it may reasonably be necessary to enable them to carry out their council duties. What has been said earlier about the times when council minutes may be inspected applies also to cabinet, committee and sub-committee minutes as it does regarding obstruction of the right of inspection.

Notes

1 Indeed, the terms of the LGA 1972, Sch. 12, para. 41, that minutes shall be signed at the same or next ensuing meeting envisages that this might be done.

2 The names of members present at a meeting must be recorded, though not necessarily in the minutes: LGA 1972, Sch. 12, para. 40.

Part 4

Miscellaneous Meetings

Chapter 13

Meetings for special purposes

Introduction

13.1 This chapter deals with a number of committees, decision-makers and related groups, whose meetings or the particular business to be transacted call for special treatment. There is no exhaustive list of these because many local authorities have set up special committees and the like for purposes that arise out of particular local circumstances, but the examples selected are thought to cover the more important of those which may concern the majority of authorities.

13.2 In several of these cases the rules governing meetings are not substantially different from those which apply to conventional local authority committees but certain of them, either in their constitution or their functions or in the procedure that they must follow, differ significantly. Also covered in this chapter are election meetings and some quasi-meetings, such as public inquiries, etc., with which local authorities are concerned indirectly.

Executive arrangements

Individual decision-making

13.3 It may be that all executive decisions are made by or at least as part of a meeting of the cabinet. Equally, however, it may be that as 'senior executive member', the leader or the mayor retains all executive decision-making to himself or herself as an individual or has delegated those decisions to a single member of the executive (cabinet) or to an officer. In such situations, the decision does not need to be made in public or, in any sense, as part of a meeting. Nonetheless, it will (and for reasons of sound governance should) fall to the democratic services officers to fulfil their role as, or on behalf of, the proper officer, and to organise an agenda of decisions to be made, organise the reports and evidence gathering that will support the making of those decisions, arrange for prior notification and publication, conduct the recording or receiving notification of the decision-making and ensure the publication of that decision record and related documentation.

13.4 For those authorities operating executive arrangements, how executive decisions are to be made falls to the leader or elected mayor, or what the Local Government Act 2000 now calls the 'senior executive member'. The Act makes no distinction between these two roles for these purposes.

13.5 As with meetings of the cabinet, the first step is to consider whether or not the decision to be taken is a key decision. A key decision will require advance publicity and public access to the papers; a non-key decision will not. Where an individual member is to make a decision, however, given all authorities' commitment to openness and transparency, it is now common practice that an authority's rules for advance publicity and access to papers applying to key decisions will also apply to non-key decisions. This makes it much simpler for democratic services officers to organise and, more importantly, apply the requirements for good governance and lawful decision-making to individual executive decisions. It also makes it easier for everyone when forward-planning decisions, providing support and collating reports, and indeed applying the principal of the requirement for reports at all.

13.6 Differentiating between key and non-key decisions remains nonetheless important, not least when considering the requirement to pre-publish papers and notice of a decision to be made by an officer.

13.7 This definition may be found, as all of the publication requirements may be, within the Local Authorities (Executive Arrangements) (Meetings and Access to Information) (England) Regulations 2012 (SI 2012/2089). Paragraph 8 provides that a 'key decision' means an executive decision, which is likely:

(a) to result in the relevant local authority incurring expenditure which is, or the making of savings which are, significant having regard to the relevant local authority's budget for the service or function to which the decision relates; or
(b) to be significant in terms of its effects on communities living or working in an area comprising two or more wards or electoral divisions in the area of the relevant local authority.

13.8 Quite what the above means in practice has been the subject of debate for several years, but authorities have generally set a figure for expenditure/savings that clarifies matters in respect of their own constitutions.

13.9 The situation differs in Wales, where the relevant regulations are the Local Authorities (Executive Arrangements) (Decisions, Documents and Meetings) (Wales) Regulations 2001 (SI 2001/2290).

13.10 As can be seen from the above, the decision taken by an individual member or officer can be no less important or of less effect than where that decision is made by a duly convened meeting. It therefore follows that the process to ensure that such decision-making is properly informed, that access to information rules are complied with and that the decision is properly recorded is no less onerous. Indeed, as such decisions can always be made in private, it is arguably more important to get such matters right. This role falls to democratic services officers in the same way that the equivalent decisions made by meetings are. It is no less onerous at times.

13.11 The rules concerning individual executive decisions are derived from the same source. Currently, this is the Local Authorities (Executive Arrangements) (Meetings and Access to Information) (England) Regulations 2012/2089.

13.12 Publicity in relation to key decisions is the same whether made by meeting or by an individual. The prior notification procedure remains the same: the publication of what is no longer formally named but widely known as 'the Forward Plan'. What differs is that, instead of referring to the meeting, the Forward Plan states that the decision-maker is to be an individual, gives the individual's name and title (if any) and the date on which, or the period within which, the decision is to be made.

13.13 The Forward Plan will also provide:

(a) a list of the documents submitted to the decision-maker for consideration in relation to the matter in respect of which the key decision is to be made;
(b) the address from which, subject to any prohibition or restriction on their disclosure, copies of, or extracts from, any document listed is available;
(c) that other documents relevant to those matters may be submitted to the decision-maker; and
(d) the procedure for requesting details of those documents (if any) as they become available.

This will be provided at least 28 clear days before a key decision is made.

13.14 The content and quality of the report for an individual executive decision should be no less rigorous than if it were being produced for a committee or cabinet. It may be helpful, however, to split the report into two parts.

13.15 The first part provides the front-sheet to the officers' report. It is set out in the way that a written record of cabinet member decision is required to be set out – the equivalent of a committee minute for the cabinet meeting but written in advance, together with a pro forma so that:

- if the cabinet member agrees with the recommended decision, he or she need only sign it, and it can be recorded and published as a decision in that form; but
- if the cabinet member makes a decision different to the recommendation, or adopts the recommendation for different reasons, the written record is amended as per the form's boxes filled out by the cabinet member at the time of making the decision. The amended written record of the decision is then published.

13.16 The second part is the body of the officer report. This sets out the evidence, information and opinion required to be put before the cabinet member to enable him or her to make a decision. This will also include the recommendation, but as a conclusion to the report.

13.17 As well as advance publication of the recommendation and report prior to the decision being taken, this second part will not subject to later amendment; it is published alongside the decision record.

13.18 As soon as reasonably practicable after an individual member has made an executive decision, that member must produce or instruct the proper officer to produce a written statement of that executive decision, and if an officer they must produce, a written statement which must include:

(a) a record of the decision including the date it was made;
(b) a record of the reasons for the decision;
(c) details of any alternative options considered and rejected by the officer when making the decision;
(d) a record of any conflict of interest declared by any executive member who is consulted by the officer which relates to the decision; and
(e) in respect of any declared conflict of interest, a note of dispensation granted by the relevant local authority's head of paid service.

13.19 That record, together with any report considered by the individual member or officer and relevant to a decision recorded or, where only part of the report is relevant to such a decision, that part, must be available for inspection by members of the public, as soon as is reasonably practicable, at the offices of the relevant local authority, and on that authority's website, if it has one (reg. 14).

13.20 Definitions of exempt information, background papers and time limits for retention and availability are the same for executive decisions as they are under the LGA 1972 for council and committees (reg. 21).

Joint committees of the authority

Power to appoint

13.21 Among the several arrangements that local authorities may make for the discharge of their functions is that which provides for two or more authorities to discharge functions jointly, so long as it is not a function that the law requires to be discharged by a specified committee (LGA 1972, s. 101(5)). For purposes of discharging a function jointly, the authorities may appoint a joint committee. The number of members of the joint committee, their term of office (which must not extend beyond their term of office with the appointing authority) and the area within which the joint committee shall exercise its authority must be fixed by the appointing authorities; the membership may include persons who are not members of the appointing authorities (so long as they are not disqualified from membership).

13.22 Joint committees are used for a variety of purposes; for example, the West Midlands Joint Committee comprises seven local authorities around Birmingham with an overall objective to coordinate actions on important issues affecting the local authorities in the West Midlands, and to provide a vehicle for communicating these actions and their needs to the government and other influential bodies, and Northamptonshire & Cambridgeshire County Councils Joint Committee for Shared Services. Since local government has been sharing services – for example, building control – joint committees have become more common.

Executive and advisory powers

13.23 Two or more authorities, in discharging any of their functions through a joint committee, may delegate executive powers to the joint committee, other than the function with respect to levying or issuing a precept for a rate. There is separate statutory power (although the terms are substantially the same) enabling two or more authorities to join in appointing a joint committee 'to advise the appointing authorities on any matter relating to the discharge of their functions'.

Expenses

13.24 The expenses incurred by a joint committee of two or more authorities, whether appointed under the LGA 1972 or any other enactment,[1] are to be defrayed by those authorities in such proportions as they may agree or in case of disagreement as may be determined:

- in any case in which those authorities are the councils of parishes or communities or groups of parishes or communities situated in the same district, by the district council; and
- in any other case, by a single arbitrator agreed on by the appointing authorities or, in default of agreement, by the Secretary of State (LGA 1972, s. 103).

Standing orders

13.25 Standing orders regarding a joint committee of two or more local authorities (irrespective of the statute under which the joint committee is appointed) may be made by those authorities, dealing with the quorum, proceedings and place of meeting of the joint committee (including any sub-committees); but, subject to any such standing orders, the quorum, proceedings and place of meeting can be such as the joint committee itself may determine.

Committees meeting jointly

13.26 There is another kind of joint committee or, more accurately, a coming together within the local authority of two committees of their own volition to discuss a matter in which they have a common interest. Such an arrangement is a purely informal one and, if procedural and other problems are to be avoided, the arrangement should be such that one committee has invited to its meeting the members of the other for an informal discussion. There can then be no dispute as to who takes the chair or how a vote should be taken, because the 'attending' councillors would have no vote.

Joint boards

Distinguishable from joint committees

13.27 A joint board or, as it is sometimes called, a joint authority, is fundamentally different from a joint committee. There is no general power permitting the establishment of joint boards, but specific power is contained in a number of statutes and in each case the rules as to its constitution are prescribed.

Joint boards

13.28 A joint board is a corporate body, created by order of a minister, requiring in many cases the approval of Parliament: it has perpetual succession, a common seal and it can hold land. Unlike a joint committee, a joint board cannot be dissolved by agreement; it has independent financial powers, including the power to borrow money, and obtains its revenue from constituent authorities by means of precepts.

13.29 The order or other instrument creating the joint board will ordinarily prescribe its constitution and the rules governing meetings procedure. As to the unique position of local authority members on a joint planning board (and other joint boards where members hold statutory office), see Chapter 5, and as to the new Police and Crime Panels, see Chapter 14.

Statutory meetings to consider officers' reports

General

13.30 There are three circumstances in particular where a relevant local authority (see Chapter 1) has a statutory duty to hold a meeting of the whole council to consider a report from an officer: a report from the head of paid service under s. 4 of the LG&HA 1989, a report from the monitoring officer under s. 5 of the LG&HA 1989, or from the chief finance (s. 151) officer under s. 114 of the LGFA 1988. In respect of the reports from either the monitoring officer or the chief finance (s. 151) officer, pending the meeting, the council must not proceed with implementation of the proposal or decision or whatever course may be intended: the subject matter is, in effect, frozen until the meeting. Because the responsibility on both the Monitoring Officer and the s. 151 officer is very similar, there needs to be in practice a close working relationship between them, together with the Head of Paid Service.

Monitoring officer's report

13.31 The duties of the monitoring officer include reporting to the authority on any proposal decision or omission by the council or a committee or sub-committee or a joint committee on which the authority is represented or by an officer of the authority that has or is likely to contravene the law or lead to maladministration (LG&HA 1989, s. 5). Where the council operates executive arrangements, then the monitoring officer must report to the executive in relation to any such proposals, decisions or omissions of the executive itself. No duty to report on any maladministration arises unless the Local Government Ombudsman has conducted an investigation in relation to the proposal, decision or omission concerned.
13.32 It is the monitoring officer's duty, during preparation of their report, to consult with the head of the paid service and the chief finance officer (who has somewhat similar duties) and as soon as practicable after it is prepared, to arrange for a copy of it to be sent to each member of the authority or the executive. The duty must be discharged by the monitoring officer personally and immediately, i.e. the circulation of the report should not wait until a meeting is summoned by the proper officer.

Chief finance (s. 151) officer's report

13.33 The duties of the local authority in regard to a report from the monitoring officer are without prejudice to the similar duties under s. 114 of the Local Government Finance Act 1988,[2] which fall on the officer designated by the authority for that purpose, i.e. the chief finance officer under s. 151 of the 1972 Act, which is why, even though the post is called the chief finance officer in the LG&HA 1989, the post is now more often than not referred to as 'the section 151 officer'.

The chief finance officer is required to report in similar manner to the council (or the executive if in relation to any function of the executive) whenever the authority, a committee or joint committee or an officer has made or is about to make a decision that involves or would involve illegal expenditure or likely to cause loss to the authority or is about to enter an illegal item or account;[3] or where it appears to the chief finance officer that expenditure in a financial year is likely to exceed the resources, including sums borrowed, available to meet that expenditure.[4] The chief finance officer is required to consult the head of the paid service and the monitoring officer in preparing their report in the case of likely illegality or loss of expenditure,[5] but in the other case, i.e. where the issue is one of financial judgement, there is no such obligation to consult.

The meeting

13.34 The duties of the monitoring officer and the chief finance officer have been set out in broad terms because this work is primarily concerned with the meeting, which in the circumstances the council is required to hold to consider any report so made. The meeting must be held within the specified period of 21 days after the report has been circulated to councillors.[6] It need not necessarily be a special meeting held solely for the purpose of considering the report: the report could quite properly be considered at an ordinary meeting of the council if one is due to be held within the prescribed period, although it would be possible to convene a special meeting for the purpose to take place immediately before the ordinary meeting. The meeting must be of the council: the duty cannot be delegated.[7] There is no detailed statutory prescription governing the convening of the meeting or the conduct of the business: what is important, of course, is that the business to be transacted, i.e. to consider the relevant report, is clearly indicated on the agenda (and a copy of the report must be circulated with the summons and agenda if it has not been sent to councillors already as will have been so in most instances), accompanied by a statement, if not set out in the report, of the consequences of failing to take requisite action. What needs to be done can be expected to be spelled out by the chief finance officer where expenditure is likely to exceed resources, but in the other cases, i.e. whether the report is made by the chief finance officer or the monitoring officer, the meeting is likely to have before it a report from the chief executive of the courses open to the council to achieve lawfully and properly whatever it may be that has been aborted. In such a report by the chief finance officer, there is an express duty on the proper officer – i.e. the officer who has been assigned responsibility for the task – to notify the authority's auditor of the date, time and place of the meeting; and if the auditor is not satisfied that the authority's decision at the meeting overcomes the problems identified in the report, they may proceed to take further action in their own right.

13.35 Subject to the provisions of the Freedom of Information Act 2000, there is no obligation to make any report by the monitoring officer or the chief finance officer available for public inspection. The necessary meeting to consider the report will, of course, be open to the press and public, and subject to the rules of exclusion in regard to confidential information and exempt information (see 3.8), the report should be made available to the press and public.

Judicial and quasi-judicial business

General considerations

13.36 There are occasions when a meeting is required to conduct business that is judicial or quasi-judicial in character: invariably a meeting of a committee or sub-committee or the like because the full council could not effectively exercise such a role. Examples include: the grant of licences where there is scope for or the need to exercise discretion (as opposed to instances where a licence or permission issues automatically, given the fulfilment of specified conditions); the exercise of powers that affect the interests of individuals whether or not they have a right to be heard and the hearing of disciplinary appeals (see *Ridge v Baldwin* (1964) and 13.42). In all such cases, while the committee or sub-committee is, strictly speaking, an ordinary administrative one, it must observe the principles of natural justice. In most instances where a committee or sub-committee is exercising a judicial or quasi-judicial function, it can properly meet in private because the subject matter will be exempt information. Care should be taken to ensure that members understand that they could be seen to be acting as an 'agent' of the council in respect of such proceedings. For example, a member can have an employment tribunal claim brought against them in respect of their actions at such a hearing, and in the case of *Moores v Bude-Stratton Town Council* (2000), the employment appeals tribunal held that common sense demands that councillors have responsibilities for the employment contract.

13.37 It is a cardinal principle that not only must justice be done, but also it must manifestly be seen to be done. There is, therefore, a responsibility on councillors when acting in a judicial or quasi-judicial capacity (and officers, too, if present) to conduct proceedings in such a way that parties appearing before them have no reason to suspect bias or be encouraged to challenge the proceedings on some grounds of impropriety.[8] Apart from the above, it is important that members of the committee or sub-committee should be present in the committee room at the outset of the meeting and remain there until a decision has been reached. It would be wholly improper for a councillor to participate in reaching the decision if they had not heard all the evidence.

13.38 Of great assistance in this has been the application of two trends, the first being the application of specific codes of conduct, practice or guidance to particular committees. In general terms, the LGA (LACoRS) published such a guide some years ago for licensing committee members and published a mini guide for development control committee members in association with LLG and the Institute of Licensing/Planning Officers Society and others. Both of these guides have proved popular and useful. More particularly, almost every relevant authority has adopted a code of conduct or protocol in relation to development control committees, which they enforce in meetings and through connection to their members' code of conduct. Importantly, these codes are published and available to anyone who wishes to see them. A Model Members' Planning Code or Protocol was first produced by ACSeS/LLG in 2003 and last updated in January 2014; a copy of this is in Appendix 4.

13.39 The second trend is now almost universal, and highly effective, whereby local authorities have introduced a standing order (or sometimes simply a convention) to the effect that members are not permitted to sit on these quasi-judicial committees until they have undergone a process of training. The level and form of training is usually as determined by the monitoring officer or by the relevant planning, licensing, or HR service director.

The Human Rights Act 1998

13.40 The Human Rights Act 1998 has particular relevance in relation to a local authority's decision-making process. Under the 1998 Act, it is unlawful for a public authority to act in a way that is incompatible with a Convention right unless, as the result of one or more provisions of primary legislation, the authority could not have acted differently.

Article 6 (1) of the Convention (Right to a Fair Trial) stipulates that:

> 'In the determination of his civil rights and obligations or of any criminal charge against him, everyone is entitled to a fair and public hearing within a reasonable time by an independent and impartial tribunal established by law. Judgement shall be pronounced publicly but the press and public may be excluded from all or part of the trial in the interest of morals, public order or national security in a democratic society, where the interests of juveniles or the protection of the private life of the parties so require, or to the extent strictly necessary in the opinion of the court in special circumstances where publicity would prejudice the interests of justice.'

Any hearing held by a local authority must comply with Article 6 and the rules of procedure should ensure that is the case subject to exceptions. This may include the right of effective access to a court and adequate disclosure of relevant evidence. At the end of the hearing, committee members should normally retire on their own to consider their decision. It will rarely be the case that it will be necessary for an officer to accompany them, as any legal or procedural advice should normally be given in the presence of all those involved. If officers do leave with members to provide advice, it should be made clear that this is the case and that advice should be repeated in public when the members return.

13.41 In addition, Article 8 of the Convention (Right to Respect for Private and Family Life) states that:

> 'Everyone has the right to respect for his private and family life, his home and his correspondence, and there shall be no interference by a public authority with the exercise of this right except such as is in accordance with the law and is necessary in a democratic society in the interests of national security, public safety or the economic well-being of the country, for the prevention of disorder or crime, for the protection of health or morals, or for the protection of the rights and freedoms of others.'

In essence, therefore, the relevant committee must ensure that any interference with such rights is proportionate, when reaching their decision.

A useful booklet entitled *Acting on Rights: A Guide to the Human Rights Act 1998* has been produced by the Local Government Association and deals with these issues.

Natural justice

13.42 Where in the exercise of a discretion by a local authority the rights and interests of an individual are affected, the authority, in practice usually through a committee, is under a duty to exercise its discretion fairly and without whim or bias. Lord Esher, in *R v West Vestry of St Pancras* (1890), said:

> '. . . they must fairly consider the application and exercise their discretion on it fairly, and not take into account any reason for their discretion which is not a legal one. If people who have to exercise a public duty by exercising their discretion take into account matters which the courts consider not to be proper for the guidance of their discretion, then in the eyes of the law they have not exercised their discretion.'

An authority, or indeed any body of persons, that has a duty in law to determine questions affecting the rights of people must act judicially and this means in general terms (the relevant law is beyond the scope of this book) that it must comply with the principles of natural justice.

13.43 These principles, as evident from decisions of the courts, are that the local authority must reach its decision fairly, without bias and in good faith, and must give a reasonable opportunity to the parties concerned to put their case, though not necessarily in person or by representative, and it may not act as a judge in its own cause. If the statute under which the authority is purporting to act lays down a procedure then that procedure must be followed; but otherwise it is not necessary for the procedure of a court of law to be followed (*R v Electricity Commissioners* (1924): any procedure that does not offend the principles of natural justice may be employed. In *R v Army Board of Defence Council, ex parte Anderson* (1991), it was held that there should not be an inflexible policy of not having oral hearings. The courts can review a decision made in a judicial or quasi-judicial capacity if there is an error in law disclosed on the face of the record (*Local Government Board v Arlidge* (1915)), except where the statute concerned provides that an order made it may not be questioned in legal proceedings. In several instances a statute gives a right of appeal to a person aggrieved by a decision of a local authority, either to a minister or to a court of law.

Staff consultative committees

General principles

13.44 Since the Information and Consultation Directive in March 2005, local authorities have had a responsibility to ensure that staff are:

- informed about the business's economic situation;
- informed and consulted about employment prospects; and
- informed and consulted about decisions likely to lead to substantial changes in work organisation or contractual relations, including redundancies and transfers.

In practice, most local authorities already had joint staff consultative committees, which carried out these functions. Two important general principles govern committees of this character: one is that their function is advisory (this type of committee can have no executive power to commit the employing authority); and the other, in conformity with the practice of all collective bargaining, is that decisions can only be reached upon the vote of a majority on each side voting separately.[9]

13.45 However, if the process of consultation is to have the confidence of employees, the local authority should ensure that its representatives are knowledgeable and can speak with authority and in expectation that when they join with the other side in recommending a course of action to the local authority, it is likely that the proposal will be accepted. Somewhat similarly, the employees' side should be truly representative of the workforce for whom they purport to speak. Such a committee's deliberations must take place in an atmosphere conducive to free and meaningful discussion. Therefore it is usual for the chairman to be chosen in turn from each side, and when an employer-side representative is serving as chairman the other side should select a vice-chairman, and vice versa.

Conflict of interest in staff negotiations

13.46 Local authorities are required[10] to secure that, so far as practicable, their interests in negotiations that govern local authority terms and conditions of employment are not represented, directly or indirectly, by persons who are both members of an authority and in such employment, i.e. with another local authority, or by persons who are both members of an authority and an official or employee of a trade union whose membership includes people in local authority employment. The term 'negotiations' is not defined but needs to be distinguished from consultation. If a staff consultative committee does enter into negotiations, the local authority must ensure that its choice of employer-side representatives does not contravene the law. It might also be wise for local authority members hearing disciplinary appeals (see 13.45) not to be councillors with an interest in staff negotiations, even though an appeals panel could hardly be said to be concerned with these negotiations.

Model constitutions

13.47 The constitution and rules of procedure of consultative committees vary considerably in detail and are always settled by agreement between the employing authority and employee representatives.

Clerking the committees

13.48 The committee's constitution will provide for the appointment of either a single secretary to clerk the committee's proceedings or joint secretaries, i.e. one appointed by each side, whose respective responsibility is to frame the matters to be placed on the agenda and to take appropriate action on decisions. Where there are joint secretaries it is usual, nevertheless, for the employer's side secretary to take charge of the dispatch of agenda, preparation of draft minutes, and servicing the committee generally.
13.49 Where there is only one secretary of the committee that officer, even if a council officer, should regard themselves as the officer of the committee collectively, and in drafting the minutes (which must be approved by both sides) must see to it that the arguments put forward by each side are fairly summarised.

Safety committees

13.50 The Health and Safety at Work, etc. Act 1974 (H&SWA 1974) makes it the duty of every employer – and that includes, of course, every local authority – to ensure, so far as reasonably practicable, the health, safety and welfare at work of all its employees (s. 2(1)). The employer has a duty to consult safety representatives, i.e. representatives of the employees,[11] with a view to the making and maintenance of arrangements enabling the employer and the employees to cooperate effectively in promoting and developing measures for this purpose and may be required by the safety representatives or may itself so elect to establish a safety committee or committees to keep health, safety and welfare measures under review.
13.51 The Safety Representatives and Safety Committees Regulations 1977 provide that an employer must establish a safety committee within three months of being requested in writing to do so by at least two safety representatives who made the request and with representatives of recognised trade unions whose members work in any workplace in respect of which the committee is to function, and is required to post a notice stating the composition of the committee and the workplace or workplaces covered by it in a place where the notice may be easily read by employees. The Health and Safety Executive has produced guidance on the objectives and functions of safety committees, their membership and conduct available at www.hse.gov.uk/involvement/hscommittees.htm. The constitution, rules and procedure of the committees should be settled by joint consultation between management and trade unions.
13.52 A safety committee will be advisory in character and should function in much the same way as other consultative committees, i.e. decisions will be made by majority vote on either side and the decisions will be recommendations, ordinarily to the staffing committee.

Staff selection panels

General considerations

13.53 Many local authorities incorporate in their standing orders a number of staffing regulations, although the regulations do not as a rule govern meetings for the interview and appointment of staff and other HR matters. Most have in the past been mainly aimed at preventing canvassing of councillors by prospective employees, or lobbying of councillors by disgruntled staff.

The selection of staff on the basis predominantly of an interview has long been the traditional way in which local authorities have made their selection of prospective staff, often by over-large appointments panels comprised not infrequently in the past by councillors with little if any training in staff selection techniques. This process was the subject of much criticism, which led to the Local Authorities (Standing Orders) (England) Regulations 2001. These regulations require the appointment, dismissal or disciplining of all staff below deputy chief officer level (apart from political assistants) to be the responsibility of the head of paid service, or an officer nominated by them.

13.54 So far as the appointment of chief officers is concerned (in England), the Local Authorities (Standing Orders) Regulations 1993 (as amended by SI 2001/3384) stipulate that:

'1 Where the authority propose to appoint a chief officer and it is not proposed that the appointment be made exclusively from among their existing officers, they shall:

(a) draw up a statement specifying:
  (i) the duties of the officer concerned, and
  (ii) any qualifications or qualities to be sought in the person to be appointed;
(b) make arrangements for the post to be advertised in such a way as is likely to bring it to the attention of persons who are qualified to apply for it; and
(c) make arrangements for a copy of the statement mentioned in paragraph (a) to be sent to any person on request.

2–1 Where a post has been advertised as provided in standing order 1(b), the authority shall:

(a) interview all qualified applicants for the post, or
(b) select a shortlist of such qualified applicants and interview those included on the shortlist.

2 Where no qualified person has applied, the authority shall make further arrangements for advertisement in accordance with standing order 1(b).

3 Every appointment of a chief officer shall be made by the authority. The regulations, in Pt. II of Sch. 1, provide for these authorised variations:

1 The standing orders may provide that:

(a) the steps taken under standing order 1 or 2 above may be taken by a committee, subcommittee or chief officer of the authority;

(b) any chief officer may be appointed by a committee or subcommittee of the authority, or a relevant joint committee.

2 The standing orders may provide that where the duties of a chief officer include the discharge of functions of two or more local authorities in pursuance of section 101(5) of the Local Government Act 1972:

(a) the steps taken under standing order 1 or 2 above may be taken by a joint committee of those authorities, a subcommittee of that committee or a chief officer of any of the authorities concerned; and

(b) any chief officer may be appointed by such a joint committee, a subcommittee of that committee or a committee or subcommittee of any of those authorities.

3 There may be excluded from the application of standing orders 1 to 3:

(a) any appointment of a non-statutory chief officer (within the meaning of section 2(7)(a) or (b) of that Act), and

(b) any appointment in pursuance of section 9 (assistants for political groups) of the Act.' All local authority staff are required to be appointed solely on 'merit' (LG&HA 1989, s. 7).

Summons and agenda

13.55 The summons and agenda for a selection panel, constituted as a subcommittee and governed by the rules as to political proportionality (with an additional member where it will include the directly elected mayor as a member), will comprise in every case:

- notification of date, time and place of the meeting;
- an indication of the panel's terms of reference and powers, e.g. 'to interview selected candidates and to recommend an appointment to the post of . . .'; and
- such documents as may be thought appropriate to enable the members to study in advance: the job description of the post; the job specification[12] of the kind of candidate sought; and a copy of the applications and/or a summary of them.

13.56 The candidates will obviously need to be invited to attend for the interview before the selection panel. They should be given advance notice (candidates should be advised of the probable date of interview when they first apply for an application form and particulars of the post), asked to come at staggered times and given directions to the offices. A waiting area should be available for them when they arrive.

Purpose of selection interview

13.57 It would be an oversimplification to say that the object of the selection interview is to select and appoint a candidate to the job concerned. The interview, in any case, is only part of the total selection process. There is likely in practice to have been some form of testing and a preliminary interview of candidates at officer level to determine a shortlist. There are enquiries to be made beforehand and formalities to be dealt with subsequently before the contract of employment is finalised: references, medical clearance and so on. Nevertheless, the interview is in most cases the critical stage in the process and will usually result in the selection of a preferred candidate.

13.58 The purposes of the interview may be summarised to:

- give each candidate information about the job (although ideally most of the information required should have been provided by the written particulars of the appointment);
- obtain or check the basic facts about the shortlisted candidates;
- permit observation of the candidates' outward appearance and manner.;
- to test by oral question and answer the candidates' capabilities as relevant to the job;
- to enable an assessment to be made of the personality of the candidates, using this term in the most general sense to include both intelligence and personal qualities; and
- to influence the favoured candidate towards accepting the job if the panel wishes them to take it.

Often candidates are asked to make a presentation to members and committee staff should check in advance with HR as to what is expected of a candidate and who will provide the IT support, projection equipment, laptop, etc., and to advise candidates whether they need to email in any presentation. A 'memory stick' is unlikely to be acceptable, as the local authority system is likely to be encrypted.

The ultimate choice of candidate ought to be a matter of mutual agreement between members of the interviewing panel. There is risk of making an unsatisfactory decision where the choice is decided on a formal vote. If the panel is a sizable one (as, regrettably, is still the case in some authorities, especially for chief officer appointments), a candidate chosen on the basis of having secured most votes may have been selected as a minority choice if the majority of interviewers have spread their votes among other candidates.

Conduct of the interview

13.59 Any member of the selection panel not present throughout the interviews ought not to cast a vote in the decision to select. In *R v Birmingham City Council ex parte McKenna* (1992), a selection panel of six members had been properly appointed under the terms of the former E(2)A 1986, ss. 35–37 and the Education (School Government) Regulations 1989 to interview and appoint a head teacher. The panel chose to make the selection process a three-stage business: first a meeting to consider the written applications, second to interview the long list of those selected, and third a meeting to interview the shortlisted candidates and make the appointment. An unsuccessful candidate challenged the decision on the grounds that one of the members of the panel did not attend the second meeting although she was present at the third when she had agreed with the unanimous decision (to reduce the longlist to a shortlist) taken in her absence at the second meeting. An application for judicial review was subsequently refused (on a number of grounds not connected with the issue we are considering) and in reaching its decision the court decided that the long list interview meeting (when the member was absent) was not an essential step in the appointment process. Though the point may be arguable, it surely seems to imply that if the member had been temporarily absent during the final interviews and had nevertheless voted to appoint the chosen candidate, the decision might well have been successfully challenged.

13.60 It used to be said that there is no restriction on the type of questions that may be put to candidates, save those that relate to religious or political views. That must now be modified. Questions that may imply that the selection could be biased on grounds of sex or race or other types of unlawful discrimination could involve the employing authority in challenge before an employment tribunal if the candidate concerned is not appointed. Alternatively, questions may be put about the social awareness of the candidate that could be interpreted as politically orientated. Clearly the interviewing process needs to be conducted in a way that will detect fitness for the job and to persuade candidates that merit has been the overriding criterion. It can often be a difficult job to ensure that members do not stray into areas that could lead the authority into potential difficulties.

13.61 The following is suggested as a checklist for the chairman on procedure:

- Preliminary discussion: clarify key qualities/competencies being sought; decide systematic approach: time to be devoted to each candidate, when to break for refreshments, apportionment of questioning, etc.; ensure no likelihood of interruptions;
- Receive candidate: introduce panel;
- Check that candidate is a firm applicant and willing to accept the job if offered;
- Invite candidate to:
  - (a) make any presentation that may have been requested;
  - (b) give outline of experience, stressing that which they consider relevant; or
  - (c) say what they do in present post;
- Ask questions of candidate; invite:
  - (a) panel members to ask questions;
- Ask candidate whether they:
  - (a) wish to add anything in support of their candidature;
  - (b) have any questions;
- Thank candidate for attending, ask them to retire and either:
  - (a) tell them to wait; or
  - (b) say they will be advised of the panel's decision in due course;
- Consider decision in light of:
  - (a) written applications; and
  - (b) impression gained at interview; and
  - (c) result of any testing; and – with reserve –
  - (d) references; against job specification;

- Call back successful candidate and offer appointment (or, if appropriate, say that a decision will be communicated to them); and
- Tell unsuccessful candidates of decision and thank them for attending.

The panel chairman should keep a check on time devoted to each candidate and ensure that all areas of necessary investigation are adequately covered by questions.

Staff appeals tribunals

General considerations

13.62 Some councils have an internal appeals machinery to deal with appeals against dismissals and redundancy. Councillors in reaching a decision in appeal cases are exercising a quasi-judicial role (see above).

13.63 The membership should be as small as the rules governing political balance permit; the councillors chosen should ideally be ones who enjoy the confidence of both council and employees, and have received the necessary training. They should be empowered to make the final decision so far as the local authority is concerned. There is advantage in establishing a pool of members from which an appeals panel can be selected because of the expertise that is built up by their experience and the greater likelihood of uniformity of approach. The council should take account of the statutory provisions relating to the conflict of interest of councillors involved in staff negotiations, even though membership of an appeals panel may, strictly, not be caught.

13.64 The constitution of the panel and the procedure adopted at its meetings will depend to some extent upon local arrangements governing employee appeals. For example, where, as is usual, the power to dismiss is delegated to senior officers, the appeals tribunal can be appointed by and out of the personnel or staffing committee or personnel sub-committee; but in the case of the dismissal of an employee, there may be a further appeal outside the local authority to an employment tribunal if the employee, having the requisite service, challenges the disallowance of their appeal and alleges unfair dismissal. (See Employment Rights Act 1996, s. 94.)

Disciplinary hearings

13.65 The arrangements that local authorities make for the hearing of appeals against dismissal are still largely for each authority to determine[13] (other than in the case of disciplinary action against the head of the paid service and other statutory officers) although the LG&HA 1989, s. 8, enables the Secretary of State to make regulations in respect of all categories of local authority employed staff. An authority's discretion is, however, constrained by considerations of natural justice and the recommendations in the ACAS code on Disciplinary Practice and Procedures in Employment. Each authority's disciplinary code should define what constitutes disciplinary action – in the case of the head of the paid service, monitoring officers and chief finance officers, a statutory definition applies – and regulate the manner in which breaches of discipline are to be handled. What is important is that employees

should know what constitutes misconduct likely to lead to disciplinary action and the probable consequences of such misconduct.
Therefore disciplinary action when necessary must be taken:

- in a manner which is fair to the employee concerned;
- in strict accordance with the council's own procedures;
- in conformity with any statutory provisions that apply; and
- in accordance with a procedure that provides a right of appeal against action taken at first instance.

13.66 The notice of the hearing sent to the appeals panel with the date, time and place of meeting (the date should have been agreed with the appellant and their trade union or other representative) should be accompanied by a report setting out the facts that led to the disciplinary action taken, the disciplinary action itself, the reasons for it and possibly also an indication of alternative courses open to the panel if it wishes to allow the appeal. The panel must also be provided with a copy of any representations made by the appellant. The appellant and their representative must be provided with a copy of all the papers made available to members of the panel.

Natural justice

13.67 When an appeals tribunal is hearing an appeal against disciplinary action (or against a salary grading claim or seeking to settle a grievance), it is acting, of course, in a quasi-judicial capacity and must observe the principles of natural justice. These principles in relation to judicial and quasi-judicial business in committee have already been discussed (see above), but their application specifically to the conduct of disciplinary proceedings was considered in *Khanum v Mid-Glamorgan Area Health Authority* (1978), in which the Employment Appeal Tribunal said:

> '. . . in the end how nearly a domestic disciplinary inquiry, a statutory inquiry by a statutory body, a public statutory inquiry, or any other inquiry which has to make decisions, must approach to the full-blown procedure of a court of justice is, no doubt, a matter of degree. But in our judgement as regards the sort of domestic tribunal with which we are concerned in this case [a domestic inquiry and disciplinary hearing by an area health authority] the law is as it was expressed by Harman J in *Byrne v Kinematograph Renters Society Ltd* (1958) 1 W.L.R. 762, and approved and applied by the Privy Council to the conduct of a university vice-chancellor's inquiry into cheating in examinations in Fernando's Case:
>
> "What then are the requirements of natural justice in a case of this kind? First, I think that the person accused should know of the nature of the accusation made; secondly, that he should be given an opportunity to state his case; and thirdly, of course, that the tribunal should act in good faith. I do not myself think that there is really anything more."'

There is, perhaps, something more to be added and it is this. Members who take the final decision must have been present throughout the hearing and therefore vote on the whole of the evidence: anyone who entered the room after the proceedings began or absented themselves for part of the hearing ought not to be allowed to vote.

13.68 It must be obvious that a tribunal cannot be regarded as acting in conditions of complete impartiality because it will always be reviewing a decision already made by the management of which it forms a part. This was well expressed in another EAT case, *Corina v Berkshire County Council* (1979):

> 'It is a fallacy to suppose that in the course of internal grievance or disciplinary procedures you can have a neutral disciplinary or appellate "tribunal" short of an express provision for recourse to outside arbitration through ACAS or otherwise, something which involves its own disadvantages. The people who have to hear and decide on the matter, in internal procedures, are limbs of the employer and so not "impartial" in any true sense. What, as a matter of natural justice you are entitled to, is that they shall come to their decisions honestly.'

Who should represent the parties?

13.69 The officer who is to represent the council at a disciplinary or grievance hearing should, ideally, be the officer who took the initial disciplinary decision against the appellant or heard their grievance at first instance (and this will ordinarily be the chief officer or a senior officer in the department). It ought not to be the HR officer because, among other reasons, they may well be the appeal tribunal's adviser. The HR officer must remain impartial until a final decision has been taken on behalf of the employing authority, i.e. after the decision of the tribunal in a disciplinary matter, when they may well represent the local authority before an industrial tribunal. The expression council's representative should thus be interpreted to mean the chief officer or their representative or investigating officer.

The role of the HR professional in relation to disciplinary hearings was considered by the EAT in *Ramphal v Department for Transport* (2015). The EAT found that HR had significantly overstepped the permitted boundaries of its involvement in that case, but in so doing gave the following important guidance:

- An investigating officer is entitled to call for advice from HR, but HR must be 'very careful' to limit advice essentially to questions of law and procedure and process, and to avoid straying into areas of culpability.
- HR can give advice in respect of consistency (e.g. advising what other decisions have been taken by the employer on similar facts) but must not advise on what the appropriate sanction is in respect of the investigator's (or decision-maker's) findings of fact. 'It was not for human resources to advise whether the finding should be one of simple misconduct or gross misconduct.'
- An employee facing disciplinary charges and a dismissal procedure is entitled to assume that the decision will be taken by the appropriate officer, without having

been lobbied by other parties as to the findings he or she should make as to culpability. He or she should be given: notice of any changes in the case he or she has to meet so that he or she can deal with them; notice of representations made by others to the dismissing officer that go beyond legal advice; and advice on matters of process and procedure.
- If the integrity of the decision to dismiss has been influenced by persons outside the procedure, it will be unfair, particularly if the claimant has no knowledge of it.

13.70 The ACAS Code of Disciplinary Practice and Procedures in Employment says that the employee should be accorded the right to be accompanied by a trade union representative or a fellow employee of their choice; and most local authority codes, likely in every case to have been agreed with employee representatives, will contain similar provisions. However, what if notwithstanding such provisions, an employee wishes to be accompanied or represented by a lawyer or a relative? Most authorities would probably not wish to place any restriction on the freedom of the individual to be represented by whoever they wish. Nevertheless, there is support for the view that a panel, which is entitled to regulate its own procedures, could properly refuse to allow legal representation, at least if the applicable code expressly forbids it.

There have been various judicial views over the years. However, the Supreme Court overturned, by a majority, the Court of Appeal's decision in the case of *R (on the application of G) v Governors of X School* (2011) and ruled that a teaching assistant at a school who was accused of sexual misconduct with a minor could not rely on the Article 6 right to a fair trial under the European Convention of Human Rights. The Supreme Court has ruled that it was not a breach of an employee's human rights to refuse him the right to be accompanied by a lawyer at a disciplinary hearing.

The case concerned a teaching assistant who was alleged to have acted inappropriately towards a pupil at the school at which he worked.

Disciplinary procedures were instigated against him; his conduct was found to have constituted an abuse of trust, and he was summarily dismissed. Subsequently, he was informed that his dismissal would be reported to the Secretary of State for Children, Schools and Families on the basis that he might be unsuitable to work with children.

The teaching assistant argued that the disciplinary hearing was in breach of his right to a fair and public hearing under the European Convention on Human Rights and that he should have been afforded legal representation during the hearing. As a result, the High Court found that the disciplinary hearing had breached his human rights, saying that his right to practise his profession might be irretrievably prejudiced in the disciplinary proceedings.

However, the Supreme Court overruled the High Court. It looked at the case law from the European Court of Human Rights and concluded that it takes 'a fact-sensitive, pragmatic approach to the right to legal representation'.

This judgement is of particular significance to local authorities, which should now be aware that an employee is not automatically entitled to legal representation at a disciplinary hearing that might result in them being referred to the authorities and potentially placed on the children's barred list.

However, the Supreme Court has stressed that the issue is fact sensitive and leaves open the possibility that legal representation may be required in limited cases, although it stopped short of providing examples where this would be the case.

Procedure

13.71 The following is an example, couched in terms of advice for the chairman, of the procedure which should be followed at the hearing of an appeal against disciplinary action by any local authority employee (but see below as regards disciplinary action in the case of the head of the paid service, monitoring officer and chief financial officer) and subject to modification in cases where a disciplinary procedure is specifically prescribed as, for example, in the case of police officers, firefighters, teachers, etc. The council's representative (CR) – the director or his representative – puts their case first and the appellant's representative (AR) puts the case for the appellant (A) afterwards:

- Call in together CR, AR and A.
- Invite CR to put the council's case.
- After each of the CR's witnesses (if any) has given evidence:
  - o ask AR whether they (or A) wish to ask questions of the witness;
  - o ask whether members of the tribunal wish to ask questions of the witness; and
  - o ask CR whether they wishes to re-examine their witness.
- After CR has completed his case:
  - o ask AR whether they have any questions they wish to put to CR; and
  - o ask whether members of the tribunal wish to ask questions of the CR.
- Invite AR to put A's case.
- If AR calls witnesses, then after each has given evidence:
  - o ask CR whether they wish to ask questions of the witness;
  - o ask whether members of the tribunal wish to ask questions of the witness; and
  - o ask AR whether they wish to re-examine their witness.
- After AR has completed their case:
  - o ask CR whether they have any questions to put to either AR or A; and
  - o ask whether members of the panel wish to ask questions of AR or A.
- Invite CR to sum up the council's case if they wish to do so.
- Invite AR to sum up A's case if they wish to do so.
- Ask all parties to withdraw except the panel's adviser.
- Deliberate upon the case.

The panel may confirm, amend or reject the original decision and may recall both parties to clear points of uncertainty on the evidence given, but if recall is necessary, both parties are to return notwithstanding that only one is concerned with the point giving rise to doubt. After a decision has been reached, call back both parties and announce either:

- the panel's decision if it possesses delegated power; or
- that the decision will be communicated to the parties as soon as possible.

In either case the decision must be confirmed in writing.

Disciplinary action against the head of the paid service, monitoring officer or chief finance officer

13.72 The Local Authorities (Standing Orders) Regulations 1993 and the Local Authorities (Standing Orders) (England) Regulations 2001, as amended by the Local Authorities (Standing Orders) (England) (Amendment) Regulations 2015/881, prescribe a mandatory standing order that relevant authorities must make regulating the investigation of alleged misconduct on the part of the head of the council's paid service,[14] its monitoring officer or its chief finance officer. The Regulations also define disciplinary action in these terms:

> '"Disciplinary action" in relation to a member of staff of a local authority means any action occasioned by alleged misconduct which, if proved, would, according to the usual practice of the authority, be recorded on the member of staff 's personal file, and includes any proposal for dismissal of a member of staff for any reason other than redundancy, permanent ill-health or infirmity of mind or body, but does not include failure to renew a contract of employment for a fixed term unless the authority has undertaken to renew such a contract.'

The Regulations had previously provided for the involvement of a designated independent person to be appointed by the authority and remunerated by it, in every case where a complaint of misconduct requires to be investigated against the head of the paid service, monitoring officer or chief finance officer. The Regulations had provided that no disciplinary action in respect of the head of the paid service, monitoring officer or chief finance officer, other than permitted suspension, i.e. suspension on full pay terminating no later than the expiry of two months beginning on the day on which suspension takes effect, may be taken by an authority other than in accordance with a recommendation in a report made by the designated independent person. The object of these Regulations was to provide a measure of protection or those three statutory governance officers whose role it was to 'speak truth unto power', introduced in the LGFA 1988 and LG&HA 1989. In practice, the involvement of the Designated Independent Person (DIP) and delays created costs, which were sometimes considerable, at this early stage in proceedings.

13.73 The result has been the amendments brought about by the Local Authorities (Standing Orders) (England) (Amendment) Regulations (SI 2015/881), which revokes the DIP provisions. The new provisions introduce a step in a disciplinary procedure whereby any dismissal of these officers is required to be considered by a panel which must contain at least two Independent Persons. The obvious response in moving any protection of these officers from the point of allegation and investigation to the final step of proposed dismissal is that, by the time an investigation is completed and dismissal is proposed, the seniority of these officers and the requirement for continuing trust and confidence in their relationships with members means that any protection so inserted is so limited as to be arguably almost pointless beyond the conceptual. There is also the point that the old standing orders remain as a term of the contract of employment of heads of paid service. The provisions of the old standing orders and the new are, however, not incompatible and many (if not most) authorities have sought to combine the two. An example is set out below.

. . .

Disciplinary Action Against Head of Paid Service, Monitoring Officer or Chief Finance Officer

1. In the following paragraphs:
   (a) 'the 2011 Act' means the Localism Act 2011;
   (b) 'chief finance officer', 'disciplinary action', 'head of the authority's paid service' and 'monitoring officer' have the same meaning as in regulation 2 of the Local Authorities (Standing Orders) (England) Regulations 2001;
   (c) 'independent person' means a person appointed under section 28(7) of the 2011 Act;
   (d) 'local government elector' means a person registered as a local government elector in the register of electors in the authority's area in accordance with the Representation of the People Acts;
   (e) 'the Panel' means a committee appointed by the authority under section 102(4) of the Local Government Act 1972 for the purposes of advising the authority on matters relating to the dismissal of relevant officers of the authority;
   (f) 'relevant meeting' means a meeting of the authority to consider whether or not to approve a proposal to dismiss a relevant officer; and
   (g) 'relevant officer' means the chief finance officer, head of the authority's paid service or monitoring officer, as the case may be.
2. A relevant officer may not be dismissed by an authority unless the procedure set out in the following paragraphs is complied with.
3. The authority must invite relevant independent persons to be considered for appointment to the Panel, with a view to appointing at least two such persons to the Panel.
4. In paragraph 3, 'relevant independent person' means any independent person who has been appointed by the authority or, where there are fewer than two such persons, such independent persons as have been appointed by another authority or authorities as the authority considers appropriate.
5. Subject to paragraph 6, the authority must appoint to the Panel such relevant independent persons who have accepted an invitation issues in accordance with paragraph 3 in accordance with the following priority order:

(a) a relevant independent person who has been appointed by the authority and who is a local government elector;
(b) any other relevant independent person who has been appointed by the authority;
(c) a relevant independent person who has been appointed by another authority or authorities.

6. An authority is not required to appoint more than two relevant independent person in accordance with paragraph 5, but may do so.
7. The authority must appoint any Panel at least 20 working days before the relevant meeting.
8. Before the taking of a vote at the relevant meeting on whether or not to approve such a dismissal, the authority must take into account, in particular:
   (a) any advice, views or recommendations of the Panel;
   (b) the conclusion of any investigation into the proposed dismissal; and
   (c) any representations from the relevant officer.
9. Any remuneration, allowances or fees paid by the authority to an independent person appointed to the Panel must not exceed the level of remuneration, allowances or fees payable to that independent person in respect of that person's role as independent person under the 2011 Act.

. . .

Disciplinary Action

(a) Suspension. The Head of Paid Service, Monitoring Officer, Chief Finance Officer and other Chief Officer(s) may be suspended while an investigation takes place into alleged misconduct. That suspension will be on full pay and last no longer than two months.
(b) Designated Independent Person. No other disciplinary action may be taken in respect of any of those officers specified above except in accordance with recommendation in a report made by a designated independent person.

Standards committee

Historical position

13.74 The Nolan Committee proposed that each local authority should establish a standards committee that would command a special position in the council's management structure. It would be composed of senior members and chaired by someone other than the leader of the council with power to examine allegations of misconduct by councillors and to recommend disciplinary action to the full assembly. These powers of recommendation would include proposing the withdrawal by particular councillors from decision-making and the suspension of a member for up to three months.

13.75 As mentioned in Chapter 1, these proposals eventually resulted in the LGA 2000 establishing an ethical framework for local authorities and, at local level, each relevant authority has the obligation to establish a standards committee that has the statutory duty to promote and maintain high standards of conduct by members and co-opted members of the authority; and to assist them in observing the authority's Code of Conduct. As it stood, and as a number of authorities have largely followed, the committee needed not to be politically balanced, and must have had at least three people on it. At least 25% of the committee members had to be independent of local government (SI 1085/2008 reg. 4) and only one member could be a member of the executive. If there are parish councils in the area covered by the local authority concerned, then there must also have been at least two parish councillors on the committee, who are also not members of the council itself (SI 1085/2008). The independent representatives must have been approved by a majority of councillors after public advertisement under the procedure set down in the Standards Committee (England) Regulations 2008.

13.76 So far as meetings of the standards committee are concerned, there is a quorum of at least three, including one independent representative. Also, a parish representative must be present when matters relating to parish councils are being discussed. Members of standards committees should not be whipped or told how to vote, but should consider matters impartially and without regard to party loyalty.

Standards Committees

13.77 There is no longer a need to have a Standards Committee designated as such, but the duties under ss. 26 to 37 of the Localism Act 2011 must be carried out by a politically balanced committee of the council. Political balance can of course be waived if the council agrees (see Chapter 9). If the council contains independent members, then these must be non-voting under s. 104 of the LGA 1972. For a number of local authorities, this has meant that they have abolished their standards committees and passed the functions to, for example, the audit and governance committee. In the majority of cases, however, it seems that standards committees have continued with revised terms of reference.

For all other matters there will be no sanctions and authorities will have to rely on the ability to censure councillors, revoke appointments and require, to the extent that they are able without statutory backing, councillors to make apologies or undertake training.

Those powers were considered by the *Court of Appeal in R v Broadland District Council ex parte Lashley* (2001). In that case a chief executive had issued instructions that apart from nominated officers, staff were not to have any dealings with Councillor Lashley and the chief executive also banned that member from entering the council offices other than to attend council meetings. In essence, the court considered such restrictions to be unlawful. The court was inclined to agree with the view, however, that the standards committee could 'name and shame' a councillor, and could recommend that a councillor be removed from a particular committee.

Meetings of governing bodies

Introduction

13.78 There is within local government an immense variety of governing bodies. These include, for example, informal groups of council and co-opted members (sometimes local residents also), and the formally constituted boards of governors of schools set up by local education authorities. It would not be useful to attempt to refer to each one of the many types of such bodies that exist. Whatever their type, however, it is a matter of good practice and convenience where such matters are not prescribed by law that each should be accorded clearly defined terms of reference, so that even if the precise constitution has not been set down on paper at least there is no uncertainty about the powers and duties of members individually and the body collectively. Preferably, too, each meeting should be minuted even if the note of proceedings is no more than a brief aide-mémoire. Ideally, standing orders or rules of procedure should be drawn up as well.

13.79 If the governing body has not been formally constituted and no rules, regulations or standing orders have been laid down, then necessarily the common law rules of meetings procedure will apply. If the body is a sub-committee of a local authority committee (and not all will be), then unquestionably the appropriate statutory provisions and the authority's standing orders will apply to its meetings, which must be open to the public.

Appeals against school admission decisions

Appeal committees

13.80 There is statutory provision allowing parents of a child to make representations when their expressed preference for a certain school or college is not complied with by the local education authority or the governing body of a voluntary school. The School Admissions Code and School Admissions Appeal Code was issued in 2009 and then amended to produce a slimmed-down version in 2012. The timing of this edition, however, means that an updated version of the School Admissions and Appeals Codes is expected shortly, so that anything recorded here will be out of date almost as soon as it is printed. This remains important work for local authorities as sensible go-to providers of central services for schools.

The chief executive's management team

Its character

13.81 It has long been a practice in many authorities for the chief executive to hold regular meetings with their directors (and in some cases this extends to heads of service). In the past these have varied in character, according to local custom, from mere social gatherings for the exchange of opinion and information largely about the officers' respective areas of involvement, to more purposeful but still informal meetings concerned with high-level coordination and the discussion of matters of policy or important principle. These meetings are now more formal meetings of properly constituted management teams of the kind originally envisaged by the Maud Committee but modelled more specifically on that sketched out by Bains. They are distinguishable from their forerunners by the fact that the management team is usually an integral part of the management process of decision-making and control.

13.82 Maud recommended that the principal officers should work as members of a team of managers and specialist advisers, and see that the same approach is adopted by their staff at all levels and it saw the principal officers working together on matters that transcend the purely professional and departmental considerations under the clerk's leadership and producing agreed and coordinated recommendations to be put to Maud's management board. Bains believed that the officers' management team:[15]

> '. . . should have a corporate identity and a positive role to play in the corporate management of the authority. It is the counterpart, at officer level, of the policy and resources committee. Its members do not attend primarily as representatives of particular departments, though on occasion it will be necessary for them to speak in that capacity; they are there as members of a body created to aid the management of the authority as a whole.'

This is still relevant today. Bains discussed the role of the management team and its size, the support it would need from interdepartmental working groups and its terms of reference. It thought the team had two broad functions. The first is the long-term strategic function of considering and advising on what policies the council should be adopting to cope with changing needs and circumstances, and the second the overall management coordination and progress-chasing role.

Proceedings and business

13.83 The business of the management team should be given some measure of formality. There should be a prearranged timetable of regular meetings and an agenda and reports circulated on each occasion to those entitled to attend; individual officers should have the opportunity of originating matters for discussion but the agenda should be controlled by the chief executive; minutes should be kept and copies circulated. The distinguishing feature of management team meetings is that business is conducted as a cabinet. The chief executive will occupy the chair as of right and there will ordinarily be no voting. The chief executive will make the decisions either on the basis of a consensus of opinion or on their view of the balance of argument on a particular issue, or may make their own judgement of what needs to be decided after taking account of what is said by their colleagues. Members of the team will usually accept collective responsibility for the decisions made.

13.84 One of the by-products, as it were, of compiling an agenda is that the chief executive can examine it in draft and delete any items they think do not warrant the attention of the management team. It is important that meetings of the team should not be cluttered up with matters that can be competently dealt with elsewhere, by chief officers individually or in consultation with others either in company or not with the chief executive. Otherwise the team will fail constantly to perform its corporate role. The mere fact that a proposal of one officer may impinge on the work of others is not itself sufficient justification for bringing the matter to the management team (or almost everything, important or otherwise, that, for example, the chief finance officer or director of children's services wants to do could be held up for management team consideration). The matter must be of major importance or affect council policy to warrant the formal attention of the team as a whole. The team exists to facilitate the business of the local authority, not to obstruct progress.

13.85 Bains thought it 'difficult to lay down specific terms of reference' for the management team, but the following is a suggested shortlist of the kind of items that would need to come before the team:

- important questions of a corporate character and matters of major importance that cannot properly be dealt with by the individual officer or officers concerned;
- matters referred to the team for consideration from the policy and resources committee (now the executive);
- policy matters on which collective advice is to be submitted to council or committee;
- formulation of proposals for linking presentation of objectives, programmes and budgets;
- identification and review of objectives and priorities;
- monitoring progress against plans; and
- strategic questions concerning the acquisition, use, motivation, development and levels of manpower resources.

13.86 There can be a problem where a management team has fairly formal meetings and minutes of its proceedings and members may express a wish to see the minutes of particular decisions and sometimes even ask for regular access to papers. When such a request is declined – as would ordinarily be the case – the member may seek to rely on their 'need to know' and this raises a difficult question. It is, however, one less likely to arise if the relationship between the management team and councillors has been spelled out and understood from the outset. The management team's deliberations are part of the authority's management arrangements, i.e. the province of officers, rather than part of the authority's decision-making process, which is the remit of members. In most instances it would seem appropriate for the chief executive to advise that members do not need to see the record of the chief executive's management team's discussions to enable them to carry out their duties as councillors.

There will also be, at many authorities, regular informal meetings between the management team and leading councillors (either cabinet members or chairs of committee, depending on the executive arrangements of the council) which will be the forum for ensuring that officers and members of the administration coordinate their respective programmes.

Election meetings

Use of local authority premises

13.87 The Representation of the People Act 1983, consolidating previous enactments to like effect, obliges a local authority to permit the use of certain schools and halls for meetings for purposes connected with parliamentary and local government elections.

Parliamentary elections

13.88 A candidate at a parliamentary or European parliamentary election is entitled,[16] for the purpose of holding public meetings to support their campaign, to use at reasonable times between the receipt of the writ for the election and the day preceding the day of election, any room that is usually let for public meetings and that is maintained wholly or mainly at public expense, and any suitable school room, e.g. at a county school, voluntary school or grant-maintained school situated in the constituency or an adjoining constituency if more reasonably accessible. Local education authorities, district councils and London borough councils must prepare lists of suitable available rooms, which should also include details of the person to whom application for the use of a room should be made. A local authority cannot refuse the use of such premises even if the candidate's views are offensive to many people – see *Webster v Southwark London Borough Council* (1983) – but the police should be contacted if it is believed that the views to be put forward at a meeting are likely to be so extreme that they may cause disruption or offence and a risk to public order. In other respects, a candidate, no matter what their political persuasion, has a relatively unfettered private law right to hire a public meeting room so long as it is for the purpose described in the statute. It must be a public meeting in furtherance of their campaign for election (see *Ettridge v Morrell* (1986)). Some local authorities provide political parties with questionnaires designed to find out precisely whether the intended meeting is a public meeting within the meaning of the Representation of the People Act 1983, and require production of a valid insurance certificate for public indemnity insurance.

13.89 Where a room is used, the person by whom or on whose behalf the meeting is convened may be required to pay for expenses incurred in preparing, heating, lighting and cleaning it, in providing attendants for the meeting and restoring the room to its usual condition, and for any damage caused.

13.90 A candidate is required to give reasonable notice if they wish to take advantage of these rights, but there cannot be any interference with the hours during which a room in school premises is used for educational purposes or with the use of a meeting room either for the purposes of the person maintaining it or under a prior agreement for its letting.

Local government elections

13.91 Similar statutory provisions apply in respect of local government elections.[17] A candidate is entitled to the use of school rooms during the period between the notice of election and the day preceding election day, free of charge, except that expenses incurred by the person having charge of the room and payment for any damage must be made.

Disturbance at election meetings

13.92 Anyone who, at a lawful public meeting held for election purposes, acts or incites others to act in a disorderly manner for the purpose of preventing the transaction of the business for which the meeting was called is guilty of an illegal practice. This applies to:

- a political meeting held in any constituency between the date of the issue of a writ for the return of a Member of Parliament for the constituency and the date at which a return to the writ is made; and
- a meeting held with reference to a local government election in the electoral area for that election on, or within three weeks before, the day of election.

Planning inquiries

Procedure

13.93 The procedure at an inquiry will be at the discretion of the inspector or whoever else may have charge of the proceedings. Most planning inquiries are by their character adversarial because the issue will ordinarily be argued out by supporters of and objectors to a proposed scheme or course of action or whatever it might be.[18]

Practical arrangements

13.94 When considering where to site a public enquiry, particular attention should be had to the location. The venue for an examination should normally be centrally located within the area that the document being examined relates to. It would be helpful for the venue to be near the appeal site – for example, to allow more residents to attend – but this needs to be weighed against the suitability of any proposed venue, such as how many people it can hold and the acoustics. There will also need to be access for the inspector to a retiring room, photocopiers, telephones (including a mobile phone signal), etc., together with internet access and the availability of cafés or restaurants. It may be that a venue in a nearby town (e.g. where local residents would usually go for routine shopping trips) would be more appropriate than a village hall in a parish venue. The room should be capable of being secured overnight if the inquiry is to last more than one day, to save papers being transported back and forwards.

In particular, there is a duty on all public bodies, under the Equality Act 2010 and the Public Sector Equality Duty to ensure facilities provided are accessible to people with disabilities, if necessary by making appropriate adjustments. It is therefore essential to ensure, for example, that the venue is wheelchair accessible, has disabled parking and has a hearing loop. Religious or licensed premises may be considered inappropriate by some groups of people and are therefore unsuitable.

There is, as it were, no standard layout of a room in which an inquiry is to be held but the room must be adequate for the purpose, easy of access, and reserved for the likely duration of the proceedings. Essential points to be borne in mind include the following:

- Seating and tables must be provided in a convenient arrangement for the participants, e.g. parallel facing table and chairs for supporters and opponents respectively, with the inspector's/chairman's table between them forming a square U is the usually preferred layout, but the size and shape of the room itself will be governing constraints.
- Reasonable facilities should be provided: notepaper, pencils, water carafes and tumblers with fresh water, display boards for maps, etc., and visual aid equipment. Direction signs should be displayed at the entrance to the building indicating the room in which the inquiry is being held, and to car parks, lavatories, etc., but attendants should also be on duty to assist those attending.
- Ample seating must be provided for witnesses and others behind the front tables for the advocates on the respective sides.
- Provision should be made for accommodating members of the public and press with easy access to telephones, etc., and the room should be capable to internet access/WiFi.

Advice from the planning inspectorate says that:

> '... the Inspector's table, which should have a modesty screen, should be located centrally at one end or side of the room, preferably on a low platform. The table should be positioned to avoid people passing behind the Inspector. The Inspector should have a comfortable workstation with enough and suitable tables and chairs. The table should be large enough to spread out plans, and a side table to accommodate documents is helpful.'

In addition, the guidance now sets out that the chair should have height and tilt mechanisms, gliders and swivels. So getting the right chair for the inspector is clearly important!

Licensing Act 2003 committees

13.95 The Licensing Act 2003 gave responsibility for licensing to local authorities. Section 6 of the Act provides that the licensing authority must establish a committee, which should consist of a least 10 but no more than 15 members. In turn the licensing committee can delegate its functions to a sub-committee that has been established by it, or by an authorised officer of the licensing authority, who would normally be the licensing officer. The licensing committee and consequently the sub-committee does not need to be politically balanced. The sub-committee would usually have three members on it, although it is arguable that the quorum for such meetings could be two, with the chairman having the casting vote. It is good practice to ensure that members of the sub-committee are chosen from the main pool of licensing committee members, in order to ensure that the same members do not hear every case.

13.96 The time and place of the hearing should be arranged by the authority, and the hearing should be held in accordance with Licensing Act 2003 (Hearings) Regulations 2005 (SI 2005/44) reg. 5. The authority is under strict timescales within which they must hold a meeting, and under reg. 6(3) the authority must give at least five working days' notice before the date of the hearing. In addition, reg. 7 sets out the information that must be sent out with the notice of hearing.

13.97 The time limits for holding a hearing differ depending on the type of application that is before the sub-committee, and these are set out in the Hearing Regulations Sch. 1.

13.98 The authority may dispense with holding a hearing (reg. 9) if all parties agree that a hearing is unnecessary. This will usually be when representations to the application have been withdrawn or when all parties have reached agreement.

13.99 All hearings should take place in public, although an authority may exclude the public where it considers that the public interest in doing so outweighs the public interest in the hearing (reg. 124(2)). The conduct of the hearing should be conducted in accordance with the hearing regulations and a decision regarding the application should be made 'forthwith'. A record of the hearing must be taken in a permanent and intelligible form and must be kept for six years from the date of determination or, where an appeal is brought against the determination, the disposal of the appeal (reg. 30).

13.100 The regulations provide for notices to be transmitted by electronic means where they are capable of being accessed by the recipient and that person has agreed to this method in advance (reg. 34) and they also allow that clerical mistakes may be corrected by the authority (reg. 33).

Health and well-being boards

13.101 The Health and Social Care Act 2012 (H&SCA) established health and well-being boards from 1 April 2013, as forums where key leaders from the health and care systems work together to improve the health and well-being of their local population and reduce health inequalities. The members are to collaborate to understand their local community's needs, agree priorities and encourage commissioners to work in a more joined-up way, to improve services that patients receive from the NHS and local authorities. In particular, a key role is to produce a joint strategic needs assessment for the area, and use this to develop a locally agreed health and well-being strategy.

13.102 They are a set committee of upper-tier local authorities to which s. 102 of the LGA 1972 applies (s. 194 (11)), although the Secretary of State may make regulations to disapply parts of s. 102. This recognises that health and well-being boards are unusual in comparison to normal s. 102 committees in having officers, clinical commissioning groups and local Healthwatch representatives sit on them.

13.103 While some boards are serviced by democratic services staff, in some local authorities this is not the norm, and they are serviced from within the social care areas.

Membership

13.104 Under s. 194 H&SCA, the health and well-being board (H&WB) must contain:

- at least one councillor of the local authority, nominated in accordance with sub-section 3;
- the director of adult social services for the local authority;
- the director of children's services for the local authority;
- the director of public health for the local authority;
- a representative of the Local Healthwatch organisation for the area of the local authority;
- a representative of each relevant clinical commissioning group (CCG); and
- such other persons, or representatives of such other persons, as the local authority thinks appropriate.

13.105 It is for the leader (in an authority with executive arrangements), elected mayor or the local authority itself (where there are alternative arrangements) to determine the precise number of elected representatives on the board, and the relevant person could decide to have a majority of elected members on the board. They may also wish to take into consideration the political balance within the council, but this is not a committee to which the political balance rules apply (reg. 7 2013/218) (see Chapter 13 for information on political balance).

13.106 Two or more CCGs may be represented by the same person on the health and well-being board, where this has the explicit agreement of the board, to avoid the need for a number of CCG (clinical commissioning group) representatives.

13.107 The provisions in s. 80 of the LGA 1972 are disapplied in that if you are disqualified from being a member of a local authority under s. 80, then you can still be a member of the Health and Well-being Board (other than if you are disqualified by reason of bankruptcy or criminal conviction). This therefore allows officers to be voting members of the Health and Well-being Board (H&WB) (reg. 5 SI 218/2013).

Sub-committees

13.108 As set out above, s. 101 of the LGA 1972 has been disapplied in respect of certain parts, by the Local Authority (Public Health, Health and Well-being Boards and Health Scrutiny) Regulations 2013 (SI 2013/218).

13.109 Functions of the Health and Well-being Board may be discharged by either a sub-committee or an officer of the local authority, and a sub-committee may also delegate its functions to an officer.

Voting rights

13.110 Members of the H&WB have voting rights unless they are disapplied by the local authority, which can only do so following consultation with the H&SB.

13.111 The NHS Commissioning Board must appoint a representative for the purpose of participating in the preparation of Joint Strategic Needs Assessments (JSNAs) and the Joint Health and Well-being Strategy (JHWS), and to join the health and well-being board when it is considering a matter relating to the exercise, or proposed exercise, of the NHS commissioning board's commissioning functions in relation to the area and it is requested to do so by the board.

Local authorities or health and well-being boards can add members to the board beyond those set out in the legislation. However, they must consult with the whole board before appointing any such non-statutory members.

13.112 A study by the King's Fund in 2012 found that of the 48 shadow boards that had already been set up, 21 had up to 12 members, 23 had between 13 and 20 members, and four had more than 20 members. Unitary authorities were more likely to have smaller boards, while shire counties and metropolitan boroughs were more likely to have larger ones. This seems to reflect the likelihood that shire county boards will be swelled by district council members and have several clinical commissioning groups. Many metropolitan boroughs will have more clinical commissioning groups than unitary authorities.

Chair of the board

13.113 The Act does not prescribe who should be the chair of the board, but in 2012, a total of 25 boards had chosen the portfolio holder for health, adult social care or children's services as their chair, 17 had opted for their local authority leader or deputy leader, and in two cases, the local elected mayor had been chosen. The seniority of these roles reflects the importance that local authorities attach to the boards.

13.114 Some boards had made imaginative and unusual choices, such as an independent chair with experience in health and social care. One board had filled this role with the local superintendent commander of police, as they felt this post-holder had a special interest in the well-being of the community. In two cases, the role was shared between an elected member and a local primary care trust (PCT) or NHS trust chair. Only one board was chaired by the director of public health.

Notes

1 The expenses of the joint planning committee for Greater London, if incurred with the approval of at least two-thirds of the local planning authorities, are to be defrayed by those authorities in such proportions as they may decide or, in default, as the Secretary of State may determine: LGA 1985, s. 5(3).
2 LG&HA 1989. s. 6, applies to the Common Council of the city of London and successor bodies to residuary bodies, the same requirements as to the other local authorities under the LGFA 1988.
3 LGFA 1988, s. 114(2).
4 Ibid., s. 114(3).
5 Ibid., s. 114(3A)
6 Ibid., s. 115.
7 Ibid., s. 115(4).
8 If there is a defect in procedure, the court will intervene. Thus in *Ex parte Ladbroke Group* (1969), the decision of a committee was quashed where, when considering a contested application for renewal of a licence under the Betting, Gaming and Lotteries Act 1963, the

chairman twice announced that he was ready to give a decision before counsel had completed cross-examination and then appeared to reach a decision without consulting the other members of the committee.

9 Although it might be thought that committees of this character could be set up under the provisions of the LGA 1972, s. 102(4), which empower the establishment of committees 'to advise . . . on any matter relating to the discharge' of an authority's function, the obligation to decide questions 'by a majority of the members . . . present and voting thereon (Sch. 12, para. 39(1), as applied to committees by para. 44) would make this impracticable. These committees are not, therefore, committees of the local authority in the ordinary sense: in a way they exist in limbo. The Community Rights Project has argued in the past that there are in practice two meetings taking place simultaneously! Then the provisions on access for the public and press would apply to the councillors' meeting but not to the officers' meeting. This would appear to strain credibility beyond the limit.

10 LG&HA 1989, s. 12.

11 These representatives must be appointed by recognised trade unions from among the employees (s. 2 and Safety Representatives and Safety Committee Regulations 1977).

12 The job description is a statement, in whatever detail circumstances may require, of the content of the job; the duties and responsibilities, its place in the organisation, the salary grade and so on. The job or person specification lists the personal qualities required in the candidate who can be expected to perform the job to the prescribed standard. A statement covering these requirements will have been prepared to meet statutory requirements in the case of chief officer appointments.

13 An interesting point of some significance arose in *Cabaj v Westminster City Council* (1994), where the EAT ruled that the hearing of an employee's appeal against dismissal had been defective because only two of the three members of the council's internal appeals panel had been present. The EAT said that the council's standing orders (which prescribed a quorum of two for a sub-committee – and the panel was a sub-committee under that) did not overrule the requirements of the council's disciplinary code, which stipulated a membership of three and which formed part of the employee's contract of employment. The Court of Appeal's decision in 1996 accepted that the council had failed to observe its disciplinary code, but said this did not necessarily mean that the dismissal was unfair because that was for an industrial tribunal to decide in relation to all the relevant facts.

14 The head of an authority's paid service is appointed by 'designation' under the LG&HA 1989, s. 4(1). The officer is in practice usually the chief executive, but not necessarily so. This means that in many instances the appointment of 'head of the paid service' is not part of an officer's contract of employment in their substantive post of chief executive or otherwise and this may lead to complications: see further *Knight's Law and Practice of Local Authority Employment*. The monitoring officer is also a designated officer under s. 5.

15 Bains Report, para. 5.38.

16 RPA 1983, s. 95 and the European Parliamentary Election Regulations 2004 (reg. 67).

17 RPA 1983 s. 97, applied, with modifications, to elections of the European Assembly by the European Assembly Regulations 1984.

18 The Secretary of State is given power to direct inquiries wherever any minister is authorised to make decisions under the LGA 1972 or any other enactment relating to the functions of local authorities: s. 250.

Chapter 14
Meetings of other public bodies

Introduction

14.1 There are many bodies, statutory and otherwise, that operate within the sphere of local government, apart from local authorities themselves, either on the fringe of local government or with functions that were at one time the responsibility of local authorities. It seemed appropriate that there should be some brief reference to the meetings procedure of certain of these bodies. In some cases their practices are indistinguishable from those that have long been part of the local government process, but in others there are distinctive features.

14.2 There are also many quasi-official and voluntary bodies in which local authorities have an interest and/or to which they provide grant aid. Among the first category is, for example, the Local Government Association, and the national negotiating bodies regulating the pay and conditions of service of local authority staff. All these bodies substantially follow local authority practice as regards their meetings procedure.

Statutory joint committees

Created out of reorganisation

14.3 As a consequence of the abolition of the Greater London Council and the metropolitan county councils, provision was made in the LGA 1985 for the establishment of joint authorities to administer county-wide a number of former county functions that it was considered could not be discharged effectively and efficiently at borough or district level. In each case the joint authority is a corporate body, similar in most respects to a joint board, except that it owes its existence to an Act of Parliament rather than to a ministerial order, and in general they are treated as local authorities. Their members are subject to the same rules as to disqualification, and the statutory provisions in regard to meetings procedure apply to them, including the obligation to admit the public and press to their meetings.

14.4 The joint authorities established under the LGA 1985 are:

- Metropolitan fire and rescue authorities;
- London Fire and Emergency Planning Authority; and
- integrated transport authorities,

There are other similar authorities, e.g. a waste disposal authority established under the LGA 1985, s. 10; the Broads Authority and National Park Authorities.

Membership

14.5 The members of the joint authorities are in most cases the elected members of the constituent borough or district councils nominated to serve on them. The numbers to be appointed are prescribed and subject to alteration by ministerial order, having regard to the number of local government electors in the constituent authorities' areas (LGA 1985 s. 29, Sch. 10). It is expressly provided – distinguishing a joint authority from a joint board in this respect – that a constituent council may at any time terminate an appointment and appoint another member of the council in their place, but where this power of replacement is exercised the council must give notice one month in advance of the new appointment and of the termination of the previous appointment to the joint authority concerned (ss. 29, 31–32). The provisions as to the filling of vacancies follow substantially the usual pattern of such arrangements for joint committees and joint boards. The joint authority is required to give public notice of changes in its membership (s. 36).

Police authorities

Statutory provisions

14.6 Parts I and II of the Police and Magistrates' Courts Act 1994 (PMCA 1994) set up new police authorities in England and Wales from 1 April 1995. What had previously been outside the Metropolitan Police area, committees of county councils, combined authorities established under individual schemes or under the LGA 1965 in metropolitan areas became independent authorities with changed membership.[1] The original concept of these authorities, as largely removed from local control with chairmen appointed by the Home Secretary as proposed by the then government, was significantly changed during the passage of the Bill through Parliament. This was particularly evident in the House of Lords where many fears were expressed at what was seen as centralising control of the police. The resultant police authorities were controlled by local elected members but with added members. For many purposes the authorities remained classified and defined as local authorities, sharing many of the practices and problems of councils, but there are also significant differences. The relevant provisions of the PMCA 1994 were repealed and incorporated in the Police Act 1996 (PA 1996).

In 2012, the Government abolished the police authorities and replaced them with directly elected Police and Crime Commissioners (PCCs).[1] The Home Office considered that individual police authority members worked hard to engage their communities, but Police Authorities remained too invisible to the public and were not directly elected – only 8% of wards elected councillors who were police authority members. The Metropolitan Police Authority was also abolished and its functions were transferred to the Greater London Authority. For all other areas, scrutiny is undertaken by newly established Police and Crime Panels. Their role is to ensure that there is a robust overview at force level, and that decisions of the Police and Crime Commissioners are tested, on behalf of the public, on a regular basis. Police and Crime Panels in each force area are drawn from locally elected councillors from constituent wards and independent and lay members, who will bring additional skills, experience and diversity to the discussions.

Police and Crime Panels

14.7 Section 28 of the Police Reform and Social Responsibility Act 2011 provides for each police force area, outside London, to have a police and crime panel (PCP) from 25 April 2012, established and maintained in accordance with Schedule 6. Each PCP is either a committee of the local authority (for single-tier areas) or established as a joint committee of the relevant local authorities, and is a committee to which the LGA 1972 Sch. 12A (Access to Information) applies.

Membership

14.8 The Act makes detailed provisions on PCP composition in Schedule 6, part 4.

Where a force area consists of ten or fewer authorities, the number of members of the PCP will be ten, not including the co-opted members. Where a force area consists of more than ten authorities, there will be as many members as there are local authorities in the force area, plus two co-opted members.

Additional councillors may be co-opted on to the PCP, as long as two lay co-optees are also included, the size of the PCP does not exceed 20 and the Secretary of State approves the co-options.

Composition should be carried out in accordance with the 'fair representation objective' – essentially, each authority in the force area must be represented by at least one member if the total number of authorities in the area is fewer than ten, and one member if the number of authorities is ten or more.

Where agreement cannot be reached (see below) the Secretary of State has the power to make nominations. The PCC cannot be a member of the PCP, and MPs, Welsh AMs, MSPs, MEPs, staff of the PCC and civilian police staff may not be co-opted on to the PCP.

The Police and Crime Panels (Nominations, Appointments and Notifications) Regulations 2012 require:

- local authorities (via a single 'host' authority) to notify the Home Office that panel arrangements have been made; and
- individual local authorities to notify the Home Office where they have failed to nominate or appoint a councillor to the panel.

When seeking Home Office approval for additional co-optees, the panel must notify the Home Office of the reasons for determining that their requested number of co-optees will aid the panel in meeting, or meeting more effectively, the balanced appointment objective. The co-option of individual additional local authority members must be unanimously agreed by the panel. All notifications must be made in writing.

The Regulations require that where a local authority has the power to nominate a councillor to the police and crime panel and fails to do so, they must notify the Home Office within set timescales. Notification must be made 21 days after the annual general meeting of the local authority, at which appointments to joint committees of the authority are considered; or 21 days after the first meeting of the authority to be held after the power to nominate arose (e.g. when a vacancy became known).

14.9 Securing appointments giving the desired party balance can be difficult, particularly when taking in mind the 'balanced appointment' approach set out in Sch. 6 para. 31. Panels should be politically proportionate, and this is no different to the previous approach to appointments to the former Police Authorities. This means that they should be proportionate according to the total number of councillors in the force area. The most straightforward process would seem to be to calculate the number of seats each party is entitled to, and then divide the total between the relevant councils on some rational basis, e.g. population or expenditure.

While the Police Authority Regulations 2008 (SI 2008/630) as amended by the Police Authority (Community Engagement and Membership) Regulations 2010 are no longer in force, they provide a useful methodology setting out how councils are to appoint members so that they reflect party membership. This can result in some PCPs being allocated members whose policies are not to their liking. It would appear that they have no rights in the matter; the decision of each local authority would seem to be unimpeachable, except perhaps by application for judicial review, should the decision be made wholly on unreasonable grounds. No provision for appeal from a joint committee's decision is allowed for in the Act. Opportunity is given in the Act to change membership from time to time in order to retain the right party balance. In *R v Joint Committee for the purpose of making appointments to Humberside Police Authority ex parte East Riding of Yorkshire Council* (2001), Mrs Justice Rafferty in a somewhat controversial judgement considered the issue as to whether the number of independent members on each constituent authority should be taken into account by the joint committee when deciding how many members of each political party should be appointed to the police authority. She decided that independent members do not enter into the calculation of the balance of political parties and are, therefore, not entitled to any proportion of seats on the police authority irrespective of the numbers of independent members on the constituent authorities.

Who should be appointed to the PCP?

14.10 There is no prescription as to who should sit on the PCP. However, if there are any executive mayors in the force area, they will have a guaranteed seat (although they can delegate a councillor from the authority in their place). The question is whether remaining seats should go to executive or non-executive members.

Authorities should properly decide which members are best placed to sit on the PC Panel, given their skills set. It would be possible to take a 'mixed' approach, with some executive and some non-executive members sitting on the panel, but this might prove complex. The authorities involved in contributing to the PCP, by virtue of being in the relevant force area, must make 'panel arrangements' and 'rules of procedure' for the PCP. These are separate documents that will need to be agreed by all the local authorities in the force area, and doing this will help enshrine arrangements for the future, so that for democratic services staff, once the arrangements are in place, it should simply be a matter of applying them for the future.

Miscellaneous meetings

The rules of procedure should cover (Sch. 6, para. 25 of the Police Reform and Social Responsibility Act 2011) chairing (including appointment, removal and resignation of the chair). This is mandatory.

In addition, they may (and should, as a matter of good practice and to make it easier for future administration of the PCP) cover the formation of sub-committees, the making of decisions, arrangements for convening meetings, systems for circulating information in the run-up to, after and between meetings.

The panel arrangements should cover all other aspects of the establishment and maintenance of a PCP. The Act sets out (Sch. 6, para. 24) specific requirements, which must form part of the panel arrangements. These include:

- arrangements about the appointment of co-optees; and
- terms of office, appointment, resignation and removal of members of the PCP, and conditions of re-appointment.

Promotion of the role of the PCP (para. 29)

14.11 Administrative and other support and guidance is to be given to the PCP and to local authorities (para. 29).

As a matter of good practice, this support and guidance should also cover expenses arrangements.

It is likely that both the panel arrangements and the rules of procedure will, in most areas, closely reflect existing local government practice on the running of committees, as they are formal joint committees of the councils in the force area.

Combined authorities

Creation

14.12 Combined authorities, like economic prosperity boards, were introduced as a consequence of the Local Democracy, Economic Development and Construction Act 2009. They were focused on the operation of transport and economic development in an area covering at least two local authorities, who become the constituent authorities for the combined authority and appoint the members of the combined authority from their elected membership. Five were established and usually incorporated the existing integrated transport authority.

14.13 The 2009 Act was amended as a result of the Cities and Local Government Devolution Act 2016, including the basis and functions of such an authority. Now, combined authorities continue to be created following a review of the area under s. 108, but it is now on the wider remit of a review of the exercise of statutory functions in relation to an area ('the review area'). The review is undertaken with a view to deciding whether to prepare and publish a scheme for the establishment of a combined authority for the area if the review concludes that the establishment of a combined authority for an area would be likely to improve the exercise of statutory functions in relation to the area. The Secretary of State then makes an order if he or she also considers that test is met, the authorities concerned consent, and public consultation required has been undertaken (s. 110). Existing combined authorities could also review their area and function under s. 111.

Governance

14.14 Governance and functions of the combined authority is a matter for the authorities to set out in their scheme, subsequently translated into the Order. The Cities and Local Government Devolution Act 2016 made amendments to the LGA 1972, now including combined authorities under the definition of 'local authorities' for the purposes of s. 99 and Sch. 12. The 2016 Act changes to the 2009 Act also provided for functions to be transferred, wholly or jointly, from other public bodies to the combined authority by the Secretary of State: s. 105A (the devolution agenda). It also allowed for the Secretary of State by order to provide for a directly elected mayor for the combined authority area and for functions of the combined authority to be transferred to the mayor: s. 107D (the policy requisite to the full devolution agenda). Such a combined authority must now have both an overview and scrutiny committee and an audit committee.

Note

1 The Police Reform and Social Responsibility Act 2011.

Appendices

Appendix 1
Call-in guidance

What is a call-in?

A call-in is simply the referral of a decision made, but not yet implemented, to the overview and scrutiny committee. It is a key way of holding the cabinet to account. A called-in decision cannot be implemented until it has been considered by the overview and scrutiny committee, which can examine the issue and question the decision-taker on the actions taken.

What can be called-in?

Call-in powers relate to executive (cabinet) functions. Subject to the exceptions listed below, any decision made by the cabinet or a *key decision* made by an officer with delegated authority from the cabinet may be called-in.

What can't be called-in?

The following categories of decision cannot be called-in:

- a decision that is not a key decision, and which has been taken by an officer under delegated powers (*If, in the future, delegation to individual members of the cabinet is permitted, this exclusion will also apply to non-key decisions taken by the Leader or a Portfolio Holder under delegated powers*);
- a decision that the decision-taker has certified as urgent (giving reasons) in accordance with the Council's Rules of Procedure;
- a decision relating to a matter which has already been the subject of a call-in during the previous six months;
- *any* decision relating to a non-cabinet function, whether taken by a committee or an officer under delegated powers;
- a decision by the full council; or
- a decision taken at stage 4 of the call-in procedure (see below).

In particular, it should be noted that the overview and scrutiny committee cannot scrutinise individual decisions made by, or on behalf of, the Regulatory Committees of the council, e.g. decisions relating to development control, licensing, registration, consents and other permissions. Nor can it scrutinise decisions relating to individual members of staff taken by the Staffing Appeals and Officer Appointments Committees. Furthermore, although they may be key decisions (and included in the Forward Plan), decisions taken by the cabinet when preparing annual budget or new policy proposals *for submission to the full council* will not be subject to call-in. In these circumstances, the full council is responsible for the final decision and, in any event, the Council's Rules of Procedure require that the overview and scrutiny and policy development committees must be consulted by the cabinet, even if they have been involved earlier in the process anyway.

When can a decision be called-in?

It is important that the call-in process is not abused, nor causes unreasonable delay; the main tool of the overview and scrutiny committee to improve the delivery of policies and services should be detailed reviews, rather than call-ins.

The Overview and Scrutiny Procedure Rules in Part Four of the council's constitution specify formal safeguards for the use of call-in. These include rules about the number of members who must request a call-in and a restriction that prevents any decision on the same matter being called-in on more than one occasion within a six-month period. The constitution also suggests that call-ins should be reserved for exceptional circumstances. Broadly, a decision can be called-in when members:

- believe it may be contrary to the normal requirements for decision-making;
- believe it may be contrary to the council's agreed policy framework and/or budget;
- need further information from the decision-taker to explain why it was taken.

Call-in checklist

The above rules and criteria can be brought together in the following checklist of questions (or tests) that can be used when a member is considering a call-in. Questions 2–5 can also be used by authors to test draft reports for cabinet.

1 Can the decision actually be called in?	*If the answer to any of questions 1(a)-(g) is yes, then the decision CANNOT be called-in.*	
	a) Does it relate to a non-executive function?	☐
	b) Was it a non-key decision taken by an officer under delegated powers?	☐
	c) Was it classified as an urgent decision?	☐
	d) Has this issue been called-in in the last six months?	☐
	e) Does the decision relate to an existing call-in (i.e. decisions taken in relation to a reference back)?	☐
	f) Does the decision relate to the formulation of a policy or budget matter that requires full council approval?	☐
	g) Was it a decision taken by full council?	☐
2 Was the decision in accordance with the council's policy framework?	a) What is the relevant policy or strategy?	☐
	b) Is the decision contrary to that policy?	☐
	c) If yes, how?	☐

3	Was the decision in accordance with the agreed budget or budget procedures?	a) Is there funding for the proposal in an agreed budget/capital programme?	☐
		b) If no, have the rules for virement and supplementary estimates been observed?	☐
4	Was the decision taken in accordance with the principles of good decision-making (Article 12 of the Constitution)?	a) Does the decision comply with the council's constitution, i.e.:	
		• Articles of Constitution	☐
		• Scheme of Delegation	☐
		• Rules of Procedure	☐
		• Codes and Protocols?	☐
		b) Was the decision reasonable within the common meaning of the word, i.e. rational, based on sound judgment?	☐
		c) Was the decision reasonable within the legal definition of 'reasonableness', i.e. was everything relevant taken into account, and was everything irrelevant disregarded?	☐
		d) Was the decision proportionate, i.e. is the action proportionate to the desired outcome?	☐
		e) Was the decision taken on the basis of due consultation?	☐
		f) Was the decision taken on the basis of professional advice from officers?	☐
		g) Were human rights respected and/or will the decision give rise to any human rights implications, i.e. without discrimination, the right of an individual to:	
		• liberty and security;	☐
		• the enjoyment of their property;	☐
		• a fair trial;	☐
		• respect for private and family life;	☐
		• freedom of thought, conscience and religion;	☐
		• freedom of expression; and	☐
		• freedom of assembly and association, etc?	☐
		h) When the decision was taken, was there a presumption in favour of openness?	☐
5	Has the decision been well explained, i.e. do you need more information?	a) Was it clear what the reasons for the decision were?	☐
		b) Was it clear what the desired outcomes were?	☐
		c) Was it clear what alternative options (if any) were considered?	☐
		d) Was it clear why the alternative options were not chosen?	☐
		e) Do you need any more information/ clarification?	☐

How does call-in work?

Every decision that is subject to potential call-in cannot be implemented until the end of the call-in period. The call-in period lasts for *five working days* after notice of the decision is published by the Head of Legal and Democratic Services.

Decision notices will normally be published on the Friday of the week in which the decision was taken. This means that the normal call-in period will expire at 5pm on the following Friday (adjusted for bank holidays as appropriate). The call-in procedure itself follows four stages.

Stage 1

A valid call-in request must be submitted in accordance with the current rules in the constitution. The request must say who is making the call-in and to which decision it relates. It must also give brief reasons why the decision is being called in. A pro-forma is available. Requests may also be submitted by electronic mail, fax or telephone. If the call-in is to be submitted by e-mail, only one member need submit the actual form. However, individual e-mails (or letters) in support of the request must also be submitted by the other Members specified on the request form before the end of the call-in period.

Call-ins submitted by fax or telephone must be followed up in writing with the required number of signatures before the end of the call-in period.

Stage 2

When the officers receive a valid call-in request with respect to a decision, then that decision may not be implemented until that decision has completed the call-in procedure. The officers will refer the call-in to the next available meeting of the overview and scrutiny committee. A special meeting may also be convened if appropriate, e.g. in cases of urgency. Members who have requested the call-in will have the right to address the committee when it deals with the issue.

Stage 3

The overview and scrutiny committee will consider the called-in decision and decide to take one of the following courses of action (the overview and scrutiny committee's decision should not be adjourned or delayed without an exceptional reason):

- to allow the decision to be implemented without further delay;
- to refer the decision back to the cabinet (irrespective of who the original decision-taker was) together with the observations of the overview and scrutiny committee.

The cabinet will then take the final decision, and that decision may not be called in:

- to request the cabinet to allow further time for the overview and scrutiny committee to consider the issue and make observations at a later date;
- to seek the advice of the Head of Legal and Democratic Services and/or the Chief

Finance Officer as to whether the decision is contrary to, or not wholly in accordance with, the policy framework or the budget and, if applicable, to refer the matter to the full council for a final decision.

Stage 4

Reference back to cabinet

Where the overview and scrutiny committee decides to refer the decision back, the cabinet must reconsider the decision in the light of any observations of the committee. Where the overview and scrutiny committee has requested more time to consider an issue, the cabinet must have regard to the urgency, and to the Budget and Policy Framework Rules, when deciding whether to implement the decision.

Reference to Head of Legal and Democratic Services and/or Chief Finance Officer

The overview and scrutiny committee may refer any called-in decision to the Head of Legal and Democratic Services (Monitoring Officer) and/or the Chief Finance Officer if it considers it to be contrary to the policy framework or budget. The officer(s) will then submit a report on the matter to the next meeting of the cabinet. A copy of this report will be sent to all members of the council. No action may be taken in respect of the decision or its implementation pending that meeting.

If, in that report, the Head of Legal and Democratic Services (Monitoring Officer) and/or the Chief Finance Officer is of the view that a decision referred to him/her by the overview and scrutiny committee is not a departure from the policy framework or budget, the decision may be implemented immediately. A report to this effect will be submitted to the overview and scrutiny committee for information. If, however, a referred matter is deemed to be a departure from the policy framework or the budget by the Head of Legal and Democratic Services and/or the Chief Finance Officer, the cabinet has two options. Firstly, it may choose to adjust its decision to bring it within the policy framework or budget, in which case it can then be implemented. In these circumstances, the cabinet would submit a report to the next meeting of the overview and scrutiny committee explaining its actions. Secondly, if the cabinet does not wish to adjust its original decision, it must prepare a report for the full council. This report must include the views of the overview and scrutiny committee. No action may be taken in respect of the decision or its implementation until the council has met to consider the matter.

Reference to full council

Subject to the provisions above, the overview and scrutiny committee may require that any called-in matter *which has been deemed to be (and remains)* contrary to the policy framework or budget is referred to the full council. The report to the full council will set out the views of the cabinet and the overview and scrutiny committee and the advice of the Head of Legal and Democratic Services and/or the Chief Finance Officer. The council may:

- decide that the decision is within the existing policy framework and/or budget (in which case it can be implemented); or

- amend the financial regulations or policy concerned to encompass the decision (in which case it can be implemented); or
- agree that the decision is contrary to the policy framework or budget and require the cabinet to reconsider the matter in accordance with the advice of the officer(s).

This document is reproduced with the kind permission of St Edmundsbury Borough Council.

Appendix 2A
Welsh Model Code of Conduct

Local Authorities (Model Code of Conduct) (Wales) Order 2008/788

Schedule 1

The Model Code of Conduct

Part 1
Interpretation

1

(1A) In this code—

'co-opted member' ('aelod cyfetholedig'), in relation to a relevant authority, means a person who is not a member of the authority but who—

(a) is a member of any committee or sub-committee of the authority, or

(b) is a member of, and represents the authority on, any joint committee or joint sub-committee of the authority,

and who is entitled to vote on any question which falls to be decided at any meeting of that committee or sub-committee;

'meeting' ('cyfarfod') means any meeting—

(a) of the relevant authority,

(b) of any executive or board of the relevant authority,

(c) of any committee, sub-committee, joint committee or joint sub-committee of the relevant authority or of any such committee, sub-committee, joint committee or joint sub-committee of any executive or board of the authority, or

(d) where members or officers of the relevant authority are present other than a meeting of a political group constituted in accordance with regulation 8 of the Local Government (Committees and Political Groups) Regulations 1990,

and includes circumstances in which a member of an executive or board or an officer acting alone exercises a function of an authority;

'member' ('aelod') includes, unless the context requires otherwise, a co-opted member;

['register of members' interests' ('cofrestr o fuddiannau'r aelodau') means the register established and maintained under section 81 of the Local Government Act 2000;]

['registered society' means a society, other than a society registered as a credit union, which is—

(a) a registered society within the meaning given by section 1(1) of the Co-operative and Community Benefit Societies Act 2014; or
(b) a society registered or deemed to be registered under the Industrial and Provident Societies Act (Northern Ireland) 1969;]

'relevant authority' ('awdurdod perthnasol') means—

(a) a county council,
(b) a county borough council,
(c) a community council,
(d) a fire and rescue authority constituted by a scheme under section 2 of the Fire and Rescue Services Act 2004 or a scheme to which section 4 of that Act applies,
(e) a National Park authority established under section 63 of the Environment Act 1995;

'you' ('chi') means you as a member or co-opted member of a relevant authority; and

'your authority' ('eich awdurdod') means the relevant authority of which you are a member or co-opted member.

[(2) In relation to a community council—

(a) 'proper officer' ('swyddog priodol') means an officer of that council within the meaning of section 270(3) of the Local Government Act 1972; and
(b) 'standards committee' ('pwyllgor safonau') means the standards committee of the county or county borough council which has functions in relation to the community council for which it is responsible under section 56(1) and (2) of the Local Government Act 2000.]

Part 2

General Provisions

2

(1) Save where paragraph 3(a) applies, you must observe this code of conduct—

(a) whenever you conduct the business, or are present at a meeting, of your authority;
(b) whenever you act, claim to act or give the impression you are acting in the role of member to which you were elected or appointed;
(c) whenever you act, claim to act or give the impression you are acting as a representative of your authority; or
(d) at all times and in any capacity, in respect of conduct identified in paragraphs 6(1)(a) and 7.

(2) You should read this code together with the general principles prescribed under section 49(2) of the Local Government Act 2000 in relation to Wales.

3

Where you are elected, appointed or nominated by your authority to serve—

(a) on another relevant authority, or any other body, which includes a . . . Local Health Board you must, when acting for that other authority or body, comply with the code of conduct of that other authority or body; or
(b) on any other body which does not have a code relating to the conduct of its members, you must, when acting for that other body, comply with this

code of conduct, except and insofar as it conflicts with any other lawful obligations to which that other body may be subject.

4

You must—

(a) carry out your duties and responsibilities with due regard to the principle that there should be equality of opportunity for all people, regardless of their gender, race, disability, sexual orientation, age or religion;
(b) show respect and consideration for others;
(c) not use bullying behaviour or harass any person; and
(d) not do anything which compromises, or which is likely to compromise, the impartiality of those who work for, or on behalf of, your authority.

5

You must not—

(a) disclose confidential information or information which should reasonably be regarded as being of a confidential nature, without the express consent of a person authorised to give such consent, or unless required by law to do so;
(b) prevent any person from gaining access to information to which that person is entitled by law.

6

(1) You must—

(a) not conduct yourself in a manner which could reasonably be regarded as bringing your office or authority into disrepute;
(b) report, whether through your authority's confidential reporting procedure or direct to the proper authority, any conduct by another member or anyone who works for, or on behalf of, your authority which you reasonably believe involves or is likely to involve criminal behaviour (which for the purposes of this paragraph does not include offences or behaviour capable of punishment by way of a fixed penalty);
(c) report . . . to your authority's monitoring officer any conduct by another member which you reasonably believe breaches this code of conduct;
(d) not make vexatious, malicious or frivolous complaints against other members or anyone who works for, or on behalf of, your authority.

(2) You must comply with any request of your authority's monitoring officer, or the Public Services Ombudsman for Wales, in connection with an investigation conducted in accordance with their respective statutory powers.

7

You must not—

(a) in your official capacity or otherwise, use or attempt to use your position improperly to confer on or secure for yourself, or any other person, an advantage or create or avoid for yourself, or any other person, a disadvantage;
(b) use, or authorise others to use, the resources of your authority—
    (i) imprudently;
    (ii) in breach of your authority's requirements;
    (iii) unlawfully;

(iv) other than in a manner which is calculated to facilitate, or to be conducive to, the discharge of the functions of the authority or of the office to which you have been elected or appointed;
(v) improperly for political purposes; or
(vi) improperly for private purposes.

8

You must—

(a) when participating in meetings or reaching decisions regarding the business of your authority, do so on the basis of the merits of the circumstances involved and in the public interest having regard to any relevant advice provided by your authority's officers, in particular by—
(i) the authority's head of paid service;
(ii) the authority's chief finance officer;
(iii) the authority's monitoring officer;
(iv) the authority's chief legal officer (who should be consulted when there is any doubt as to the authority's power to act, as to whether the action proposed lies within the policy framework agreed by the authority or where the legal consequences of action or failure to act by the authority might have important repercussions);
(b) give reasons for all decisions in accordance with any statutory requirements and any reasonable additional requirements imposed by your authority.

9

You must—

(a) observe the law and your authority's rules governing the claiming of expenses and allowances in connection with your duties as a member;
(b) avoid accepting from anyone gifts, hospitality (other than official hospitality, such as a civic reception or a working lunch duly authorised by your authority), material benefits or services for yourself or any person which might place you, or reasonably appear to place you, under an improper obligation.

Part 3

Interests

Personal Interests

10

(1) You must in all matters consider whether you have a personal interest, and whether this code of conduct requires you to disclose that interest.
(2) You must regard yourself as having a personal interest in any business of your authority if—
(a) it relates to, or is likely to affect—
(i) any employment or business carried on by you;
(ii) any person who employs or has appointed you, any firm in which you are a partner or any company for which you are a remunerated director;

(iii) any person, other than your authority, who has made a payment to you in respect of your election or any expenses incurred by you in carrying out your duties as a member;

(iv) any corporate body which has a place of business or land in your authority's area, and in which you have a beneficial interest in a class of securities of that body that exceeds the nominal value of £25,000 or one hundredth of the total issued share capital of that body;

(v) any contract for goods, services or works made between your authority and you or a firm in which you are a partner, a company of which you are a remunerated director, or a body of the description specified in sub-paragraph (iv) above;

(vi) any land in which you have a beneficial interest and which is in the area of your authority;

(vii) any land where the landlord is your authority and the tenant is a firm in which you are a partner, a company of which you are a remunerated director, or a body of the description specified in sub-paragraph (iv) above;

(viii) any body to which you have been elected, appointed or nominated by your authority;

(ix) any—

(aa) public authority or body exercising functions of a public nature;

(bb) company, [registered society], charity, or body directed to charitable purposes;

(cc) body whose principal purposes include the influence of public opinion or policy;

(dd) trade union or professional association; or

(ee) private club, society or association operating within your authority's area,

in which you have membership or hold a position of general control or management;

(x) any land in your authority's area in which you have a licence (alone or jointly with others) to occupy for 28 days or longer;

(b) . . .

(c) a decision upon it might reasonably be regarded as affecting—

(i) your well-being or financial position, or that of a person with whom you live, or any person with whom you have a close personal association;

(ii) any employment or business carried on by persons as described in 10(2)(c)(i);

(iii) any person who employs or has appointed such persons described in 10(2)(c)(i), any firm in which they are a partner, or any company of which they are directors;

(iv) any corporate body in which persons as described in 10(2)(c)(i) have a beneficial interest in a class of securities exceeding the nominal value of £5,000; or

(v) any body listed in paragraphs 10(2)(a)(ix)(aa) to (ee) in which persons described in 10(2)(c)(i) hold a position of general control or management,

to a greater extent than the majority of—

(aa) in the case of an authority with electoral divisions or wards, other council tax payers, rate payers or inhabitants of the electoral division or ward, as the case may be, affected by the decision; or

(bb) in all other cases, other council tax payers, ratepayers or inhabitants of the authority's area.

Disclosure of Personal Interests

11

(1) Where you have a personal interest in any business of your authority and you attend a meeting at which that business is considered, you must disclose orally to that meeting the existence and nature of that interest before or at the commencement of that consideration, or when the interest becomes apparent.

(2) Where you have a personal interest in any business of your authority and you make—

(a) written representations (whether by letter, facsimile or some other form of electronic communication) to a member or officer of your authority regarding that business, you should include details of that interest in the written communication; or

(b) oral representations (whether in person or some form of electronic communication) to a member or officer of your authority you should disclose the interest at the commencement of such representations, or when it becomes apparent to you that you have such an interest, and confirm the representation and interest in writing within 14 days of the representation.

(3) Subject to paragraph 14(1)(b) below, where you have a personal interest in any business of your authority and you have made a decision in exercising a function of an executive or board, you must in relation to that business ensure that any written statement of that decision records the existence and nature of your interest.

(4) You must, in respect of a personal interest not previously disclosed, before or immediately after the close of a meeting where the disclosure is made pursuant to sub-paragraph 11(1), give written notification to your authority in accordance with any requirements identified by your authority's monitoring officer[, or in relation to a community council, your authority's proper officer] from time to time but, as a minimum containing—

(a) details of the personal interest;

(b) details of the business to which the personal interest relates; and

(c) your signature.

(5) Where you have agreement from your monitoring officer that the information relating to your personal interest is sensitive information, pursuant to paragraph 16(1), your obligations under this paragraph 11 to disclose such

information, whether orally or in writing, are to be replaced with an obligation to disclose the existence of a personal interest and to confirm that your monitoring officer has agreed that the nature of such personal interest is sensitive information.

(6) For the purposes of sub-paragraph (4), a personal interest will only be deemed to have been previously disclosed if written notification has been provided in accordance with this code since the last date on which you were elected, appointed or nominated as a member of your authority.

(7) For the purposes of sub-paragraph (3), where no written notice is provided in accordance with that paragraph you will be deemed as not to have declared a personal interest in accordance with this code.

Prejudicial Interests

12

(1) Subject to sub-paragraph (2) below, where you have a personal interest in any business of your authority you also have a prejudicial interest in that business if the interest is one which a member of the public with knowledge of the relevant facts would reasonably regard as so significant that it is likely to prejudice your judgement of the public interest.

(2) Subject to sub-paragraph (3), you will not be regarded as having a prejudicial interest in any business where that business—

(a) relates to—

(i) another relevant authority of which you are also a member;

(ii) another public authority or body exercising functions of a public nature in which you hold a position of general control or management;

(iii) a body to which you have been elected, appointed or nominated by your authority;

(iv) your role as a school governor (where not appointed or nominated by your authority) unless it relates particularly to the school of which you are a governor;

(v) your role as a member of a Local Health Board where you have not been appointed or nominated by your authority;

(b) relates to—

(i) the housing functions of your authority where you hold a tenancy or lease with your authority, provided that you do not have arrears of rent with your authority of more than two months, and provided that those functions do not relate particularly to your tenancy or lease;

(ii) the functions of your authority in respect of school meals, transport and travelling expenses, where you are a guardian, parent, grandparent or have parental responsibility (as defined in section 3 of the Children Act 1989) of a child in full time education, unless it relates particularly to the school which that child attends;

(iii) the functions of your authority in respect of statutory sick pay under Part XI of the Social Security Contributions and Benefits Act 1992, where you are in receipt of, or are entitled to the receipt of such pay from your authority;

[(iv) the functions of your authority in respect of an allowance or payment made in accordance with the provisions of Part 8 of the Local Government (Wales) Measure 2011, or an allowance or pension provided under section 18 of the Local Government and Housing Act 1989;]

(c) your role as a community councillor in relation to a grant, loan or other form of financial assistance made by your community council to community or voluntary organisations up to a maximum of £500.

(3) The exemptions in subparagraph (2)(a) do not apply where the business relates to the determination of any approval, consent, licence, permission or registration.

Overview and Scrutiny Committees

13

You also have a prejudicial interest in any business before an overview and scrutiny committee of your authority (or of a sub-committee of such a committee) where—

(a) that business relates to a decision made (whether implemented or not) or action taken by your authority's executive, board or another of your authority's committees, sub-committees, joint committees or joint sub-committees; and

(b) at the time the decision was made or action was taken, you were a member of the executive, board, committee, sub-committee, joint-committee or joint sub-committee mentioned in sub-paragraph (a) and you were present when that decision was made or action was taken.

Participation in Relation to Disclosed Interests

14

(1) Subject to sub-paragraphs (2), [(2A),] (3) and (4), where you have a prejudicial interest in any business of your authority you must, unless you have obtained a dispensation from your authority's standards committee—

(a) withdraw from the room, chamber or place where a meeting considering the business is being held—

(i) where sub-paragraph (2) applies, immediately after the period for making representations, answering questions or giving evidence relating to the business has ended and in any event before further consideration of the business begins, whether or not the public are allowed to remain in attendance for such consideration; or

(ii) in any other case, whenever it becomes apparent that that business is being considered at that meeting;

(b) not exercise executive or board functions in relation to that business;

(c) not seek to influence a decision about that business;

(d) not make any written representations (whether by letter, facsimile or some other form of electronic communication) in relation to that business; and

(e) not make any oral representations (whether in person or some form of electronic communication) in respect of that business or immediately cease to make such oral representations when the prejudicial interest becomes apparent.

(2) Where you have a prejudicial interest in any business of your authority you may attend a meeting but only for the purpose of making representations, answering questions or giving evidence relating to the business, provided that the public are also allowed to attend the meeting for the same purpose, whether under a statutory right or otherwise.

[(2A) Where you have a prejudicial interest in any business of your authority you may submit written representations to a meeting relating to that business, provided that the public are allowed to attend the meeting for the purpose of making representations, answering questions or giving evidence relating to the business, whether under a statutory right or otherwise.

(2B) When submitting written representations under sub-paragraph (2A) you must comply with any procedure that your authority may adopt for the submission of such representations.]

(3) Sub-paragraph (1) does not prevent you attending and participating in a meeting if—

- (a) you are required to attend a meeting of an overview or scrutiny committee, by such committee exercising its statutory powers; or
- (b) you have the benefit of a dispensation provided that you—
  - (i) state at the meeting that you are relying on the dispensation; and
  - (ii) before or immediately after the close of the meeting give written notification to your authority containing—
    - (aa) details of the prejudicial interest;
    - (bb) details of the business to which the prejudicial interest relates;
    - (cc) details of, and the date on which, the dispensation was granted; and
    - (dd) your signature.

(4) Where you have a prejudicial interest and are making written or oral representations to your authority in reliance upon a dispensation, you must provide details of the dispensation within any such written or oral representation and, in the latter case, provide written notification to your authority within 14 days of making the representation.

Part 4

The Register of Members' Interests

[Registration of Personal Interests

15

[(1) Subject to sub-paragraph (4), you must, within 28 days of—

- (a) your authority's code of conduct being adopted or the mandatory provisions of this model code being applied to your authority; or
- (b) your election or appointment to office (if that is later),

register your personal interests, where they fall within a category mentioned in paragraph 10(2)(a), in your authority's register of members' interests by providing written notification to your authority's monitoring officer.

(2) Subject to sub-paragraph (4), you must, within 28 days of becoming aware of

any new personal interest falling within a category mentioned in paragraph 10(2)(a), register that new personal interest in your authority's register of members' interests by providing written notification to your authority's monitoring officer.

(3) Subject to sub-paragraph (4), you must, within 28 days of becoming aware of any change to a registered personal interest falling within a category mentioned in paragraph 10(2)(a), register that change in your authority's register of members' interests by providing written notification to your authority's monitoring officer, or in the case of a community council to your authority's proper officer.

(4) Sub-paragraphs (1), (2) and (3) do not apply to sensitive information determined in accordance with paragraph 16(1).

(5) Sub-paragraphs (1) and (2) do not apply if you are a member of a relevant authority which is community council when you act in your capacity as a member of such an authority.

(6) You must, when disclosing a personal interest in accordance with paragraph 11 for the first time, register that personal interest in your authority's register of members' interests by providing written notification to your authority's monitoring officer, or in the case of a community council to your authority's proper officer.]

Sensitive Information

16

(1) Where you consider that the information relating to any of your personal interests is sensitive information, and your authority's monitoring officer agrees, you need not include that information when registering that interest, or, as the case may be, a change to the interest under paragraph 15.

(2) You must, within 28 days of becoming aware of any change of circumstances which means that information excluded under sub-paragraph (1) is no longer sensitive information, notify your authority's monitoring officer[, or in relation to a community council, your authority's proper officer] asking that the information be included in your authority's register of members' interests.

(3) In this code, 'sensitive information' ('gwybodaeth sensitif') means information whose availability for inspection by the public creates, or is likely to create, a serious risk that you or a person who lives with you may be subjected to violence or intimidation.

Registration of Gifts and Hospitality

17

You must, within 28 days of receiving any gift, hospitality, material benefit or advantage above a value specified in a resolution of your authority, provide written notification to your authority's monitoring officer[, or in relation to a community council, to your authority's proper officer] of the existence and nature of that gift, hospitality, material benefit or advantage.

Appendix 2B
Old Model Code of Conduct

Statutory Instrument 2007 No. 1159 [Repealed]

The Local Authorities (Model Code of Conduct) Order 2007

Schedule

The Model Code of Conduct

Part 1: General provisions

Introduction and interpretation

1–(1) This Code applies to **you** as a member of an authority.

(2) You should read this Code together with the general principles prescribed by the Secretary of State.

(3) It is your responsibility to comply with the provisions of this Code.

(4) In this Code, 'meeting' means any meeting of–

(a) the authority;

(b) the executive of the authority;

(c) any of the authority's or its executive's committees, sub-committees, joint committees, joint sub-committees, or area committees;

'member' includes a co-opted member and an appointed member.

(5) In relation to a parish council, references to an authority's monitoring officer and an authority's standards committee shall be read, respectively, as references to the monitoring officer and the standards committee of the district council or unitary county council which has functions in relation to the parish council for which it is responsible under section 55(12) of the Local Government Act 2000.

Scope

2–(1) Subject to sub-paragraphs (2) to (5), you must comply with this Code whenever you–

(a) conduct the business of your authority (which, in this Code, includes the business of the office to which you are elected or appointed); or

(b) act, claim to act or give the impression you are acting as a representative of your authority, and references to your official capacity are construed accordingly.

(2) Subject to sub-paragraphs (3) and (4), this Code does not have effect in relation to your conduct other than where it is in your official capacity.

(3) In addition to having effect in relation to conduct in your official capacity, paragraphs 3(2)(c), 5 and 6(a) also have effect, at any other time, where that conduct constitutes a criminal offence for which you have been convicted.

(4) Conduct to which this Code applies (whether that is conduct in your official capacity or conduct mentioned in sub-paragraph (3)) includes a criminal offence for which you are convicted (including an offence you committed before the date you took office, but for which you are convicted after that date).

(5) Where you act as a representative of your authority–
- (a) on another relevant authority, you must, when acting for that other authority, comply with that other authority's code of conduct; or
- (b) on any other body, you must, when acting for that other body, comply with your authority's code of conduct, except and insofar as it conflicts with any other lawful obligations to which that other body may be subject.

General obligations

3–(1) You must treat others with respect.

(2) You must not–
- (a) do anything which may cause your authority to breach any of the equality enactments (as defined in section 33 of the Equality Act 2006);
- (b) bully any person;
- (c) intimidate or attempt to intimidate any person who is or is likely to be–
  - (i) a complainant,
  - (ii) a witness, or
  - (iii) involved in the administration of any investigation or proceedings,

  in relation to an allegation that a member (including yourself) has failed to comply with his or her authority's code of conduct; or
- (d) do anything which compromises or is likely to compromise the impartiality of those who work for, or on behalf of, your authority.

(3) In relation to police authorities and the Metropolitan Police Authority, for the purposes of sub-paragraph (2)(d) those who work for, or on behalf of, an authority are deemed to include a police officer.

(4) You must not–
- (a) disclose information given to you in confidence by anyone, or information acquired by you which you believe, or ought reasonably to be aware, is of a confidential nature, except where–
  - (i) you have the consent of a person authorised to give it;
  - (ii) you are required by law to do so;
  - (iii) the disclosure is made to a third party for the purpose of obtaining professional advice provided that the third party agrees not to disclose the information to any other person; or
  - (iv) the disclosure is (aa) reasonable and in the public interest; and (bb)

made in good faith and in compliance with the reasonable requirements of the authority; or

(b) prevent another person from gaining access to information to which that person is entitled by law.

(5) You must not conduct yourself in a manner which could reasonably be regarded as bringing your office or authority into disrepute.

(6) You–

(a) must not use or attempt to use your position as a member improperly to confer on or secure for yourself or any other person, an advantage or disadvantage; and

(b) must, when using or authorising the use by others of the resources of your authority–

(i) act in accordance with your authority's reasonable requirements;

(ii) ensure that such resources are not used improperly for political purposes (including party political purposes); and

(c) must have regard to any applicable Local Authority Code of Publicity made under the Local Government Act 1986.

7–(1) When reaching decisions on any matter you must have regard to any relevance provided to you by–

(a) your authority's chief finance officer; or

(b) your authority's monitoring officer, where that officer is acting pursuant to his or her statutory duties.

(2) You must give reasons for all decisions in accordance with any statutory requirements and any reasonable additional requirements imposed by your authority.

Part 2: interests

Personal interests

8–(1) You have a personal interest in any business of your authority where either–

(a) it relates to or is likely to affect–

(i) any body of which you are a member or in a position of general control or management and to which you are appointed or nominated by your authority;

(ii) any body–

(aa) exercising functions of a public nature;

(bb) directed to charitable purposes; or

(cc) one of whose principal purposes includes the influence of public opinion or policy (including any political party or trade union), of which you are a member or in a position of general control or management;

(iii) any employment or business carried on by you;

(iv) any person or body who employs or has appointed you;

(v) any person or body, other than a relevant authority, who has made a payment to you in respect of your election or any expenses incurred by you in carrying out your duties;

(vi) any person or body who has a place of business or land in your authority's area, and in whom you have a beneficial interest in a class of securities of that person or body that exceeds the nominal value of £25,000 or one hundredth of the total issued share capital (whichever is the lower);

(vii) any contract for goods, services or works made between your authority and you or a firm in which you are a partner, a company of which you are a remunerated director, or a person or body of the description specified in paragraph (vi);

(viii) the interests of any person from whom you have received a gift or hospitality with an estimated value of at least £25;

(ix) any land in your authority's area in which you have a beneficial interest;

(x) any land where the landlord is your authority and you are, or a firm in which you are a partner, a company of which you are a remunerated director, or a person or body of the description specified in paragraph (vi) is, the tenant;

(xi) any land in the authority's area for which you have a licence (alone or jointly with others) to occupy for 28 days or longer; or

(c) a decision in relation to that business might reasonably be regarded as affecting your well-being or financial position or the well-being or financial position of a relevant person to a greater extent than the majority of–

(i) (in the case of authorities with electoral divisions or wards) other council tax payers, ratepayers or inhabitants of the electoral division or ward, as the case may be, affected by the decision;

(ii) (in the case of the Greater London Authority) other council tax payers, ratepayers or inhabitants of the Assembly constituency affected by the decision; or

(iii) (in all other cases) other council tax payers, ratepayers or inhabitants of your authority's area.

(2) In sub-paragraph (1)(b), a relevant person is–

(a) a member of your family or any person with whom you have a close association; or

(b) any person or body who employs or has appointed such persons, any firm in which they are a partner, or any company of which they are directors;

(c) any person or body in whom such persons have a beneficial interest in a class of securities exceeding the nominal value of £25,000; or

(d) any body of a type described in sub-paragraph (1)(a)(i) or (ii).

Disclosure of personal interests

9–(1) Subject to sub-paragraphs (2) to (7), where you have a personal interest in any business of your authority and you attend a meeting of your authority at which the business is considered, you must disclose to that meeting the existence and nature of that interest at the commencement of that consideration, or when the interest becomes apparent.

(2) Where you have a personal interest in any business of your authority which relates to or is likely to affect a person described in paragraph 8(1)(a)(i) or 8(1)(a)(ii)(aa), you need only disclose to the meeting the existence and nature of that interest when you address the meeting on that business.

(3) Where you have a personal interest in any business of the authority of the type mentioned in paragraph 8(1)(a)(viii), you need not disclose the nature or existence of that interest to the meeting if the interest was registered more than three years before the date of the meeting.

(4) Sub-paragraph (1) only applies where you are aware or ought reasonably to be aware of the existence of the personal interest.

(5) Where you have a personal interest but, by virtue of paragraph 14, sensitive information relating to it is not registered in your authority's register of members' interests, you must indicate to the meeting that you have a personal interest, but need not disclose the sensitive information to the meeting.

(6) Subject to paragraph 12(1)(b), where you have a personal interest in any business of your authority and you have made an executive decision in relation to that business, you must ensure that any written statement of that decision records the existence and nature of that interest.

(7) In this paragraph, 'executive decision' is to be construed in accordance with any regulations made by the Secretary of State under section 22 of the Local Government Act 2000.

Prejudicial interest generally

10–(1) Subject to sub-paragraph (2), where you have a personal interest in any business of your authority you also have a prejudicial interest in that business where the interest is one which a member of the public with knowledge of the relevant facts would reasonably regard as so significant that it is likely to prejudice your judgement of the public interest.

(2) You do not have a prejudicial interest in any business of the authority where that business–

(a) does not affect your financial position or the financial position of a person or body described in paragraph 8;

(b) does not relate to the determining of any approval, consent, licence, permission or registration in relation to you or any person or body described in paragraph 8; or

(c) relates to thc functions of your authority in respect of–

(i) housing, where you are a tenant of your authority provided that those functions do not relate particularly to your tenancy or lease;

(ii) school meals or school transport and travelling expenses, where you are a parent or guardian of a child in full time education, or are a parent governor of a school, unless it relates particularly to the school which the child attends;

(iii) statutory sick pay under Part XI of the Social Security Contributions and Benefits Act 1992, where you are in receipt of, or are entitled to the receipt of, such pay;

(iv) an allowance, payment or indemnity given to members;

(v) any ceremonial honour given to members; and
(vi) setting council tax or a precept under the Local Government Finance Act 1992.

Prejudicial interests arising in relation to overview and scrutiny committees

11 You also have a prejudicial interest in any business before an overview and scrutiny committee of your authority (or of a sub-committee of such a committee) where–

(a) that business relates to a decision made (whether implemented or not) or action taken by your authority's executive or another of your authority's committees, sub-committees, joint committees or joint sub-committees; and
(b) at the time the decision was made or action was taken, you were a member of the executive, committee, sub-committee, joint committee or joint sub-committee mentioned in paragraph (a) and you were present when that decision was made or action was taken.

Effect of prejudicial interests on participation

12–(1) Subject to sub-paragraph (2), where you have a prejudicial interest in any business of your authority–

(a) you must withdraw from the room or chamber where a meeting considering the business is being held–
    (i) in a case where sub-paragraph (2) applies, immediately after making representations, answering questions or giving evidence;
    (ii) in any other case, whenever it becomes apparent that the business is being considered at that meeting; unless you have obtained a dispensation from your authority's standards committee;
(b) you must not exercise executive functions in relation to that business; and
(c) you must not seek improperly to influence a decision about that business.

(2) Where you have a prejudicial interest in any business of your authority, you may attend a meeting (including a meeting of the overview and scrutiny committee of your authority or of a sub-committee of such a committee) but only for the purpose of making representations, answering questions or giving evidence relating to the business, provided that the public are also allowed to attend the meeting for the same purpose, whether under a statutory right or otherwise.

Part 3: registration of members' interests

Registration of members' interests

13–(1) Subject to paragraph 14, you must, within 28 days of–

(a) this Code being adopted by or applied to your authority; or
(b) your election or appointment to office (where that is later), register in your authority's register of members' interests (maintained under section 81(1) of the Local Government Act 2000) details of your personal

interests where they fall within a category mentioned in paragraph 8(1) (a), by providing written notification to your authority's monitoring officer.

(2) Subject to paragraph 14, you must, within 28 days of becoming aware of any new personal interest or change to any personal interest registered under paragraph (1), register details of that new personal interest or change by providing written notification to your authority's monitoring officer.

Sensitive information

14–(1) Where you consider that the information relating to any of your personal interests is sensitive information, and your authority's monitoring officer agrees, you need not include that information when registering that interest, or, as the case may be, a change to that interest under paragraph 13.

(2) You must, within 28 days of becoming aware of any change of circumstances which means that information excluded under paragraph (1) is no longer sensitive information, notify your authority's monitoring officer asking that the information be included in your authority's register of members' interests.

(3) In this Code, 'sensitive information' means information whose availability for inspection by the public creates, or is likely to create, a serious risk that you or a person who lives with you may be subjected to violence or intimidation.

Appendix 2C
LGA Template Code of Conduct

As a member or co-opted member of [X authority] I have a responsibility to represent the community and work constructively with our staff and partner organisations to secure better social, economic and environmental outcomes for all.

In accordance with the Localism Act provisions, when acting in this capacity I am committed to behaving in a manner that is consistent with the following principles to achieve best value for our residents and maintain public confidence in this authority.

SELFLESSNESS: Holders of public office should act solely in terms of the public interest.

INTEGRITY: Holders of public office must avoid placing themselves under any obligation to people or organisations that might try inappropriately to influence them in their work. They should not act or take decisions in order to gain financial or other material benefits for themselves, their family, or their friends. They must declare and resolve any interests and relationships.

OBJECTIVITY: Holders of public office must act and take decisions impartially, fairly and on merit, using the best evidence and without discrimination or bias.

ACCOUNTABILITY: Holders of public office are accountable to the public for their decisions and actions and must submit themselves to the scrutiny necessary to ensure this.

OPENNESS: Holders of public office should act and take decisions in an open and transparent manner. Information should not be withheld from the public unless there are clear and lawful reasons for so doing.

HONESTY: Holders of public office should be truthful..

LEADERSHIP: Holders of public office should exhibit these principles in their own behaviour. They should actively promote and robustly support the principles and be willing to challenge poor behaviour wherever it occurs.

The Act further provides for registration and disclosure of interests and in [X authority] this will be done as follows: [to be completed by individual authorities]

As a Member of [X authority], my conduct will in particular address the statutory principles of the code of conduct by:

- championing the needs of residents – the whole community and in a special way my constituents, including those who did not vote for me – and putting their interests first;
- dealing with representations or enquiries from residents, members of our communities and visitors fairly, appropriately and impartially;
- not allowing other pressures, including the financial interests of myself or others connected to me, to deter me from pursuing constituents' casework, the interests

of the [county][borough][Authority's area] or the good governance of the authority in a proper manner;

- exercising independent judgement and not compromising my position by placing myself under obligations to outside individuals or organisations who might seek to influence the way I perform my duties as a member/co-opted member of this authority;
- listening to the interests of all parties, including relevant advice from statutory and other professional officers, taking all relevant information into consideration, remaining objective and making decisions on merit;
- being accountable for my decisions and cooperating when scrutinised internally and externally, including by local residents;
- contributing to making this authority's decision-making processes as open and transparent as possible to enable residents to understand the reasoning behind those decisions and to be informed when holding me and other members to account but restricting access to information when the wider public interest or the law requires it;
- behaving in accordance with all our legal obligations, alongside any requirements contained within this authority's policies, protocols and procedures, including on the use of the Authority's resources;
- valuing my colleagues and staff and engaging with them in an appropriate manner and one that underpins the mutual respect between us that is essential to good local government;
- always treating people with respect, including the organisations and public I engage with and those I work alongside; and
- providing leadership through behaving in accordance with these principles when championing the interests of the community with other organisations as well as within this authority.

Appendix 2D
DCLG Illustrative text for local code of conduct

From: Department for Communities and Local Government
First published: 11 April 2012
Last updated: 20 September 2013

Illustrative text for code dealing with the conduct expected of members and co-opted members of the authority when acting in that capacity

You are a member or co-opted member of the [name] council and hence you shall have regard to the following principles – selflessness, integrity, objectivity, accountability, openness, honesty and leadership.

Accordingly, when acting in your capacity as a member or co-opted member:

You must act solely in the public interest and should never improperly confer an advantage or disadvantage on any person or act to gain financial or other material benefits for yourself, your family, a friend or close associate.

You must not place yourself under a financial or other obligation to outside individuals or organisations that might seek to influence you in the performance of your official duties.

When carrying out your public duties you must make all choices, such as making public appointments, awarding contracts or recommending individuals for rewards or benefits, on merit.

You are accountable for your decisions to the public and you must cooperate fully with whatever scrutiny is appropriate to your office.

You must be as open as possible about your decisions and actions and the decisions and actions of your authority and should be prepared to give reasons for those decisions and actions.

You must declare any private interests, both pecuniary and non-pecuniary, including your membership of any Trade Union, that relate to your public duties and must take steps to resolve any conflicts arising in a way that protects the public interest, including registering and declaring interests in a manner conforming with the procedures set out in the box below.

You must, when using or authorising the use by others of the resources of your authority, ensure that such resources are not used improperly for political purposes (including party political purposes) and you must have regard to any applicable Local Authority Code of Publicity made under the Local Government Act 1986.

Appendix 2D. DCLG illustrative text for local code of conduct

You must promote and support high standards of conduct when serving in your public post, in particular as characterised by the above requirements, by leadership and example.

Registering and declaring pecuniary and non-pecuniary interests

You must, within 28 days of taking office as a member or co-opted member, notify your authority's monitoring officer of any disclosable pecuniary interest as defined by regulations made by the Secretary of State, where the pecuniary interest is yours, your spouse's or civil partner's, or is the pecuniary interest of somebody with whom you are living with as a husband or wife, or as if you were civil partners.

In addition, you must, within 28 days of taking office as a member or co-opted member, notify your authority's monitoring officer of any disclosable pecuniary or non-pecuniary interest which your authority has decided should be included in the register or which you consider should be included if you are to fulfil your duty to act in conformity with the Seven Principles of Public Life. These non-pecuniary interests will necessarily include your membership of any Trade Union.

If an interest has not been entered onto the authority's register, then the member must disclose the interest to any meeting of the authority at which they are present, where they have a disclosable interest in any matter being considered and where the matter is not a 'sensitive interest'.[1]

Following any disclosure of an interest not on the authority's register or the subject of pending notification, you must notify the monitoring officer of the interest within 28 days beginning with the date of disclosure.

Unless dispensation has been granted, you may not participate in any discussion of, vote on, or discharge any function related to any matter in which you have a pecuniary interest as defined by regulations made by the Secretary of State. Additionally, your must observe the restrictions your authority places on your involvement in matters where you have a pecuniary or non pecuniary interest as defined by your authority.

Note

1 A 'sensitive interest' is described in the Localism Act 2011 as a member or co-opted member of an authority having an interest, and the nature of the interest being such that the member or co-opted member, and the authority's monitoring officer, consider that disclosure of the details of the interest could lead to the member or co-opted member, or a person connected with the member or co-opted member, being subject to violence or intimidation.

Appendix 3

How do I register and declare interests, and register gifts and hospitality?

3A Old Code

DECLARING INTERESTS FLOWCHART – QUESTIONS TO ASK YOURSELF

(Non-overview and Scrutiny Meetings)

Personal Interest

What matters are being discussed at the meeting?

↓

Does the business relate to or is it likely to affect any of your registered interests? These will include

- persons who employ you, appointed you or paid your election expenses;
- your business, company ownership, contracts or land; or
- gifts or hospitality received (in the previous three years of this Code)

↓ *or*

Might a decision in relation to that business be reasonably be regarded as affecting, to a greater extent than the majority of other council tax payers, ratepayers or inhabitants of the ward affected by the decision (or the Authority's area as a whole if there is no electoral ward or division that you represent),

- your well-being or financial position; or
- the well-being or financial position of:
  - o a member of your family or any person with whom you have a close association; or
    - any person or body who employs or has appointed such persons, any firm in which they are a partner, or any company of which they are directors;
    - any person or body in whom such persons have a beneficial interest in a class of securities exceeding the nominal value of £25,000;
  - o any body of which you are a member or in a position of general control or management and to which you are appointed or nominated by your authority; or
  - o any body exercising functions of a public nature, directed to charitable purposes or whose principal purposes includes the influence of public opinion or policy (including any political party or trade union) of which you are a member or in a position of general control or management?

↓ *Yes* (*No* → You can participate in the meeting and vote)

<u>**YOU HAVE A PERSONAL INTEREST**</u>

You must disclose the existence and nature of your personal interests as a member of the meeting (subject to certain exemptions [para 9(2)])

↓

Prejudicial Interest

Would a member of the public, with knowledge of the relevant facts, reasonably regard your personal interest to be so significant that it is likely to prejudice your judgement of the public interest?

No → **You can participate in the meeting and vote** (or remain in the room if not a member of the meeting)

↓ *Yes*

- Does the matter affect your financial position or the financial position of any person or body through whom you have a personal interest?
- Does the matter relate to an approval, consent, licence, permission or registration that affects you or any person or body with which you have a personal interest?
- Does the matter <u>not</u> fall within one of the exempt categories of decisions?

No → You can participate in the meeting and vote

↓ *Yes*

<u>**YOU HAVE A PREJUDICIAL INTEREST**</u>

↓

Are members of the public allowed to make representations to the meeting, give evidence or answer questions about the matter by statutory right or otherwise?

↓ *Yes*

You can attend the meeting for that purpose *[if your parish/town council has adopted that provision]* but IMMEDIATELY after you have finished (or when the meeting decides that you have finished) …

→

No ↓

You must leave the room
You cannot remain in the public gallery to observe the vote on the matter. You must not seek to improperly influence the decision

3B: New Codes – DPI Only

Members' Interests Flowchart – Questions to ask yourself: 1

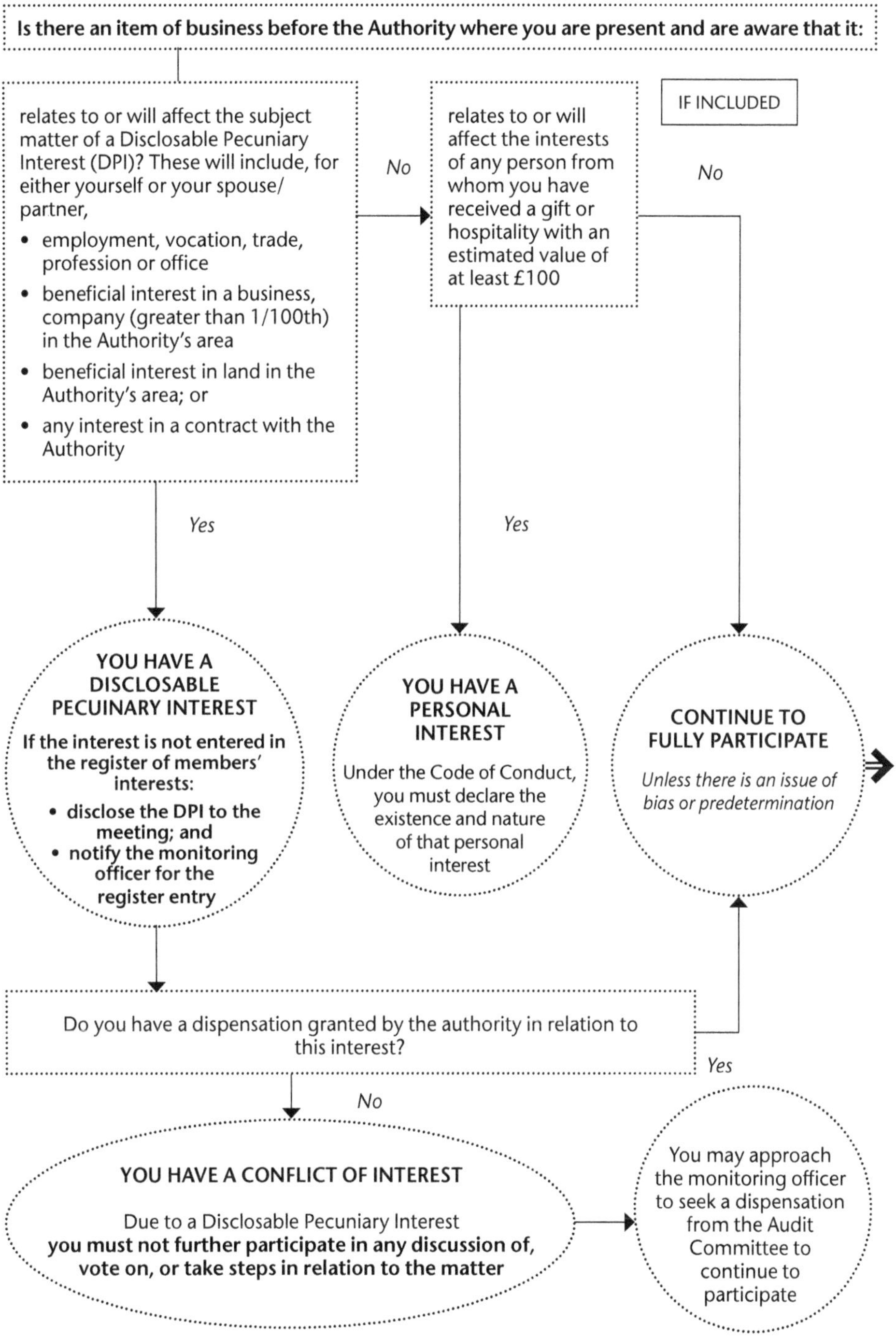

Members' Interests Flowchart – Questions to ask yourself: 2

Is there an item of business before the Authority where you are present and are aware that it:
relates to or will affect a subject matter in which you have a personal interest of another kind, such as

– Does it relate to or will it affect the subject matter of what would be a Disclosable Pecuniary Interest, but it is in respect of a member of your family or a person with whom you have a close association rather than yourself or your spouse/ partner?

No

– Might it otherwise be reasonably regarded as affecting the well being or financial standing of

(i) yourself;

(ii) a member of your family;

(iii) a person* with whom you have a close association; or

(iv) a person* from whom you have in the previous [twelve months] received a gift or hospitality with an estimated value of at least £100 as a Member (other than when as part of their approved duties)

to a greater extent than it would affect the majority of the Council Tax payers, ratepayers or inhabitants of the ward or electoral area for which they have been elected (or otherwise of the authority's administrative area)?

* A person includes a natural person and also a legal person in the form of a company, a charitable, other incorporated body or, for these purposes, an unincorporated association

No

Yes

Yes

Would a fair-minded and informed observer, having considered the facts, conclude that there was a real possibility that your decision-making would be biased?

No

CONTINUE TO FULLY PARTICIPATE

Unless there is an issue of predetermination

Yes

Your continued involvement would mean the decision-making is tainted by

APPARENT BIAS

and if challenged it would be likely that the Council's decision would be quashed in the courts, or there would be a finding of maladministration against the Council by the Local Government Ombudsman, because

YOU HAVE A CONFLICT OF INTEREST

because you cannot be a judge in your own cause within the rules of natural justice.

You should not take part in the meeting's debate or vote on the decision.

You are free to advocate your view or concerns as a member of the public,

but you should be careful not to improperly take advantage of, or be seen to misuse, the additional access or influence you have as a councillor

Appendix 3. How do I register and declare interests, gifts and hospitality

Members' Interests Flowchart – Questions to ask yourself: 3

Is there an item of business before the Authority where you are present and are aware that it:
is a matter which you are predisposed to vote/decide one way or the other?

- Have you actively campaigned for or against the proposal or a significant aspect of it; or
- Have you spoken out and told anyone how you would or would be likely to vote on the issue?

No →

- Have you been involved in other meetings where this item has been the topic of a recorded debate or decision; and
- Have you taken part in that debate or decision (including Council meetings, external meetings and political group meetings?

No → CONTINUE TO FULLY PARTICIPATE

Yes ↓

Will this affect your ability to fairly hear all of the evidence, advice and opinion and then weigh up those relevant factors to come to a decision at the meeting?

No → CONTINUE TO FULLY PARTICIPATE

So that, rather than it being a predisposition to vote or decide one way or the other, you will have a closed mind as to what your vote or decision will be?

No → CONTINUE TO FULLY PARTICIPATE

CONTINUE TO FULLY PARTICIPATE

You should carry on as normal, taking full part in the discussion, debate and vote or decision

Yes ↓

Your continued involvement would mean the decision-making is tainted by

PREDETERMINATION

and if challenged it would be likely that the Council's decision would be quashed in the courts, or there would be a finding of maladministration against the Council by the Local Government Ombudsman, because

↓

YOU HAVE A CONFLICT OF INTEREST

You cannot judge an issue within the rules of natural justice without first hearing all sides of the debate and then weighing the relevant considerations

You should not take part in the meeting's debate or vote on the decision

→

You are free to advocate the views or concerns of yourself or your constituents

as a Member, a ward member or as a member of the public

Appendix 4
LLG Model Members' Planning Code of Protocol

Background

The Members' Planning Code of Good Practice was originally prepared in response to a series of successful court challenges concerning themselves with local planning authorities and the Members' conduct or conflicts of interests. It replaced what was a number of individual and sometimes haphazard approaches in individual councils at the time.

The drafting of the model code was subject to consultation and comment from a number of local authorities through the machinery of the Association of Council Secretaries and Solicitors (now LLG), the Local Government Association, the Local Government Ombudsman, Audit Commission and from firms of solicitors or counsel acting on their behalf.

This 2013 update takes into account the update to the the Seven Principles of Public Life (the 'Nolan principles') and commentary from the Committee on standards in public life, the changes in the approach to codes of conduct and also to predetermination introduced by the Localism Act 2011 and the guide on 'Openness and transparency on personal interests' published by the Department for Communities and Local Government 2013.

For further reading, please refer to 'Probity in Planning' issued by the Local Government Association.

Introduction

The aim of this Code: to ensure that in the planning process there are no grounds for suggesting that a decision has been biased, partial or not well founded in any way. One of the key purposes of the planning system is to regulate the development and use of land in the public interest. **Your role as a Member of the Planning Authority** is to make planning decisions openly, impartially, with sound judgement and for justifiable reasons. You are also a democratically accountable decision-taker who had been elected to provide and pursue policies. You are entitled to be predisposed to make planning decisions in accordance with your political views and policies **provided** that you have considered all material considerations and have given fair consideration to relevant points raised.

When the Code applies: this code applies to Members at all times when involving themselves in the planning process. (This includes when taking part in the decision-making meetings of the Council in exercising the functions of the Planning Authority or when involved on less formal occasions, such as meetings with officers or the public and consultative meetings.) It applies as equally to planning enforcement matters or site specific policy issues as it does to planning applications.

If you have any doubts about the application of this Code to your own circumstances you should seek advice early, from the Monitoring Officer or one of his or her staff, and preferably well before any meeting takes place.

1. Relationship to the Members' Code of Conduct

- **Do** apply the rules in the Members' Code of Conduct first, which must always be complied with. This is both the rules on interest, Disclosable Pecuniary Interests (DPIs) and any other interests identified by your Authority, and the general rules giving effect to the seven principles of public life: selflessness, integrity, objectivity, accountability, openness, honesty and leadership.
- **Do** then apply the rules in this Members' Planning Code, which seek to explain and supplement the Members' Code of Conduct and the law on decision making for the purposes of planning control. If you do not abide by this Members' Planning Code, you may put:
  - the Council at risk of proceedings on the legality of the related decision or maladministration; and
  - yourself at risk of being named in a report made to the Council or, if the failure is also likely to be a breach of the interest provisions of Localism Act 2011, a complaint being made to the police to consider criminal proceedings.

2. Development Proposals and Personal Interests

- Do disclose the existence and nature of your interest as required by your Authority's Member Code of Conduct.
- Do take into account when approaching a decision that the Principle of Integrity is defined in terms that:

  'Holders of public office must avoid placing themselves under any obligation to people or organisations that might try inappropriately to influence them in their work. They should not act or take decisions in order to gain financial or other material benefits for themselves, their family, or their friends. ***They must declare and resolve any interests and relationships****.'*

  It is therefore advisable that you:

  - **don't** seek or accept any preferential treatment, or place yourself in a position that could lead the public to think you are receiving preferential treatment, because of your position as a councillor. This would include, where you have a disclosable or other personal conflict of interest in a proposal, using your position to discuss that proposal with officers or Members when other members of the public would not have the same opportunity to do so;
  - **do** note that you are not prevented from seeking to explain and justify a

proposal in which you may have a conflict of interest to an appropriate officer, in person or in writing, but that your role as a councillor may place additional limitations on you in representing the proposal in which you have a personal interest; and

- **do** notify the Monitoring Officer in writing where it is clear to you that you have a disclosable pecuniary interest or other personal conflict of interest and note that:

- you should send the notification no later than submission of that application where you can;
- the proposal will always be reported to the Committee as a main item and not dealt with by officers under delegated powers;
- you must not get involved in the processing of the application; and
- it is advisable that you employ an agent to act on your behalf in respect of the proposal when dealing with officers and in public speaking at Committee.

3. **Fettering Discretion in the Planning Process**
(natural justice, predisposition and predetermination)

- **Don't** fetter your discretion by approaching the decision with a closed mind.
- **Do** be aware that in your role as an elected Member you are entitled, and are often expected, to have expressed views on planning issues and that these comments have an added measure of protection under the Localism Act 2011.
- **Do** keep at the front of your mind that, when you come to make the decision, you:
  - are entitled to have and to have expressed your own views on the matter, provided you are prepared to reconsider your position in the light of all the evidence and arguments;
  - must keep an open mind and hear all of the evidence before you, both the officers' presentation of the facts and their advice as well as the arguments from all sides;
  - are not required to cast aside views on planning policy you held when seeking election or otherwise acting as a Member, in giving fair consideration to points raised;
  - are only entitled to take account a material consideration and must disregard considerations irrelevant to the question and legal context at hand; and
  - are to come to a decision after giving what you feel is the right weight to those material considerations.
- Do be aware that you can be biased where the Council is the landowner, developer or applicant if you have acted as, or could be perceived as being, a chief advocate for the proposal. (This is more than a matter of membership of both the proposing and planning determination committees, but that through your significant personal involvement in preparing or advocating the proposal you will be, or perceived by the public as being, no longer able to act impartially or to determine the proposal purely on its planning merits.)

- **Do** consider yourself able to take part in the debate on a proposal when acting as part of a consultee body (where you are also a member of the parish council, for example, or both a district/borough and county councillor), provided:
  - the proposal does not substantially effect the well being or financial standing of the consultee body;
  - you make it clear to the consultee body that:
    - your views are expressed on the limited information before you only;
    - you must reserve judgement and the independence to make up your own mind on each separate proposal, based on your overriding duty to the whole community and not just to the people in that area, ward or parish, as and when it comes before the Committee and you hear all of the relevant information; and
  - you will not in any way commit yourself as to how you or others may vote when the proposal comes before the Committee.
- **Do** explain that you do not intend to speak and vote as a member of the Committee because you will be perceived as having judged (or you reserve the right to judge) the matter elsewhere, so that this may be recorded in the minutes. (*Use the disclosure form provided for disclosing interests.*)
- **Do** take the opportunity to exercise your separate speaking rights as a Ward/ Local Member (*where this is granted by the authority's standing orders or by the consent from the Chair and Committee*) where you have represented your views or those of local electors and fettered your discretion, but do not have a disclosable or other personal conflict of interest. Where you do:
  - advise the proper officer or Chair that you wish to speak in this capacity before commencement of the item;
  - remove yourself from the seating area for members of the Committee for the duration of that item; and
  - ensure that your actions are recorded.

4. Contact with Applicants, Developers and Objectors

- **Do** refer those who approach you for planning, procedural or technical advice to officers.
- **Don't** agree to any formal meeting with applicants, developers or groups of objectors where you can avoid it. Where you feel that a formal meeting would be useful in clarifying the issues, you should seek to arrange that meeting yourself through a request to the [Development Control Manager] to organise it. The officer(s) will then ensure that those present at the meeting are advised from the start that the discussions will not bind the authority to any particular course of action, that the meeting is properly recorded on the application file and the record of the meeting is disclosed when the application is considered by the Committee.
- **Do** otherwise:

- follow the Authority's rules on lobbying;
- consider whether or not it would be prudent in the circumstances to make notes when contacted; and
- report to the [Development Control Manager] any significant contact with the applicant and other parties, explaining the nature and purpose of the contacts and your involvement in them, and ensure that this is recorded on the planning file [a pro-forma has been supplied to you for this purpose].

In addition in respect of presentations by applicants/developers:

- **Don't** attend a planning presentation without requesting an officer to be present.
- **Do** ask relevant questions for the purposes of clarifying your understanding of the proposals.
- **Do** remember that the presentation is not part of the formal process of debate and determination of any subsequent application, this will be carried out by the appropriate Committee of the planning authority.
- **Do** be aware that a presentation is a form of lobbying and, while you may express any view on the merits or otherwise of the proposal presented, you should never state how you or other Members would intend to vote at a committee.

5. Lobbying of Councillors

- **Do** explain to those lobbying or attempting to lobby you that, while you can listen to what is said, it may subsequently prejudice your impartiality, and therefore your ability to participate in the Committee's decision-making, to make any sort of promise to vote one way or another or such a firm point of view that it amounts to the same thing.
- **Do** remember that your overriding duty is to the whole community not just to the people in your [ward][division] and, taking account of the need to make decisions impartially, that you should not improperly favour, or appear to improperly favour, any person, company, group or locality.
- **Don't** accept gifts or hospitality from any person involved in or affected by a planning proposal. If a degree of hospitality is entirely unavoidable, ensure it is of a minimum, its acceptance is declared as soon as possible, including its addition to your register of interests where relevant.
- **Do** copy or pass on any lobbying correspondence you receive to the Development Control Manager at the earliest opportunity.
- **Do** promptly refer to the [Development Control Manager] any offers made to you of planning gain or constraint of development, through a proposed s. 106 Planning Obligation or otherwise.
- **Do** inform the Monitoring Officer where you feel you have been exposed to undue or excessive lobbying or approaches (including inappropriate offers of gifts or hospitality), who will in turn advise the appropriate officers to follow the matter up.

- **Do** note that, unless you have a disclosable or overriding other personal conflict of interest, you will not have fettered your discretion or breached this Planning Code through:
  - listening or receiving viewpoints from residents or other interested parties;
  - making comments to residents, interested parties, other Members or appropriate officers (making clear that you must keep an open mind when it comes to making the decision);
  - seeking information through appropriate channels; or
  - being a vehicle for the expression of opinion of others in your role as a [Ward][Division] Member.

6. Lobbying by Councillors

- **Don't** become a member of, lead or represent an organisation whose primary purpose is to lobby to promote or oppose planning proposals unless it is your intention to openly campaign on the matter and will therefore step away from the Committee when it comes to make it's decision.
- **Do** join general interest groups which reflect your areas of interest and which concentrate on issues beyond particular planning proposals (such as the Victorian Society, CPRE, Ramblers Association or a local civic society), but you should normally seek to disclose that interest on the grounds of transparency where the organisation has made representations on a particular proposal.
- **Don't** excessively lobby fellow councillors regarding your concerns or views nor attempt to persuade them that they should decide how to vote in advance of the meeting at which any planning decision is to be taken.
- **Don't** decide or discuss how to vote on any application at any political group meeting, or lobby any other Member to do so. Political Group Meetings should never dictate how Members should vote on a planning issue.

7. Site Visits/Inspections

- **Do** try to attend site visits organised by the Council where possible.
- **Don't** request a site visit unless you feel it is strictly necessary because:
  - particular site factors are significant in terms of the weight attached to them relative to other factors or the difficulty of their assessment in the absence of a site inspection; or
  - there are significant policy or precedent implications and specific site factors need to be carefully addressed.
- **Do** ensure that you report back to the Committee any information gained from the site visit that you feel would benefit all Members of the Committee.
- **Do** ensure that you treat the site visit only as an opportunity to seek information and to observe the site.
- **Do** ask the officers at the site visit questions or seek clarification from them on matters which are relevant to the site inspection.

- **Don't** hear representations from any other party, with the exception of the Ward Member(s) whose address must focus only on site factors and site issues. Where you are approached by the applicant or a third party, advise them that they should make representations in writing to the authority and direct them to or inform the officer present.
- **Don't** express opinions or views.
- **Don't** enter a site which is subject to a proposal other than as part of an official site visit, even in response to an invitation, as this may give the impression of bias unless:
  - you feel it is essential for you to visit the site other than through attending the official site visit;
  - you have first spoken to the Development Control Manager about your intention to do so and why (which will be recorded on the file); and
  - you can ensure you will comply with these good practice rules on site visits.

8. Public Speaking at Meetings

- **Don't** allow members of the public to communicate with you during the Committee's proceedings (orally or in writing) other than through the scheme for public speaking or through the Chair, as this may give the appearance of bias.
- **Do** ensure that you comply with the Council's procedures in respect of public speaking.

9. Officers

- **Don't** put pressure on officers to put forward a particular recommendation. (This does not prevent you from asking questions or submitting views to the [Development Control Manager], which may be incorporated into any committee report).
- **Do** recognise that officers are part of a management structure and only discuss a proposal, outside of any arranged meeting, with a Head of Service or those officers who are authorised by their Head of Service to deal with the proposal at a Member level.
- **Do** recognise and respect that officers involved in the processing and determination of planning matters must act in accordance with the Council's Code of Conduct for Officers and their professional codes of conduct, primarily the Royal Town Planning Institute's Code of Professional Conduct. As a result, planning officers' views, opinions and recommendations will be presented on the basis of their overriding obligation of professional independence, which may on occasion be at odds with the views, opinions or decisions of the Committee or its Members.

10. Decision-making

- Do ensure that, if you request a proposal to go before the Committee rather than be determined through officer delegation, that your planning reasons are recorded and repeated in the report to the Committee.

- **Do** come to meetings with an open mind and demonstrate that you are open-minded.
- **Do** comply with section 38 of the Planning and Compulsory Purchase Act 2004 and make decisions in accordance with the Development Plan unless material considerations indicate otherwise.
- **Do** come to your decision only after due consideration of all of the information reasonably required upon which to base a decision. If you feel there is insufficient time to digest new information or that there is simply insufficient information before you, request that further information. If necessary, defer or refuse.
- **Don't** vote or take part in the meeting's discussion on a proposal unless you have been present to hear the entire debate, including the officers' introduction to the matter.
- **Do** have recorded the reasons for Committee's decision to defer any proposal [and that this is in accordance with the Council's protocol on deferrals].
- **Do** make sure that if you are proposing, seconding or supporting a decision contrary to officer recommendations or the development plan that you clearly identify and understand the planning reasons leading to this conclusion/decision. These reasons must be given prior to the vote and be recorded. Be aware that you may have to justify the resulting decision by giving evidence in the event of any challenge.

11. Training

- **Don't** participate in decision-making at meetings dealing with planning matters if you have not attended the mandatory planning training prescribed by the Council.
- **Do** endeavour to attend any other specialised training sessions provided, since these will be designed to extend your knowledge of planning law, regulations, procedures, Codes of Practice and the Development Plans beyond the minimum referred to above and thus assist you in carrying out your role properly and effectively.
- **Do** participate in the annual review of a sample of planning decisions to ensure that Members' judgements have been based on proper planning considerations.

Adopted by Lawyers in Local Government, January 2014

Appendix 5

Scrutiny checklist – some dos and don'ts

DO

- Remember that scrutiny:
  - is about learning and being a 'critical friend'; it should be a positive process;
  - is not opposition; and
  - should result in improved value and enhanced performance.
- Take an overview and keep an eye on the wider picture.
- Check performance against local standards and targets and national standards, and compare results with other authorities.
- Benchmark performance against local and national performance indicators, using the results to ask more informed questions.
- Use panels to get underneath performance information.
- Take account of local needs, priorities and policies.
- Be persistent and inquisitive.
- Ask effective questions – be constructive, not judgemental.
- Be open-minded and self-aware – encourage openness and self-criticism in services.
- Listen to users and the public, seek the voices that are often not heard, seek the views of others – and balance all of these.
- Praise good practice and performance improvement – and seek to spread this throughout the authority.
- Provide feedback to those who have been involved in the review and to stakeholders.
- Anticipate difficulties in Members challenging colleagues from their own party and officers challenging their colleagues.
- Take time to review your own performance.

DON'T

- Witch-hunt or use performance review as punishment.
- Be party political/partisan.
- Blame valid risk taking or stifle initiative or creativity.
- Treat scrutiny as an add-on.
- Get bogged down in the detail.
- Be frightened to ask basic questions.
- Tackle too many issues in insufficient depth.
- Start without a clear objective and brief.
- Underestimate the task.
- Lose track of the main purpose of scrutiny.
- Lack sensitivity towards other stakeholders.
- Succumb to organisational inertia.
- Duck facing failure – learn from it and support change and development.
- Be driven by data or be paralysed by analysis – keep a strategic overview, and expect officers to provide high level information and analysis to help.

This document is reproduced with the kind permission of St Edmundsbury Borough Council.

Index

Index

Index

Index

www.ingramcontent.com/pod-product-compliance
Ingram Content Group UK Ltd.
Pitfield, Milton Keynes, MK11 3LW, UK
UKHW021840100926
8556IPUK00004B/466

9 781860 726798